THE WAY OF THE WARRIOR

MARTIAL ARTS AND FIGHTING STYLES FROM AROUND THE WORLD

CHRIS CRUDELLI

DK

CONTENTS

London, New York,
Munich, Melbourne, Delhi

**Dedicated to Yung Lee-Crudelli
and Heron Lee-Crudelli**

Project Editor Bob Bridle
Senior Art Editors Gillian Andrews, Michael Duffy
Editors Tarda Davison-Aitkins, Chris Hawkes, Philip Morgan, Nicky Munro, Chris Stone, Clare Weber
US Editor Margaret Parrish
Designers Sarah Arnold, Brian Flynn, Carolyn Hewitson, Thomas Keenes, Angela Won-Yin Mak, Hugh Schermuly, Vicki Smith

Production Editors Lucy Baker, Phil Sergeant
Senior Production Controller Shane Higgins

Managing Editor Stephanie Farrow
Managing Art Editor Lee Griffiths

SOUTHEAST ASIA AND OCEANIA

First American Edition, 2008

Published in the United States by
DK Publishing, 375 Hudson Street
New York, New York 10014

TD375—Oct. 08

08 09 10 11 10 9 8 7 6 5 4 3 2 1

Published in Great Britain by Dorling Kindersley Limited

A catalog record for this book is available from the Library of Congress

ISBN 978-0-7566-3975-4

DK books are available at special discounts when purchased in bulk sales promotions, premiums, fundraising, or educational use. For details, contact: DK Publishing Special Markets, 375 Hudson Street, New York, New York, 10014 or SpecialSales@dk.com

Proofing by Altaimage, United Kingdom
Printed and bound in Hong Kong

Discover more at **www.dk.com**

CONTENTS CONTINUED

INTRODUCTION

 Despite the fact that we live in an age of incredible technology, ready availability of quality information, air travel, advanced scientific understanding, and electronic communication, the ancient warrior arts—and their associated cultures—are still widely misunderstood. While it is true that the martial arts have been surrounded by mystery, myth, and disinformation for millennia, today we live in a fascinating time of change. Since the 1970s, major changes have started to take place, fueled by economic, social, and educational freedoms. The landscape of martial arts is shifting fast. While they retain their ancient heart, the arts are constantly and rapidly evolving, and this book is a significant example of that sweeping change.

Myth and legend do form an important aspect of the rich fabric of the martial arts, much of which has been passed down through strict teaching methods and oral tradition. Good, clear, factual information is needed to help individuals make informed choices, and to raise the standard of the martial arts in general. It is, however, unnecessary to be overly clinical in our approach to understanding and explaining the martial arts. On the contrary, knowledge does not have to be won at the expense of a culture's color and texture. I believe we can both recognize the facts and still enjoy the fables.

It is my goal with the publication of *The Way of the Warrior* to start a definitive end to the era of disinformation in the martial arts by writing the most comprehensive, picture-rich, readily available, affordable, and clear guide to every definable martial art in the world.

Writing this book is the culmination of 25 years of training, teaching, and research in the martial-arts world, combined with every conceivable modern method of gathering and disseminating reliable information. Most importantly, it's the result of good old-fashioned legwork and obsessive, dogged effort.

As a martial artist, my hope is that, when reading about the fascinating arts featured in this book, you will also keep in mind the absolute fragility and preciousness of human life by remembering that the ultimate goal of studying the arts of war is not to harm but rather to heal, enhance, and preserve life.

Chris Crudelli

THE WORLD OF MARTIAL ARTS

THE TERM "MARTIAL ART" CAN BE DEFINED as an art of combat that combines codified fighting techniques with philosophy, strategy, and cultural traditions. A martial art may be an offensive art for combat or a defensive art for self-defense. It may also be practiced to promote health and fitness, as a means of personal and spiritual development, and as a form of sport or entertainment. Martial arts can be performed both with and without weapons.

Styles of martial art

There are many different styles of martial art practiced throughout the world. Generally, however, they can be categorized into three broad types: traditional martial arts, sport-based martial arts, and weapons-based martial arts.

The traditional martial arts—such as jujutsu (see pp. 216–17), which was used by Japan's samurai warriors, or La Scuola della Spada Italiana (the Italian School of Swordsmanship, see p. 255)—evolved from battlefield training syllabuses. Employed in combat situations, these arts had the sole goal of equipping a practitioner with the skills and techniques necessary to kill or incapacitate the enemy. Sport-based martial arts, on the other hand, incorporate training regimes that prepare a practitioner for sporting competitions rather than solely life-threatening situations. Muay Thai, Western boxing, judo, mixed martial arts, and tae kwon do (see pp. 158–65, 256–63, 234–35, 318–27, 134–35), are

▲ BROAD-BASED SYSTEM
The art of kalarippayattu (see pp. 24–31) combines unarmed combat with dance, weapons-based combat, and healing.

prime examples. Weapons-based arts concentrate specifically on the use of weapons. The techniques learned here can then be applied in either traditional battlefield arts or in sporting competitions. Kendo, bataireacht, and escrima (see pp. 220–21, 250, 180–81) are all examples of weapons-based arts. Depending on the style of martial art, the school, and the individual teacher, varying amounts of emphasis will be placed on each of these aspects, with some martial arts combining elements of all three.

Ancient arts, modern myths

Fighting and humankind's need to dominate and defend is as old as life itself. Our ancestors' survival instincts undoubtedly sowed the seeds for the development of martial arts. Primarily methods of cultivating effective battlefield

❯ RITES AND RITUALS
When they fight, laamb wrestlers in Senegal (see p. 288) believe that they are protected from evil by their spiritual leader, or "juju man."

❯ PREPARING FOR A BOUT
The national sport of Thailand, muay Thai (see pp. 158–65) was first practiced with bare knuckles, or with hemp binding the fists. Today, most fighters wear boxing gloves, first wrapping their hands in cloth for added protection.

> "HE WHO OVERCOMES OTHERS IS STRONG. HE WHO OVERCOMES HIMSELF IS MIGHTY."

CHINESE PROVERB

techniques, and first codified to ensure high-quality and consistent teaching across the troops, many of the martial arts practiced today have a surprisingly long history, which is believed to span approximately 5,000 years. Furthermore, contrary to popular belief, they are not solely defined by the traditions of the East. While extensive archeological evidence points to the millennia-old practice of martial arts in China and India, many other nations and cultures can make similar claims. In Egypt, for example, tombs dating from approximately 2000 BCE show that stick-fighting arts were highly evolved, and the ancient full-contact art of pankration (see p. 276) is thought to have already been considered an ancient sport at the time of its first appearance at the ancient Olympics in 648 BC.

A global phenomenon

In more recent times, the Olympic movement has further championed both Eastern and Western martial arts. Greco-Roman wrestling (see p. 270) and fencing, for example, featured at the first modern Games in 1896, while Western archery (see p. 268), boxing, judo, and tae kwon do made their inaugural appearances in 1900, 1904, 1964, and 2000 respectively. The Asian Games can add karate and wushu (see pp. 202, 93–99) to the list of martial arts practiced at the highest level.

Global commercial TV coverage means that Western boxing has long pulled in huge audiences, with legendary status being awarded to champion boxers such as Muhammad Ali. In the 1990s, mixed martial arts (MMA), in which fighting is conducted inside a cage, introduced millions of people to interdisciplinary forms of martial arts. The Ultimate Fighting Championship (UFC), which runs the sport's foremost competition, brings together the most talented competition fighters from around the

▲ OLYMPIC SPORT
Judo was the first martial art to be thoroughly codified. This made it possible to teach the art to a high standard, and paved the way for its acceptance as an Olympic sport.

world. From its somewhat controversial beginnings, when it was forced underground for being too violent, fighters now come together in front of massive pay-per-view TV audiences to compete, bringing with them their experience in a variety of arts, from boxing, Brazilian jujutsu, and Greco-Roman wrestling, to judo, karate, and various styles of kung fu.

The paradox of martial arts

The world of martial arts is full of complex contradictions. Arguably the greatest paradox of all is that many practitioners—regardless of the style or origin of their particular art form—regularly seek peace, enlightenment, and a deep understanding of the self through the practice of

violent, often lethal skills. The inclusion of philosophical concepts such as Confucianism, Buddhism and Daoism in many Eastern arts has also had a profound effect on the evolution of martial arts around the world. It may seem ironic that—once training is over for the day—some of the world's most accomplished martial artists are also some of the world's gentlest people. Perhaps it is because there is so much violence involved with mastering a martial art that practitioners have a strong desire to avoid confrontation in everyday life.

MARTIAL ARTS AND THE MOVIES

Mainstream contemporary interest in the martial arts in the West can, arguably, be traced back to the popularity and iconic status of Bruce Lee in the 1970s. His most popular films—*The Big Boss*, *Fist of Fury*, *Way of the Dragon*, and *Enter the Dragon*—put martial arts firmly on the movie map and introduced many previously secretive and exclusive arts to a wider audience.

Chuck Norris came to the attention of US film audiences just as Lee's star was rising, and he acted alongside Lee in the film *Way of the Dragon*. Norris was a renowned martial artist in his own right, and played an important part in creating the martial-arts "action hero."

A number of successful television series have also helped to broaden knowledge of Chinese and Asian philosophy and martial arts in the West, influencing many Western filmmakers. The influence of long-running series such as "The Water Margin," "Monkey," and "Kung Fu," are continually referenced in contemporary Hollywood films such as *The Matrix*, and the *Kill Bill* series, and the success of these films has led to increased interest in foreign-language films such as *Crouching Tiger, Hidden Dragon*, and *Hero*.

"PERSEVERANCE AND YEAR-ROUND TRAINING — IN THE DOG DAYS OF SUMMER AND THE COLDEST DAYS OF WINTER — IS THE WAY TO LEARN REAL KUNG FU."

SAYING FROM THE SHAOLIN TEMPLE

◄ ANCIENT ORIGINS
Shaolin kung fu as practiced today refers to a number of systems that have their origins in the famed Shaolin temple in China. Dating back more than 1,000 years, the art is believed to have its roots in the yogic exercises introduced to the temple by the Indian Buddhist monk, Bodhidharma.

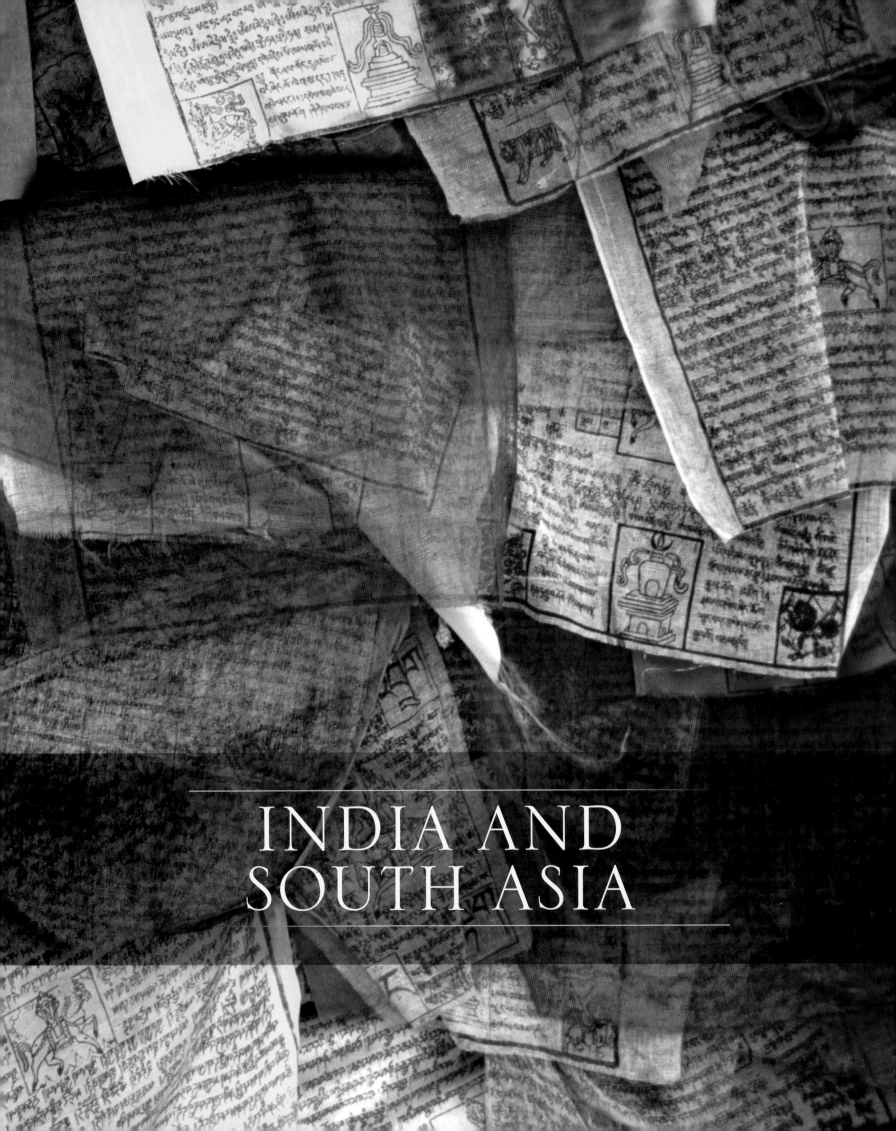

INDIA AND SOUTH ASIA

INDIA AND SOUTH ASIA

THE WORLD'S MOST POPULOUS democracy and the seventh largest country by geographical land mass, the Republic of India shares its borders with China, Nepal, and Bhutan in the northeast; Bangladesh and Myanmar in the east; and Pakistan to the west. It has given birth to four major world religions—Sikhism, Buddhism, Hinduism, and Jainism—and the region's long history and diverse culture has spawned many philosophies, great thinkers, brave warriors, and influential martial artists.

INDIA IS OFTEN CONSIDERED the birthplace of martial arts and, although this claim may not be strictly true, it could be said that the existence of many of today's martial arts is due to the actions of an Indian monk called Bodhidharma, who was also known as "Da Mo" in China.

Born around 440 CE in Kanchi (at that time the capital of the southern Indian kingdom of Pallava) into the warrior caste, Bodhidharma received Buddhist teachings from a young age and was also said to be proficient in kalarippayattu, an empty-hand and weapons-based form of Indian martial arts (see pp. 24–31). He later traveled to China and started what became known as the Chan (or Zen) School of Buddhism.

Arriving at the Shaolin temple in Song Shan in Henan province, Bodhidharma was initially refused entry but, according to legend, he went off to meditate in a cave close to the temple for nine years, not speaking for the entire time. The monks, realizing Bodhidharma's dedication

> **THE FOUNDING FATHER**
Bodhidharma is credited in some quarters as introducing both Zen and martial arts to China.

and wisdom, eventually allowed him to enter the temple. While he was there he taught a number of Zen principles and yogic martial-art exercises to strengthen the weak and sickly monks who, after years of static meditation, lacked physical strength and vigor.

Bodhidharma was later credited, somewhat contentiously, with writing the Chinese classics *Yi Jin Jing* and *Xi Sui Jing*. These books were effectively the first "qi-gong" manuals and are thought to form the basis of modern Shaolin kung fu (see p. 57–67).

India's varied landscape—it is pocketed with mountains, vast plains, jungles, and deserts—has also had a major influence on the country's martial-arts scene. Various cultures evolved in isolation and the martial arts that grew within them were influenced by the terrain, the religious beliefs, and the philosophical practices of each particular region. As a result, a number of unique indigenous martial arts—such as aki kiti and mukna (see p. 23)—have evolved over the centuries.

A wealthy past

Although the country now suffers from high levels of poverty, illiteracy, and malnutrition, India was a wealthy nation for much of its history and one that was home to vast empires lured to the area by historic trade routes. The vibrant

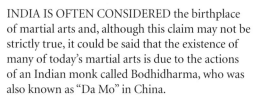

REGION AT A GLANCE

1 POPULATION BOOM
The second-largest country by population in the world, through sheer numbers alone India has had an enormous influence on the global martial-art scene.

2 RELIGIOUS MELTING POT
The birthplace of four of the world's major religions—Sikhism, Buddhism, Hinduism, and Jainism—India has had a major impact on global philosophies and thought.

3 BIRTHPLACE OF MARTIAL ARTS
According to legend, in the early 6th century CE Bodhidharma traveled from southern India to China and introduced Zen thought and martial techniques to monks in the Shaolin temple.

4 DIVERSE LANDSCAPE
Indian martial arts have been heavily influenced by the great diversity of the country's terrain: separate indigenous art forms have evolved in the forests of the south, the deserts of the west, and the mighty Himalayas in the north.

5 CENTER OF WORLD TRADE
India's former status as a global trading epicenter saw the exchange of spices, silk, new religious ideas, weapons, and fighting techniques.

6 INDIGENOUS TRIBES
Several diverse and individual indigenous martial arts have been developed by numerous isolated tribes in the region as a means of self-defense.

7 TRADITIONAL DANCE
Throughout the centuries many of the region's performing art forms—such as the kathakali dance in the southern Indian state of Kerala—have been influenced by martial arts.

8 RELIGIOUS FESTIVALS
Several Indian martial arts have strong links with religious movements. Gatka (see pp. 20–21), for example, is predominantly practiced by Sikhs in the Indian state of Punjab.

TEMPLE CURTAIN DEPICTING A BATTLE SCENE

"WE WANT TO COME IN CONTACT WITH THE SUPREME CONSCIOUSNESS… THEREFORE WE HAVE TO BUILD UP A BODY SOLID, HEALTHY, ENDURING, SKILLFUL, AGILE, AND STRONG."

PRINCIPLES OF KALARIPPAYATTU, ONE OF THE WORLD'S OLDEST MARTIAL ARTS

MAP OF INDIA AND SOUTH ASIA

▼ ANCIENT CIVILIZATION

Archeological evidence suggests that martial arts have been practiced in India for at least 5,000 years. As it was at the center of a historic trade route, the region has had a huge impact on global martial arts.

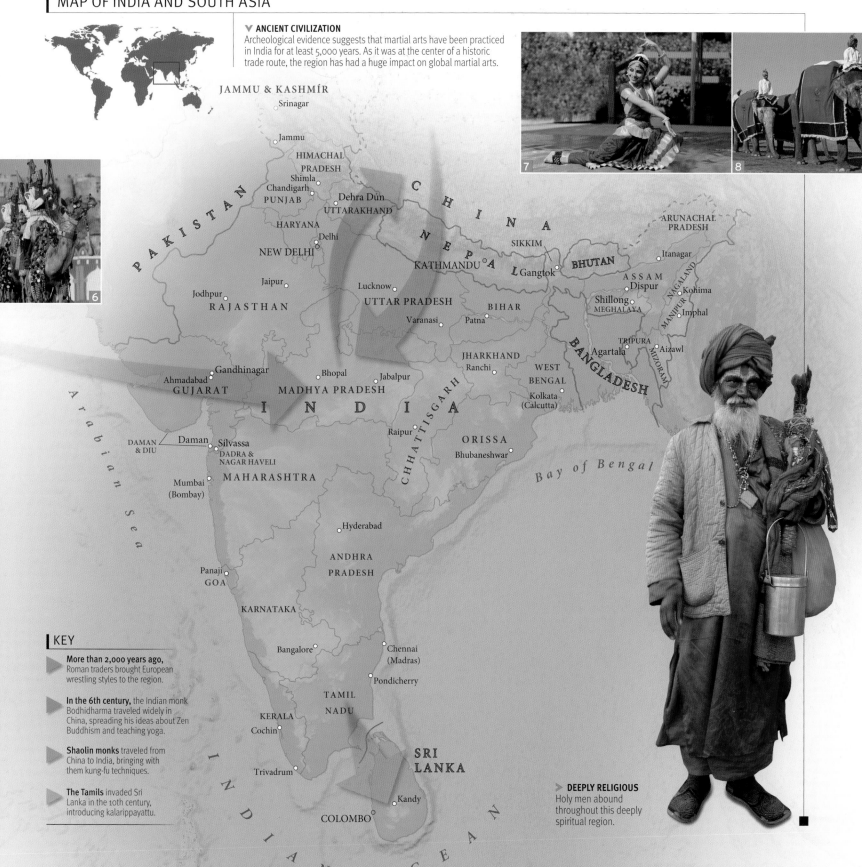

KEY

▶ **More than 2,000 years ago,** Roman traders brought European wrestling styles to the region.

▶ **In the 6th century,** the Indian monk Bodhidharma traveled widely in China, spreading his ideas about Zen Buddhism and teaching yoga.

▶ **Shaolin monks** traveled from China to India, bringing with them kung-fu techniques.

▶ **The Tamils** invaded Sri Lanka in the 10th century, introducing kalarippayattu.

▷ DEEPLY RELIGIOUS

Holy men abound throughout this deeply spiritual region.

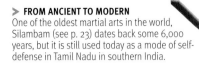

> **FROM ANCIENT TO MODERN**
One of the oldest martial arts in the world, Silambam (see p. 23) dates back some 6,000 years, but it is still used today as a mode of self-defense in Tamil Nadu in southern India.

commercial scene would have brought new religious ideas, weapons, and fighting techniques to the region from many different sources. For example, wrestling was a popular sport in India even before the advent of Buddhism and is proof that the region came into contact with people from the outside world—such as the ancient Greeks, Persians, and Romans—several centuries ago. Doubtless, many similar cross-cultural exchanges would have taken place over the years.

Religious associations

Many of the martial arts popular in India today have strong connections with religious movements. Gatka (see pp. 20–21), for example, is a martial art associated with the Sikh religion and is commonly practiced in the Punjab. It was originally used to train Sikh warriors to protect

their communities and, although it is now largely only practiced as a sport and demonstration art at festivals and public gatherings to the accompaniment of music, like many of the region's other religion-based martial traditions, it has a strong connection with its battlefield origins.

Ancient dynasties

The Chola and Tamil Chera were two important dynasties central to the development of Indian martial arts. During its zenith of power in the 10th, 11th, and 12th centuries, the Chola dynasty was a cultural, militaristic, and economic powerhouse throughout Asia, but primarily in southern India. A Tamil dynasty that stretched south to the Malay Archipelago, it excelled in maritime activity and much trade was conducted with Southeast Asia—particularly China—and some parts of the Middle East. It is safe to assume that the technological and militaristic advances made during the Chola period were in large part due to contact with the outside world. The Tamil Chera

▼ **RELIGIOUS CONNECTIONS**
Gatka (see pp. 20–21) is closely associated with the Sikh religion. The art is thought to be based on an ancient Indian military training curriculum.

< MEN AT ARMS
India and South Asia have produced a vast array of unique weaponry, such as this 17th-century battleaxe.

> "AS LONG AS THERE HAVE BEEN PEOPLE THERE HAS BEEN FIGHTING, AND AS LONG AS THERE HAS BEEN FIGHTING, PEOPLE HAVE DEVISED WAYS OF HELPING THEMSELVES FIGHT."
>
> UNKNOWN

dynasty, which ruled southern India (the modern-day regions of Tamil Nadu and Kerala) from ancient times until around the 15th century, saw a further expansion in both trade and contact with the wider world, most notably with Mesopotamia, Persia, Greece, Rome, Egypt, and much of the Arab world. Trade in spices, gems, lumber, and pearls from Kerala fuelled much of this expansion, and the cross-fertilization of militaristic ideas, weaponry, armour, and hand-to-hand combat techniques was inevitable.

DANCE AND INDIAN MARTIAL ARTS

The introduction of firearms in the 17th century saw a decline in many Indian martial arts, but many lived on in other forms. Kalarippayattu (see pp. 24–31), for example, has had a major influence on kathakali, the traditional Keralan dance-drama. Not only are kathakali's dance postures taken straight from kalarippayattu, but its training methods also bear a strong resemblance to those found in India's 3,000-year-old martial art.

∧ ROOTED IN TRADITION
The wrestling art of kushti (see pp. 39–45) plays a major part in the annual Dussehra festival in Mysore, which celebrates the triumph of good over evil.

> NATURAL EVOLUTION
Formerly a battlefield art, gatka is now mainly seen as an exhibition martial art and sport. The art combines elements of physical martial arts and self-defense techniques.

Gatka

EXPLANATION
"FREEDOM; MEMBER OF A
GROUP" IN PUNJABI
DATE OF ORIGIN
INDIGENOUS ART
FOUNDER
NO KNOWN FOUNDER

PLACE OF ORIGIN
PUNJAB, PAKISTAN, AND INDIA

A martial art of Sikh origin, which
is thought to have derived from an
ancient Indian military training
curriculum called shaster vidiya (see
p.22), gatka originated in the Punjab.
It is rarely used for actual combat
today but has gained notoriety as
an exhibition martial art and sport.
Although the name gatka also refers
to a stick that is used when practicing
sword-fighting, the art combines
elements of physical martial arts and
self-defense techniques. It also
features spiritual practices and
meditative mental exercises.

Music and dance

Gatka demonstrations are usually
accompanied by music and, integral
to the art, a unique and exotic dance
in which practitioners participate
prior to fighting. The art shares
many common principles with other
warlike arts used in the training of
troops; one of these principles is to
instil in a participant the ability to
defend himself against multiple
opponents attacking from all sides.

An element of basic gatka
training features the use of a
combination of weapons, such as
two sticks or a stick and a sword,
simultaneously. The principles of
using both hands at once while in
combat enhances the body's ability
to be dexterous.

Maintaining the art's link to
Sikhism, gatka is still often taught
and practiced in "gurdwaras," or
Sikh temples.

▼ GATKA DEMONSTRATION
Two practitioners perform gatka in
Andapur, Punjab, as part of the official
celebrations to mark the tercentenary
of the Sikh faith.

AUTHOR'S NOTE

I spent time training at the Guru Nanak
gurdwara in the Punjab with a religious
group of gatka practitioners. I remember
being struck by their ability to master
quickly a wide range of traditional
weapons and employ them to good
effect, while at the same time dancing,
singing, and chanting religious songs.
I also remember being deeply affected
by the sincere environment of brotherly
camaraderie of this religious, martial
group—an environment from which
many ancient and traditional martial
arts were born.

DAGGER DUEL

Perfectly suited for swift attacks at close quarters, the "katar" (short punching dagger) was traditionally an armor-piercing weapon. Potentially lethal, today the katar is used by only the most experienced kalarippayattu players.

SWORD, SHIELD, AND SPEAR TRAINING

By the time students reach the third aspect of kalarippayattu training, known as "ankathari," they are instructed in the art of three further weapons—"paricha" (round shield), "val" (long sword), and "kuntham" (spear). Students must be especially competent with the paricha as its relatively small size means it can only offer limited protection from sword and spear attacks.

▼ LEAP OF FAITH

The standing jump is a popular technique used by kalarippayattu practitioners to increase agility. It is often deployed in combat as a means of avoiding attacks aimed at the middle or lower part of the body.

▼ ART OF AVOIDANCE

An experienced kalarippayattu fighter demonstrates the effectiveness of the standing jump on an Keralan beach. As he watches his opponent prepare, then execute, a staff strike, he leaps to safety.

>>>

WEAPONS AND ARMOR

INDIAN WEAPONS

INDIAN WEAPONS ARE RENOWNED for their distinctive shapes, high-quality metalwork, and ornamentation. Swords are elegantly curved, handles and grips ornately shaped, and weapons often delicately covered in gold damask. In kalarippayattu, the weapon chosen by a practitioner—either a wooden stick or club, a metal sword, or a dagger—depends on the level of skill that he or she has reached; only the most capable fighters experience fighting with daggers. These "katar" daggers were originally developed for use in battle situations; traditionally used to pierce armor, they are extremely dangerous weapons during close combat. As the only protection kalarippayattu practitioners have against oncoming attacks is their "paricha"—a very small shield—the need for skill, focus, and accuracy is heightened.

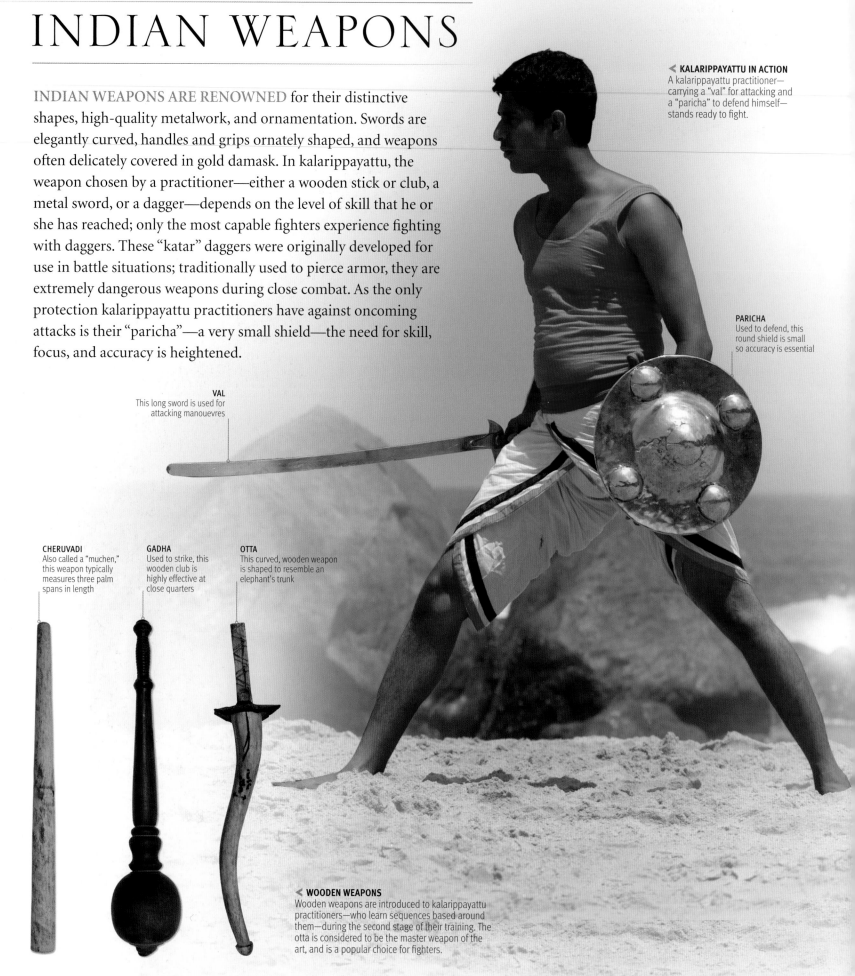

< KALARIPPAYATTU IN ACTION
A kalarippayattu practitioner—carrying a "val" for attacking and a "paricha" to defend himself—stands ready to fight.

PARICHA
Used to defend, this round shield is small so accuracy is essential

VAL
This long sword is used for attacking manouevres

CHERUVADI
Also called a "muchen," this weapon typically measures three palm spans in length

GADHA
Used to strike, this wooden club is highly effective at close quarters

OTTA
This curved, wooden weapon is shaped to resemble an elephant's trunk

< WOODEN WEAPONS
Wooden weapons are introduced to kalarippayattu practitioners—who learn sequences based around them—during the second stage of their training. The otta is considered to be the master weapon of the art, and is a popular choice for fighters.

▼ DAGGERS AND BLADES

Made to a high standard, Indian daggers—of which there are many types—are often highly detailed and intricately shaped. "Katar" daggers (see right) are used by only the most experienced kalarippayattu practitioners. They are extremely dangerous weapons, ideal for swift attacks in close-combat situations.

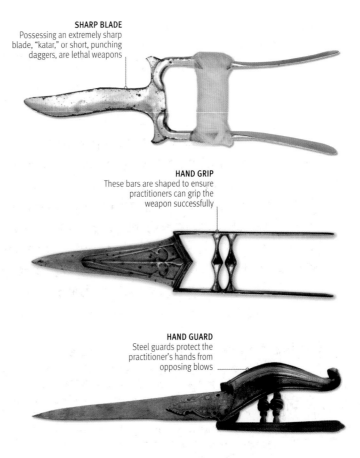

SHARP BLADE
Possessing an extremely sharp blade, "katar," or short, punching daggers, are lethal weapons

JAMBIYA DAGGER
Usually worn on a belt, this curved dagger is covered in gold damask

FINGER GRIPS
The ornate grips on this dagger enable accurate maneuvers

HAND GRIP
These bars are shaped to ensure practitioners can grip the weapon successfully

BICH'HWA DAGGER
Named after the Indian word for scorpion, bich'hwa daggers have recurved double-edged blades

HAND GUARD
Steel guards protect the practitioner's hands from opposing blows

▼ SWORDS AND SHEATHS

The curved nature of these swords is representative of the Indian style. Wielded in martial arts as well as in warfare situations, the swords—typically made of silver or steel—are often highly ornate. When practicing martial-arts techniques, fighters will generally use a blunter sword, such as the val below.

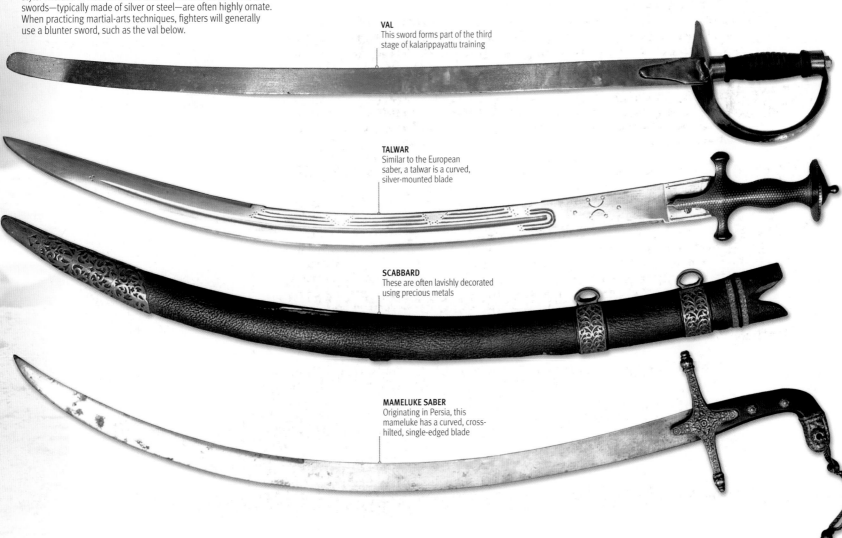

VAL
This sword forms part of the third stage of kalarippayattu training

TALWAR
Similar to the European saber, a talwar is a curved, silver-mounted blade

SCABBARD
These are often lavishly decorated using precious metals

MAMELUKE SABER
Originating in Persia, this mameluke has a curved, cross-hilted, single-edged blade

◄ INTENSE STAND-OFF
Two kalarippayattu (see pp.24–31) fighters
adopt low stances to grapple during training
in Kerala. The "katar" (dagger) is a popular
weapon in Indian martial arts.

Malyutham

EXPLANATION
TAMIL WRESTLING

DATE OF ORIGIN
INDIGENOUS ART

FOUNDER
NO KNOWN FOUNDER

PLACE OF ORIGIN
TAMIL NADU

Malyutham is a wrestling art of the Tamil people that focuses on grappling and throwing techniques. Although its origin is unclear, it is noted in ancient Tamil literature. Evidence suggests it reached a peak of popularity in Tamil Nadu during the Pallava period in the 4th century CE. Although many variations and sets of rules existed during its peak, generally a victory was signified either if one wrestler threw his opponent to the ground and forcefully held him down so that he could not move, or if the combatant was injured and withdrew from the match.

Challenge matches were widespread, and well-known wrestlers traveled from town to town, winning respect and fortune, a phenomenon that still exists in wrestling and mixed martial arts competitions today.

Marma Adi

EXPLANATION
TRADITIONAL BOXING

DATE OF ORIGIN
INDIGENOUS ART

FOUNDER
NO KNOWN FOUNDER

PLACE OF ORIGIN
KERALA

Marma adi is a traditional Indian boxing school that relies on the principles of striking the "marma" (secret vital energy) points, similar to those shared in the Chinese art of dim mak, otherwise known as "the death touch."

The art is based around the theory that a number of vulnerable points exist on the human body. Depending on periodic energy flows through the body on lines known as meridians, strikes centered powerfully at key areas can cause damage that is disproportionate to the amount of power issued from the actual physical strike.

A number of body parts are used, including the foot, knuckles, ridge part of the hand, the palm, fingertips, elbows, insteps, and even the big toe. As is usually the case with southern styles of kung fu (see p. 57) in China, southern styles of marma adi rarely make use of kicks above the waist.

Medicine and massage
As with many Oriental martial arts, a common training tool used by practitioners of this art form is the use of set forms, or "katas", whereby players fight a series of imaginary opponents using predetermined techniques. Ayurvedic medicine, along with massage and folk remedies, are also commonly taught in the system and practitioners believe strongly in the motto: "what can cure can kill, and what can kill can cure."

▼ **THE ROUTE TO BETTER HEALTH**
The art of marma adi is closely linked to marma therapy, which is practiced by ayurvedic doctors. Here, a patient is treated with medicinal oil.

Vajra Mushti

EXPLANATION
"GRASPING A THUNDERBOLT" IN HINDI

DATE OF ORIGIN
5TH CENTURY CE

FOUNDER
NO KNOWN FOUNDER

PLACE OF ORIGIN
INDIA

The art of vajra mushti is a collection of grappling and striking techniques. It is also the Sanskrit name for a knuckleduster weapon that historically was used by fighters. The earliest recorded writings on the art date

▲ **FIGHT TO THE DEATH**
An artist's impression of a particularly vicious vajra mushti bout in the late 19th century. Both fighters are wearing spiked knuckledusters.

back to the 5th century and can be found in the religious text Buddharata Sutra, although it is thought that the system predates those writings and was regularly practiced by the Kshatriya warrior caste.

Ancient roots
Closely related to the ancient Tibetan martial art known as lion's roar, vajra mushti is claimed to be the martial art of the historical Buddha's bloodline.

Kuttu Varisai

EXPLANATION
"EMPTY HAND COMBAT" IN TAMIL

DATE OF ORIGIN
1ST CENTURY BCE

FOUNDER
NO KNOWN FOUNDER

PLACE OF ORIGIN
TAMIL NADU

Although often taught alongside the stick-fighting art of silambam (see p. 23) kuttu varisai is also a stand-alone martial art; it resembles other empty-hand martial arts such as kung fu and karate (see pp. 57, 202).

It employs techniques based on the movements of aggressive animals, as well as grappling and striking arts. Some weapons—notably the stick, trident dagger, double sword, shield, steel whip, and knuckleduster—are also used. In addition, kuttu varisai features the more peaceful pursuits of yoga, breathing exercises, and meditation.

The first recorded literature relating to the art dates from the 1st century BCE. It is believed to have been a uniquely Tamil practice, popular in Tamil Nadu and northeastern Sri Lanka.

Bothati

EXPLANATION
SPEAR ART ON HORSEBACK

DATE OF ORIGIN
INDIGENOUS ART

FOUNDER
NO KNOWN FOUNDER

PLACE OF ORIGIN
INDIA

Although its origins are unclear, this ancient martial art focuses on cavalry disciplines such as the fighting techniques employed with the use of the long spear while riding on horseback.

Competitors race toward each other on their steeds and seek to dismount one another. There are similiarities in this art to jousting (see p. 264), which was popular in most parts of medieval Europe.

SUPREME HORSEMANSHIP
A Nihang, or ancient Sikh, warrior exhibits his riding skills during a three-day religious event called "Hola Mohalla," held annually after the Hindu Diwali festival.

Angampora

EXPLANATION
"BODY COMBAT" IN HINDI

DATE OF ORIGIN
6TH CENTURY CE

FOUNDER
NO KNOWN FOUNDER

PLACE OF ORIGIN
SRI LANKA

A Sri Lankan grappling and submission martial art, angampora includes a number of physical combat techniques and strength-building techniques aimed at enhancing the efficiency of combatants. It was traditionally practiced by Sinhala warriors.

Practitioners were noted for their courage and physical prowess. They often found employment in the gathering of rock bee honey or the noosing of elephants—both pursuits that require great agility, physical strength, and courage.

Lethal weapon
Today, weapons are studied and practiced in the art, the most common of which is the "velayudaya," a whiplike weapon that has four long, double-edged, flexible, metal strips attached to a handle and is devastatingly lethal. It cuts and thrashes opponents, is effective in battle against opponents armed

with swords or long staffs, and is difficult to block because there are four instruments attacking at any one moment.

The basic footwork that informs the system is called "mulla panina" and it is often learned and practiced to the beat of traditional Indian drums. It is believed that the rhythm of the drums helps a fighter understand the spirit of a caged tiger, a spirit he may employ when fighting opponents of greater strength. The envisaging of oneself in another form, most often an aggressive animal, is a common psychological tactic integral to many martial arts.

Bandesh

EXPLANATION
TRADITIONAL COMBAT ART

DATE OF ORIGIN
INDIGENOUS ART

FOUNDER
NO KNOWN FOUNDER

PLACE OF ORIGIN
INDIA

Thought to have originated several hundred years ago, bandesh is a system of grappling, locking, choking, disarming, and forced-submission techniques, commonly used against an armed assault. It is a martial art that stresses non-lethal use of force; practitioners are encouraged to reduce the risk of injury to their attacker. While practice matches can involve hand-to-hand combat, they generally include weapons—the winner is deemed to be the practitioner who successfully disarms his opponent.

But Marma Atti

EXPLANATION
TRADITIONAL STRIKING ART

DATE OF ORIGIN
INDIGENOUS ART

FOUNDER
NO KNOWN FOUNDER

PLACE OF ORIGIN
SOUTHERN INDIA

The principles of but marma atti consists of two-pronged attacks on opponents—both physical and mental. Practitioners first aim to erode their opponent's will to fight by psychological means—reasoning with them and discouraging them—before striking, kicking, knifing, or clubbing them, or attacking with any other improvised weapon. Humiliation of the opponent during the fighting process is also of primary importance and it is believed that this can help effect a swift victory.

Inner peace
Taught and practiced widely in rural south India, but marma atti is a holistic and practical method of self-defense rather than a sporting art. Practitioners are taught to maintain an impeccable character of high moral standing to cultivate inner strength and an understanding of one's own ego. This in turn engenders an attitude of avoiding aggressive individuals. But marma atti is, in essence, an evolution of natural defensive mind-and-body practices.

Nata

EXPLANATION
DANCE-BASED MARTIAL ART

DATE OF ORIGIN
INDIGENOUS ART

FOUNDER
NO KNOWN FOUNDER

PLACE OF ORIGIN
INDIA

Nata is a martial art form in which finger movements, taken from an ancient Indian dance, are used alongside yogic movements. Although little is known about the art today, it is quite likely that it included finger- and wrist-locking maneuvers and weapons disarms based on joint locks and pain-compliance techniques.

The practitioners of ancient Indian dance possessed a good understanding of the physiological make up of the joints, in particular the arms, hands, and fingers, as these types of movements were stressed in ancient Indian dance. It is likely that the arts were included in other ancient Indian martial arts such as weapon forms and grappling sports.

In the 3rd century BCE, the author Patanjali wrote the *Yoga Sutras*, the ancient foundational text of yoga. These yogic elements, as well as finger movements in the nata dances, were later incorporated into various martial arts. Furthermore, there are several references in early historical Buddhist texts such as the Lotus Sutra, written in the 1st century CE, which refer to Indian martial arts of boxing and, in particular, techniques of joint locking, fist strikes, grapples, and throws.

Although the subject of speculation among historians, it is possible that these elements describe the evolution of hand movements and locking techniques from the early nata dances into later martial-art forms.

◀ **LORD OF THE DANCE**
The depiction of Shiva, one of the principal deities of Hinduism, as Nataraja ("Lord of the Dance") is the inspiration for nata.

Cheena Adi

EXPLANATION
"CHINESE PUNCH" IN MALAYALAM

DATE OF ORIGIN
INDIGENOUS ART

FOUNDER
NO KNOWN FOUNDER

PLACE OF ORIGIN
SRI LANKA

Experts believed that this ancient system of martial arts, which closely resembles Chinese kung fu, was passed on by a Shaolin monk. When visiting the sacred relic of the tooth of the Buddha, housed in Sri Lanka, he taught the system openly to a number of students. It is said that cheena adi takes 15 years to master and, because of this, other martial arts such as aikido, judo, and karate (see pp. 238–39, 234–35, 202–03) have become more popular in Sri Lanka.

Lathi

EXPLANATION
"CANE" IN HINDI

DATE OF ORIGIN
INDIGENOUS ART

FOUNDER
NO KNOWN FOUNDER

PLACE OF ORIGIN
EASTERN AND SOUTHERN INDIA

Lathi is a martial art and is also the name given to a bamboo pole, 6–8 ft (1.8–2.8 m) long, with a metal tip at the end, which is wielded like a sword. Lathi is thought to have originated from an ancient and peaceful yogic practice in which practitioners try to release "kundalini" (coiled-up energy) through the body via circular and figure-eight movements. It later became a martial art and was initially popular in eastern and southern India.

The stick was originally used to help keep buffalo in order—in fact, a common Hindi saying goes "jiski lathi, uski bhains," meaning, "he who wields the lathi gets to keep the buffalo." Farmers skilled with the stick were often called to become militia and settle disputes on behalf of regional warlords and landowners. The art later evolved into a sport and duels, in which practitioners could show their prowess and possibly gain employment or enhanced status among the men of their village, were common.

Today, the term "lathials," derived from the art form, is commonly used as a word to describe men for hire who will fight, settle scores, and restore honor among farmers who feel slighted.

It was the British, during the colonial rule of India, who introduced the lathi as a weapon to be used in crowd control and during riots. In present day India, the lathi is used as a weapon by the national police for similar purposes.

▼ **FRENZIED FIGHTING**
Performers demonstrate their fighting prowess with lathis (bamboo poles) at the Desert Festival in Rajasthan.

Kushti

EXPLANATION
INDIAN WRESTLING

DATE OF ORIGIN
C. 5TH CENTURY BCE

FOUNDER
NO KNOWN FOUNDER

PLACE OF ORIGIN
INDIA

Sometimes known as Indian wrestling, or "pehlwani," this Aryan and Hindu form of wrestling dates from the 5th century BCE. Although indigenous to the Indian population, it is thought that it was originally influenced by the Persian wrestling arts. Hindu teachers of kushti are known as "gurus," whereas Muslim teachers are known as "ustad." Training, which is held in a sand-pit area, is extremely physical and designed to build bulk, strength, fluidity of movement, technique, and flexibility.

Strength conditioning

Resistance-training exercises are fundamental to kushti. Traditionally, practitioners carried large stone rings while training, sometimes worn around the neck, to develop neck and upper-body strength. Blocks of stone or logs were also commonly lifted. Today it is more usual for practitioners to pull a large log, sometimes with their master standing on top of it, around the sand-pit ring a number of times. This serves both as a warm-up exercise and to flatten the surface of the sand prior to training.

Training regime

The training area is known as an "akhara." Training sessions are generally between four to six hours in length, starting at 5am, when the temperature is cooler and more conducive to physical exertions. The training day may start with a 5–10 mile (8–16 km) run. This is followed by a climbing exercise using ropes of approximately 50 ft (15 m) in length tied to trees. Practitioners climb up and down these ropes using nothing but their arms, which builds great upper-body strength. Students also partake in jumping exercises and push-ups. Stretches and yoga are followed by actual wrestling bouts; the day's training ends with strength conditioning, including weight training and resistance exercises.

Strict diet

The eating of certain foods is prohibited for kushti practitioners, as underlined in the Samkhya school of philosophical thought; this states that all things can be classified into three areas: "sattva" (calm), "rajas" (passionate), and "tamas" (lethargic). It is thought that a good wrestler must take a large quantity of sattva foods, such as almonds, milk, ghee (a type of Indian butter), figs, apples, bananas, water melons, lemons, and gooseberries. These, alongside green vegetables and orange juice, are said to be good for wrestlers. Spiced food is discouraged, however, as is the use of alcohol and tobacco.

Wrestling status

Although considered a national sport, kushti does not yet have its own stadium in India. There is not much money to be made in the art, but numerous

FIGHTING FOR A HOLD
A kushti wrestler grapples for a secure hold across the full length of his opponent's upper body prior to executing a pinning maneuver.

practitioners have traveled to the West to fight in commercial and Olympic bouts with much success. Many modern Western wrestling experts have made the pilgrimage to Indian wrestling schools and, indeed, modern forms of wrestling such as shoot fighting and some catch systems borrow throws and submissions from kushti.

BEHIND THE SCENES
KUSHTI WRESTLERS

AT KUSHTI SCHOOLS ACROSS INDIA—such as Delhi's Guru Hanuman Akhara, shown here—hundreds of wrestlers, both young and old, uphold the proud traditions of their art. Their dedication ensures that kushti will continue to thrive.

The practices and beliefs inherent in kushti are far removed from the brash, highly publicized world of American professional wrestling, even though they are both major styles of wrestling. Kushti wrestlers are humble fighters, known for their lifelong dedication to training and competition, and for the respect they show to their masters and the school. Typically, a wrestler's day begins at approximately 5 a.m. with a 5 mile (8 km) run. Returning to the gym, the wrestlers split into groups, with the older fighters lifting weights to improve their strength and the younger members of the school spending time stretching.

Suitably limbered up, the young wrestlers then form pairs to practice their techniques. Later on, all the kushti players change into loincloths and continue their training outside, focusing on rope-climbing and push-ups. Finally, at lunchtime, the wrestlers receive some respite from their training regime. They take the chance to shower, eat, and then rest for several hours. When they emerge, they continue training in a special dirt-filled pit, which they must first prepare. Heavy logs or concrete blocks are dragged across the surface of the pit to level it, before the wrestlers put their training to the test with competitive bouts.

EARLY MORNING EXERCISES

Preparing the body for exercise, or warming down after it, is vital for physical pursuits, particularly for a sport as strenuous as kushti. Once back at the gym after their morning run, the young wrestlers spend around 30 minutes warming down their legs and stretching their upper bodies in preparation for the exertions of the day ahead. The head stand (far right) is particularly good for strengthening neck and shoulder muscles.

TROPHY HAUL
Kushti schools compete against one another on a regular basis in order to measure the relative abilities of the wrestlers. The Guru Hanuman Akhara school in Delhi is very proud of its collection of trophies, and displays them in a corner of the gym.

WEIGHT TRAINING

Good upper-body strength is vital for kushti wrestlers because it helps them to out-muscle opponents during grapples and to better execute throws and lifts. Wrestlers therefore usually spend at least an hour every morning lifting weights to maintain their supreme levels of strength.

PRACTICE MAKES PERFECT

After the trainers are satisfied that their students are fully conditioned, the wrestlers team up in pairs to practice specific techniques. Students rehearse a variety of holds, pinning maneuvers, locks, and throws that they will aim to use in one-on-one bouts later in the day. Although these morning training sessions can be competitive, the primary focus is on the wrestlers working together to refine their techniques.

CLIMBING THE ROPE

The rope climb is a defining feature of kushti training. Using only their hands and arms the students must climb up and down a rope that is sometimes 50 ft (15 m) long. The exercise constitutes great conditioning for the upper body and, following the physical exertions of morning training, it is a supreme test of stamina.

BUILDING MUSCLE

Following the exacting rope climb, the masters expect their students to perform push-ups and to lift a heavy stone bound to wood with their arms extended. Sometimes also included in training is an exercise in which the student must stand with his head inside a hollowed-out stone disk. This generates an almost unbearable weight on the neck muscles, so only the strongest wrestlers are deemed capable of this training.

END OF THE SESSION

Morning training at a kushti school usually ends with some preliminary preparation of the fighting pit, prior to afternoon wrestling. Here, a student breaks up sand that has become compacted. With those duties completed, it's time for a refreshing shower before lunch.

FOOD AND REST

After training, the students cook and eat together. The kushti wrestlers' diet is subject to the Samkhya school of philosophical thought, which means that the menu consists entirely of sattva (calm), rajas (passionate), and tamas (lethargic) foodstuffs. After a nourishing meal, the students take a well-earned rest.

PREPARING THE RING

The work done to prepare the wrestling pit for action is not a menial chore; in fact, it forms a core part of a student's training. After moistening the ground with water, students take turns leveling the surface by dragging around a large stone block. This process further aids the wresters' strength conditioning. The strongest students are not limited merely to the weight of the block, they are handicapped with the additional weight of a fellow student.

PREPARING THE BODY

In grappling arts such as kushti, it is vital that the wrestlers are able to establish a secure hold. So, before each contest begins, the wrestlers cover their own body—and that of their opponent—with wet dirt from the pit floor.

SEEKING A HOLD

After a long day's training, the wrestlers now have an opportunity to put their technique and strength training into practice. A convivial handshake starts the bout, and then each wrestler begins slowly looking for a way to gain an advantage over his opponent. A common tactic involves trying to get a secure hold on the opponent's sturdy cotton trunks.

WINNING MANEUVER

With a sound hold over his opponent, the wrestler in blue trunks attempts to end the contest. With his opponent slightly off-balance, he uses his superior strength and technique to throw him to the floor and win the contest with a pinning maneuver. The victor will sleep well tonight; the loser knows he must redouble his efforts in the gym tomorrow.

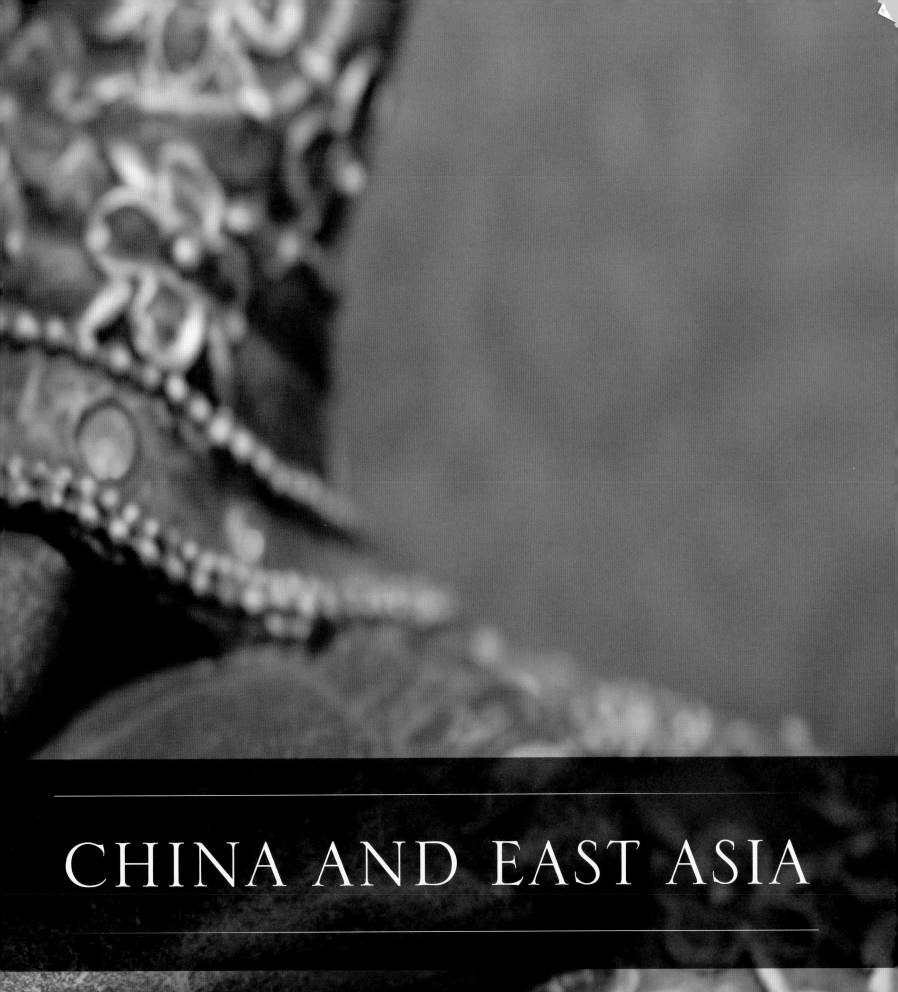

CHINA AND EAST ASIA

CULTURE AND INFLUENCES

CHINA AND EAST ASIA

CHINA AND KOREA have both made vast contributions to the global body of martial arts. China, the world's largest country by population, is widely regarded as the home of martial arts and is the birthplace of numerous diverse styles. Korea, on the other hand, has given us tae kwon do (see pp. 134–35), an Olympic sport since the 2000 Games, and the world's most popular martial art—one that is officially practiced by approximately 50 million people in 120 countries worldwide.

MODERN CHINESE MARTIAL ARTS can trace their origins to a number of sources, including ancient military skills, the Buddhist martial arts that evolved out of the Shaolin temple, the Daoist martial arts that originate from the Wudang temple in Hubei province, and a number of other techniques used by bandits, militia, secret societies, invaders, and marauding pirates throughout China's turbulent history.

According to legend, the Indian monk Bodhidharma (known as "Da Mo" in China) traveled from southern India to China in the 6th century CE carrying sutras (collections of dialogs and discourses). He then settled in the Shaolin temple in Song Shan, and introduced martial exercises and Zen Buddhism to China. However, there is evidence to suggest that the practice of martial arts in the country dates back to well before that time.

A longer history

Although Bodhidharma may well have been one of the first to record martial-art techniques—he also introduced techniques such as meditation to existing fighting systems—experts believe that Chinese martial arts gradually developed from ancient hunting skills and from one tribe's need to

ZI-WU—SHAOLIN DEER-HORN KNIVES

> "TO WIN ONE HUNDRED VICTORIES IN ONE HUNDRED BATTLES IS NOT THE HIGHEST SKILL, TO SUBDUE THE ENEMY WITHOUT FIGHTING IS THE HIGHEST SKILL."
>
> SUN TZU, *THE ART OF WAR*

defend itself from another. These fighting forms developed slowly over the years: punches and kicks were incorporated and, in time, so was the use of weapons.

The first evidence of martial-art practice in China comes in 2698 BCE during the reign of the Yellow Emperor, Huangdi, who developed the practice of jiao di ("horn-butting") among his soldiers. In the 5th century BCE—some 1,000 years before Bodhidharma's arrival in Song Shan—Confucius mentions martial arts in his texts; Daoist literature from the 4th century BCE contains principles applicable to martial arts; and there is evidence to suggest that physical exercises similar to taijiquan (see pp. 80–87) have been practiced in the region since at least 500 BCE. In contrast, the earliest textual evidence of Shaolin martial arts comes in 728 CE.

Putting soldiers to the test

The development of martial arts in China is indelibly linked to the military. The first military martial-arts tests were established in 702 CE. These challenged a soldier's physical strength, horsemanship, and skills with a lance, spear, and bow and arrow. Such a premium was placed on them that regular soldiers were categorized according to their ability and courage in hand-to-hand combat and weapons skills, particularly their swordsmanship.

Various military generals have added their expertise to China's martial-arts mix. Even Genghis Khan, the Mongol warrior whose armies had conquered much of South Asia—including all of China—by the 13th century, believed that bkyukl bökh (also known as Mongolian wrestling, see p. 54) was the best

MAP OF CHINA AND EAST ASIA

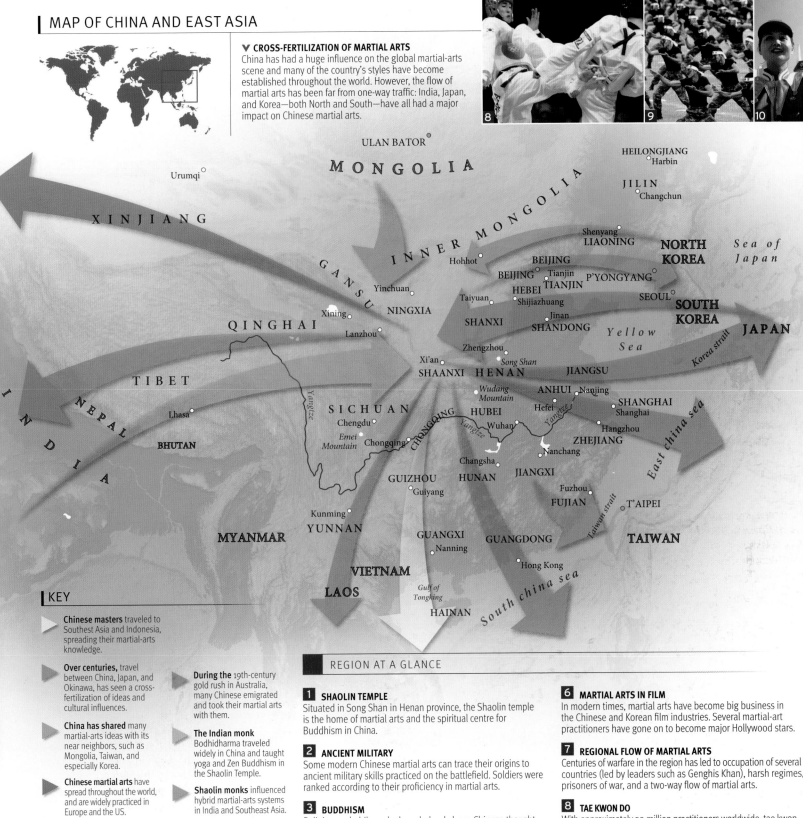

▼ CROSS-FERTILIZATION OF MARTIAL ARTS
China has had a huge influence on the global martial-arts scene and many of the country's styles have become established throughout the world. However, the flow of martial arts has been far from one-way traffic: India, Japan, and Korea—both North and South—have all had a major impact on Chinese martial arts.

8

9

10

ULAN BATOR

MONGOLIA

Urumqi

HEILONGJIANG
Harbin

JILIN
Changchun

XINJIANG

INNER MONGOLIA

Shenyang
LIAONING

NORTH KOREA

Sea of Japan

Hohhot

BEIJING

GANSU

Yinchuan

BEIJING
Tianjin
TIANJIN

P'YONGYANG

Taiyuan
HEBEI

Shijiazhuang

SEOUL

SOUTH KOREA

NINGXIA

Xining

SHANXI

Jinan

JAPAN

QINGHAI

Lanzhou

SHANDONG

Yellow Sea

Zhengzhou

TIBET

Yangtze

Xi'an
SHAANXI

Song Shan
HENAN

JIANGSU

Korea strait

INDIA

NEPAL

Lhasa

SICHUAN

Chengdu

Wudang Mountain

HUBEI

ANHUI
Hefei

Nanjing

SHANGHAI
Shanghai

BHUTAN

Emei Mountain
Chongqing

CHONGQING

Yangtze

Wuhan

Yangtze

Hangzhou

ZHEJIANG

East china sea

Nanchang

Changsha

JIANGXI

GUIZHOU

HUNAN

Fuzhou

MYANMAR

Kunming
YUNNAN

Guiyang

FUJIAN

T'AIPEI

GUANGXI

GUANGDONG

Taiwan strait

TAIWAN

Nanning

VIETNAM

Hong Kong

LAOS

Gulf of Tongking

South china sea

HAINAN

KEY

▷ **Chinese masters** traveled to Southeast Asia and Indonesia, spreading their martial-arts knowledge.

▷ **Over centuries,** travel between China, Japan, and Okinawa, has seen a cross-fertilization of ideas and cultural influences.

▷ **China has shared** many martial-arts ideas with its near neighbors, such as Mongolia, Taiwan, and especially Korea.

▷ **Chinese martial arts** have spread throughout the world, and are widely practiced in Europe and the US.

▷ **During the** 19th-century gold rush in Australia, many Chinese emigrated and took their martial arts with them.

▷ **The Indian monk** Bodhidharma traveled widely in China and taught yoga and Zen Buddhism in the Shaolin Temple.

▷ **Shaolin monks** influenced hybrid martial-arts systems in India and Southeast Asia.

6

7

REGION AT A GLANCE

1 SHAOLIN TEMPLE
Situated in Song Shan in Henan province, the Shaolin temple is the home of martial arts and the spiritual centre for Buddhism in China.

2 ANCIENT MILITARY
Some modern Chinese martial arts can trace their origins to ancient military skills practiced on the battlefield. Soldiers were ranked according to their proficiency in martial arts.

3 BUDDHISM
Religion and philosophy have helped shape Chinese thought throughout the centuries and have played a significant role in the evolution of martial arts in the region.

4 WUDANG MOUNTAIN
Located in Hubei province, Wudang Mountain is considered the Holy Land of Daoism in China and is the source of many martial arts and traditional practices.

5 CULTURAL REVOLUTION
The nationalistic government of China has been eager to use some martial arts for propaganda purposes, in particular wushu (see pp. 93–99), which became popular after 1949.

6 MARTIAL ARTS IN FILM
In modern times, martial arts have become big business in the Chinese and Korean film industries. Several martial-art practitioners have gone on to become major Hollywood stars.

7 REGIONAL FLOW OF MARTIAL ARTS
Centuries of warfare in the region has led to occupation of several countries (led by leaders such as Genghis Khan), harsh regimes, prisoners of war, and a two-way flow of martial arts.

8 TAE KWON DO
With approximately 50 million practitioners worldwide, tae kwon do (see pp. 134–35), Korea's national sport and an Olympic event since 2000, is the most-practiced martial art in the world.

9 ISOLATIONIST TENDENCIES
Some martial arts in the region have evolved independently from outside influence and technological advances and remain unchanged to this day.

10 BUILDING BRIDGES
Martial arts have been used as a way of establishing relations between North and South Korea. Competitions are now starting to take place between the two countries.

way to keep his troops ready for battle. Two styles of the art are still practiced today, one in Mongolia, the other in Inner Mongolia.

Boom in popularity

It was not until the Republican Period (1912–1949), a time when China was recovering from the fall of the Qing dynasty, the invasion by Japan, and the Chinese Civil War, that martial arts became more accessible to the general public. In a wave of national pride, the Chinese government classified all martial arts under the banner "guosho," meaning "national art." Martial artists were encouraged to teach, numerous training manuals were published, examinations in martial arts were created, and demonstration teams started to travel the world—the first martial-art demonstration in front of an international audience took place at the 1936 Olympic Games in Berlin.

Under pressure

The founding of the People's Republic of China on October 1, 1949—and the Cultural Revolution between 1966 and 1976 in particular—saw dramatic changes in the Chinese martial-arts scene. The widespread practice of traditional martial arts was discouraged and some systems were altered to reflect Maoist doctrine. Many well-known practitioners chose to escape the country. They went on to teach their systems in overseas Chinese communities, then to non-Chinese pupils, and so Chinese martial-art forms began to seep into communities throughout the world. But the PRC government was eager to make the most of one of the country's most iconic symbols.

In 1949, the term "wushu"—a generic term for a number of martial arts, meaning "martial skill" or "martial art"—started to become popular in China. The Physical Culture and Sports Commission used the term to govern and standardize versions of the traditional arts and develop routines for use in competition. These routines consist of three main categories: chang quan, taijiquan, and nan quan (see pp. 89, 80–87, 121). Chang quan uses acrobatic martial-art styles that originated in the north of China. Taijiquan comprises slow, fluid, and graceful movements, and is considered both a martial art and a health regime. Nan quan features short, heavy-hitting styles, and is generally thought to have originated in southern China.

^ ANCIENT TRADITIONS
Monks practice with the Shaolin long staff, one of the most important weapons in Shaolin kung fu (see p. 57–67). Cudgels and sticks were always readily available, so it was common for monks to take them with them on their travels as a means of protecting themselves.

< SHAOLIN DOUBLE DAGGERS
Only taught to more experienced practitioners, the double-dagger forms require power, speed, good stances, and aggression. They are equally effective in attack and defense.

"KNOWING OTHERS IS INTELLIGENCE; KNOWING YOURSELF IS TRUE WISDOM; MASTERING OTHERS IS STRENGTH; MASTERING YOURSELF IS TRUE POWER."

LAO-TZU, THE FATHER OF DAOISM

Modern Chinese arts

Today Chinese martial arts can be placed into different "families." Some styles mimic the movements of animals, while some take their names from their founders. Some arts are categorized according to whether they are internal ("soft") or external ("hard"). Others are grouped by their geographic location: styles that developed north of the Yangtze River, or "northern styles," which generally contain fast, powerful kicks with fluid and rapid movements, and those which developed south of the river, "southern" styles, where emphasis is placed on strong arm and hand techniques, stable stances, and fast footwork.

Philosophy, religion, traditional Chinese medicinal and herbal theories, as well as folk medicine, have all played a large role in the evolution of Chinese martial arts. China is the world's most populated country, and its 1.3 billion people—including some 55 ethnic minorities, in addition to the Han majority—

⋀ AN ANNUAL EVENT
Practitioners gather for the biggest event in the bkyukl bökh (also known as Mongolian wrestling, see p. 54) calendar: the annual Nadaam Festival held in Ulan Bator in northern Mongolia—an event that commonly features over 1,000 wrestlers. Genghis Khan used the sport in the 13th century to help his troops prepare for battle.

◄ MASS PARTICIPATION
Up to 18,000 people perform fan taiji (see pp. 80–87) during the opening ceremony of the 2007 Foshan Tourism and Cultural Festival in the city of Foshan in Guangdong province.

have all brought their traditions, cultures, and beliefs into the tremendous mixing pot that is Chinese martial arts.

Korean martial arts

Martial arts enjoy enormous popularity in Korea. Nearly every street corner in Seoul has a "dojang," a martial training school, and tae kwon do has been taught in the country's primary schools since the 1970s. Today, approximately 50 million people around the world practice this Olympic sport, making it the most popular martial art in the world.

Korea's long and turbulent history has also played its part in the development of martial arts, as have the numerous wars that have taken place on the peninsula, from early Chinese domination to the 20th-century occupation by Japan.

Korean martial arts have been shaped by religion and philosophy, most notably Buddhism and Confucianism. The Buddhist element gave the country its martial code during the Silla dynasty (57 BCE–935 CE): loyalty to one's king; obedience to one's parents; honorable conduct to one's friends; never to retreat in battle; and only to kill for a good reason.

Origins of Korean martial arts

Because of its early isolationist policies, many of Korea's fighting cultures developed independently of any technological advances. Favoring the bow, the Koreans did not develop sword and bladed-weapon arts to the same degree as China and Japan. The wooden staff, or "bo," also failed to find popularity in the country.

The earliest evidence of Korean martial arts dates back to the Koguryo dynasty, founded in 37 BCE. The disputed tombs of the Sambo-Chong, located in Jilin province in modern-day China,

> "ALL MUST STAY CONNECTED;
> IF ONE PART OF THE BODY
> MOVES, ALL PARTS MUST MOVE.
> IF ONE PART OF THE BODY IS
> STILL, ALL PARTS MUST BE STILL."
>
> TAIJIQUAN GRAND MASTER CHENG MAN CHING

depict fighters engaging in unarmed combat. Korean wrestling competitions, similar to sumo (see pp. 226–33), were common occurrences on national holidays in ancient Korea, and ssireum (see p. 126), the traditional form of Korean wrestling, is still popular today. Koreans are also noted for their archery skills and have won many international and Olympic titles.

▲ OCCUPYING FORCES
Japanese officials march through the Korean streets in the early 1900s. Many of Korea's indigenous martial arts were banned during the Japanese period of occupation after the Sino-Japanese war in 1894.

Japanese influences

The Japanese occupation of Korea following the Sino-Japanese war of 1894 led to a number of significant developments in the evolution of Korean martial arts. Following liberation, many martial arts were codified and popularized, most famously tae kwon do. The nation, and particularly the military, recognized the importance of this process, not only for unarmed combat, but also as a means of building morale among the army and civilian population.

After the war, many of the Koreans who had been living in Japan—either as laborers or inductees in the Japanese military—stayed on and played their part in influencing Japanese and world martial arts.

Since 1945, the country has been divided into two sections: the communist north and the democratic south. Differing governing bodies of martial arts exist on both sides of the cultural divide and recently there have been a number of friendly sporting and educational exchanges between the two sections.

◄ NATIONAL SPORT
Korea's oldest sport, ssireum (see p. 126) is still a common sight at national festivals. The goal is to force an opponent to touch the ground with any part of his body above the knee.

Bkyukl Bökh

EXPLANATION
"WRESTLING" IN MONGOLIAN
DATE OF ORIGIN
INDIGENOUS ART
FOUNDER
NO KNOWN FOUNDER
PLACE OF ORIGIN
MONGOLIA

There are two styles of bkyukl bökh: the first is practiced in Mongolia, while the second is popular in Inner Mongolia. Practitioners typically perform a ritual dance before entering the tournament. There are numerous dancing styles (all of them imitating animal movements), but a wrestler from Mongolia will usually imitate the falcon or phoenix, while those from Inner Mongolia are more likely to mimic the lion, tiger, or deer. Although the dance is generally regarded as a warm-up and a psychological preparation rite, its origins can be found in the shamanistic rituals of the Mongols.

Alongside archery and horseback riding, wrestling is seen as one of the three most important skills of manhood in all Mongolian societies,

and the great Mongol warrior Genghis Khan believed it to be the most effective method of keeping troops readied for battle.

Mongolians have not lost sight of the art's historical importance: in former times on the steppe, their countrymen had to be constantly prepared for war, and the art is closely related to the pastoral, nomadic traditions of central Asian steppe clans. Although bkyukl bökh is no longer used for military purposes, it remains the national sport of Mongolia and has retained its cultural prestige.

The correct dress

A wrestler wears three main items of clothing when fighting: the "jodag," a short-sleeved jacket traditionally made from silk, wool, or cotton, and which is open at the front to expose the chest of the wrestler; the "gutal," which are traditional leather boots with upturned toes that are sometimes tied to the leg of the fighter with cord so that they do not loosen during fighting; and the "shuudag," a pair of tight-fitting shorts that allow ease of movement.

The Naadam Festival

The biggest and most popular bkyukl bökh competition, the Naadam Festival, takes place near Ulanbataar in nothern Mongolia. Bkyukl bökh is a "winner takes all" sport and no weight categories or time limits are imposed, and the ultimate winner is the wrestler who remains undefeated through each stage of the competition. The

▲ THE GAMES BEGIN
The opening ceremony of the Naadam Festival sees all the competitors dress in their national costume before the tournament begins.

winner of a bout is the wrestler who is able to force an opponent's knee, back, or elbow to the ground. This contrasts with the competitions that take place in Inner Mongolia, where any part of the body touching the ground is a defeat. Hitting and locking are illegal in both styles.

▼ WRESTLING MONGOLIAN-STYLE
Two wrestlers battle it out at the Naadam Festival, where there is no time limit and no weight categories.

Tien Shan Pai

EXPLANATION
NAMED AFTER TIEN SHAN MOUNTAIN IN XINJIANG PROVINCE

DATE OF ORIGIN
UNKNOWN

FOUNDER
HUNG YUN TZU

PLACE OF ORIGIN
XINJIANG PROVINCE, CHINA

This northern Chinese system was created by Hung Yun Tzu in the Tien Shan mountains in Xinjiang province in the northwest of China. He was fanatical about martial arts and, as a boy, once knelt outside a temple for two days in order to learn an old monk's fighting style.

Double blocks

The art is known for its hidden footwork steps and for the unique way in which practitioners double-block attacks—meaning that if

▲ **CLASSICAL HORSE STANCE**
In this stance, the left hand defends an attack from above, and the right hand thrusts the weapon (yin-yang hooks) toward an opponent.

the first block should fail to stop an attack, a second hand always covers the first. Emphasis is placed on single strikes and, alongside the empty-hand forms, the art teaches a number of weapons forms.

Boabom

EXPLANATION
NOT KNOWN

DATE OF ORIGIN
INDIGENOUS ART

FOUNDER
NO KNOWN FOUNDER

PLACE OF ORIGIN
TIBETAN HIMALAYAS

Boabom is a system that does not advocate repetition as a way of learning, and there is no contact between practitioners. They are encouraged instead to focus on achieving a feeling of self-confidence while avoiding fighting.

Exercises are designed to improve agility, balance, speed reflexes, spontaneity, and breathing. Movements with the aid of a stick are also taught. The weapon should be thought of as an extension of the body and the principles of movement—both with and without the stick—are the same.

Hop Gar Kung Fu

EXPLANATION
"CANNON FIST" IN TIBETAN

DATE OF ORIGIN
15TH CENTURY

FOUNDER
A DA TUO

PLACE OF ORIGIN
TIBET

Hop gar is closely related to the lama pai system and the Tibetan white crane system, both of which derive from an original system called lion's roar (see pak hok pai below). The system is now practiced mostly in southern China rather than Tibet, and hand techniques such as the "backfist" and the "overhead punch" are perfected by the practice of forms.

The main characteristics are: no blocking; keeping opponents at arms length; deft changes of direction; and the idea of clarity of intention behind all movement.

Pak Hok Pai

EXPLANATION
"WHITE CRANE BOXING" IN CANTONESE

DATE OF ORIGIN
UNKNOWN

FOUNDER
A DA TUO

PLACE OF ORIGIN
TIBET

This system was first created in Tibet during the Ming Dynasty (1368–1644). It is thought that a Tibetan Lama (spiritual leader) named A Da Tuo, while in a meditative state, witnessed a white crane and a black ape fighting. He was so impressed by the quick and easy movement of the ape and the gracefulness of the crane, that he was inspired to create a new system, which he called "lion's roar."

It was originally named after the Buddhist principle that is best translated as "sounds that shake the Earth are like the lion's roar"—the lion's roar is seen as being the creation or the starting point of a significant event.

In the 1800s, the system was improved and renamed "white crane sect" by Lama Du Luo Ji Tan.

Guiding principles

Much of the original syllabus is still taught today. The four main underlying concepts upon which the system is based are: "chan," literally translated as cruel, and meaning that fighters must adopt a dominant mentality and never retreat until the fight is ended; "sim," the principle of skilled use of body movement to dodge any attacks; "jit," meaning to stay one move ahead of the fight; and "cheung," which is the concept of powerful strikes punching through opponents and targets. Typically, punches are aimed to land 3 in (7.5 cm) behind (i.e. through) the opponent's body.

Emei Quan

EXPLANATION
"EMEI FIST" IN MANDARIN

DATE OF ORIGIN
INDIGENOUS ART

FOUNDER
NO KNOWN FOUNDER

PLACE OF ORIGIN
SZECHWAN PROVINCE, CHINA

This system is named after the Emei Mountains, located in the Szechwan province of western China, and it incorporates low, strong stances, hopping movements, and powerful flipping actions that are generated from the wrists. Training involves the use of forms and weapons. One of the system's main characteristics is the way that practitioners use force both to divert attacks from, and

deliver strikes to, opponents. Emei incorporates a number of techniques from monkey-style kung fu (see p. 102) and its forms are particularly spectacular and officious.

Although not as popular outside Asia as Shaolin kung fu (see p. 57), emei quan is one of the five major systems recognized inside China.

▼ **ABUNDANT WILDLIFE**
Emei Mountain is famed for its wildlife and animal styles of kung fu.

> "PAK HOK PAI'S TRAITS ARE THE NO BLOCKING PRINCIPLE, LONG-ARM TECHNIQUES, DEFT CHANGES IN DIRECTION, AND CLARITY OF MOVEMENT."
>
> LAMA A DA TUO

Bak Fu Pai

EXPLANATION
"WHITE TIGER KUNG FU" IN CANTONESE

DATE OF ORIGIN
UNKNOWN

FOUNDER
FUNG DO DUK

PLACE OF ORIGIN
SZECHWAN PROVINCE, CHINA

According to legend, Fung Do Duk, the founder of the system, was one of the few monks to escape with his martial-arts knowledge from the brutal burning of the southern Shaolin temple in 1723. While meditating on Emei Mountain, he was visited by a goddess on a golden throne. She demonstrated a set of meditations called "fae fung sunn gung," which were said to greatly benefit the health of mankind, but also warned the monk that, because the exercises and meditations were heaven-sent, he had to choose who he taught them to with great care. Consequently, a tradition of secrecy has always surrounded the art.

Bak fu pai as it is taught today includes a number of southern-style Chinese punches and kicks, including the "reverse punch." Low shin kicks and knee kicks are a commonly employed tactic and, alongside the study of meditation and nutrition, "iron-palm" practices are widespread. The most spectacular iron-palm strike is the coconut break, in which, after a number of years of iron-palm practice, practitioners are able to smash coconuts with the fist or the back of the hand—a clean break indicates good, solid iron-palm technique.

▲ TIGER-CLAW STANCE
Here, the right hand has pulled an imaginary opponent inward, while the left hand claws the face.

Liu He

EXPLANATION
"SIX HARMONIES" IN MANDARIN

DATE OF ORIGIN
MID-19TH CENTURY

FOUNDER
JI LONGFENG

PLACE OF ORIGIN
SHAANXI PROVINCE, CHINA

The guiding principle of this art is the belief that the received impact of a strike or a force is far greater when the body is working as a harmonious unit.

There are two elements to this martial art—the external and the internal, both of which have three harmonies, or combinations. "San wai he" (the external harmonies), refer to the coordination between hips and shoulders, knees and elbows, and feet and hands. If the maximum amount of power is to be delivered by the strike, all parts of the body and mind must act in complete harmony with each other. "San nei he" (the internal aspects) relate to how the spirit harmonizes with intention, how intention harmonizes with physical energy, and how physical energy harmonizes with strength.

These six harmonies must work together in order to deliver the most effective strikes.

> "NOW THAT WE ARE IN A TIME OF PEACE, IF I AM UNARMED AND MEET THE UNEXPECTED, HOW SHALL I DEFEND MYSELF?"
>
> LIU HE FOUNDER, JI LONGFENG

Bak Mei

EXPLANATION
"WHITE EYEBROW" IN CANTONESE

DATE OF ORIGIN
BETWEEN 1650 AND 1700

FOUNDER
BAK MEI

PLACE OF ORIGIN
SZECHWAN PROVINCE, CHINA

The system is said to have been developed by a Shaolin monk nicknamed Bak Mei, meaning "white eyebrow." Some practitioners, however, claim he was a traitor to the Shaolin temple and worked as a spy for the Qing dynasty (1644–1911), an allegiance that resulted in the burning down of the temple and Bak Mei's subsequent escape.

Some animosity remains among kung-fu stylists to this day, and some teachers refuse to teach Shaolin arts to students who have previously trained in bak mei.

Powerful principles

This important and powerful system is characterized by close-contact, aggressive, explosive punches and blocks that are often thrown in decisive combinations. Hand movements whip, cut, and poke, and practitioners exhale hard when throwing punches.

At its core the system is a close-range fighting art founded on four principles: to float, to sink, to swallow, and to split. These power principles refer directly to the forward, sideways, and up-and-down motions of movement, and in particular the delivery, or splitting, of power and the swallowing, or absorption, of force. Further important fighting techniques used within the system are sinking, springing, thrusting, and neutralizing.

The style has been fictionalized in popular Hong Kong movies such as *The Shaolin Heroes* or *Shaolin Ying Xiong* (1980) and more recently by the character Pai Mei, as played by Gordon Liu, in the Hollywood film *Kill Bill: Volume 2* (2004).

AUTHOR'S NOTE

Bak mei is a no-nonsense, direct striking system and training involves the practice of violent jabbing and thrusting moves in partner drills. It is the only one in which I have trained where the teacher would give you a tissue before the class, to blow your nose, because of the large exhaling movements you make when training—and one afterward, to wipe the blood from your nose because, inevitably, one or the other of you gets punched on the nose.

▼ BLOCKBUSTER FILMS
Mainstream Hollywood films have contributed to the growing popularity of bak mei, and in Chinese martial arts in general.

Shaolin Kung Fu

EXPLANATION
SKILL OF THE SHAOLIN TEMPLE
DATE OF ORIGIN
C. 6TH CENTURY CE
FOUNDER
BODHIDHARMA
PLACE OF ORIGIN
SONG SHAN, HENAN PROVINCE, CHINA

Shaolin kung fu is a generic term that refers to a number of different types of kung fu that all trace their origins back to the famed Shaolin temple. The style is generally considered to have external characteristics, which emphasize physical power, speed, agility, and athleticism.

The founding father

Bodhidharma—the Indian Buddhist monk sometimes known as Da Mo—is thought to have been responsible for the introduction of yogic exercises at the Shaolin temple. Although disputed, it is claimed that these exercises eventually became what is now known as kung fu. Experts can be certain, however, that a monk named Da Mo did reside at the temple and became the Temple Master between 512 and 527 CE, and that he introduced an exercise regime known as "18 lohan hands."

The fighting monks

It was during the first millennium CE that the Shaolin monks began to earn themselves a fearsome reputation due to their prowess in fighting. Records show that in 621 CE, for example, they played a decisive role in the defeat of Wang Shi Chong at the battle of Hulao but, although records at the temple do show that the monks engaged in actual combat during that period, there is no recorded evidence to show that their daily training regime included martial-arts practice.

North versus south

Two main variations of Shaolin kung fu exist, known as "northern-style boxing" and "southern-style boxing." The former uses a combination of hand and foot techniques, while the latter focuses on hand-based techniques. Both utilize strengths and weaknesses of bone, muscle, sinew, and the mind, to create the best-known of all the Chinese martial-arts systems.

THE LEGEND OF BODHIDHARMA

Bodhidharma arrived in China from India to spread Zen Buddhism throughout the country. After visiting Emperor Wu-ti, who had supported Buddhism and was anxious to discuss its guiding principles, Bodhidharma traveled to, and settled in, the Shaolin temple of Song Shan in Henan province. He felt that the monks there lacked sufficient stamina to meditate properly or defend themselves from the roving bandits in the area, so he taught them the "18 lohan hands", a system of dynamic tension exercises that was eventually published in 550 CE as the *Yi Jin Jing*.

▼ MAIN ENTRANCE
To show their commitment, potential disciples must kneel outside the temple for three days. But this alone does not guarantee admittance.

> **IRON-PALM TECHNIQUE**
A monk from the Shaolin Monastery in
Henan province, China, destroys an ice-
filled vat with a single strike of his fist.
A combination of muscular strength and
control of the vital energy of "qi" enables
him to perform the movement unharmed.

BEHIND THE SCENES

SHAOLIN MONKS

THE ORANGE-ROBED, SHAVEN-HEADED MONKS of the Shaolin temple have been synonymous with fighting prowess and spirit for millennia. The arts that they developed have inspired hundreds of martial-arts systems around the world.

The monks' exploits, and the battles they have fought, have earned them near-mythological status in China and around the world, and monk warriors have been used as central figures in many films and books.

Traditionally, the training structure among the monks was relatively limited, with fighters being divided into three categories: students, disciples, and masters. As a rule, students were given menial tasks such as washing clothes, preparing food, sweeping, and cleaning. From this group, masters would choose their disciples—those who they

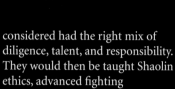

"LIVE A GOOD, HONOURABLE LIFE. THEN WHEN YOU GET OLDER AND THINK BACK, YOU'LL BE ABLE TO ENJOY IT A SECOND TIME."

considered had the right mix of diligence, talent, and responsibility. They would then be taught Shaolin ethics, advanced fighting techniques, and the traditional medicinal arts. From these disciples, those who excelled by mastering the arts and philosophical teachings were promoted to be masters.

Much of this framework of teaching is still in place and, although there are commercial schools in the area teaching Shaolin kung fu, there still exists a core of genuine Shaolin monks who train in the traditional arts.

WORSHIPING THE BUDDHA
Participating in religious activities is a principal part of life at the temple, but Shaolin is the only Buddhist temple to also encourage training in martial arts. Praying and endurance training are of equal importance as a pure mind and physical strength are crucial skills for mastering kung fu.

BIRTH OF A LEGEND
Situated at the foot of Songshan Mountain in Henan province, the Shaolin temple is often cited as the crucible of Chinese martial arts. It has been destroyed and rebuilt many times, but its training methods and Buddhist teachings live on.

CREATIVE STUDY
The study of sacred Shaolin texts and the practice of calligraphy (left) is integral to learning martial arts at the temple. Such creative undertakings help the monks foster moral integrity, martial prowess, and also help to fortify the mind and cultivate "qi." The traditions of the temple and the feats of its monks, past and present, are also kept alive through music and song.

A LABOR OF LOVE
Practical labor is part of the monks' daily training regime. A number of them will have been instructed to retrieve bundles of straw—which will be used to stuff mattresses—from the agricultural land that surrounds the temple. A simple breakfast will sustain the monks after early-morning training and before the commencement of their chores, meditation, and further training.

CONTINUOUS TRAINING

Shaolin monks may have as many as four training sessions every day. Practice with dummies and long cudgels, one of the most important Shaolin weapons (see p. 66), feature heavily during these sessions. Physical endurance also forms a very important part of their conditioning.

HEAD STRONG

As part of their mental and physical endurance training, the monks are taught to stand on their heads for long periods of time. Eventually they will be able to perform this exercise without the help of a wall to support them. Head-butting and weight-training with everyday objects comprise more aspects of their exercise regime.

STRONGER HANDS
The physical conditioning of the monks' hands is a crucial part of their instruction. One of the training methods involves thrusting hands into iron sand to toughen up finger joints. Without strong hands, wrists, and joints, many of the techniques that the monks learn would be impossible to carry out effectively.

"THE MIND IS THE ROOT FROM WHICH ALL THINGS GROW. IF YOU CAN UNDERSTAND THE MIND, EVERYTHING ELSE IS INCLUDED"

ATTRIBUTED TO THE LEGENDARY MONK BODHIDHARMA

TRAINING WITH WEAPONS

There are 18 original Shaolin weapons, which originate from ancient military weapons and from adapted farming implements. Of the "18 Arms" (see p. 66), the term used to describe Shaolin kung fu weaponry, a selection are shown here, including the "guan dao" (below and bottom middle), the "rope dart" (right), the "broadsword" (bottom left), and the "monk's spade" (bottom right).

>>

WEAPONS AND ARMOR

SHAOLIN MONKS

ACCORDING TO THEIR BUDDHIST PRINCIPLES, Shaolin monks practice nonviolence, although their weapons are famed for their variety. Legend dictates that 18 of these— "The 18 Arms" (see pp. 64–65)—were invented behind the walls of the Shaolin temple. The four most important of these are the staff (known as "the father of all weapons"), the broadsword ("the marshall"), the spear ("the king"), and the straight sword ("the gentleman"). Used over the centuries for practice and self-defense, the vast array of weapons can be classified into five categories: long, short, soft, rare, and hidden.

< CHIU
The "chiu," or hammer, is a classic example of a simple yet incredibly useful weapon.

∨ SHAOLIN MONK UNIFORM
Shaolin monks wear a standard uniform in either blue-gray (the color commonly worn by students) or orange. Famously, the tunic can, and does, hide a vast array of armory.

> THREE-SECTIONED STAFF
Consisting of three linked staves, this is a formidable weapon at long or short range.

∨ TWO-SECTIONED STAFF
One of the most celebrated Shaolin weapons, Shaolin kung fu contains 36 forms for the two-sectioned staff.

∨ GOU
This "gou," or hook, is used to disarm an opponent. The crescent-shaped handle can also be used for attacks.

Hook

∨ BAMBOO STICKS
Owing to the fact that they can be found anywhere in the forest, sticks have played a key role in Shaolin fighting methods.

HANDLE
These are effective for both attack and defense

∨ ZI-WU
"Zi-wu," or deer-horn knives, are deadly, multibladed weapons designed for use against multiple attackers.

GROUND TIP
Ground tips are ideal for stabbing an opponent

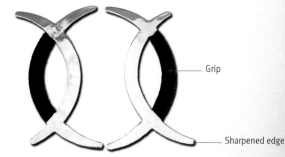

Grip

Sharpened edge

> **GUAN DAO**
The "guan dao", or halberd, is one of 18 Shaolin weapons. It consists of a long crescent-shaped blade (for cutting and slashing) and a sharp point (for stabbing).

POINTED TIP
The sharp tip is ideal for stabbing thrusts

DRAGON ENGRAVING
The dragon is a mythological symbol standing for happiness, immortality, fertility, and activity

> **SAN JIAN LIANG REN DAO**
This three-pointed halberd is suitable for both stabbing and cutting.

POINTED SPEAR
This tip is lethal if thrust toward an opponent at close quarters

> **TIGER FORK**
Similar to the forks used by farmers, this weapon is made of metal and was originally used as a fishing instrument.

ELEPHANT
In Chinese mythology, the elephant is a symbol of strength and astuteness

> **BODHIDHARMA STAFF**
Unique to Shaolin martial arts, this staff is used as a hand-held stabbing instrument. It was named after the Buddhist monk Bodhidharma, who is thought to have come to China from southern India in the 6th century CE.

TIGER
The tiger is symbolic of courage and bravery

Decorative pommel

CRESCENT BLADE
As well as being an effective weapon, this blade acts as a counterweight

∧ **MONK'S SPADE**
A versatile weapon that can be used for both defense and attack. Techniques for learning the spade are not taught to outsiders.

SPADE
Monks typically carried spades with them on their travels so they could perform burial duties

∧ **STAFF**
Known as "the father of all weapons," the staff is indelibly linked to the legend of the Shaolin monks.

FLAG
The flag adds visual appeal and covers the handle

∧ **NINE-SECTIONED STEEL WHIP**
Known as "the dragon of weapons," a practitioner will need complete coordination between the eyes, hand, and feet, if he is to master the use of the nine-sectioned whip.

METAL DART
This is swung around in a wide arc to ward off opponents

Ba Ji Quan

EXPLANATION
"EIGHT EXTREME FISTS" IN MANDARIN

DATE OF ORIGIN
UNKNOWN

FOUNDER
NO KNOWN FOUNDER

PLACE OF ORIGIN
HEBEI PROVINCE, CHINA

The origin of this art is unclear, but the earliest recorded use was during the Qing dynasty (1644–1911) by a Chinese Muslim from Mong village in Hebei province, northern China.

The current system is an amalgamated form that was once taught alongside what is now known as piguazhang, or "chopping, hanging palm." Today, the systems are generally taught as one system due to their complementary nature. Practitioners are encouraged to learn techniques that aim to defeat opponents with a single strike, and low stances to develop strength in the legs. A ruthless and direct style, the art is well-known for its extremely powerful blows.

Loud and deadly

A feature of this art is the loud, stomping action that is designed to scare opponents while at the same time developing the practitioner's internal energy. Attacks are released at close range and eight different parts of the body are used to deliver them: elbows, shoulders, head, hands, feet, buttocks, hips, and knees.

It is thought that the bodyguards of three of China's recent most important historical figures—Mao Tse Dong, Chiang Kai Shek, and Sun Yat Sen were all practitioners of this brutally effective killing art.

Leopard-style Kung Fu

EXPLANATION
A TRADITIONAL SHAOLIN ANIMAL SYSTEM

DATE OF ORIGIN
INDIGENOUS ART

FOUNDER
JUEYUAN (WITH HELP FROM BAI YUFENG AND LI SOU)

PLACE OF ORIGIN
HENAN PROVINCE, CHINA

Leopard-style kung ku is one of the five traditional Shaolin animal systems and, due to its quick and penetrating strikes, it is likened to tiger claw and white crane.

The style is based around observations of the movements of the leopard, and one of the main characteristics of the style is its unique leopard fist—an unusual fist that mimics the leopard's paw as it is thrust into an opponent's ribs or throat. Another feature of this kind of kung fu is aggression, combined with repetitive strikes with little regard being paid to one's own welfare. Consequently, it contains fewer blocks than other systems. However, despite it being primarily an external attacking system, some of the attacks do in fact contain blocks within them, blocks that will not necessarily be noticed by the untrained eye.

Deflecting an opponent's moves is another common characteristic of the leopard style. The system relies on speed to be effective at close-quarters. Rhythm, deftness, staying low, and attacking from a crouching position before attacking the "soft" areas of the opponent's body, are all essential ingredients.

◀ **ONE-STRIKE WONDER**
This explosive system is designed to kill with just one strike.

KING LI YEN

Master King Li Yen is Taiwan's most acclaimed Secret Service master. His fighting method is da nei ba ji quan, which is a specialized style of ba ji quan that was once used to train emperor's bodyguards from the Ming dynasty onward, and is now practiced by presidential bodyguards. Having served four Taiwanese presidents over a 21-year period, King is now an instructor to various Taiwanese police agencies and says that in his next life he would be very pleased to be a bodyguard to the president again.

"LIAN HUAN QUAN" (CONTINUOUS FISTS)

1 The form starts with double palms to repel an imaginary attack. Seventy percent of the weight is distributed on the back leg to maintain balance.

2 The defender kicks with his heel, thrusting his leg to an opponent's midsection while blocking an overhead strike, or a hair-grab attempt.

3 Taking a firm low stance, he thrusts down his right palm to block a knee strike or a kick.

4 Imagining a second attacker to his right, he drops his body to the ground, dodging a punch aimed at his face and swinging his torso 90 degrees to the right.

5 Springing back upright, he delivers a stomping kick to his second opponent's groin or lower abdomen.

6 Standing between his two fallen adversaries (one directly to his right another to his left) in a ready stance, he decides if further action is required.

Duan Quan

EXPLANATION
"SHORT DISTANCE FIGHTING"
IN MANDARIN
DATE OF ORIGIN
INDIGENOUS ART
FOUNDER
NO KNOWN FOUNDER

PLACE OF ORIGIN
HEBEI PROVINCE, CHINA

Duan quan, or "short-style" boxing, is popular in Hebei province, China, and, as the name suggests, the system focuses on close-range techniques. Practitioners aim for continual fluid movement, and the routines typically range from three to five steps with a dozen or so movements during which stances are kept low and strikes are thrown in sudden barrages. The unusually low stances from which practitioners fight is designed to disorientate opponents. Jumping and midair actions are discouraged and power is generated from the legs and body.

Da Cheng Quan

EXPLANATION
"THE GREAT ACCOMPLISHMENT"
IN MANDARIN
DATE OF ORIGIN
1940s
FOUNDER
WANG XIANG ZHAI

PLACE OF ORIGIN
SHENXIAN COUNTY, HEBEI PROVINCE, CHINA

This is a form of yiquan ("mind" or "intent" boxing) first developed by Wang Xiang Zhai who, at the age of 14 and in poor health, began a lifelong study of martial arts before creating his own unique system in the 1940s. His motivation for developing a new system came from his frustration at students putting postures and form ahead of mind and spirit training. To this end, exponents of da cheng quan believe that every action must be guided by "yi" (will or spirit), including walking, standing, sitting, and eating, as well as fighting.

Yau Kung Moon

EXPLANATION
"THE STYLE OF FLEXIBLE
POWER" IN MANDARIN
DATE OF ORIGIN
C. 800 CE
FOUNDER
UNKNOWN

PLACE OF ORIGIN
SONG SHAN, HENAN PROVINCE, CHINA

Although this ancient art is thought of as being internal—because of its Buddhist origin—those learning yau kung moon today should expect long hours of physical training. The system teaches stance work, physical conditioning, conditioning of the limbs, reflex training, and weapons training. Iron palm, iron body, dit dar medicine, and qi gong healing methods—along with learning forms, and understanding pressure points—are also taught.

Modern yau kung moon is heavily influenced by the yin and yang philosophy. Hard and soft techniques are interchangeable during combat, opponent's forces are often redirected against them, and striking actions are delivered with an explosive power known as "ging." Ging power in this art is developed by rigorous breathing exercises.

AUTHOR'S NOTE

Yau kung moon is relatively unknown in the West but it is one of my favourite arts because of my early experiences training in Hong Kong as a teenager with Master Ha Tak Kin, grandson of Ha Hon Hung, the first layperson to learn the system.

Mian Quan

EXPLANATION
"CONTINUOUS FIST" IN
MANDARIN
DATE OF ORIGIN
INDIGENOUS ART
FOUNDER
NO KNOWN FOUNDER

PLACE OF ORIGIN
HEBEI PROVINCE, CHINA

Mian quan, known as the "continuous-fist" style, is most popular in Hebei province in the northeast of China, but the art became globally popular after 1936 when the Chinese wushu (see p. 93) team demonstrated the system at the Olympic games in Berlin.

Preference for punching

Mian quan is an effective fight-orientated art that relies on punches and kicks rather than grappling, which is avoided. It is thought of as a relatively simple art to learn and practice when compared to other popular Chinese martial arts.

The system's underlying principle is characterized by soft movements and continuous attacks that are similar to techniques used in Western boxing (see pp. 256–63), such as when a jab is used to set up a combination of heavy, confrontation-deciding blows.

Luohan Quan

EXPLANATION
"WORTHY ONE"
IN MANDARIN
DATE OF ORIGIN
INDIGENOUS ART
FOUNDER
BODHIDHARMA

PLACE OF ORIGIN
HENAN PROVINCE, CHINA

It is believed that this system was developed by monks in the Shaolin temple who copied the facial expressions of the statues of "Arhats" (saints or sages) and developed 18 movements based on those expressions. A further 24 movements of advancing and retreating during actual combat were also developed, and the system now has a total of 108 different movements. These include six forms, which are punctuated throughout with locks, kicks, punches, throws, and takedowns.

It is possible that luohan is the only Chinese, Buddhist kung-fu system to be based on human expressions and emotions. The style also found popularity among Buddhist practitioners in Japan, Indonesia, Malaysia, and Singapore.

◀ READY TO DEFEND
A Shaolin monk in the "ready" position. The low stance and right hand defend against kicks, while the left hand covers attacks from behind.

THE FOUR FORMS

The four forms of da nei ba ji quan, or eight extremes boxing, are: "xiao baji" (small frame); "da baji" (large frame); "liu da kai" (six large openings); and "Lian huan quan" (continuous fists, see p. 68). Each form builds on the foundations of the previous form.

SIMPLICITY WITH POWER

Da nei ba ji quan is known for its forcefulness and simplicity. It is made up of short, powerful techniques for both attack and defense. Debilitating blows and throws are delivered from elbows and shoulder in close combat. The sequence below is called "wrapped by snake."

BEHIND THE SCENES

BEIJING OPERA

COLORFUL, LAVISHLY DECORATED costumes, elaborate facial painting, amazing acrobatics, and martial prowess all combine to make the Beijing Opera both the foremost style of opera in China and a cultural institution.

Traditionally, the Beijing Opera was seen as a way of strengthening China's cultural identity. This form of "public education" was achieved through the dramatization of folk tales, historical battles, and literature. In recent years, however, it is thought that the television and film industries have undermined the influence of the opera.

Historians also believe that the opera contributed to the cross-fertilization and spread of martial arts around China. Skilled martial artists were key members of the opera, and they would invariably share their knowledge as the troupes traveled across the country.

> "BOTH JACKIE CHAN AND SAMMO HUNG ARE THE PRODUCT OF A STRICT OPERATIC EDUCATION."

The necessary skills required to become a performer cannot be underestimated. Performers must be able to sing, dance, act, and perfectly execute martial-art techniques. As a result, it can take an aspiring performer over 10 years of training to hone the right skills to fulfill a role in the opera.

In recent years, because of the physical demands and martial-arts skills that are required to become an opera performer, the opera circuit has become a recruiting ground for the expanding Chinese film industry. The opera has proved a breeding ground for homegrown talent, such as Jackie Chan and Sammo Hung.

THE NEW OPERAGOER

The Cultural Revolution (1966–1976)—Chairman Mao's imposition of a return to basic communist values—was, ironically, a period of stagnation for the arts in China. In the years that followed, the opera suffered from poor audiences and a severe lack of technical expertise. This, however, is constantly changing and, as standards improve and performance are brought up to date, new and younger audiences are attracted to the performances.

CULTURAL EXCHANGE

The Beijing Opera has become increasingly popular with people all over the world, and it has made an important contribution to cultural exchange between China and the West. As more people come to visit the opera and are exposed to the performances it showcases, the more they will understand and appreciate China's people and their way of life.

THE PRINCIPAL PLAYERS

There are four major types of role at the Beijing Opera: "Sheng," which are male roles; "Dan," which are female roles; "Jing," which are male characters with painted faces, such as warriors, heroes, statesmen, or demons; and "Chou," which are clowns or comic characters. There are two types of chou: "wen chou," which are civilian clowns; and "wu chou," which are clowns with martial skills. Both types are instantly recognizable by a patch of white paint on their noses.

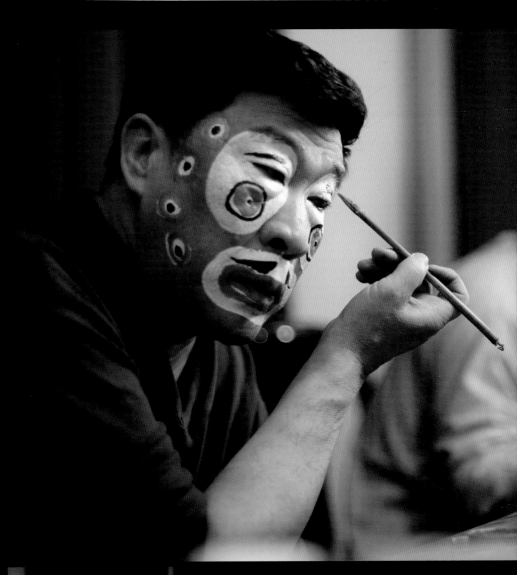

PAINTING A CHARACTER

In the Beijing Opera, facial paint applied to the jing roles helps the audience to identify each character. The color of their makeup reveals how old they are, their profession and, most importantly, their personality. Red denotes loyalty, yellow is for rashness and fierceness, and white is for cunning. If characters are painted gold or silver, they are gods or demons.

>>>

CULTURAL HERITAGE
There are hundreds of operas that describe historical, political, and military events throughout China's history. In recent times, books written by indigenous and foreign authors have also made it to the stage in order to update the form and increase its popularity.

Ba Gua Zhang

EXPLANATION
"EIGHT TRIGRAM PALM" IN MANDARIN

DATE OF ORIGIN
1850

FOUNDER
DONG HAICHUAN

PLACE OF ORIGIN
BEIJING, CHINA

Often called "ba gua" for short, this is one of the most distinctive Chinese internal martial arts. Practitioners walk around in what appears to be a circle as they practice their hand movements, following the octagon shape of the ba gua, or eight trigram, which is used in Chinese philosophy, divination, and magic. The system involves a number of grappling and striking techniques that—to the untrained eye—are often concealed. Weapons training includes the standard Chinese broadsword, staff, and double sword, along with some unique and unusual weapons, such as the "lu jiao dao"—the spear hook sword. Although relatively new, the art has quickly established itself in mainland China due to its grace and efficiency.

▼ WALKING THE CIRCLE
As a major internal system, the generation of "qi" is central to this art. In this system, qi is cultivated by the practice of "walking the circle."

Chuo Jiao

EXPLANATION
"POKING FOOT" IN MANDARIN

DATE OF ORIGIN
INDIGENOUS ART

FOUNDER
DENG LLANG

PLACE OF ORIGIN
NORTHERN CHINA

It is believed this ancient martial art evolved out of wen quan during the days of the Sung dynasty (960–1279). The famous Chinese martial-arts saying, "Hands of the south and legs of the north and even the gods will fear you," commonly referred to the northern leg system of chuo jiao. The system's coiling method relies heavily on the use of forms and routines, as well as on stretching and isometric strengthening exercises.

Shared heritage

Many point to the similarities between chua jiao and xing yi quan (see p. 92). This is possibly because a wen quan master may have developed both systems. Wu Bin Lou, who is well known for his abilities in martial arts and weaponry, and who popularized the art in the Chinese capital Beijing during the 1920s, is largely responsible for the art's wider recognition across China today

Although rarely taught outside China, chuo jiao is a fascinating and beautiful system that focuses on kicks from extremely unusual angles, sweeps, blocks, and throws.

The system may include a range of quickfire, straight-line punches aimed at the center line of the opponent's body, but the style has earned its reputation among martial artists for its large range of unusual but accurate kicks. The system is very demanding physically and requires strong and flexible legs.

Standout features

One of the style's most common styles is the unusual back kick, sometimes known as the "swallow tail kick," which sees the practitioner turn his back on his opponent and release a swinging kick, arching his back, while at the same time lashing out with one of his arms. The theory behind the kick is that because the opponent is distracted by the arm movement, the kick has more chance of finding its target.

Jiu Fa Men

EXPLANATION
"NINE METHOD GATE" IN MANDARIN

DATE OF ORIGIN
1994

FOUNDER
CHRIS CRUDELLI

PLACE OF ORIGIN
BEIJING, CHINA

Sometimes referred to as "alphabet boxing," jiu fa men (JFM) was developed by Chris Crudelli (who lived and studied in China for ten years) in Beijing in 1994. It is a collection of fighting techniques aimed at ending life-threatening situations quickly and decisively.

A practitioner of traditional Shaolin fu jow, nan quan, lau gar, and Southern mantis (see pp. 116, 121–23), Crudelli gained practical insight into the effectiveness of his own methods while working as a bodyguard at an illegal gambling den. He quickly found out which techniques did and didn't work.

JFM utilizes a unique alphabet boxing exercise in which combinations of difficult punches,

palms, chops, elbows, and blocks are taught and explained by following the letters of the English alphabet.

Filling a void

Crudelli developed the system after noting that many trained martial artists struggled to gain sufficient striking power to defend themselves against blows at extreme close quarters, which in turn decreased their chances of victory. This simple discovery formed the basis for much of the system.

He later blended elements of taijiquan (see pp. 80–87), qi gong, and muay Thai (see pp. 158–65) into the system, along with techniques for restraining, locking, throwing, choking, and joint-dislocating, as well as a set of elbow drills, including nine different close-quarter elbow strikes. The style emphasizes correct body alignment to generate power and conceal the move. Weapons training includes the broadsword and staff, knifework, stick and gun disarms.

▼ A FIGHTING STANCE
In this stance, the right hand is extended to deflect attacks to the torso while the left hand provides a secondary line of defense. The hands are splayed for clawing.

> "IF FEAR IS AN UNTESTED THOUGHT, TEST IT, TEST IT, AND THEN TEST IT AGAIN."
>
> CHRIS CRUDELLI

Hua Quan

EXPLANATION
"CHINA STYLE BOXING SYSTEM"
IN MANDARIN

DATE OF ORIGIN
INDIGENOUS ART

FOUNDER
CAI MAO

PLACE OF ORIGIN
SHANDONG PROVINCE, CHINA

The hua quan, also known as "China style boxing system," is one of the chang quan (see p. 89) external northern Chinese kung-fu systems. It is thought that an ancient warrior by the name of Cai Mao, a skilled fighter and swordsman of noble birth, created the system in Shandong province. The art was further developed 400 years later by the brothers Cai Tai and Cai Gang (descendents of Mao), and the art was first documented by Cai

Wanzhi, who described the system in his 16th-century book *The Secrets of Hua Quan*. The book combines the original and revised martial techniques and philosophy, while also extolling the benefits of qi gong breathing exercises. (Practitioners breathe deeply to oxygenate the blood and build "qi".)

Hua quan is characterized by its smooth, well-connected movements, and its techniques are executed with great pace from a solid foundation.

Kept in the family

The system serves as a perfect example of how, through many centuries, Chinese kung-fu systems have evolved and been taught behind closed doors and often only to close family members. This influence is still evident in the teaching methodology of many traditional Chinese martial-art systems.

Di Tang Quan

EXPLANATION
"GROUND TUMBLING BOXING"
IN MANDARIN

DATE OF ORIGIN
12TH CENTURY

FOUNDER
NO KNOWN FOUNDER

PLACE OF ORIGIN
SHANDONG PROVINCE, CHINA

Although little is known about the origin of di tang quan, it is thought to have become popular in China during the Southern Song dynasty (1127–1279).

Acrobatic nature

Di tang quan is an incredibly dynamic martial arts form. It is characterized by an acrobatic nature that includes flips, somersaults, and twists. Many elements of the art have been amalgamated into other Chinese martial arts and exercises.

However, what separates this art from a standard acrobatic routine is that every somersault, twist, jump, or flip contains a surprise punch, kick, grab, or throw.

Conditioning the body

An unusual exercise characteristic of the art is that the practitioner will repeatedly jump backward up into the air as high as he can and land on his back.

Although it might seem strange, this is an exercise of central importance to the understanding of Chinese martial arts and students are encouraged to practice the exercise rigorously. When a martial artist's body receives an impact, he must exhale violently to contract the muscle and constrict the rib cage, emptying the lungs of air as quickly as possible in order to protect the vital organs from damage and prevent, or diminish, the effects of being "winded."

Despite the fact that many may consider this method of training unnecessarily dangerous, and even potentially damaging to one's health, it is said that, if practiced properly, repetition of the exercise will teach the body to exhale instinctively, relax, and allow the impact to travel through the body without harming or disrupting the practitioner's ability to function.

> "THE WAY IS SO SMALL AND SIMPLE, BUT THE MEANING IS TIMELESS AND PROFOUND."
>
> YUH NIUY, LEGENDARY CHINESE WARRIOR

Jing Quan Do

EXPLANATION
POLICE COMBAT METHOD

DATE OF ORIGIN
1995

FOUNDER
ALEXANDER TAO

PLACE OF ORIGIN
SHANDONG PROVINCE, CHINA

Developed by Alex Tao, jing quan do is a combination of practical martial arts designed for the Chinese police. It includes a number of effective quick throws, joint locks, palm strikes, kicks, and punches that are aimed at disarming or disabling dangerous criminals quickly.

GRAND MASTER ALEX TAO

Grand Master Tao grew up in Shandong province in northern China, a region famous for its kung fu. Tao studied fighting strategies from childhood and spent many years at the Shaolin temple honing his skills. Being influenced by Bruce Lee and his fighting style jeet kune do (see pp. 316–17), Tao set about creating his own system, which has been endorsed by the Chinese police and military.

▼ EXTREME MEASURES
Tao's elite military group specializes in security and rescue techniques. They train to overcome opponents with maximum force and speed.

Taijiquan

EXPLANATION
"SUPREME ULTIMATE FIST" IN MANDARIN

DATE OF ORIGIN
12TH CENTURY

FOUNDER
CHANG SAN FENG

PLACE OF ORIGIN
HUBEI PROVINCE, CHINA

A martial art and health regime with an underlying Daoist philosophy, taiji (often written as tai chi) is practiced by millions of people in China and around the world. It is characterized by slow, fluid, and graceful movements, which conform to the Daoist notion of naturalism.

Health benefits

In China the art is seen as a way of restoring health or curing illness, as well as a form of socializing, particularly for older people.

Although the exact origins of this martial art are not clear it is a widely held belief that the original 13 postures of taiji were invented by the Daoist Master Chang San Feng, who resided at the famous Wudang Mountain, a center for the study and practice of Daoist arts (see box opposite). It is said that the master took refuge at Wudang while being pursued by bandits and, in a dream one night, learned the method of taiji. Putting it into practice, he was able to defeat hundreds of attackers.

Chen-style taijiquan

What we can be more certain of is that Chen Wang Ting, a successful warrior and a garrison commander in the 1640s, choreographed much of what we recognize as taiji today.

◄ TAIJIQUAN FAN
The fan is used in more advanced forms of the art.

His original chen-style taijiquan forms the basis of the art's most popular form.

Over the last few centuries different styles have emerged and although they follow Daoist principles there are some striking differences in the forms, most notably the removal of quick, powerful, thrusting, and twisting actions that are found in the original chen style.

Modern taiji

More recent styles of the art employ a higher stance and focus less on fighting, joint locking, and throwing, and emphasize the cultivation of health through slow, rhythmical movements that increase the flow of "qi," or energy, throughout the body. The four major schools are chen, yang, wu, and sun style.

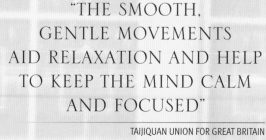

> "THE SMOOTH, GENTLE MOVEMENTS AID RELAXATION AND HELP TO KEEP THE MIND CALM AND FOCUSED"
>
> TAIJIQUAN UNION FOR GREAT BRITAIN

Each school has a number of variants; yang, for example, has a number of subsets that range in terms of complexity; yang 24 step, also known as Beijing style, is the most popular and simple to learn.

Learning the art

Typically, classes emphasize the three main aspects of taiji, which are health, education, and martial art. The stances and the degree of concentration required when exercising movements correctly regulate blood pressure and develops muscular strength, coordination, and balance to a higher degree than when the movements are executed quickly. In addition, each action must be visualized, which enhances strategic thinking.

A major characteristic of this style of martial art is its self-defense aspect. The pupil is taught how to divert and change the direction of opponents' force, rather than directly opposing the force head-on.

The daily practice of moving the joints slowly in a circular fashion greatly helps their mobility, while the qi-building movements built into the form are relaxing and refreshing.

▼ TAIJI FORMS
Hidden within the calm and graceful movements are techniques for defense and attack.

WUDANG MOUNTAIN

Located in Shiyan, in China's Hubei province, Wudang Mountain is well-known for its deep-rooted martial-arts tradition. As an old saying goes: "Shaolin wushu is the best in the north, while Wudang wushu is the best in the south." The mountain is the center for the internal martial-arts training of taijiquan and for training in the healing power of qi gong.

∨ INCREASING THE "QI"
Starting at the top left-hand picture and finishing at the bottom right, this taijiquan master performs eight different movements, beginning with the evocatively named "sated tiger going back to the mountain."

TAIJIQUAN MASTER

MASTER WANG IS A RESPECTED MASTER of taijiquan and yue-style sanshou. Born to a farming family with a martial-arts tradition in the Hunan province of China, he was taught by his father, who had been a Shaolin disciple since the age of eight.

Master Wang is dedicated to the restoration of traditional martial arts. As the founder and director of the Academy of Martial Arts of Restoration (AMAR) in Taipei, Taiwan, his teaching is heavily influenced by the traditional martial arts he learned as a young boy. He later went on to refine and teach them while serving with the Hunan guerrilla force, a clandestine, highly mobile, lightly armed special unit of the Chinese military. Under the command of General Yin Li Yan, they were tasked with conducting guerrilla activities against the Japanese army in occupied China during the 1940s.

> "PUNCHES AND KICKS ARE NOT A FEATURE OF THIS FORM OF TAIJIQUAN. SUCCESS IN PUSHING HANDS IS ACHIEVED BY UPSETTING THE BALANCE OF ONE'S OPPONENT."

Each man was armed with only two daggers, a saber, and a German-made pistol. In keeping with guerrilla tactics, fighting methodology was simple, brutal, and disruptive, relying on good intelligence. His team's actions were to be swift and silent, favoring hand-to-hand combat techniques that avoided redundant, flowery movements. Much of the practicality of his former training informs his teaching methods today. Master Wang still teaches students from around the world on a daily basis at Xing Long Park in Taipei.

THE START OF THE DAY
Before making his way to Xing Long Park for his daily practice and teaching sessions, Master Wang prepares by supping tea and consulting texts. His family and background are very important and act as a constant reinforcement of his heritage.

EARLY DAYS
Master Wang was taught how to use the saber in 1944, when he joined the Hunan guerrilla force. The standard equipment for each member of this special unit included one saber made by the Hanyang Arsenal.

TEACHING AT THE PARK

Master Wang teaches "pushing hands," which is an art that does not seek to fight force with force. Students are encouraged to move with an incoming force, until it is exhausted. When performing this art, the use of force is not encouraged, but control, sensitivity, and skill are highly regarded.

THE BENEFITS OF CONTROLLED MOVEMENT

Taiji is a moderate exercise that has beneficial effects on cardiovascular and respiratory function, immune capacity, mental control, flexibility, and balance control. It is commonly regarded as an internal martial art, with emphasis on the use of the mind to coordinate a relaxed body, as opposed to reliance on brute strength to achieve a required movement. The system is recognizable for its smooth, flowing movements, and the gentle postures and absence of jumping techniques make it suitable exercise for older people.

Northern Praying Mantis

EXPLANATION
NORTHERN CHINESE
KUNG-FU SYSTEM

DATE OF ORIGIN
C. 1650

FOUNDER
WANG LANG

PLACE OF ORIGIN
SHANDONG PROVINCE, CHINA

Northern praying mantis was created by a Shaolin master called Wang Lang in the mid-17th century when he combined footwork techniques from monkey-style kung fu (see p. 102) with hand techniques from praying mantis (see p. 122). The system went on to become one of the most well-known and best-loved Chinese kung-fu systems.

Based around the movements of the praying mantis and its aggressive, forward-thrusting nature, the art is often linked with an old story of a Daoist wise man who observed a praying mantis trying to hold back the wooden wheels of a cart laden with fruit. The mantis, locked in a futile battle with the huge wooden wheel, was constantly pushed back, but refused to give in.

To some Daoists this story is a call to stop fighting against life. To martial artists, however, it symbolizes the spirit of pushing and fighting, even if the struggle might bring about their demise. This particular characteristic is a prized asset among traditional martial artists: if a practitioner is aggressive and decisive he can assume control in many circumstances and emerge victorious.

Shared characteristics

Although there are a number of different styles of northern praying mantis, the differing systems share a number of key characteristics. All are characterized by a unique poking-hand posture imitating the leg of a mantis. This very distinctive hand posture uses a hooking, clawlike action to divert incoming threats before quickly changing into a vicious attack aimed at vital points of an opponent's body— the eyes, or various acupuncture points. In combat, northern mantis body movements are similar to those found in monkey-style kung fu. This may be due to the fact that northern praying mantis includes a complex set of footwork that was originally taken from monkey-style kung fu.

The three main styles of northern praying mantis are known as: six-harmony style, eight-steps style, and seven-star style.

▼ PROTECTING THE GROIN
In this stance, the knee protects the groin area, while the fingers hook around an attacker's hand to unbalance him.

"IF THE PRAYING MANTIS, WHILE STRIVING FOR EXISTENCE, DID NOT REVEAL ITS SECRETS TO US, WE WOULD NEVER HAVE DEVELOPED THIS NEW STYLE."

NORTHERN PRAYING MANTIS FOUNDER WANG LANG

Tiger Kung Fu

EXPLANATION
TIGER-STYLE KUNG FU

DATE OF ORIGIN
INDIGENOUS ART

FOUNDER
NO KNOWN FOUNDER

PLACE OF ORIGIN
SHANDONG PROVINCE, CHINA

Inspired by the clawing motions of tigers and said to strengthen the bones, tiger kung fu is one of the five animal systems of Chinese kung fu (see p. 124) and is closely associated with bak fu pai (see p. 56). The system focuses on quick attacking movements aimed at resolving a conflict swiftly, but places no emphasis on blocking or evasive defensive techniques. It is not taught as a sport. Traditional practitioners rely solely on deadly and shocking power and do no stamina training. This vicious system is characterized by direct movements, grabs, chokes, scrapes, and punches, combined with straight, side, and crescent kicks.

Pigua Quan

EXPLANATION
"CHOP-HANGING FIST" IN MANDARIN

DATE OF ORIGIN
INDIGENOUS ART

FOUNDER
NO KNOWN FOUNDER

PLACE OF ORIGIN
HEBEI PROVINCE, CHINA

Sometimes known as "chopping fist" because of its emphasis on chopping fist and palm techniques, pigua quan uses a number of sweeping actions to generate speed through the hips and arms to produce powerful strikes. It is sometimes taught alongside ba ji quan (see p. 68), and the two forms are thought to have been a single art before diverging some centuries ago.

Power with simplicity

Sometimes accused of being an impractical martial art because of the exaggerated nature of its opening moves, pigua quan's value lies in its simplicity and its ease to master. In its original form, it would have differed markedly from the routines seen in competitive wushu (see pp. 93–99), but even in modern demonstrations the principles of generating power through speed and rotation are clear to see.

Chang Quan

EXPLANATION
"LONG FIST" IN MANDARIN

DATE OF ORIGIN
10TH CENTURY

FOUNDER
ZHAO KUANGYIN

PLACE OF ORIGIN
NORTHERN CHINA

Sometimes known as "long fist" or as "extended arm boxing," chang quan is one of the oldest kung-fu striking systems. Emphasizing large, extended, and sometimes circular movements, the system relies on strong muscles, tendons, and joints to generate striking power.

Forms also contain joint locks, throws, and a number of high kicks, jumps, and flips. It is an acrobatic style and in modern wushu competitions (see pp. 93–99) the forms are often the most spectacular and memorable to watch. Many of the tumbling and flipping kicks have been allotted exotic names, such as the "whirlwind kick," "butterfly jump," and "tornado kick," and many of them are used by characters in video games.

Although many of the movements predate the system's foundation (it was founded in the 10th century by Zhao Kuangyin), chang quan's contemporary form combines elements of cha quan, hong quan, and hua quan (see p. 79).

Alternative meaning

The name chang quan is also used as a generic term for a number of different Chinese martial schools—such as cha quan, Shaolin chuan, fan zi quan, hong quan, hua quan, and others—to denote systems thought of as being of northern origin and which are external as opposed to internal. These arts all employ similar large, extended, circular movements and physical athleticism. They also use offence-driven techniques, where the fighter rarely remains stationary, throwing attacking strikes, before moving position to continue the attack.

▲ STAYING THE DISTANCE
Zhao Kuangyin's style has survived for centuries and now, along with two other systems, forms the basis for modern wushu.

Black Crane Kung Fu

EXPLANATION
BLACK CRANE-STYLE KUNG FU

DATE OF ORIGIN
C. 206 BCE

FOUNDER
DR. HUA TO

PLACE OF ORIGIN
CHINA

Black crane kung fu is a hybrid system incorporating white crane techniques (see p. 111) and tui na locks. It places heavy emphasis on strength and stance training. Practitioners will typically use deflection techniques before striking their opponent and using a lock. The system also incorporates qi gong breathing meditation techniques and the teaching of weapons, the most popular of which are the baton, sword, spear, staff, and the cane. Elements of xing yi quan and ba gua zhang (see p. 92, 78) can also be identified in the system's footwork routines.

Mei Huaquan

EXPLANATION
"PLUM FLOWER FIST" IN MANDARIN

DATE OF ORIGIN
17TH CENTURY

FOUNDER
NO SINGLE FOUNDER

PLACE OF ORIGIN
NORTHERN CHINA

Although the exact origins of this system are unclear, mei huaquan is thought to have originated in the 17th century in northern China. Typically the 18 traditional weapons are taught alongside fist, hand, and foot forms, which are built around five static training positions. The system is noted as much for its health-giving benefits as for its self-defense skills.

A secretive fighting style

A popular variant of the system is "mei hua zhuang," where zhuang means "trunks" or "pillars." The name of this branch, it is said, comes from the ancient training method in which all the moves were executed while standing on top of wooden pillars, thus encouraging good balance and quick, light, deft footwork. It was thought that training for long hours on the pillars would improve overall coordination and increase practitioners' confidence when they came to fight at ground level.

Originally a secret style, the system gradually began to open its doors to outsiders, and in time fixed training regimes were employed to ensure that practitioners had the necessary determination, moral qualities, and skills to study the art as required by their teachers.

In the first three years of training students were carefully observed, and those found lacking would no

◄ STRENGTH IN BALANCE
This ancient training method is designed to help develop the balance, footwork, and the confidence of the fighter.

longer receive instruction. Those who made it through the rigorous induction period would spend the next two years adding to the boxing skills they had learned during the first year.

Historical significance

During the 1900 Boxer Rebellion— a violent reaction to the work of foreign missionaries, high taxes, and corruption—mei huquan played an important role among the peasant martial artists, which resulted in the practice of the art being banned. Schools moved underground and the system was taught in secret for many generations.

During the 1920s, when famine was at critical proportions, the underground martial societies banded together to form village militias and provided protection for the common people. The art was again banned during the Cultural Revolution, due to alleged connections with religious cults, such as The White Lotus Sectarians, although this is strongly denied by elderly practitioners of the art.

STICKY HANDS
This wing chun (see p. 122) training exercise known as "sticky hands" aims to help practitioners predict an opponent's next move. It is a sensitivity drill that teaches a practitioner to sense rather than see physical movements.

Xing Yi Quan

EXPLANATION
"FORM/INTENTION BOXING"
IN MANDARIN

DATE OF ORIGIN
17TH CENTURY

FOUNDER
NO KNOWN FOUNDER

PLACE OF ORIGIN
SHAANXI PROVINCE, CHINA

Widely practiced in northern China, this well-known internal martial art is often taught alongside ba gua zhang (see p. 78) and sometimes in combination with taijiquan (see pp. 80–87). Known as "form" or "intention boxing," the art is characterized by aggressive, seemingly linear movements followed by bursts of explosive power. The goal is to make contact with an opponent quickly and to defeat him in a single movement.

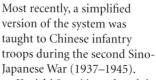

XING YI QUAN

Mythical origins
According to legend, General Yue Fei created the system during the Sung dynasty (920–1127) by basing the art's hand form on the thrusting movements of a spear. He then taught the system to his officers; the second system he created, northern eagle claw (see p. 102), he taught to his foot soldiers.

Finding a wider audience
Knowledge of the art was passed on in secret until, in the early 17th century, a wandering Daoist taught it to General Ji Ji Ke. The system was then passed on to Cao Jiwu, a commanding officer in the Shaanxi army, who incorporated it into his officers' core training. This version of the art—known as the Shaanxi xing yi quan—achieved widespread popularity.

Among the numerous regional xing yi systems, a popular variation is the Henan style, which has become closely associated with Chinese Muslims and goes by the name "xing yi liuhe quan." The Hebei style of the art absorbed many of the province's local boxing techniques, including some ba gua zhang movements.

Guiding principles
Weapon training typically includes the staff, the spear, the broadsword, and the straight sword. The art aims to develop three main skills: to unbalance an opponent while maintaining one's own; to act, strike, and think in unity; and to use sound to shock an opponent and fill him with dread.

Modern use
Most recently, a simplified version of the system was taught to Chinese infantry troops during the second Sino-Japanese War (1937–1945).

Kenichi Sawai introduced the system to Japan under the name "taiki ken," and classic xing yi techniques were adapted for use with both the bayonet and the saber.

◄ **NO BLOCKING**
With no regard for blocking incoming attacks, this is an uncomplicated, direct style.

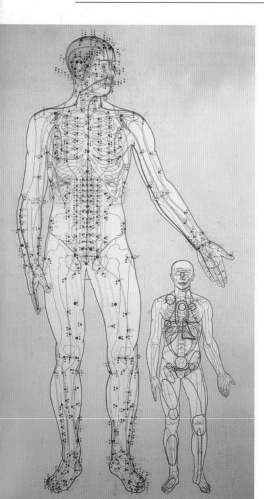

◄ **DEATH IN AN INSTANT**
This image, from the earliest-known medical manual, the *Nei Tsing*, shows all the body's acupuncture and pressure points.

Dim Mak

EXPLANATION
"POKE POINT" IN MANDARIN

DATE OF ORIGIN
INDIGENOUS ART

FOUNDER
NO KNOWN FOUNDER

PLACE OF ORIGIN
CHINA

Dim mak is an ancient art that consists of hitting various points on the body—known as "vital points" or "pressure points"—to cause injury, illness, or death. Although disputed, it is claimed that the art—famously described as "the death touch"—was created by Chang San Feng, who also founded taijiquan (see pp. 80–87). However, its close associations with traditional Chinese medicine, which has a recorded history of over 5,000 years, suggests that its origins are much older.

The technique depends on striking precise locations along an appropriate meridian (or artery) at a time when specific points are "open" and vulnerable to attack. To be a master of the art, a practitioner needs to have a sound understanding of acupressure points and circadian rhythm—the 24-hour biochemical, physiological, and behavioral process of all living things.

Shrouded in secrecy
Because of the serious nature of the injuries it can cause, dim mak was only taught to the most advanced and trusted students. As a result, the art is considered to be highly secretive and has been the subject of much speculation and debate. For example, after the death of Bruce Lee, rumors flooded Hong Kong that he had been killed by a dim mak master. It is more likely, however, that these unfounded suggestions were fueled by fans struggling to come to terms with the death of a legend in his prime.

AUTHOR'S NOTE

Since there is little scientific evidence to prove whether dim mak is genuine or simply a myth, I traveled to Beijing in the winter of 2003 to study with one of the art's last living practitioners. Obsessed with finding a definitive answer, I decided to gamble my life to find out. I invited the master to perform a lethal, or near-lethal, move on me. It was a short, sharp jab to a point on my front torso. It instantly winded me and I collapsed to my knees in an unusual way. Fortunately, I quickly regained my composure, thanked the master and, after a few slaps on the back, seemed to have regained full awareness. I returned to the UK believing the art to be nothing more than a painful, acupressure point-based fighting system. Three months later, however, I was admitted to the hospital suffering from chest pains and an irregular heartbeat was detected. The condition cleared after a short period of rest. Further research with Western-trained doctors showed that the exact timing and the amount of pressure applied to the point at which I was struck could have caused the heart muscle to spasm and could have been responsible for the physical problems that ensued. In order to obtain conclusive proof, though, proper testing under strict laboratory conditions should be conducted—but I, for one, will not be participating in them.

Wushu

EXPLANATION
"MARTIAL ART" IN MANDARIN

DATE OF ORIGIN
1949

FOUNDER
NO KNOWN FOUNDER

PLACE OF ORIGIN
CHINA

This is a generic term for a number of martial arts—performed for either exhibition or as full-contact sports—which were derived from ancient Chinese martial arts and recreated in the People's Republic of China after 1949. The two main disciplines are "taolu," meaning forms, and "san shou" (see p. 120), which means sparring. The forms have a gymnastic flavor and, although they involve martial-arts patterns, they are primarily carried out before judges, who award points based on a set of specific rules and, most importantly, on aesthetic value. The sparring disciplines take place on a "lei tei" (a raised platform) and are considered a sport. Practitioners compete mainly in three different categories: "chang quan" (long fist), "nan quan" (southern fist),

> **GOOD ALL-AROUNDERS**
Practitioners should be proficient in empty-hand and weapons forms, and must entertain.

> **ENTER THE DRAGON**
Dragon dancing features heavily in Chinese folklore. "Wenshi" (civil lion) style is most often seen at wushu competitions

and taijiquan (see pp. 80–87). Both empty-hand and weapons forms are judged in competition.

Standardizing kung fu
The introduction of wushu caused a major divergence among Chinese martial-arts practitioners, with traditionalists viewing it as an attempt to eradicate traditional clan-based systems of martial arts and neutralize the more subversive aspects of martial arts.

Promoters of wushu claim to have developed it as a way of preserving the art forms by standardizing the syllabus and the quality of the teaching—an important practice, if arts are to be spread effectively across the nation.

Wushu competitions are spectacular, with gymnastic aerial techniques including dramatic jumps, twists, and somersaults. Jet Li (see p. 103) is the most recognized wushu practitioner, having won five Chinese national wushu gold medals between 1974 and 1979.

"WUSHU IS A MOVE IN CHINESE, A PHYSICAL MOVE, AN ATTACK. WUSHU IS LIKE AN ART."

JET LI, WUSHU'S MOST FAMOUS PRACTITIONER

WUSHU SCHOOL

TYPICALLY, AMBITIOUS YOUNG CHILDREN will begin their training at a wushu school at the age of seven, and those with exceptional talent may even win a scholarship to one of the more prestigious schools or universities to be found throughout China.

For the young martial artists, the day will usually start at 6 a.m. with one hour of aerobic conditioning. This includes a long run, kicking exercises, and stretching. After a brief rest and time out for breakfast, the morning's main wushu training begins. During these sessions, the children are taught how to become well-rounded martial artists. The students typically learn 18 weapons systems, as well as the main wushu competition arts: "chang quan" (long fist), "nan quan" (southern fist), and taijiquan (see pp. 80–87). Their intensive training runs until lunchtime, after which the students begin their studies.

> "THE SPORT IS WIDESPREAD THROUGHOUT CHINA, ENABLING THE COUNTRY TO DEVELOP SOME OF THE BEST WUSHU ATHLETES IN THE WORLD."

Conventional academic lessons last all afternoon until, at 5 p.m., the students sit down together to eat their evening meal. Between 7 p.m. and 9 p.m., the final two-hour wushu training session commences.

The day is very long and the students must often train in extreme temperatures. During the summer months temperatures can reach up to 104°F (40°C), while in the depths of winter they can plunge to -22°F (-30°C). The reward, however, can be great if a student has both the ability and the talent to excell. There are a number of national and international wushu championships in which to compete, and students may find a career as a wushu instructor or even as a movie star—Jet Li (see p. 103) did just that.

ONE-TO-ONE TEACHING
Most schools teach a combination of traditional and modern wushu. If a pupil's main consideration is self-defense, then a school that specializes in traditional wushu may be more suitable, as their focus will be concentrated toward teaching sparring disciplines.

SCHOOL DAYS

Children that are sent to wushu schools are encouraged to discover their true potential in martial arts, which will also help them in their daily lives. The art of performance, with its attendant benefits of endurance, flexibility, coordination, health, and strength, are the main focus of contemporary wushu.

ALL FOR ONE

Classmates eat and train together and will form lasting bonds during their time at the school. Many schools provide primary, junior, and secondary education for children who attend them, and many pupils have graduated and become famous teachers and movie stars.

ORIGINAL STYLES

Modern wushu preserves is a standardized and acrobatic version of the original styles. Standard routines were created around various styles—such as "chang quan" (long fist), "nan quan" (southern fist), "jian shu" (swordplay), "gun shu" (cudgel play), and "dao shu" (broadsword play)—as well as various hand form routines.

NATIONAL SUCCESS

Members of a performance team take part in a dress rehearsal prior to a performance at their school. Those who excell may one day join one of the professional teams—like the Beijing wushu team—that take part in national and international competitions. Places on professional wushu teams are fiercely contested.

MIND GAMES
Members of the team engage in a "qi gong" (a regulated breathing technique) performance to increase their strength and stamina. This style of act has its roots in the training regime of the Shaolin monks (see pp. 57–65).

THE LION KING
The lion dance is probably the most performed martial folk dance in China. The lion, as the king of animals, is regarded as a good-luck mascot. There are two types of performance: "wenshi" (civil lion) and "wushi" (martial lion). Wushi portrays the power of the lion. Besides the usual jumping, falling, and tumbling, performers will also show their acrobatic ability by climbing on to a high table or by stepping on stakes. This is all performed to the rhythm provided by the drummer.

Drunken Monkey

EXPLANATION
DRUNKEN MONKEY-STYLE
KUNG FU

DATE OF ORIGIN
EARLY 1960s

FOUNDER
NO SINGLE FOUNDER

PLACE OF ORIGIN
CHINA

This is a variation of the popular monkey-style kung fu (see p. 102) that aims to imitate the movements of a monkey that is drunk in order to confuse an opponent. Although forms are short, there are a number of rolling, tumbling, and falling techniques to master alongside mid-level kicks aimed at the stomach and groin. Practitioners are encouraged to relax when executing techniques such as the palm-facing-down striking technique.

Unusually for drunken-style systems, the "drunkenness" of drunken monkey does not start until halfway through the form. When it

begins, the action punctuates the movements, showing a clear change in tactics, style, and execution.

The classic novel

Inspiration for the style derives from the central character in the 16th-century Chinese novel *Journey to the West*, Sun Wu Kong, who was later popularized in the 1970s' television series *Monkey*. In one part of the book, the monkey steals the spiritual peaches from heaven's peach tree and then drinks the wine that was reserved for a heavenly party for the immortals. After eating and drinking to his heart's content, the monkey defeats heaven's warriors, before he is finally subdued by Buddha.

Enhanced effectiveness

Those who developed the system clearly understood the connection between alcohol and violence—and

> **THE MISCHIEVOUS MONKEY**
The monkey king, shown here in the middle of a garden of women, was thrown out of heaven for stealing the peaches of immortality.

its emboldening qualities in particular—and, although practitioners are aiming to mimic the actions of a drunken monkey when fighting, drinking alcohol is not encouraged when training.

Five guiding principles

The five main principles uniting the system are: the monkey must be deceptive and poisonous to his

▲ MONKEY IS FUNKY
Journey to the West was dramatized in the 1970s. The series followed the exploits of the monkey king (center), Sandy (right), Pigsy, and Tripitaka.

opponents, he must destroy their attacks, he must be unpredictable, he must bluff them, and he must frighten them. Practitioners are encouraged to demonstrate all of those characteristics when fighting and when performing routines.

Tong Bei Quan

EXPLANATION
"POWER FROM THE BACK FIST" IN MANDARIN

DATE OF ORIGIN
17TH CENTURY

FOUNDER
NO KNOWN FOUNDER

PLACE OF ORIGIN
NORTHERN CHINA

Much of tong bai quan's power source and many of its techniques come from the back, through the shoulders, through the arms, and finally emerge from the fists or hands. It is thought to have originated during the Qing dynasty, when it was called "qi boxing."

Originally, the name possibly referred to a set of exercises or warm-ups for general health that developed into a system of martial arts. The style is comprised of a number of different ways of issuing force through the hands that include boring or twisting movements as well as heavy thudding blows.

There are two main styles of tong bei quan: the "father" style is the traditional system that emphasizes power, movement, development, discipline, and secrecy, and it is taught in a clandestine way; the "young" style is a wushu (see pp. 93–99) performance-based art often taught in the Chinese sports universities.

Tai Sheng Men

EXPLANATION
"GREAT SAINT" IN MANDARIN

DATE OF ORIGIN
20TH CENTURY

FOUNDER
KAU TZE

PLACE OF ORIGIN
NORTHERN CHINA

This system is named after the monkey king, Sun Wu Kong, a mythological figure who features in the book *Journey to the West*. Developed by

Kau Tze while he was serving a prison sentence for murder, legend has it that he observed a colony of chattering monkeys from his prison-cell window. He watched their fighting and playful tactics in the trees, incorporated their characteristics into his own knowledge of tei tong, and created tai sheng men. The five personality types of monkeys as observed by the creator still exist in the movements today, and are called: tall monkey, wooden monkey, lost money, stone monkey, and drunken monkey (see opposite).

◀ REALISTIC EXPRESSIONS
The fighter must mimic the facial expressions of the monkey style that they have chosen.

Pao Chui

EXPLANATION
"CANNON FIST" IN MANDARIN

DATE OF ORIGIN
UNKNOWN

FOUNDER
NO KNOWN FOUNDER

PLACE OF ORIGIN
HENAN PROVINCE, CHINA

Pao chui is a pounding Chinese martial art known for its powerful fist punch, which has been compared by some to hung quan. According to legend, the style originated from the "Three August Ones"—three demigods in ancient Chinese mythology—who used their magical powers to improve the fortunes of Chinese people.

Virtuous and kind

It is believed that these gods were successful in achieving their goals and ruled over a period of great prosperity and peace in China. Although their actual existence is hard to confirm, these three wise demigods are mentioned in the *Shi Ji*—the first recorded Chinese historical text—and were known as the "Heavenly Sovereign," the "Earthly Sovereign," and the "Human Sovereign." In honor of these immortals, chen-style taijiquan (see pp. 80–87)—one of the four major schools—includes a pao chui routine in its training syllabus.

▷ Nü WA AND FU XI
The worship of deities and demigods was common in ancient China. This couple are sometimes known as the "parents of mankind."

Ba Faquan

EXPLANATION
"EIGHT METHOD STYLE" IN MANDARIN

DATE OF ORIGIN
1906

FOUNDER
LI BE MAO

PLACE OF ORIGIN
NORTHERN CHINA

Li Be Mao, who was a practitioner of chang chuan, fan zi, xing yi, pigua, tong bei, and tan tui (see pp. 103, 92, 88, 101, 102), combined these systems toward the end of the Qing dynasty in the early 20th century. The system he created came to be used by militia when they were engaged in organizing and training rebel armies (particularly in the northern Shaanxi province) to overthrow the unpopular Qing government.

The system was simplified as a hand-to-hand combat training program, designed to be an effective killing art, and to instill confidence in the militias. Many of the techniques were designed for use on either foot or horseback, and training with the spear, sabre or broadsword (all weapons with which the militias would have been familiar), featured heavily in the system.

Hou Quan

EXPLANATION
"MONKEY BOXING" IN MANDARIN

DATE OF ORIGIN
200 BCE

FOUNDER
NO KNOWN FOUNDER

PLACE OF ORIGIN
CHINA

Although there are conflicting arguments about the origins of this art, many believe that hou quan was created by Wang Lang who imitated the expressions and movements of the monkeys he saw coming out of a cave. The various monkeys were playing, picking fruits, play-fighting, caught by surprise, and running away into the caves. He then incorporated his observations into the traditional kung fu he already knew and founded "hou quan," meaning monkey kung fu. Hou quan has a lot of similarities with tai sheng men (see p. 101).

One of the style's characteristics is that players adopt monkey expressions and make monkey noises, often expressing their anger, fear, fright, confusion, or happiness. The style is also known for its deft movements and open-hand strikes. Most of the attacks are aimed at the groin, eyes, nose, throat, and knees.

> **MONKEY STYLE**
This Shaolin novice is posed in a classic monkey kung fu pose.

Tan Tui

EXPLANATION
"SPRINGING LEGS" IN MANDARIN

DATE OF ORIGIN
16TH CENTURY

FOUNDER
NO KNOWN FOUNDER

PLACE OF ORIGIN
NORTHERN CHINA

Sometimes known as "northern springing legs," tan tui is characterized by springing, kicking movements that require a great degree of flexibility, coordination and skill. Known for its abundant and diverse tactics in combat, the art has four major areas of study—handwork, bodywork, legwork, and footwork—and, as the name suggests, popular techniques include kicking and hook-kicking from standing or springing positions. Other favored techniques include sweeping and stamping.

Northern Eagle Claw

EXPLANATION
"TAO LUN" IN MANDARIN

DATE OF ORIGIN
12TH CENTURY

FOUNDER
GENERAL YUE FEI

PLACE OF ORIGIN
ZUEJIANG PROVINCE, CHINA

General Yue Fei, the creator of northern eagle claw, is said to have credited his victories in battle to the arts he taught to his men. Alongside the usual military skills of archery, the use of a spear, and horsemanship, they learned the hand-to-hand combat art compiled from 108 techniques that became known as "eagle's claw."

There are three main sets of the art, and many of the movements can be characterized by their similarity to the perceived movements of an eagle in flight and in pursuit of its prey.

Attack rather than defense

Although the eagle-claw system contains a number of kicking techniques, the system focuses on clawing, striking, punching, throwing, and unbalancing an opponent in a quickfire succession of rapid attacks.

Defensive postures may have been built into the set forms and techniques, but northern eagle claw remains primarily an offensive, rather than a defensive, martial art that has clearly evolved from the tried-and-tested battlefield techniques of ancient China.

▼ **THE ART OF WAR**
This martial art was invented for use on the battlefield by General Yue Fei (left). The art focuses on attacking rather than defense.

Fan Zi Quan

EXPLANATION
"TUMBLING FIST" IN MANDARIN

DATE OF ORIGIN
INDIGENOUS ART

FOUNDER
NO KNOWN FOUNDER

PLACE OF ORIGIN
CHINA

The kicking system fan zi quan contains both "hard" and "soft" power techniques. The routines and set forms focus on hand techniques, punches, and jumps, and the wide range of flowing and tumbling punches, many of which come from unusual angles, is particularly effective.

A typical fan zi quan routine involves quickfire combinations of offensive and defensive manoeuvres ending with short bursts of punches that are thrown from unusual angles and are aimed at the opponent's body.

JET LI

Fan zi quan's most famous practitioner, Jet Li, was born in Beijing on April 26, 1963. His mother took him to the Beijing Amateur Sports School at the age of eight and, after three years training in wushu, he won his first national championship. He left the school as a multiple champion aged 17, made his first film, *Shaolin Temple*, in 1982, and went on to become one of China's biggest exports, featuring in *Lethal Weapon 4* and *Romeo Must Die*.

Boxing techniques

Fan zi quan includes a number of uppercuts similar to those found in Western boxing (see pp. 256–63). These uppercuts are delivered if the opponent closes his guard and crouches down in a protective manner and are followed by head punches and lower-body punches.

Two common branches of fan zi quan are practiced today—one in the northeast of China and the other in the northwest. Although both bear a strong resemblance to each other, the latter focuses on force drawn from the waist, whereas the style from the northeast tends to focus on a strong surging power coupled with the technical ability to perform all techniques at speed.

The system's motto can be translated as: "Two fists are fast like the falling raindrops and fast like a slapping whip."

Go-Ti Boxing

EXPLANATION
EARLY CHINESE WRESTLING

DATE OF ORIGIN
C. 2600 BCE

FOUNDER
NO KNOWN FOUNDER

PLACE OF ORIGIN
HENAN PROVINCE, CHINA

Primarily a wrestling system, the style of combat known as go-ti boxing came into being in approximately 2600 BCE. At the same time, religious practitioners were developing a physical and mental training regime called "cong fu."

Both arts eventually became associated with Daoist monks and, over the years, eventually fused into one system. As many Daoist monks are experts in the system, most practitioners also follow Daoism. Many believe go-ti boxing to be a precursor to modern kung fu.

Shuai Jiao

EXPLANATION
"TO THROW TO THE GROUND THROUGH WRESTLING WITH THE LEGS" IN MANDARIN

DATE OF ORIGIN
C. 2700 BCE

FOUNDER
NO KNOWN FOUNDER

PLACE OF ORIGIN
NANJING, JIANGSU PROVINCE, CHINA

Shuai jiao is the most ancient of all Chinese martial arts, with a history of over 4,000 years—its first recorded use came in 2697 BCE. It is a throwing and grappling system that has probably been influenced by bkyukl bökh (see p. 54). In its earliest form it was known as "jiao di," or "horn butting"; the soldiers would wear headgear with horns, which they would use to gore their opponents while fighting. Later, it became an art form practiced without the headgear, and finally became a public sport during the Qin dynasty (221–207 BCE), during

which time winners of national competitions won the right to serve as one of the emperor's bodyguards.

Modern-day shuai jiao

Today, the art is commonly taught in police and military institutions in both China and Taiwan, and many of the techniques used in the ancient battlefields are still employed today, including seizing and grabbing maneuvers, joint locks, and pressure-point holds. Although some of the unique lock-breaking throws have been banned during competition, it still remains a tactical and deadly combat art incorporating vigorous snapping actions from the hips that result in eye-catching and dramatic moves.

> **FROM THE HIP**
The hip is used to lift and overbalance the opponent, and the right leg forces him to fall to the floor.

"THERE ARE A LOT OF METHODS ... [BUT] YOU CANNOT TEACH [STUDENTS] KILLING METHODS THAT THEY CANNOT USE."

MASTER DAVID CHANG

BEHIND THE SCENES

SHUAI JIAO MASTER

DAVID CHANG IS A WELL-KNOWN and well-regarded teacher of Chinese wrestling, or shuai jiao. He is a Chinese Muslim who teaches his art to cadets at the Central Police Academy in Taiwan. As a young boy, David began to show a keen interest in kung fu, and has now developed his own shuai jiao system.

Learning the art from his grandfather, Chang Tung Sheng, considered one of the greatest Chinese grapplers during his lifetime, David also studied herbalism from him, and still grows the ingredients from his small plot of land in Ho Lung Mountain in Miaoli County. He uses the recipes to brew a traditional herbal wine (or "yaojiu") for his fighters. It is believed that this yaojiu wine builds strong "qi" and enhances the student's ability to overcome physical punishment.

> "SOME OF THE TECHNIQUES HE TEACHES TO THE CADETS ARE IN FACT KILLING MOVES. THROWING OPPONENTS SO THAT THEY LAND ON THEIR HEAD"

Although David started physical training as an infant, one of the early important aspects of his method was the memorization of a shuai jiao poem. Every character mentioned in the poem directly relates to a movement in his grandfather's set form, with the forms making up the basis of the art.

David's training is brutally simple and effective and, although he teaches the art in a sporting way and engages in friendly competitions, a number of safety rules are in place to ensure the well-being of his pupils. This is especially important given the millennia-old killing techniques in use, such as throwing an opponent onto his head with the intention of breaking the neck.

CENTRAL POLICE ACADEMY
Admission into the Central Police Academy is restricted to 250 places per year. With over 10,000 people applying for admittance to the residential course, competition is fierce.

INTENSIVE TRAINING
David Chang's teaching of shuai jiao is tailored specifically for the police, with arrest in mind. The students are drilled in how to take down an aggressor with speed and efficiency.

TEAM PREPARATION

The warm-up is an important part of the training regime. Stretches, running, lifting, and push-ups all aim to improve the student's balance, strength, and endurance, since sessions can last up to one hour without a break.

GOING THROUGH THE CROTCH

This move is called "chuan dang," which roughly translates as "your movement passing through someone's crotch." The throw is primarily used when a practitioner is confronted by a taller opponent who grabs him around the neck. In this case, the shorter man drops to one knee and reaches between his opponent's legs. He grabs the back of one leg (called "clipping"), to move his opponent on to his shoulder, then he throws him over his shoulder.

BELTS AND ROPES

Shuai-jiao practitioners use a rope or the belt from their uniform as a weapon. It can be used for binding, apprehending, or in extreme circumstances, striking criminals. A leather rope or even iron chains are used in advanced training.

USING A DUMMY

Practitioners perform moves, such as this throw, with a specially designed dummy. This is useful if a partner is not available, and helps prevent injury.

USE OF EVERYDAY OBJECTS
Shuai-Jiao training often makes use of everyday objects. Here, a clay pot is used to strengthen the hands and arms while a wooden pole keeps the practitioner's hands the correct distance apart.

Mizongyi

EXPLANATION
"LOST TRACK FIST" IN MANDARIN

DATE OF ORIGIN
UNKNOWN

FOUNDER
NO KNOWN FOUNDER

PLACE OF ORIGIN
NORTHERN CHINA

Of Shaolin origin, and belonging to the chang quan school of martial arts (see p. 89), mizongyi's most unique movement is its "fajing" (the discharging of body force). This is a spectacular technique that is brought about by the simultaneous twisting of the practitioner's knees, hips, waist, elbows, and hands in a corkscrewlike action toward an off-balance target. During sparring, it is common to see masters issuing fajing into their opponents and knocking them backward by up to 6½ ft (2 m). Another characteristic is that practitioners are quite willing to engage in combat in order to establish their reputation as good fighters.

Jing Wu martial-arts school

Mizongyi has been growing in popularity since 1901 due to the deeds of master Huo Yuanjia, who was a practitioner and head of the renowned Jing Wu martial arts school in Shanghai. In tournaments and in arranged fights against other

masters, he defeated martial artists from all over the world. Yuanjia and his school have been the subject of many films, in which Jet Li and Bruce Lee have played lead roles. Another possible reason for the style's popularity is the the well-

known legend that tells the story of an ancient kung-fu practitioner who mastered the mizongyi style and joined the famed "Outlaws of the Marsh." This was a group of bandits who revolted against the emperor of the time and went on to do good

◀ **INSPIRATIONAL LEADER**
Huo Yuanjia and his famous Jing Wu martial arts school in Shanghai have provided the inspiration for many films.

THE LEGEND BRUCE LEE

The martial artist Bruce Lee (above) played the role of Chen Zhen—a student of mizongyi practitioner Huo Yuanjia at the Jing Wu school—in the film *Fist of Fury*. Jet Li took the role in *Fist of Legend*.

deeds: robbing the rich and giving to the poor, and using their skills in martial arts to help the weak and oppressed. Despite numerous attempts by the authorities to capture this group of martial outlaws, they proved elusive.

Five Ancestors Fist

EXPLANATION
COMBINED ELEMENTS OF FIVE SHAOLIN SYSTEMS

DATE OF ORIGIN
13TH CENTURY

FOUNDER
BAI YUFENG

PLACE OF ORIGIN
HENAN PROVINCE, CHINA

Bai Yufeng, a 13th-century Shaolin monk, combined five Shaolin systems into a single syllabus in order to create his own system, known as "five ancestors fist." The art borrows elements of footwork from hou quan, the power-generation techniques of luohan quan, the breathing methods of iron

OPIUM PIPE

qi gong, the hand techniques of Fujian white crane, and the striking methods of chang quan (see pp. 102, 69, 111, 89).

The system is also known for its various improvised weapons, such as the use of chop sticks, rice bowls, and even opium pipes.

Guiding principles

The system relies on a central "Three Battles" principle, which, at its core, teaches practitioners the simple methodology to achieve success in battles: combat preparation and training; combat techniques and tactics; and, finally, overall combat strategy. The Three Battles principle also equates to the inner three battles a practitioner must face in life: the conceptual battle, the physical battle, and the spiritual battle.

Black Tiger System

EXPLANATION
A SYSTEM OF KUNG FU

DATE OF ORIGIN
C. 10TH CENTURY

FOUNDER
NO KNOWN FOUNDER

PLACE OF ORIGIN
HENAN PROVINCE, CHINA

The forms of black tiger system include an extensive range of tripping and kicking footwork, often performed in hopping movements, aimed at unbalancing an opponent before striking or clawing him or her.

In order to master this art, huge emphasis is placed on maintaining physical strength and health, almost to the exclusion of internal training. The system's most important aspect is the development of the spirit of the tiger and, while fighting, it is said that

a practitioner must never give up ground, but must pursue the enemy with ferocity. A practitioner will unleash a nonstop barrage of attacks, kicks, punches, and claws, yet these must be performed without tension.

Basic training

Iron-palm and knocking-limb exercises are common parts of training. These help the practitioner develop strong hands capable of smashing objects, and powerful forearms that can block attacks effectively. One of the classic knocking-limb exercises is called "three star hitting," in which two practitioners stand face to face and smash their forearms into each other to practice the blocking techniques. The action of clashing limbs together, although very painful, develops tenacity, quick reactions, and sharp eyesight, as well as the ability to withstand pain.

Fujian White Crane

EXPLANATION
SYSTEM INSPIRED BY THE FIGHTING STYLE OF THE CRANE

DATE OF ORIGIN
18TH CENTURY

FOUNDER
FANG QINIANG

PLACE OF ORIGIN
FUJIAN PROVINCE, CHINA

The origins of this system date back to the 18th century, when Fang Qiniang, the daughter of a well-known martial-arts master, moved to the Fujian province after the death of her mother. When her father was killed in a kung-fu challenge match defending her honor she determined to dedicate herself to the study of martial arts in order to exact revenge.

One night she dreamed that a white crane had landed near her and that she used her father's martial-arts techniques and a stick to usher it away. The crane evaded the attacks, used its claw to grab the stick, and struck back at every attack, strongly and gracefully. After she woke up, she set about developing a system of kung fu based on the crane.

The system includes a number of strikes to vulnerable areas of the body, such as the temple, and chopping actions to the throat. The art's philosophy emphasizes a strict moral code to help students cope with the responsibility of the deadly skills they learn.

> "BECAUSE IT WAS FOUNDED BY A WOMAN, IT DOES NOT RELY ON BRUTE STRENGTH FOR ITS EFFECTIVENESS."
>
> FWCKUNGFU.COM

Hung Gar

EXPLANATION
FAMILY NAME OF FOUNDER

DATE OF ORIGIN
17TH CENTURY

FOUNDER
HUNG HEI-GUN

PLACE OF ORIGIN
FUJIAN PROVINCE, CHINA

This external art is loosely based around the tiger style (see p. 56, 88), and is characterized by strong hand techniques and the tiger's claw movement.

Continuous attack

The system's techniques stress the use of simultaneous striking and blocking, with blocks often used as a means of attacking opponents. A typical example of this can be seen when the hung gar practitioner is on the receiving end of a wild punch to the upper body or head: he will meet the incoming force and, with an accelerating blocking maneuver, crash into a vulnerable area with a force greater than his opponent can defend. The object of this is to either seriously damage the opponent or to send a shockwave of pain through him, thus diminishing his will to continue the attack.

The art is extremely strenuous, and a strong body and the will to overcome pain are of primary importance if the practitioner is to master it. A common exercise is the horse stance, in which practitioners are required to remain in a squatting position with each leg bent at a 90-degree angle, as if they are sitting on an imaginary horse. This particular exercise is extremely difficult to perform correctly, even for 60 seconds, but traditionally students would have been expected to hold the position for a period of half an hour to an hour before serious training commenced. It can take a student up to one year to achieve this degree of skill.

HUNG GAR

Gou Quan

EXPLANATION
"DOG FIST" IN CANTONESE

DATE OF ORIGIN
17TH CENTURY

FOUNDER
WU MEI

PLACE OF ORIGIN
FUJIAN PROVINCE, CHINA

The most common name associated with gou quan's origins is Wu Mei, a martial arts teacher and nun. Having absorbed movements from observing fighting dogs to create this dog-style kung-fu system, the system rapidly began to grow in popularity soon after its conception.

The system utilizes a number of rolling movements, scissor kicks, leg wraps and takedowns, stomping kicks, knee attacks, grappling, and leg hooking techniques. It is unpopular in the West, and still quite rare in China, except in Fujian province. The modern version of the art includes iron-shirt and iron-palm techniques (to help the body and hand withstand blows) that would probably not have been included in the original training.

◀ **UNUSUAL NAME**
A practitioner demonstrates a classic dog pose.

Hung Fut

EXPLANATION
A HYBRID SYSTEM

DATE OF ORIGIN
17TH CENTURY

FOUNDER
LEI JO FUNE

PLACE OF ORIGIN
FUJIAN PROVINCE, CHINA

Lei Jo Fune, a Buddhist monk, created this southern Shaolin-based kung-fu system. The art combines techniques and training methods from other systems—namely tiger, leopard, snake, dragon, fut gar, crane, and hung gar (see pp. 56, 88, 68, 124, 114, 123, 89, above)—and uses eight "drunken immortal" forms, four "cripple forms," and a left-hand fighting form. Generally, students are taught the use of 20 weapons, and undergo iron-rings training—a method of solidifying technique and strengthening the arms and shoulders, in which heavy iron rings are placed over the arms of the student, who then starts performing punching drills. Over time the student's forearms become stronger, which increases their effectiveness as striking and blocking tools.

∨ SUPPLE MAN

This performer, dressed in Shaolin uniform, practises his routine outside the Temple of Heaven Park in Beijing. His performance, which is as much about flexibility as martial arts, typically draws huge crowds.

∨ SHAPES AND FORMS

Although he is not performing any specific martial-art forms, his body shapes (from left to right below) are reminiscent of: monkey-style kung fu, the "sleeping Buddha" pose, the monkey king from the novel *Sun Wu Kong* (*Journey to the West*), and the classic Shaolin warrior pose.

Lai Tung Pai

EXPLANATION
"FAMILY OF LAI TUNG VILLAGE" IN CANTONESE

DATE OF ORIGIN
17TH CENTURY

FOUNDER
CHI SEM

PLACE OF ORIGIN
HENAN PROVINCE, CHINA

Originally known as "poon kuen" or "encircling fist," lai tung pai is a martial art of external Shaolin origin, developed, it is thought, by a monk called Chi Sem. His disciple, Yuen Mau, took the art south to Canton and, while anonymously hiding in a village, got into a skirmish with a group of unruly soldiers. With the help of the villagers, he emerged triumphant. The "soldiers" must have been either deserters or bandits (posing as soldiers), since there seems to be no record of retaliation for their defeat, but in honor of the villagers' help, Yuen Mau changed the name of his art form to lai tung pai, or "family of lai tung village," the village's name.

A short-form system

Although the system contains many long-arm techniques, it is considered a southern art and is sometimes compared to wing chun because of its use of close-combat techniques, in particular the one- and three-inch punches. The forms, 12 of which are empty-handed, tend to be short, ranging from between 24 to 36 moves, except for one long set of over 300 prearranged individual moves. Weapons taught include the staff, broadsword, and butterfly knives, and lai tung pai uses a "mook jong," or "eight different wooden men." This training aid is a solid wooden "sparring partner" that is now most commonly found in wing-chun schools. The similarites in terms of weapons use, and fighting style, has led people to suggest that Ng Mui, the inventor of wing chun (see p. 122), contacted lai tung pai practitioners to discuss both systems.

Qi gong Chinese medicine theory and lion dancing are also integrated into the training regime.

▶ WOODEN DUMMY
Having been designed for lai tung pai, the mook jong is a piece of sparring equipment that has since also been adopted for wing chun training.

Choy Li Fut

EXPLANATION
NAMED AFTER THE FOUNDER'S TEACHERS AND IN HONOR OF ITS BUDDHIST ROOTS

DATE OF ORIGIN
19TH CENTURY

FOUNDER
CHAN HEUNG

PLACE OF ORIGIN
SOUTHERN CHINA

Choy li fut was developed in 1836 by Chan Heung, who was taught martial arts by his uncle, a very well-known boxer from the legendary Shaolin temple in Henan province.

Choy li fut is primarily known as a southern system that includes both southern and northern styles. The art includes techniques from the five Shaolin animals: tiger, crane, leopard, snake, and dragon (see pp. 56, 88, 89, 111, 68, 124, 114). It employs wide stances as its source of power, and the hand techniques typical of the southern arts, combining them both with the footwork, kicking, and leg maneuvers from systems founded in the north.

Early syllabus

It is thought that the original curriculum, on which Heung based his system, was designed by antigovernment rebels to enable fighters to learn efficient combat techniques quickly and to help them teach the methods effectively to others. Several of the techniques have specific shouting sounds associated with a particular form: for example, practitioners who are punching from a horse stance may shout "wah"; practitioners using the tiger claw may shout "dik"; and other sounds such as "sik" and "yik" are also commonly heard. It seems most likely that the sounds were incorporated into the system so that friendly forces might be able to recognize each other when they are in battle.

CHOY LI FUT

Meditation and weapons

Virtually every type of kung fu weapon is taught to students, including the nine dragon trident that was designed by Heung himself. Internal training exercises, such as meditation and breathing exercises are also taught to practitioners.

> "MY ONLY INTEREST IS TO SHARE MY KNOWLEDGE ... SO OTHERS CAN APPRECIATE THIS MARTIAL ART STYLE."
>
> GRAND MASTER LAY WING SUNG

Dragon Fist

EXPLANATION
FIGHTING WITH THE SPIRIT OF A DRAGON

DATE OF ORIGIN
17TH CENTURY

FOUNDER
WU MEI

PLACE OF ORIGIN
WUDANG MOUNTAIN, HUBEI PROVINCE, CHINA

Although the exact origins of the art are unclear, many believe the Shaolin Buddhist nun Wu Mei created the system, basing it on techniques required to overcome opponents of greater physical capacity, making it especially relevant for women.

There are limited kicks and jumps, and the system's main focus is on fist, palm, and claw techniques, which aim to cripple or kill opponents.

"Qi gong" movements are a central aspect of the art and some practitioners, when training, can be heard exhaling a sharp hissing sound—something that can be very frightening to hear.

Among the array of traditional Chinese weapons taught in the art, such as the sword and spear, the dragon system also uses a unique staff that is 9 ft (2.7 m) long. Known as the "king dragon half-piercing pole," this weapon serves both as an effective weapon and as a tool for teaching the student how to generate the weight, power, and control utilized in the main empty-hand body of learning.

▼ DRAGON SPIRIT
The kung-fu system may not be based on the dragon's physical movements, but it is based on its spiritual qualities.

Do Pi Kung Fu

EXPLANATION
"STYLE OF THE WAY" IN CANTONESE

DATE OF ORIGIN
1930s

FOUNDER
CHAN DAU

PLACE OF ORIGIN
GUANGDONG PROVINCE, CHINA

Do pi kung fu is a relatively new system of kung fu founded by Chan Dau in Guangdong province (otherwise known as Canton province), in southern China in the late 1930s. Chan Dau did not have the best start in life (see right), but he was a very determined and talented martial artist. He started learning martial arts from the age of nine, and had been a practitioner of hung gar (see p. 115), hop gar (see p. 55), and choy li fut (see opposite), before he created his own system.

Do pi has many form routines to help practitioners progress in their development. The most well-known sets include "drunken eight fairies," and "drunken fan."

> "SIMPLE MOVEMENTS ARE ALWAYS THE MOST EFFECTIVE IN BATTLE."
>
> GRAND MASTER CHAN DAU

(see right)

SHAM SHUI PO: HOME OF DO PI KUNG FU

Kidnapped as a small boy in Guangdong and sold to the powerful Yu family, Chan Dau started to study martial arts as a child on the encouragement of the Yu family's grandfather. He began to learn hung kuen, but one day, while training, he accidentally struck the grandfather and was ejected from the house.

Chan took refuge in the local monastery and one of its monks became his new martial-arts teacher. He then left the monastery after two years to try and find his family; times were so tough he was forced to sell peanuts on the streets to survive. But, having impressed in a martial-arts exhibition and gained recognition, Chan went on to open a gymnasium in Sham Shui Po, a then-seedy district of Kowloon, Hong Kong (right), and taught a combination of all the martial arts he had learned: do pi kung fu.

Fu Jow Pai

EXPLANATION
"TIGER CLAW SYSTEM" IN CANTONESE

DATE OF ORIGIN
1934

FOUNDER
WONG BIL HONG

PLACE OF ORIGIN
HENAN PROVINCE, CHINA

Also called the "tiger claw system," fu jow pai is characterized by ripping, tearing, and clawing techniques, combined with grasping and squeezing applications to vulnerable areas of an opponent's body. The system, which was founded in the Shaolin temple (see p. 57) in Henan province, aims to develop both physical and spiritual growth through strenuous exercise and training. "Be aggressive in attacking, whether it is a feint or a direct attack," is one of the guiding principles of this art. The art is also said to encourage a positive mental attitude in its practitioners.

> **BIG IN CHINA**
> Jet Li, in the film *Once upon a time in China*, shows how popular the tiger claw system is in China.

A constantly evolving system
The system was originally known as "hark fu moon," or "black tiger system," but Grand Master Wong Bil Hong, the system's founder, renamed it in honor of his Shaolin monk teacher. Wong Bil Hong, who had already mastered hung gar (see p. 111), took much of that system's core and developed his own system.

Resistance training
Physical conditioning through the practice of "iron hand" techniques (to help the body and hand withstand blows), are an important part of this system's training regime. Torturous exercises target the strengthening of ligaments, fingers, muscles, and skin.

It is not uncommon for teachers to beat students around the body with bamboo sticks, before moving on to more unforgiving implements, such as sticks, and baseball bats, in order to toughen both mind and body.

During one particularly brutal outdoor training exercise, practitioners are encouraged to beat their forearms against trees, and then to claw at the bark of the tree in order to remove it with only their fingers.

△ OUTDOOR TRAINING
Intensive training methods encourage a positive mental attitude among practitioners. This enables them to deliver powerful blows.

WEAPONS AND ARMOR

CHINESE WEAPONS

OFTEN REFERRED TO as "the gentleman of weapons," the "jian," or sword, is one of the most common Chinese weapons, along with the "dao," or knife. Traditional martial artists preparing for battle in China aimed to carry at least three weapons on their person at any one time: a visible primary weapon, such as a sword or a knife; a concealed secondary weapon to be used if the primary weapon is lost, such as a whip or a chain; and a third type of weapon—including "bi shou" daggers, or darts—that can be utilized from long distances. To become proficient in so many weapons required much patience and practice. Early Chinese weapons were manufactured to a high standard, and Chinese forging technologies quickly spread to Japan and Korea.

SCABBARD
Often very ornate, scabbards are commonly tipped with gold

DOUBLE EDGED
Both edges of the blade are sharp, and the weapon typically tapers slightly at one end

∧ BI SHOU
These small daggers could easily be concealed inside a pair of boots. If the weapon is used as a projectile, the tassel helps to balance it in flight.

HANDLE
Early dagger handles were manufactured using jade, although wood is now also a popular choice

Sharp tip

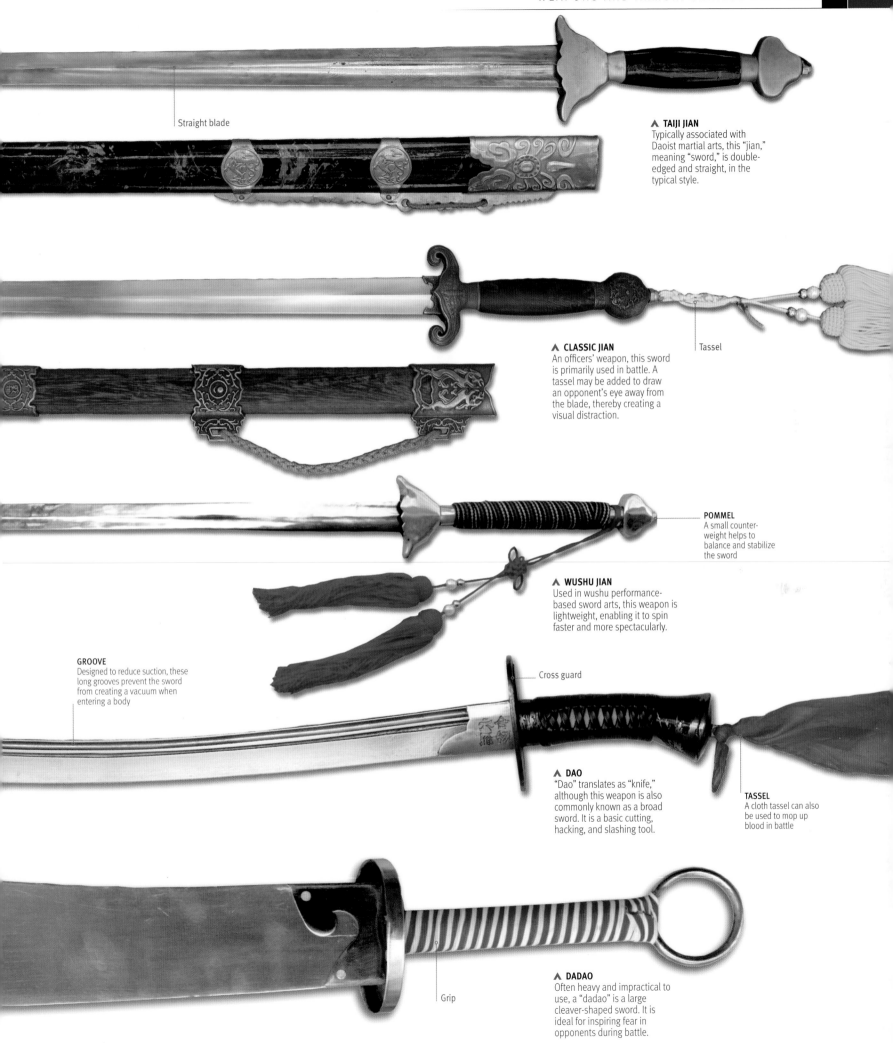

Straight blade

⌃ TAIJI JIAN
Typically associated with Daoist martial arts, this "jian," meaning "sword," is double-edged and straight, in the typical style.

Tassel

⌃ CLASSIC JIAN
An officers' weapon, this sword is primarily used in battle. A tassel may be added to draw an opponent's eye away from the blade, thereby creating a visual distraction.

POMMEL
A small counter-weight helps to balance and stabilize the sword

⌃ WUSHU JIAN
Used in wushu performance-based sword arts, this weapon is lightweight, enabling it to spin faster and more spectacularly.

GROOVE
Designed to reduce suction, these long grooves prevent the sword from creating a vacuum when entering a body

Cross guard

⌃ DAO
"Dao" translates as "knife," although this weapon is also commonly known as a broad sword. It is a basic cutting, hacking, and slashing tool.

TASSEL
A cloth tassel can also be used to mop up blood in battle

Grip

⌃ DADAO
Often heavy and impractical to use, a "dadao" is a large cleaver-shaped sword. It is ideal for inspiring fear in opponents during battle.

◀ **FINDING THE TARGET**
A wushu practioner (see pp. 93–99) recoils after executing one of chang quan's (see p. 89) many memorable, spectacular, and acrobatic high-kicking techniques.

Sansoo

EXPLANATION
"UNBOUND HAND" IN CANTONESE

DATE OF ORIGIN
1ST CENTURY BCE

FOUNDER
NO SINGLE FOUNDER

PLACE OF ORIGIN
GUANGDONG PROVINCE, CHINA

According to legend, sansoo was originally developed by monks 2,000 years ago in Kwan Yin temple in Guangdong province. The unarmed monks were regularly set upon by bandits when they were taking the food and money they had collected—and which they needed to survive—back to the temple. The monks developed the system for self-defense and it eventually evolved into what is now known as sansoo.

Coming to America

Chinese Grand Master Jimmy Woo took the art with him to the US in 1937 and opened his first school in Los Angeles' Chinatown in 1962. It is from that point that sansoo became popular with people in the West.

Interestingly, because there are no set patterns in the system, it is a highly adaptable style. It is based on a sound knowledge of physics—using principles of leverage, power, and speed—and has two main goals: to disable or cripple an opponent within three strikes, and to end the fight in no more than 10 seconds.

Common moves

A sansoo practitioner will produce a barrage of punches, kicks, and throws in an attempt to finish off an opponent quickly. A fighter will employ some unusual throwing techniques when on the receiving end of a punch. A standard move will see the practitioner evade the first strike, grab his opponent, and throw him to the ground, using either the opponent's head or waist as the access point. The practitioner will then unleash a flurry of punches and strikes to his opponent's vital points.

> "YOU CAN TAKE MY LIFE, BUT YOU CAN NEVER TAKE MY CONFIDENCE."
>
> GRAND MASTER JIMMY WOO

San Shou

EXPLANATION
"FREE HAND" OR "UNBOUND HAND" IN MANDARIN

DATE OF ORIGIN
1960s

FOUNDER
NO SINGLE FOUNDER

PLACE OF ORIGIN
CHINA

San shou, sometimes called "sanda," is the full-contact sport of modern wushu (see pp. 93–99) as practiced in China after 1949, and it is growing in popularity throughout the world.

The system was formulated during the 1960s in an attempt to standardize full-contact fighting rules in China and to provide a forum in which martial artists from all styles could complete. Kicks, punches, throws, and grappling are regarded as legal techniques, but chokes, arm locks, and finishing holds are not allowed. Fighters can win by a knockout or by a points decision, with points awarded for the effectiveness of technique.

▼ FAST AND DIRECT
This fast and furious art is similar to kickboxing (see p. 331) but includes throws. The aim is to down an opponent in the fastest possible time.

Tamo Sho

EXPLANATION
"TAMO'S PALMS"—TAMO BEING ANOTHER NAME FOR BODHIDHARMA

DATE OF ORIGIN
UNKNOWN

FOUNDER
NO KNOWN FOUNDER

PLACE OF ORIGIN
CHINA

Sometimes known as "tamo's palms," the fighting system tamo sho incorporates meditation and herbal medicine. Training of the arms and hands is characterized by open-hand techniques that use the five fingers and the back of the hand in association with the heel of the palm, the "knife hand," and the "ridge hand" as primary attacking weapons. The knife hand is the area from the little finger to the wrist, while the ridge hand is formed when the thumb is tucked under the fingers and a strike is made with the heel of the palm.

The style uses meditation and herbal medicines to train the hands and arms instead of iron-palm training methods (techniques that condition the body to deliver heavy blows without sustaining injury).

The art's origins are unclear, but this little-known art is named after Bodhidharma, the monk who taught yogic exercises to the Shaolin monks, from which Shaolin kung fu (see pp. 57–67) is thought to have evolved.

Choy Gar

EXPLANATION
RAT AND SNAKE STYLE COMBINED

DATE OF ORIGIN
17TH CENTURY

FOUNDER
CHOY GAU LEE

PLACE OF ORIGIN
SOUTHERN CHINA

Although the exact origins of choy gar are unclear, the art is believed to have developed from the rat style of kung fu, known as "cai jia quan," as taught in the Shaolin temple (see pp. 57–67). The system was then developed further to include techniques from snake kung fu (see p. 124).

This southern style, which utilizes low stances and footwork, is often taught alongside a strict moral code that aims to help students mold and strengthen their character.

Nan Quan

EXPLANATION
"SOUTHERN FIST" IN CANTONESE

DATE OF ORIGIN
1960s

FOUNDER
NO KNOWN FOUNDER

PLACE OF ORIGIN
GUANGDONG PROVINCE, CHINA

Nan quan or southern fist is popular in China's Guangdong and Fujian provinces and emphasizes quick changes of direction to encourage the arms to swing and generate momentum and power. Strikes should be repetitive and aimed downward, and followed by whipping uppercuts known as "tao quan." Due to its emphasis on strengthening every part of the body, it is particularly popular with young practitioners.

The modern wushu (see pp. 93–99) form of the art was developed in the 1960s and contained elements from hung quan, choi lei fut (see p. 114), li, liu, mo, and cai styles. Famed for its "fasheng," or release shout, similar to the "kiai" of Korean and Japanese external martial arts, the art is also renowned for its shouting as a means of releasing power into the strikes and to frighten opponents.

> **COMPETITION FIGHTING**
This nan quan competitor, performing at a wushu event at the Asian Games, demonstrates "fasheng" while practicing a strike.

Shaolin Nam Pai Chuan

EXPLANATION
"NORTHERN SOUTHERN FIST" IN CANTONESE

DATE OF ORIGIN
1978

FOUNDER
SIFU LAI

PLACE OF ORIGIN
CHINA

Shaolin nam pai chuan is a hybrid kung-fu style that combines elements of judo, wado ryu, and tae kwon do (see pp. 324, 205, 134). The name translates as "northern southern fist," because of its combination of northern and southern chinese hand techniques. The system teaches weapons and unarmed combat techniques alongside set traditional forms and sequences.

Tang Shou Dao

EXPLANATION
SPIRIT OF THE DRAGON, WAY OF THE CHINESE HAND

DATE OF ORIGIN
1950s

FOUNDER
HONG YIXIANG

PLACE OF ORIGIN
TAIWAN

After taking a trip to Japan, Hong Yixiang, a Taiwanese internal Chinese martial artist, felt that the Japanese systems of teaching and grading would be useful when it came to teaching internal arts. As a result, tang shou dao incorporates major elements from Chinese internal arts such as xing yi (see p. 92), ba qua, and taijiquan (see p. 80–87), alongside external elements of Shaolin kung fu (see pp. 57–65). Full-contact competitions

▲ BORN IN THE FIFTIES
Having studied under Chang Chun-Feng, a master of internal Chinese martial arts, Hong Yixiang (left) developed his own art.

mostly take place in Taiwan and the US (where the system is most used) and students typically wear fixed body armor and helmets with pads on their fists and on their feet.

Feng Shou

EXPLANATION
"HAND OF THE WIND" IN CANTONESE

DATE OF ORIGIN
C. 1ST CENTURY CE

FOUNDER
NO KNOWN FOUNDER

PLACE OF ORIGIN
SHANDONG PROVINCE, CHINA

Feng shou is an internal taijiquan (see pp. 80–87) self-defense system, based on a mythological character called Feng Bo, who, it is said, had control of the wind. Utilizing the posture and blending hand from li-style taiji, feng shou is a deceptive style with the motto: "The softness of a butterfly's wings, but with the hardness of steel." The system is characterized by circular movements of the hands and fast, continuous attacks and blocks.

Wing Chun

EXPLANATION
"ETERNAL SPRINGTIME" IN CANTONESE

DATE OF ORIGIN
17TH CENTURY

FOUNDER
YIM WING CHUN

PLACE OF ORIGIN
GUANGDONG PROVINCE, CHINA

Wing chun is an extremely popular, close-range style that formed the basis of Bruce Lee's fighting arts and philosophy. According to legend, it was invented by a Buddhist nun who taught the system to Yim Wing Chun, a young Chinese woman from the south who had been offered the opportunity to fight against a local warlord; if she won, she would gain her freedom, would not be forced to marry him, and could choose her own suitor. Surprisingly, she did win the fight, married her childhood sweetheart, and taught him the system. He went on to teach it to a number of other people and named it "wing chun" in her honour.

Common thread

There are many different forms of wing chun, but most include six forms: three empty hand, one wooden-dummy form, and two weapons forms. The underlying principle is economy of movement, and practitioners are encouraged to feel their way through an opponent's guard and exploit targets with rapid-fire punches and finger thrusts. Slapping and deflecting movements are used to disorientate opponents and to shift their guard away from the centre line.

> WING CHUN FORM
There are two weapons forms taught in the wing chun art: the butterfly knife (pictured), and the long staff.

When fighting, practitioners deflect or intercept strikes and then go on to trap or strike an opponent. The wing chun punch is quite unique – it is thrown from the centre of the chest, as opposed to all other styles, which are thrown from the hip, the waist, or the guard.

Softness and relaxation are stressed throughout training and practice. Brute force should be avoided, as it is believed that stiff limbs allow the opponent to gain an advantage: he will be able to anticipate movements, divert the force, and use it to his advantage.

永春

WING CHUN

Training aid

The "muk joong", or wooden dummy, is a great aid in helping students understand the system and its 108 movement forms. The art's great advantage is that it can be practised without the use of a training partner, and the dummy serves to condition hands, fists, arms, and feet through repeated quick-fire strikes and blocks against its heavy, wooden body. Training in this way with the muk joong also encourages students to think deeply about angles of entry and attack.

In 1967, Master Ip Chun, head of the wing chun art, began teaching wing chun in Hong Kong. Between 1985 and 2001, he travelled the world conducting wing chun seminars, before semi-retiring in 2001 to concentrate on teaching small groups and individuals.

WING CHUN TRAINING FORM

1	2	3	4	5	6
Turning 90 degrees right to face an imaginary opponent, the practitioner's body stance is low and the hands perform a double block.	By snapping his wrists upwards from their previous position, he can break free from an opponent's grip.	The right hand pulls back to the ready position. Then, twisting back 90 degrees to face the front, he kicks out at waist height.	The right hand blocks a kick, while the left hand covers the "core" – the centre of the torso – which is the primary focus of attack in this system.	The left hand punches while the right hand covers the core from possible attack. Then the right hand punches while the left hand covers the core.	The left hand pulls back to the ready position while the right hand delivers a dynamic tension punch (tightening the arm muscles while punching).

Hong Cha

EXPLANATION
SOUTHERN CHINESE
MARTIAL ART
DATE OF ORIGIN
UNKNOWN
FOUNDER
NO KNOWN FOUNDER

PLACE OF ORIGIN
SOUTHERN CHINA

Hong cha is a Southern Chinese kung-fu style of unknown origin that bears some resemblance to hung gar (see p.111). Heavily influenced by the five animals systems – in particular, the tiger and the dragon – the art emphasizes a range of kicks, punches, and ground-fighting techniques characterized by low stances, deep-breathing techniques (each animal is performed with its own unique breath), and the philosophy of five elements: wood, water, fire, metal, and earth.

Fut Gar Kung Fu

EXPLANATION
"BUDDHA'S PALM" IN
CANTONESE
DATE OF ORIGIN
UNKNOWN
FOUNDER
NO KNOWN FOUNDER

PLACE OF ORIGIN
SOUTHERN CHINA

Fut gar kung fu is a southern style of kung fu characterized by evasive footwork, low kicks, and palm strikes. Although no one person is credited with originating the style, it is believed to have grown from luohan kung fu (see p.69).

As the name suggests, the art was originally a generic term for the kung-fu style used by monks, although it is now taught as a distinct style in its own right. It is thought of as both an internal and external system, meaning that elements of physical strength and soft "qi gong" movements are incorporated into its comprehensive syllabus of attacking and defensive movements.

Well-known offensive techniques (including the hook and the hammer fist), evasive footwork, and the use of some unusual weapons – such as the dragon-well sword – give the system a traditional tone and one that is full of character.

> "OFFENCE SHOULD INSTANTLY FOLLOW DEFENCE IN ONE CONTINUOUS MOTION."
>
> FUT GAR KUNG FU TRAINING MANTRA

Southern Praying Mantis

EXPLANATION
SOUTHERN CHINESE
MARTIAL ART
DATE OF ORIGIN
18TH CENTURY
FOUNDER
NO KNOWN FOUNDER

PLACE OF ORIGIN
SOUTHERN CHINA

There are numerous variants of this southern kung-fu system, the most popular of which are chow gar, chu gar, bamboo forest, and iron ox.

Southern praying mantis is a brutally effective fighting system with no aesthetic value. Kicks are performed at waist level and below and are aimed at vulnerable spots, such as the groin, hips, knees, ankles, and insteps, while the hands pick off targets above the waist – the kidneys, ribs, solar plexus, throat, eyes, and temples. These principles are informed by the theory that split seconds should not be wasted attacking targets that are far from the striking weapons.

Conditioning the body
Training usually consists of fist forms, two-man drills, the execution and drilling of basic moves, and harsh conditioning exercises aimed at hardening the striking and blocking instruments of the body, such as the fists, fingers, and forearms.

Practitioners are forced to endure gruelling, grinding arm and leg exercises, whereby players exert large amounts of force on their body at unusual angles. The aim is to help the student practise breathing and "qi gong" exercises and will ultimately help strengthen the body's resistance to impact. Practitioners are expected to develop an understanding of basic Chinese traditional medicine concepts and, in particular, knowledge of acupuncture points.

Lau Gar

EXPLANATION
"LAU FAMILY FIST" IN
CANTONESE
DATE OF ORIGIN
18TH CENTURY
FOUNDER
LAU SAM-NGAN

PLACE OF ORIGIN
KONG SAI PROVINCE, CHINA

Lau gar, sometimes known as "lau family fist", is one of the major family systems in southern China. Its origin can be traced to its practice at the Kuei Ling temple, situated in Kong Sai province, western China. Three-eyed lau, a tiger hunter from the area who studied at the temple, is credited with being the style's founding father. The fighting techniques of the style are based upon the movements of the five Shaolin animals (see p.125), with the mental training, and fighting strategy derived from Buddhist philosophy and "qi gong".

Serving time
Traditionally there was no grading system in the Chinese martial arts. Rather, students in a Chinese martial arts school would be ranked according to the length of time they had spent at the school instead of according to their martial arts abilities. Thus, students entering such a school would be expected to

> **LEADING BY EXAMPLE**
> Master Yau, head of the lau gar kung fu system, perfoms the systems tiger claw posture.

pay respect to their seniors, even if in time they became more proficient than those seniors.

Depending on the aspirations of the student, harsh physical training exercises may be incorporated into training alongside routine running, jumping, and weight-bearing

stances, and some modern classes incorporate boxing and kickboxing into their fighting syllabus.

The current head of the system, Master Jeremy Yau, brought the style to the UK in 1961, and it is now one of the most popular styles of kung fu practised in the UK.

AUTHOR'S NOTE

My earliest memory of studying this art is of performing a laborious training technique. To learn the correct footwork, my teacher made me walk up and down a stretch of carpet, marked with spots, for three months. As a teenage, I just wanted to jump like Bruce Lee, but later realized that correct footwork is the key to effective combat.

Hung Sing

EXPLANATION
"GLORIOUS VICTORY" IN CANTONESE

DATE OF ORIGIN
19TH CENTURY

FOUNDER
HUNG-SING JEUNG

PLACE OF ORIGIN
SOUTHERN CHINA

Hung sing is a variant of choi li fut (see p. 114), which, it is thought, teaches over 100 "kata," or forms. The system was taken to the US in 1931 by Professor Law Bun, who taught defensive maneuvers for fighting at the Hop Sing Tong Benevolent Association in San Francisco.

Known for its explosive and direct fighting style, it was developed by Hung-Sing Jeung using his experiences working as a security

▲ US HEADQUARTERS
A view of the Hop Sing Tong Association building in San Francisco, where the style was first taught in the US.

guard. For decades, it was only taught to people of Chinese origin, but it is now enjoying a growing practitioner base in the US, particularly in San Francisco.

Snake Kung Fu

EXPLANATION
THE FIGHTING STYLE OF THE SNAKE

DATE OF ORIGIN
UNKNOWN

FOUNDER
NO KNOWN FOUNDER

PLACE OF ORIGIN
CHINA

One of the popular five animal martial arts of China (see right), there are two main branches of snake kung fu, the "northern style" and the "southern style," both of which are characterized by the practitioner adopting the fluidity of the snake in both offensive and defensive maneuvers. Its fluid motion is in line with internal martial-art theories and its different hand postures, with the fingertips typically acting as the primary striking weapon, imitate movements of the cobra and the python.

Thrusting movements

Power is generated from the spine through a whipping action that flows to the fingertips. Jabbing and poking strikes are aimed at vulnerable areas of the opponent, such as the groin, eyes, and throat. The feet need to be solidly placed, but their movement must be fluid in order to get into the correct position. Many other Asian

martial arts have adopted these thrustinglike movements of the fingers toward opponents at unusual angles, and there is a strong possibility that the origin of these actions lies in the snake-style movements of this particular style of kung fu.

▼ FIRST STANCE
The fingers are thrust toward an opponent's weak areas.

Quan Fa

EXPLANATION
"FIST METHOD" IN MANDARIN

DATE OF ORIGIN
UNKNOWN

FOUNDER
NO SINGLE FOUNDER

PLACE OF ORIGIN
HENAN PROVINCE, CHINA

The origins of quan fa remain unclear, although some experts trace its roots back to Shaolin kung fu (see pp. 57–65). Others credited with founding the art are the physician Hu'a To (190–265 CE) and Sung dynasty general Yue Fei (960–1279 CE). Quan fa, which is also commonly known as Chinese Kempo, is a no-holds-barred system of

offensive and defensive methods that emphasizes striking with the hands and feet, immobilization and control, takedowns, weaponry, and spiritual and healing arts such as "qi gong." There are many styles of quan fa, but the five animals of Chinese martial arts—tiger, crane, leopard, snake, and dragon (see pp. 56, 88, 89, 111, 68, 124, 114) inform the basic techniques of the system. The balance of many systems is made up of "18 luohan hands" (see p. 56), fuijian white crane (see p. 111), and jujutsu (see pp. 216–17). Weapons training focuses on the knife, stick, "jo" (half staff), the six-inch staff, and the chain.

◄ POSSIBLE ORIGINATOR
The Chinese physician Hu'a To is thought to be one of the originators of quan fa.

Five Animals

EXPLANATION
A MIXTURE OF THE FIVE TRADITIONAL SHAOLIN ANIMAL STYLES

DATE OF ORIGIN
13TH CENTURY

FOUNDER
JUEYUAN, LI SON, BAI YUFENG

PLACE OF ORIGIN
HENAN PROVINCE, CHINA

The five-animals style is a popular form of martial art that is commonly found in southern China. The style includes elements of tiger, crane, leopard, snake, and dragon kung fu (see pp. 56, 88, 89, 111, 68, 124, 114).

The five-animals style has its roots in the Shaolin temple in Henan province. In the 13th century, one of the temple's monks, Jueyuan, started with the "18 luohan

hands"—the original 18 techniques of Shaolin martial arts—and expanded them to 72 forms. Seeking to develop his art further, he traveled and met Li Sou, a master of hong quan. They both traveled back to Henan province, and Li Sou introduced Jueyuan to Bai Yufeng, a master of the internal arts. Together, all three expanded Jueyuan's 72 forms into approximately 170, and organized them into the five-animals style.

Power generation

As a martial-arts style, five animals can be categorized by its use of palm, fist, and claw techniques, and by the effective way in which power is generated in the waist, before being whipped violently into the hand and used against opponents. "Qi gong" breathing exercises are also commonly found in this style.

Zui Quan

EXPLANATION
"DRUNKEN FIST" IN MANDARIN

DATE OF ORIGIN
UNKNOWN

FOUNDER
NO KNOWN FOUNDER

PLACE OF ORIGIN
CHINA

Zui quan is a popular and exotic system of kung fu and wushu. The style is designed to hide combative strikes with drunkenlike, unsteady movements and actions in order to confuse an opponent.

One of the unusual striking weapons in the system is the "cup hand," which, as the name suggests, is the back of the hand twisted in toward the body, with the thumb and forefinger slightly curved around an imaginary thimbleful cup of rice wine. As well as being a striking move, this is also an effective block to counter straight and round punches. The style was probably created either at the Shaolin temple

(see pp. 57–67) or by warriors posing as Shaolin monks who, no doubt, would often drink alcohol, and who later developed a system based on the emboldening qualities of alcohol.

Recent popularity

The system has become well known in the West through one of the popular characters in the video game "Jackie Chan Stuntmaster," who uses the system to dramatic effect. The system has also been the subject of many popular martial-arts movies in Hong Kong, and famously

▲ **FUELED BY ALCOHOL**
This practitioner is fighting two opponents while pretending to be drunk. This gives him the upper hand as they may drop their guard.

featured in the 1978 Jackie Chan film *Drunken Master* and in Jet Li's more recent film *Last Hero in China*.

Modern wushu drunken boxing routines are acrobatic, whereas the traditional forms focus on rough fighting techniques involving stumbling and staggering. It is a deceptive system and its unorthodox moves often disrupt the concentration of the opponent.

"MY SKULL, MY EYES, MY NOSE, MY JAW, MY SHOULDER, MY CHEST, TWO FINGERS, A KNEE, EVERYTHING FROM THE TOP OF MY HEAD TO THE BOTTOM OF MY FEET."

JACKIE CHAN, LISTING THE BODY PARTS HE HAS BROKEN

Liq Chuan

EXPLANATION
"MIND, BODY, ART" IN CANTONESE

DATE OF ORIGIN
1970s

FOUNDER
CHIN LIK KEONG

PLACE OF ORIGIN
CHINA

Liq chuan is a modern Chinese hybrid martial art founded by Chin Lik Keong. Further developed in Malaysia, it places emphasis on internal power through mental attitude and awareness, and is a distillation of lee gar phoenix eye fist and feng yang lu yi. There are two main forms in the system: the 21-move form and the butterfly form, both of which emphasize different aspects of the art.

Esoteric concepts are introduced at an early stage, as are the yin and yang philosophies from Daoism. It is thought of as an internal art and is most popularly practiced in the US.

Ssireum

EXPLANATION
"TO OVERCOME" IN KOREAN

DATE OF ORIGIN
C. 3000BCE

FOUNDER
NO KNOWN FOUNDER

PLACE OF ORIGIN
KOREA

▼ FIGHTING IN THE SAND
Two ssireum contestants pull each other's satba, or sash, as they try to grapple their opponent to the ground.

A 5,000-year-old form of traditional wrestling, ssireum has become a widely practiced and much-loved national sport of Korea. It is an art that sets two contestants against each other in a circular sandpit. It provides a safe structure for students to grasp the principles of leverage and redirection of force.

No one knows where the name came from. Some think that the term "ssireum" probably evolved from "silum," referring to Mongolian wrestling. Another theory suggests that it originates from the verb "ssirunda," meaning "to struggle against others in the hope of achieving power."

Wrestling matches

Professional ssireum teams attract sponsorship from large Korean companies, but they do not command the same amount of publicity and

▲ MANCHURIAN MURAL
Murals found in Manchuria that date from the 4th century show ssireum players battling in exactly the same way as they do today.

prize funds as the sumo experts in Japan (see pp. 226–33). In fact, it is not unusual for ssireum players to compete in other wrestling matches as well as taking part in mixed martial arts (see pp. 318–25).

In order to win a ssireum match, a contestant must force his opponent to touch the ground with any part of his body above the knee. Kicking, head-butting, and striking are not allowed. Uniquely, the players wear a "satba" (a sash around the waist and right thigh), which forms a gripping point for throwing techniques. Sometimes more than one fall is required: in a three-minute match the first to score three falls advances to the next round.

Subak

EXPLANATION
"HAND SKILL" IN KOREAN

DATE OF ORIGIN
INDIGENOUS ART

FOUNDER
NO KNOWN FOUNDER

PLACE OF ORIGIN
KOREA

Subak is an ancient martial art that is said to have given tae kwon do (see pp. 134–35) much of its character. Little is known about subak, but historians indicate that it flourished approximately 500 years ago during the Yi dynasty and was important in the evolution of Korean martial arts. Some accounts record that subak's emphasis on kicking came about because subak players originally came from mountains in the north where

they developed strong legs. Others point to the fact that, as babies, Koreans are carried on their mother's back in a posture that encourages flexible hips. This is supported by the Korean tradition of eating while sitting cross-legged and upright on the floor, and explains the tradition of men wearing loose-fitting pants for easy movement.

▶ FLEXIBLE HIPS
Korean mothers carry their babies on their backs. This encourages flexible hips that may help in subak.

New schools

During the Japanese occupation of Korea in 1909, the indigenous martial arts were banned. However, Koreans carried on practicing in secret until liberation came in 1945, when new schools opened in the capital, Seoul. Each school taught its own version of the traditional martial arts, and this made it difficult to form a regulatory board. In 1957, many of the schools came together under the single name of tae kwon do.

Yusul

EXPLANATION
"SOFT ART" IN KOREAN

DATE OF ORIGIN
INDIGENOUS ART

FOUNDER
NO KNOWN FOUNDER

PLACE OF ORIGIN
KOREA

An ancient grappling art, yusul has similarities with modern jujutsu (see pp. 216–17). Players divert their opponent's force with throws and locks, and use leverage to apply pressure to their joints. The style that is practiced today is known as gong kwon yusul. It borrows heavily from Japanese jujutsu and contains very effective judolike throws and follow-ups, with arm breaks and arm bar-locking techniques.

Tukong Moosul

EXPLANATION
"SPECIAL COMBAT MARTIAL ARTS" IN KOREAN

DATE OF ORIGIN
1970s

FOUNDER
GENERAL CHANG OE

PLACE OF ORIGIN
KOREA

Tukong moosul is a special forces' combat art developed by General Chang Oe from South Korea's Tu Kong unit to train troops in deadly martial arts. It was developed in response to North Korea's 8th Attack Commando unit. Its four areas of training techniques depend on combat distance: throwing, punching, kicking, and weaponry. Today, the art draws influence from Daeyeon Sa Temple, a Buddhist temple with an excellent martial tradition, and from the Chinese arts of taijiquan (see pp. 80–87) and qi gong, known in Korea as "ki kong." Tukong moosul is also gaining popularity in the US.

Kyu Ki Do

EXPLANATION
"THE WAY OF STRIKING ENERGY" IN KOREAN

DATE OF ORIGIN
1979

FOUNDER
GRAND MASTER OK HYUNG KIM

PLACE OF ORIGIN
KOREA

A hybrid martial art, kyu ki do combines striking elements from tae kwon do, throwing and grappling techniques from judo and jujutsu, and joint locks from hapkido (see pp. 134–35, 234–35, 216–17, 131).

> OK HYUNG KIM

Grand Master Ken Ok Hyung Kim is the founder and chairman of the American Kyuki-Do Federation (AKF). A black belt (9th Dan) in kyu ki do and black belt (9th Dan) in judo, Grand Master Kim was one of the first people to recognize the value of studying more than one martial art. He graduated from the Korea Yudo College with a black belt in judo and tang soo do. He introduced the concept of kyu ki do to the US in 1967, and developed the name in 1979.

The use of traditional Korean weapons may also be taught. Students of this art memorize and explore choreographed defensive and offensive methods and forms. Practitioners abide by six tenets: courtesy, humility, integrity, perseverance, self-control, and indomitable spirit. Students are encouraged to concentrate force on the smallest target area and focus energy at the point of impact with a shout called a "kihap." They also learn how to maintain balance and stability, and to heighten power by increasing either the speed of the technique or the weight behind it.

Kwon Bup

EXPLANATION
"FIST METHOD" IN KOREAN

DATE OF ORIGIN
INDIGENOUS ART

FOUNDER
NO KNOWN FOUNDER

PLACE OF ORIGIN
KOREA

Kwon bup is a collection of fist-fighting techniques, most probably of ancient Chinese origin. Murals in northeast China depict Korean warriors boxing in a style similar to kwon bup. Incorporating joint locks, elaborate footwork, and jumping attacks, advanced kwon bup resembles Shaolin systems, and is difficult to master. Training involves set sequences and forms that are thought of as self-defense movements and as keys to one's own consciousness. The esoteric goal is to help practitioners understand the transitory nature of all things and that the universal principle of change is inescapable.

Kumdo

EXPLANATION
"THE WAY OF THE SWORD" IN KOREAN

DATE OF ORIGIN
1920s

FOUNDER
NO KNOWN FOUNDER

PLACE OF ORIGIN
KOREA

Kumdo is the popular modern Korean art of fencing, and is similar in training methods, apparel, and competition rules to kendo (see pp. 220–21). After the Japanese occupied Korea in 1909, kendo was included in the first national physical education system. During the early part of the 1920s, the name kumdo came into popular usage among Korean martial artists.

Kumdo and kendo

A distinct difference between kumdo and kendo is that kumdo players are encouraged to attack dynamically, focusing on both small and large combinations of aggressive forward attacks and thrusts. This is because the art developed from the needs of the battlefield, in which practitioners had to strike multiple attackers. By contrast, kendo practitioners favor the perfect single strike, which was popular in Japan during the Edo period (1603–1868) when duelling was common. Kumdo players wear helmets and body guards similar to those of their Japanese counterparts. However, the kumdo armory is often simplified and sometimes the forms are practiced alongside specific movements or techniques. Many Korean sword-fighting techniques were influenced by Chinese martial arts, particularly those from the Ming general, Qi Jiguang, who developed a system from the "katana" (Japanese sword) and its training methods.

> **LEARNING SWORDPLAY**
Regular practice with bamboo or wooden swords helps to develop the fine art of kumdo.

> **KUMDO IN THE MOUNTAINS**
Alone among the clouds and the mountains, a kumdo
practitioner stands motionless like an eternal sentinel
with her sword pointing to the heavens and her calm
mind seeking inner strength.

Taekyon

EXPLANATION
"FOOT STRIKING" IN KOREAN
DATE OF ORIGIN
INDIGENOUS ART
FOUNDER
NO KNOWN FOUNDER

PLACE OF ORIGIN
KOREA

Recognized by the Korean government in 1983, but little known outside of Korea, taekyon is a traditional dancelike and athletic martial art. It uses highly effective and deadly accurate kicks for both attacking and defending maneuvers.

It may be accompanied by dancing and singing—in a three-three rhythm as opposed to the four-four timing of other martial arts—that recall its Mongol ancestry. The basic stepping pattern is unique

and extremely difficult to learn, with unusual angles of attack that are very effective in felling opponents.

Some experts regard taekyon as a sport because matches were held as form of entertainment in the 19th and 20th centuries.

Triangular footwork

Combat techniques include "sonkisul"(a grabbing action), head-butting, grappling, and trapping moves, as well as kicks, pushes, sweeps, stamps, and "palgisul" (trips). These are combined with "pumbalki," the triangular footwork that is supposed to mimic the timing of a galloping horse. One startling fact about taekyon is that players are taught to be happy and relaxed during fighting and must not focus overly on aggression or negative mental attitudes, such as hate or anger. The attitude reduces muscular tension, leading to quicker responses and reflexes. It also reduces fear, which further enhances performance.

AUTHOR'SNOTE

I travelled to Seoul in South Korea to learn taekyon from one of the few remaining teachers. I discovered a unique training method that features a full-contact competition known as a taekyon gang battle. In 25 years of studying, researching, and teaching martial arts, I have never come across such a dramatic training method: two teams of five men battling against each other without the use of pads. This realistic situation encourages the development of peripheral vision as each man learns to flow naturally in combat with single or multiple opponents who may attack him at any time. In addition, each man ensures that other members of his team are not overwhelmed.

Renewed popularity

Taekyon's popularity has fluctuated over the centuries—at one point it was even banned—but recently there has been a renewed interest in the art. However, in the past it was practiced mainly by farmers, peasants, and gangsters, so training was random and there were many teachers. With success in combat as the primary objective, today's practitioners focus on learning and using a handful of effective techniques with a high degree of proficiency.

> "INTANGIBLE, CULTURAL ASSET, NUMBER 76."
>
> KOREAN GOVERNMENT TITLE, AWARDED IN 1983

▼ **TAEKYON KICK**
As two students demonstrate the traditional art of taekyon; one unleashes a classic kick that appears to penetrate her opponent's defensive arm movement.

Hapkido

EXPLANATION
"THE WAY OF COORDINATED POWER" IN KOREAN

DATE OF ORIGIN
1950s

FOUNDER
CHOI YONG SHUL

PLACE OF ORIGIN
KOREA

Hapkido is a systemized form of combat that uses throws, restraints, locks, chokes, kicks, and strikes. The system is sweetly and succinctly described in the hapkido poem: "As the flowing stream penetrates and surrounds its obstructions, and dripping water eventually penetrates the stone, so does the hapkido strength flow in and through his opponents." The principles of focus, balance, and leverage underpin hapkido. Timing and motion on the physical plane can also be adopted into the intellectual, emotional, and spiritual realms.

Influences on hapkido

Over 2,000 years of tradition have influenced hapkido, including the ancient tribal techniques (or "sado moosul") of archery, and sword and knife-fighting, which may have been practiced on horseback. Confucian doctrine shaped its philosophy, while Buddhism taught warriors to meet their responsibilities and act with benevolence. Martial arts, such as judo, jujutsu, and karate (see

pp. 234–35, 216–17, 202) contributed to hapkido's techniques. Added to this, the kicking and striking techniques from Korean arts, such as taekyon and subak (see pp. 130, 126), fermented hapkido's collection of techniques into a way of living rather than just a fighting method.

Modern hapkido

After Choi Yong Shul founded the modern art of hapkido in the 1950s, only small groups practiced it. Later, through Jihan Jae, the head hapkido instructor to the presidential bodyguard, hapkido became very popular in Korea and abroad.

Hapkido's emphasis is on self-defense as opposed to sport. Students learn to use weapons as well as ways of defending themselves against an untrained opponent—who is likely to mount an unusual, smothering-type attacks rather than a more coordinated, linear one. They learn to strike the pressure points of acupuncture in order to unbalance opponents prior to a throw or lock, or to disable them.

To become a master of hapkido, practitioners must grasp, apply, and live by three principles: water moves around an object, yet never loses force; the circle represents never-ending, continuous movement; and harmony applied internally must also be directed externally to every situation.

▲ OCCUPYING FORCE
The Japanese occupied Korea from 1909 to 1945, suppressing the country's martial arts, but bringing judo, jujutsu, and karate with them.

▼ HAPKIDO THROWS
Two hapkido students practice a throwing technique, combined with wrist manipulation.

CHOI YONG SHUL

As a boy Choi Yong Shul studied daito ryu aiki jujutsu in Japan. After he returned to Korea he began teaching yu sool, which is a soft-fist technique. He went on to develop modern hapkido in the 1950s with his first student, Suh Bok Sub.

"IF THERE IS BEAUTY IN THE CHARACTER THERE WILL BE HARMONY IN THE HOME. IF THERE IS HARMONY IN THE HOME THERE WILL BE ORDER IN THE NATION."

OLD CHINESE PROVERB ATTRIBUTED TO CONFUCIUS

Sun Kwan Moo

EXPLANATION
"ZEN CONTEMPLATION OF ENEMIES" IN KOREAN

DATE OF ORIGIN
1945

FOUNDER
YANG-IK

PLACE OF ORIGIN
KOREA

> **TEA CEREMONY**
The most unusual aspect of sun kwan moo training is the tea ceremony, which aims to develop a cultivated mind and disciplined movement.

A little-known, Buddhist-based martial art, sun kwan moo includes meditation and physical training with the aim of advancing students toward enlightenment. Probably of Zen origin (called "sun" in Korean), it started after 1945 and, in the 1960s, was taught at Bom Oh Temple in Korea.

Uniquely, students engage in a remarkable exercise known as "tol palki," which involves hopping from rock to rock on a mountain top, with the hope of achieving the elusive state of "no mind."

"THE TEA WAY'S ESSENCE:
TO BOIL WATER, TO WHISK TEA,
AND TO DRINK IT—NO MORE!
THIS IS WELL WORTH KNOWING."

ZEN TEA POEM

Yongmudo

EXPLANATION
"THE MARTIAL ARTS OF YONG" IN KOREAN

DATE OF ORIGIN
1999

FOUNDER
YONG-IN UNIVERSITY

PLACE OF ORIGIN
KOREA

Developed by professional sport scientists and former gold medalists at Yong-In University in Korea, Yongmudo is a new hybrid martial art aimed at enhancing physical action, mental endurance, and functions requiring both. It has become a compulsory element in the physical education of students, with three levels of difficulty or rank—beginner, moderate, and advanced. Yongmudo combines kicking techniques from tae kwon do (see pp. 134–35), shifting and throwing techniques from hapkido (see p. 131), and throwing techniques from judo (see p. 234–35). This art also includes elements of ssireum (see p. 126) and fencing (see pp. 268–69).

Gwon Gyokdo

EXPLANATION
"THE WAY OF FIST ATTACK" IN KOREAN

DATE OF ORIGIN
1970s

FOUNDER
JUNG DO MO

PLACE OF ORIGIN
KOREA

Also known as "kun gek do," gwon gyokdo is a hybrid art incorporating techniques from traditional Korean martial arts and muay Thai (see pp. 158–65). Founded by Jung Do Mo, who studied muay Thai, gwon gyokdo combines kicks from tae kwon do (see pp. 134–35) with kicking and boxing techniques from muay Thai. Unusually, open-hand techniques are removed due to the danger of injury to fingers.

Still in its infancy in Korea, gwon gyokdo is a competitive sport that includes ring fighting and 27 self-defense techniques, some of which defend against a staff, iron bar, and knife. Training includes boxing-style techniques, such as lunging knee and elbow strikes, practiced with protective gear. Unlike other Asian martial arts, it focuses solely on "wai gong," or external energy skill. Students increase physical strength through weight training and drilling of techniques, and condition their hands and feet with heavy-bag work and by repeatedly striking a wooden plank wrapped in rice-straw rope.

Hwa Rang Do

EXPLANATION
"THE WAY OF FLOWERING MANHOOD" IN KOREAN

DATE OF ORIGIN
1950s

FOUNDER
JOO BANG LEE & JOO SANG LEE

PLACE OF ORIGIN
KOREA

This system of defense and offense is named after an élite officer warrior unit called the Hwa Rang, which existed during the Three Kingdoms period of Korean history (57 BCE to 668 CE) and was unique to the Silla region in the south of the country.

Modern style
Two brothers, Joo Bang Lee and Joo Sang Lee, developed the syllabus after studying with a monk named Suahm Dosa at the Suk Wang Sa Temple in Ham Nam, North Korea. They escaped to South Korea when the Communists took over and then, during the 1960s and 70s, appeared in documentaries that were broadcast around the world. Viewers watched in amazement as they demonstrated extraordinary feats of strength and concentration, such as smashing bricks on their foreheads and withstanding the weight of trucks driving over their abdomens.

The brothers' system teaches the use of 108 different weapons, along with three categories of distancing: striking with the hand, foot, head, or weapon; close-quarter leverage, grappling, and throwing techniques; and ground fighting.

> **OUTDOOR SESSION**
The founders of hwa rang do conducting an outdoor training session for masters and instructors, in 1967.

Students learn qi gong ("ki gong" in Korean), meditation, breathing, full- and semicontact sparring, drills, and routines. The ultimate aims are balance in life and harmony with others and with nature. Proper alignment is a focus of training when using strikes, throws, and holds. To achieve a first-degree black belt takes up to 15 years of continuous training. Joo Bang Lee is currently the leading exponent of hwa rang do and the only holder of the black belt (10th Dan)—the highest grade.

Kun Mudo

EXPLANATION
"THE ART OF PUNCHING"
IN KOREAN

DATE OF ORIGIN
1957

FOUNDER
JONG-HYO HA

PLACE OF ORIGIN
KOREA

Kun mudo is a Korean martial art based on dance and music that was modernized by Jong-Hyo Ha in 1957. Similar in essence to taijiquan (see pp. 80–87), this meditative art also includes weapons training and various explosive, quick-fire, striking techniques similar to those found in Shaolin-based arts.

Kun mudo's origins probably lie in the dance and music traditions of the soldiers of the Silla kingdom in the 4th century CE, particularly the "musa chum" (sword dances) of the élite officer corps known as the Hwa Rang (see p. 132).

To the ethereal sound of the zitherlike gayageum, practitioners empty their minds completely and "act the void." Recent archeological finds indicate that the gayageum was already in use during the 1st century BCE. The instrument consists of a board of paulownia wood with 12 strings of twisted silk thread. "Tolgwae" (pegs) can be turned to adjust the tension of the strings. The player pinches or plucks the strings, shaking and bending them as they vibrate.

> **SANJO GAYAGEUM**
The gayageum that accompanies kun mudo is similar to this sanjo gayageum, developed in the 19th century for playing sanjo music.

Kuk Sool Won

EXPLANATION
"NATIONAL MARTIAL ART"
IN KOREAN

DATE OF ORIGIN
1958

FOUNDER
IN HYUK SUH

PLACE OF ORIGIN
KOREA

This relatively new martial art draws heavily on ancient traditions and techniques, but integrates them with modern elements of physical training, such as stretching of ligaments and tendons, muscle toning, flexibility, and cardiovascular conditioning, as well as joint and bone conditioning. Kuk sool won incorporates many high kicks and spinning techniques, including the concrete-smashing kicks for which it has become famous. Particularly noteworthy is its use of weapons, including short and long knife, single or double sword, staves of varying lengths, rice flail, spear, rope, cane, fan, and bow and arrow. Many of the hand methods are drawn from martial arts based on animals, including praying mantis, crane, dragon, bear, snake, eagle, and tiger. Students also study herbal medicine, acupuncture, acupressure, and internal energy systems such as qi gong ("ki gong" in Korean).

▽ **DOUBLE-SWORD TECHNIQUE**
A kuk sool won practitioner in traditional dress gives a spectacular demonstration of the double sword in use.

Tae Kwon Do

EXPLANATION
"THE WAY OF HAND AND FOOT" IN KOREAN

DATE OF ORIGIN
1955

FOUNDER
CHOI HONG HI

PLACE OF ORIGIN
KOREA

Tae kwon do is an unarmed combat method with origins that date back at least 2,000 years. In 1955 it was modernized by Choi Hong Hi, and in the latter part of the 20th century, it received influences from other arts so that it now exists as both a sport and a self-defense martial art. This spectacular and dynamic art blends hand and foot techniques, and focuses on attacking opponents with kicks. In fact, it is one of the few martial arts that emphasizes kicking

< **EXHIBITION ART**
A soldier demonstrates martial arts from the book *Muye Dobo Tongji*, in which techniques used in tae kwon do are illustrated.

become one of the most popular martial arts in the world—in 2008 there were an estimated 50 million practitioners. It joined the ranks of the events in the Olympic Games when it became a full-medal sport at Sydney in 2000.

Two ancient arts
Most of tae kwon do's teaching comes from two ancient arts: taekyon (see p. 130), a kicking art and sport noted for fast combinations of kicks from unusual angles and for rapid-fire takedowns; and subak (see p.126), a fist-orientated art designed for the battlefield and for the training of early Korean warriors. Northern Chinese systems of boxing, which relied heavily on kicking as a battle tactic, also influenced tae kwon do—for example, the flying sidekick or jumping sidekick was originally used as a technique to fell warriors on horseback.

The first book of martial arts
In 1392, shortly after the expulsion of the Mongols when the Yi dynasty established their rule over Korea, the country adopted a Confucian philosophy that stressed the importance of

result, martial arts in Korea all but disappeared from the public eye. Masters and teachers withdrew from society but continued practicing their arts in remote mountain locations, including Buddhist monasteries. In 1790, the first martial arts book was made available to the public in Korea. Called *Muye Dobo Tongji*, it contains 24 martial disciplines known as "muyi 24 gi," which are often demonstrated inside Suwon Fortress near Seoul by soldiers in

traditional dress (see below left). In the book there are 38 illustrations of hand techniques that form part of the practice of tae kwon do.

Modern tae kwon do
In 1909, Japan occupied Korea, banning the Korean language and forcing martial arts underground. At the end of the occupation, in 1945, Korean martial arts resurfaced and gradually began to unite and grow in popularity under a nationalistic theme. Several new and different systems ("kwans") emerged.

> "BE LOYAL TO YOUR COUNTRY.
> HONOR YOUR PARENTS.
> BE FAITHFUL TO FRIENDS.
> NEVER RETREAT IN BATTLE.
> USE GOOD JUDGMENT
> BEFORE KILLING."

FIVE TAE KWON DO COMMITMENTS

CHOI HONG HI

General Choi Hong Hi learned the ancient foot-fighting technique of taekyon in his teens and then went to Japan, where he studied karate. He returned to Korea and developed his new system, which he taught to army personnel and to Americans fighting in Korea. In 1955 tae kwon do was accepted as the name for his new martial art and, in 1960, he introduced the art to the US. Later, he founded the International Tae Kwon Do Federation.

In 1955, General Choi Hong Hi (see p. 134), often referred to as the father of modern tae kwon do, revealed his new art to the public. Although controversy surrounds the inclusion of certain punching techniques into tae kwon do, most notably the reverse punches that bear a resemblance to karate (see pp. 198–99), these hand techniques were most probably of Chinese origin. They were introduced into the Japanese islands of Okinawa, and then later incorporated into karate, before they were returned to Korea. The name tae kwon do was chosen because of its resemblance to the original kicking art, taekyon. Many of the acrobatic martial techniques in movies such as *Enter the Dragon* derive from tae kwon do and so stunt men have developed a familiarity with its practice. In the 360-degree spinning round kick, for example, the practitioner spins and jumps into a turning roundhouse kick that is placed on to either the temple or jaw of an opponent, often with devastating results. Bruce Lee probably incorporated tae kwon do kicking techniques into his art of jeet kune do (see pp. 316–17).

Rules and regulations

There are two important but separate systems in modern tae kwon do. One is promoted by the International Tae Kwon Do Federation (ITF), with centers in Austria, North Korea, and Canada. The other is the World Tae Kwon Do Federation (WTF), which has its headquarters in South Korea and coordinates the international competitions, including the tae kwon do events at the Olympics.

Practitioners of tae kwon do wear a uniform called the "dobahk," which is similar to a long-sleeved T-shirt. Unlike the "gi" worn by karate practitioners, this one-piece top does not tie from side to side and is often made from lighter material because there is little grappling taught in tae kwon do.

Under the WTF rules, as commonly practiced in the West, two competitors fight three rounds on a square matted area of 328 ft x 328 ft (10 m x 10 m). Junior ranks fight one-minute rounds with 30 seconds in between. Senior ranks fight two-minute rounds with one minute in between.

Scoring points

Kicks or punches must make contact with a reasonable amount of force in order to score points. A kick or punch to the body scores one and a kick to the head scores two. An extra point is scored for knocking an opponent to the ground with a clean technique. Punches to the head are not allowed. To win a match a competitor must have either a seven-point lead or be the first to reach 12 points. In the event of a tie, the winner is the first to score in a sudden death match.

∨ FIST TECHNIQUES
Two black-belt practitioners demonstrate their tae kwon do fist techniques as they spar with each other during training.

∨ SYDNEY OLYMPICS
Kim Kyong-Hun attacks Australia's Daniel Trenton on his way to securing gold for South Korea in the men's over 80 kg (176 lb) event at the Sydney Olympics in 2000.

> SPECTACULAR FORCE
South Korean soldiers show off their spectacular tae kwon do skills during the 59th Armed Forces Day ceremony at Gyeryong, south of Seoul.

Tang Soo Do

EXPLANATION
"THE WAY OF THE CHINESE HAND" IN KOREAN

DATE OF ORIGIN
INDIGENOUS ART

FOUNDER
NO KNOWN FOUNDER

PLACE OF ORIGIN
KOREA

Tang soo do is an extremely popular martial art that evolved from the kicking arts of taekyon (see p. 130) and subak (see p. 126). It is similar to tae kwon do (see pp. 134–35) and maintains its heritage as a traditional way of promoting the values of self-control, respect, and discipline in the pursuit of self-improvement. Important characteristics that underpin the art include humanity, wisdom, etiquette, and trust.

Tang soo do is particularly popular in the US, where it is sometimes advertised under the name of karate or Korean karate. Chuck Norris is probably its most well-known practitioner in the West. He is the six-time undefeated world professional middleweight karate champion and one-time martial teacher of Steve McQueen, Priscilla Presley, and Donny Osmond.

> **IN THE MOVIES**
Tang soo do practitioner Chuck Norris challenges Bruce Lee in a scene from the 1978 US movie *Game of Death*.

Han Kum Do

EXPLANATION
"THE WAY OF KOREAN SWORDSMANSHIP" IN KOREAN

DATE OF ORIGIN
1986

FOUNDER
MYUNG JAE NAM

PLACE OF ORIGIN
KOREA

Han kum do (HKD) is a sword system in which the basic cutting techniques mimic the Korean script known as "hangul". It follows the fundamental principles of multiple strikes on multiple opponents. Developed by Myung Jae Nam, the art came to popular attention during the third international HKD Games in 1997.

Hangul, known as the most scientific alphabet in existence, is very easy to learn and has 24 characters (10 vowels and 14 consonants). Making the sword cuts on the letters of the alphabet is an ingenious training aid that helps students to memorize the various cuts and enables them to perform the required movements instinctively in very little time.

Won Hwa Do

EXPLANATION
"THE WAY OF CIRCULAR HARMONY" IN KOREAN

DATE OF ORIGIN
1972

FOUNDER
BONG KI HAN

PLACE OF ORIGIN
KOREA

Won hwa do is a hybrid art that relies on 360-degree rotations to generate power, supporting the key philosophy that, in nature, there are no straight lines or angles of attack. Long-term practice, however, damages the joints and ligaments. Weapons such as the short stick, knife, and sword are routinely taught, with attacks and defends born from "bi son"—the rhythm used during traditional prayer and dance. The circular attacking motions of the art belong to the same tradition as those used for massaging injuries.

▼ **CIRCULAR POWER**
Whirling fan dancers demonstrate the effortless beauty and power that can be generated by practitioners of won hwa do.

Han Mu Do

EXPLANATION
"THE WAY OF KOREAN MARTIAL ART" IN KOREAN

DATE OF ORIGIN
1990

FOUNDER
HE-YOUNG KIMM

PLACE OF ORIGIN
KOREA

Han mu do is a modern hybrid art of open-hand combat that combines a number of techniques, including joint locks from hapkido (see p. 131), and kicks and strikes from tae kwon do (see pp. 134–35). It is not to be confused with the similar-sounding art of han moo do (see p. 280).

A range of techniques

This comprehensive system is rapidly growing in popularity, with 44 schools worldwide. Its founder, Dr. He-Young Kimm, was a 5th-degree black belt in kodokan judo and a respected practitioner of tae kwon do and hapkido. He aimed to develop a system where practitioners could briskly pound their opponent with potent strikes, then unbalance them before delivering an impressive throw or joint manipulation as a finisher. Blocking techniques typically target the wrist and elbow, but leg-locking techniques and manipulations are applied and often practiced from a sitting position. Dr. Kimm included hand techniques from tae kwon do, particularly the "spear hand" and chops, and encouraged training in traditional weapons, such as the sword, long and short poles, and knives.

Hankido

EXPLANATION
"THE WAY OF KOREAN ENERGY"
IN KOREAN

DATE OF ORIGIN
1980s

FOUNDER
MYUNG JAE NAM

PLACE OF ORIGIN
KOREA

Hankido is a hybrid martial art that incorporates aspects of aikido (see pp. 238–39), with kicking and striking techniques, acrobatic flips, and kicks reminiscent of tae kwon do (see pp. 134–35). Students develop "ki"—Korean for "qi"—and learn 12 basic self-defense moves and 24 breathing techniques. They also spin and dance to develop coordination, rhythm, timing, and softness. The art's philosophy centers on the principles of "circle," "flow," and "heart," and each has a specific exercise. "Jeon hwan bup" (the circle exercise) teaches circular moves for defense, leverage, and throwing. "Young nyu bup" (the flow exercise) encourages students to see moves as a continual interaction between themselves and their opponents, promoting an attitude of fearless, relaxed action. "Shim hwa bup" (the rowing exercise) encourages the heart to develop a fighting spirit.

Hoi Jeon Moo Sool

EXPLANATION
"THE REVOLVING MARTIAL ART"
IN KOREAN

DATE OF ORIGIN
1960s

FOUNDER
MYUNG JAE OK

PLACE OF ORIGIN
KOREA

Hoi jeon moo sool uses circular and revolving movements to generate power. A wide range of complex maneuvers, particularly with weapons, enhances brain function, memory, and spatial awareness. Traditional weapons include swords, staves, fans, and canes. Students learn internal strength training ("nae ki"), which focuses on breathing exercises to develop the strong "ki"—Korean for "qi"—needed to withstand blows. Techniques for self-defense include throwing, choking, striking with the hands, and kicking with the feet.

◄ SYMBOLIC LOGO
Red symbolizes the sky, blue is the Earth, and white is the human being. The character for "ki" is in the center.

Haedong Gum Do

EXPLANATION
"THE WAY OF HAEDONG SWORDSMANSHIP" IN KOREAN

DATE OF ORIGIN
1982

FOUNDER
KIM JEONG-HO

PLACE OF ORIGIN
KOREA

Haedong gum do is a Korean art of swordsmanship and is noted for its quick-fire, rapid succession of cuts and slashes. Practitioners use a "mokgum" (a wooden sword), a "jukdo" (a bamboo sword), and a "jingum" (a real sword). It is said to be based on gicheon, an older martial art similar to taijiquan (see pp. 82–83), as described in the *Myue Bobo Tongji*, the ancient book of martial arts (see p. 134). The ultimate aim is to achieve "shim gum," the unification of mind, body, and spirit. Public demonstrations often show a seasoned practitioner cutting straight through a target of bamboo or a damp, tightly wound bundle of straw. The target remains balanced while the practitioner performs other cuts, before it falls to the ground in pieces. This multiple-strike practice is born of battlefield experiences in which many opponents may attack simultaneously. By contrast, swordsmanship in Japan focuses on perfecting the single cut, as duels were common among warriors and the first strike often distinguished winner from loser.

▼ ART OF THE SWORD
Master Youn Ja-kyung, who has been practicing haedong gum do since she was 13, demonstrates her sword skill.

SOUTHEAST ASIA
AND OCEANIA

SOUTHEAST ASIA AND OCEANIA

THE SHEER DIVERSITY OF CULTURES in Southeast Asia and Oceania has played a large part in the evolution of martial arts in the region. At the same time, a wealth of religious practices—including shamanism, Christianity, Islam, Sikhism, Hinduism, and, in particular, Buddhism—have all contributed to the philosophical underpinnings of indigenous, imported, and hybrid art forms. These have been influenced by Chinese traditions and martial arts, and have flowered into a wide-ranging catalogue of fighting systems, each with its own distinct flavor and cultural identity.

SOME MARTIAL-ARTS TRADITIONS in the region, such as arnis and kali (see pp. 187, 175), have provided the inspiration for other, more modern arts. For example, today there are more than 800 schools across Indonesia's 13,000 islands teaching the indigenous martial art pencak silat (see pp. 172–73) and the majority of them teach different styles. In the Philippines, eskrima (see pp. 180–81) contains a multitude of stick-fighting, knife-fighting, and empty-hand techniques that were developed in the past, but which have been adapted to cope with the risks and dangers of modern life on the country's mean city streets.

Southeast Asian arts range from full-contact aggression to a more gentle focus on self-development. For example, muay Thai (see pp. 158–65), the direct and effective kickboxing sport that uses elbows and knees, is a simple yet brutal art. In contrast, the Myanmarian art of pongyi thaing (see p. 145) is nonviolent and stresses

Hindu and Buddhist principles in an attempt to develop a practitioner's mind, body, and spirit. Those who practice the ancient Myanmarian art of bando yoga (see p. 145) seek to cultivate their health—and in former times their readiness for battle—by defending themselves against both armed attack from without and internal disease from within, leading to a more peaceful existence free from confrontation and conflict. This philosophical concept was captured succinctly by the legendary Bruce Lee (see pp. 316–17) when he said: "If you don't fight, you cannot lose."

The past meets the present
Many of the older indigenous martial-art forms in Southeast Asia were practiced alongside music, dance, and drama. These traditions live on today, although in a slightly different form. For example, muay thai practitioners engage in a dancelike ritual before they fight to protect themselves and hex their opponent during a bout. The fight itself is always accompanied by hypnotic and distinctive music. In Indonesia and Malaysia, silat is often practiced to a musical accompaniment and often features in folk dramas.

> ⯈ EARLY RELIGIOUS INFLUENCES
These young children are Buddhist monks from a monastery at Lake Inle in Myanmar. They receive instruction in religion and martial arts from the older monks.

REGION AT A GLANCE

1 RELIGIOUS MIX
The region's numerous religions, from animism and shamanism to Christianity, Islam, and Buddhism, have all added considerably to the region's martial-arts mix.

2 TRADITIONAL DANCE
In the past, many indigenous Southeast Asian martial arts co-existed with music. It is a tradition that still lives on in some art forms to this day.

3 KEEPING TRADITIONS ALIVE
As has been the case for centuries, muay-Thai practitioners today consider themselves to be protected by magic when they fight.

4 INDIGENOUS INFLUENCES
Many of the region's cultures have evolved in almost total isolation and have developed unique rituals. The Maoris of New Zealand, for example, have an initiation rite that often sees young warriors having to endure painful tattooing.

5 MIND, BODY, AND SPIRIT
The Chinese influence on some of the region's martial arts is evident. Pongyi thaing, for example, is a nonviolent art that stresses Buddhist and Hindu principles.

6 MOVING WITH THE TIMES
Some of the region's martial arts, such as eskrima from the Philippines, have evolved over the years to cater for the needs of the modern-day practitioner.

7 STEEPED IN ANTIQUITY
The importance of martial arts in the region is clear. Depictions of men performing martial arts have been found in many ancient temples, including the world-famous Angkor Wat in Cambodia.

8 MUSICAL ACCOMPANIMENT
In keeping with ancient traditions, some of the region's martial arts—such as muay Thai and silat—are still practiced to the accompaniment of music.

MAP OF SOUTHEAST ASIA AND OCEANIA

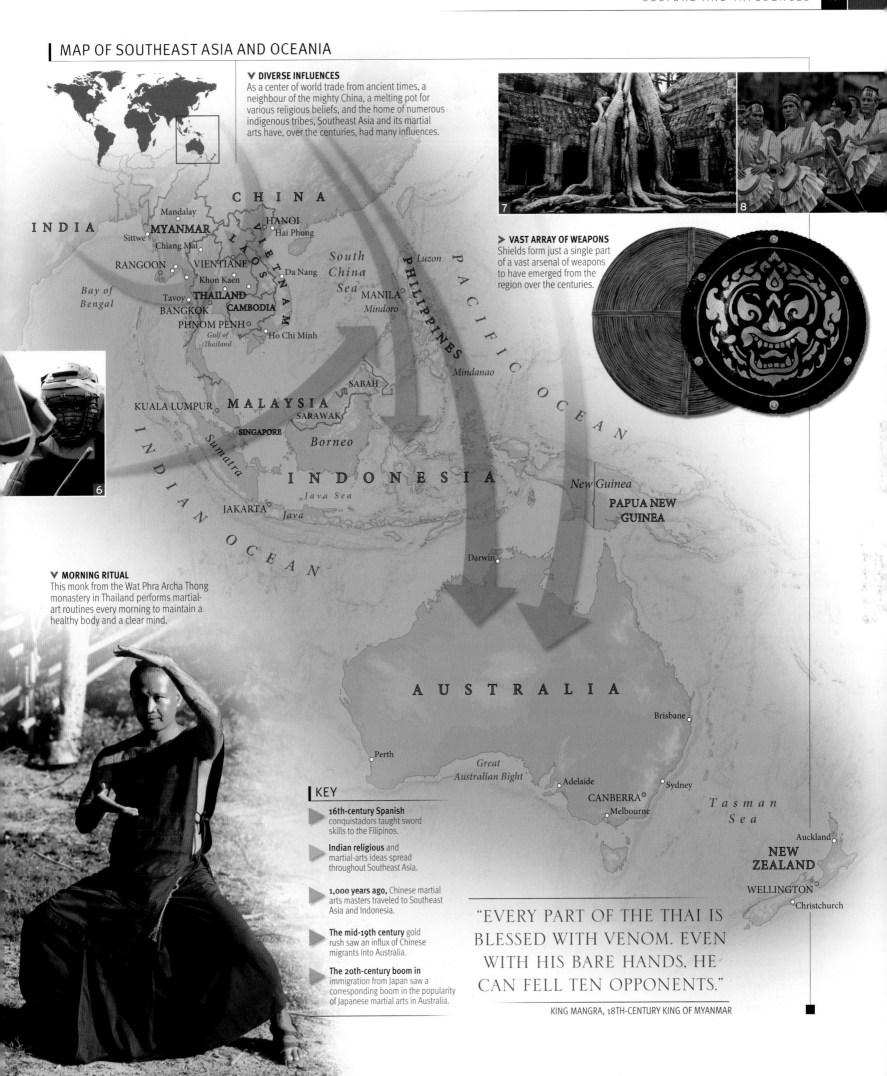

▼ **DIVERSE INFLUENCES**
As a center of world trade from ancient times, a neighbour of the mighty China, a melting pot for various religious beliefs, and the home of numerous indigenous tribes, Southeast Asia and its martial arts have, over the centuries, had many influences.

▷ **VAST ARRAY OF WEAPONS**
Shields form just a single part of a vast arsenal of weapons to have emerged from the region over the centuries.

▼ **MORNING RITUAL**
This monk from the Wat Phra Archa Thong monastery in Thailand performs martial-art routines every morning to maintain a healthy body and a clear mind.

KEY

▶ **16th-century Spanish** conquistadors taught sword skills to the Filipinos.

▶ **Indian religious** and martial-arts ideas spread throughout Southeast Asia.

▶ **1,000 years ago,** Chinese martial arts masters traveled to Southeast Asia and Indonesia.

▶ **The mid-19th century** gold rush saw an influx of Chinese migrants into Australia.

▶ **The 20th-century boom in** immigration from Japan saw a corresponding boom in the popularity of Japanese martial arts in Australia.

"EVERY PART OF THE THAI IS BLESSED WITH VENOM. EVEN WITH HIS BARE HANDS, HE CAN FELL TEN OPPONENTS."

KING MANGRA, 18TH-CENTURY KING OF MYANMAR

Renewed life

As nations and their people in the region emerge from years of conflict and suppression, traditional martial arts have begun to flower once again. Cambodia's ancient martial-art traditions can be seen in the figures that adorn the temples of Angkor Wat, which dates back to the 12th century CE. The arts in Myanmar are mostly animal-based techniques and have survived with relatively little influence from the other modern sporting arts in the region. Many styles of thaing—the generic term for defense or all-out fighting systems in Myanmar—are largely based on grappling and striking. Lethwei (see pp. 146–47), a traditional Myanmarian sport similar to muay Thai, has been practiced in Myanmar for centuries and continues to grow in popularity.

Jingoistic trends

Throughout Vietnam's turbulent history, both culturally and philosophically, the country's Chinese-influenced martial arts were never standardized. Instead they were primarily passed along family lines and, during the French occupation from 1859 to 1954, were driven underground. They are now enjoying a reemergence and many have strong nationalistic

▲ RITE OF PASSAGE
Many of the region's indigenous tribes require their members to pass through an initiation rite, often involving painful tattooing, before they can be classified as true warriors.

▼ BRINGING IN THE CROWDS
Contestants in a bare-knuckle boxing fight in the Myanmarian village of Phayathonzu—less than 1.2 miles (2 km) from the border with Thailand—attract the crowds on Karen Day (February 11), a national holiday in Myanmar.

"AT THE CORE OF THE THAI MARTIAL ARTS EXISTS THE BELIEF THAT IF FIGHTING MUST TAKE PLACE, THE WHOLESALE DESTRUCTION OF THE OPPONENT IS WARRANTED."

JASON WEBSTER, FAMOUS KRABI KRABONG PRACTITIONER

⋁ ONE ART, MANY DIFFERENT FORMS
Martial artists on the Indonesian island of Bali practice bali silat, one of the many forms of the primarily defensive art of silat.

elements, such as vovinam (see p. 168), which was founded in 1938 as a Vietnamese martial art for Vietnamese people.

Martial arts "down under"

In Oceania, most of the ancient fighting techniques and systems not only use simple weapons, such as stones, slingshots, and sticks, but also metal spears, swords, and other bladed weapons. Mau rakau (see p. 186), the traditional Maori martial art, is of particular interest. The art is seen as being a useful way of cultivating self-discipline and social responsibility and practitioners often have to endure painful tattooing as a rite of passage to warriorhood. A number of hybrid martial arts have evolved in Australia and New Zealand, especially during the early 1970s when the martial-arts craze reached its zenith and films and television series featured central characters who were skilled in combat or self-defense techniques. Many of these arts remain popular today.

▲ **MILITARY TRAINING**
Soldiers of the Karen National Union (KNU) are drilled in traditional Burmese martial arts at their headquarters in Manerplaw.

Bando Thaing

EXPLANATION
"SELF-PROTECTION STYLE" IN BURMESE

DATE OF ORIGIN
INDIGENOUS ART

FOUNDER
NO KNOWN FOUNDER

PLACE OF ORIGIN
MYANMAR (BURMA)

Also known simply as "bando," this martial art is inspired by the bull, eagle, cobra, panther, and monkey, with the characteristics of each animal reflected in its forms or set movements. Key aspects of training include strict discipline, self-development, and self-defense.

According to legend, Indian monks brought their martial arts to Southeast Asia; bando thaing originated among martial arts'

disciples in Buddhist temples. Indeed, Buddhist thought informs much of the system's philosophy. Bando thaing is governed by the International Bando Association, which was formed in 1946 in memory of those people from Myanmar, China, and India who died during World War II.

Weapons and schools

Practitioners use weapons such as spears, sticks, knives, and swords. They always try to withdraw from the range of their attacking opponent, before reentering, often at a different angle, and delivering a three-tier response. The first response is a block or evasive move followed by sudden attack; the second response is the use of a locking or grappling technique; finally a throw is employed or a weapon is used.

"BEAUTIFULLY BRUTAL ART ... I'M HAPPY THEY'RE ON OUR SIDE."

LORD MOUNTBATTEN, AFTER WATCHING BANDO FIGHTERS AT THE MILITARY ATHLETIC CLUB, 1937

A number of different schools practice various forms of bando across Myanmar. The most common are the Hard and Soft Way School, the Royal Palace School, and the Snake School. The Shan Province School may have more Chinese influences than other schools because the province is close to the Chinese border. Most schools have a belt ranking system. Generally, black-belt status is not reached until students have at least five years' experience.

> **IN THE BEGINNING...**
The discovery of ancient engravings and religious texts have enabled scholars to chart the history of Burmese martial arts.

Bando Yoga

EXPLANATION
"YOGA OF SELF-PROTECTION" IN BURMESE
DATE OF ORIGIN
C. 1000 CE
FOUNDER
NO KNOWN FOUNDER

PLACE OF ORIGIN
MYANMAR (BURMA)

Bando yoga is an ancient system that was practiced specifically by ancient warriors of northern Myanmar. It appears to imitate tantric and Buddhist yoga forms, and may have evolved in Buddhist monasteries more than a thousand years ago.

Self-protection

Bando yoga is an essential part of the bando system of self-protection. It emphasizes the maintenance of health and protection against illness and disease in order to encourage battle readiness. It was essential for recovery from illness and, more importantly, from injury sustained while fighting. Key aspects include yoga, the use of a staff, partner-assisted exercises, and stretches.

Banshay

EXPLANATION
WEAPONS-BASED ART
DATE OF ORIGIN
INDIGENOUS ART
FOUNDER
NO KNOWN FOUNDER

PLACE OF ORIGIN
MYANMAR (BURMA)

A weapons-based martial art, banshay is influenced by Chinese and Indian systems. It is part of the body of martial knowledge known

Min Zin

EXPLANATION
ART THAT PROMOTES OVERALL HEALTH AND WELL-BEING
DATE OF ORIGIN
INDIGENOUS ART
FOUNDER
NO KNOWN FOUNDER

PLACE OF ORIGIN
MYANMAR (BURMA)

Min zin is a martial art that focuses on the promotion of health and internal energies through stretching and realigning of posture. Many of

as "thaing," the collective name for Burmese martial arts. The main goal of training in defensive techniques is to disarm an opponent. Offensive battlefield techniques include stabs, slashes, thrusts, strikes, parries, and blocks with weapons such as the sword, spear, and staff. Uniquely, training and fighting often include many techniques with a sheathed sword—indeed, warriors of old were known to fight with their sword sheathed so they could defeat their opponent without killing them.

the exercises appear to have been heavily influenced by Chinese qi gong (therapeutic breathing exercises). It may be based on the teachings of traveling Buddhist monks between 500 BCE and 300 CE.

Min zin's primary principles are to control one's own destructive and negative aspects of mind, to harness health and well-being, and to achieve overall balance of spirit. As a self-defense art it places emphasis on protecting the physical, mental, and spiritual aspects of an individual.

Pongyi Thaing

EXPLANATION
NONVIOLENT MONK SYSTEM
DATE OF ORIGIN
INDIGENOUS ART
FOUNDER
NO KNOWN FOUNDER

PLACE OF ORIGIN
MYANMAR (BURMA)

A martial art firmly rooted in Hindu and Buddhist traditions, pongyi thaing advocates principles of nonviolence. It is also sometimes known as the "bando monk system." Although pongyi thaing is not a religion, it stresses methods of developing the mind, body, and spirit of individuals so that they can become fully attuned to their surroundings. Pongyi thaing's underlying philosophy is not to harm others. A key aspect of training is to develop emotional control in a confrontation and to generate emotional discipline that informs the reaction to a given threat. A confident and friendly smile, coupled with a calm, steady voice in the face of aggression, is often enough to de-escalate the threat of violence.

Naban

EXPLANATION
BURMESE WRESTLING
DATE OF ORIGIN
INDIGENOUS ART
FOUNDER
NO KNOWN FOUNDER

PLACE OF ORIGIN
MYANMAR (BURMA)

Naban is a Burmese grappling-based martial art. It is practiced at festivals by tribes such as the Kachin, Karen, and the Chin. Naban is probably based on ancient Indian styles of wrestling and may have taken root in local villages following contact with travelling monks from India and China. It is now often practiced alongside lethwei or Burmese boxing (see pp. 146–7).

Joint locks, pressure holds, point strikes, and chokes are common. The traditional art includes submission techniques such as gouging, biting, and strikes to the groin area, but these are considered inappropriate in friendly festival bouts.

> SUBMISSION MANEUVER
A Burmese wrestler endeavors to break the resistance of his opponent with a prolonged neck hold, while the referee looks on.

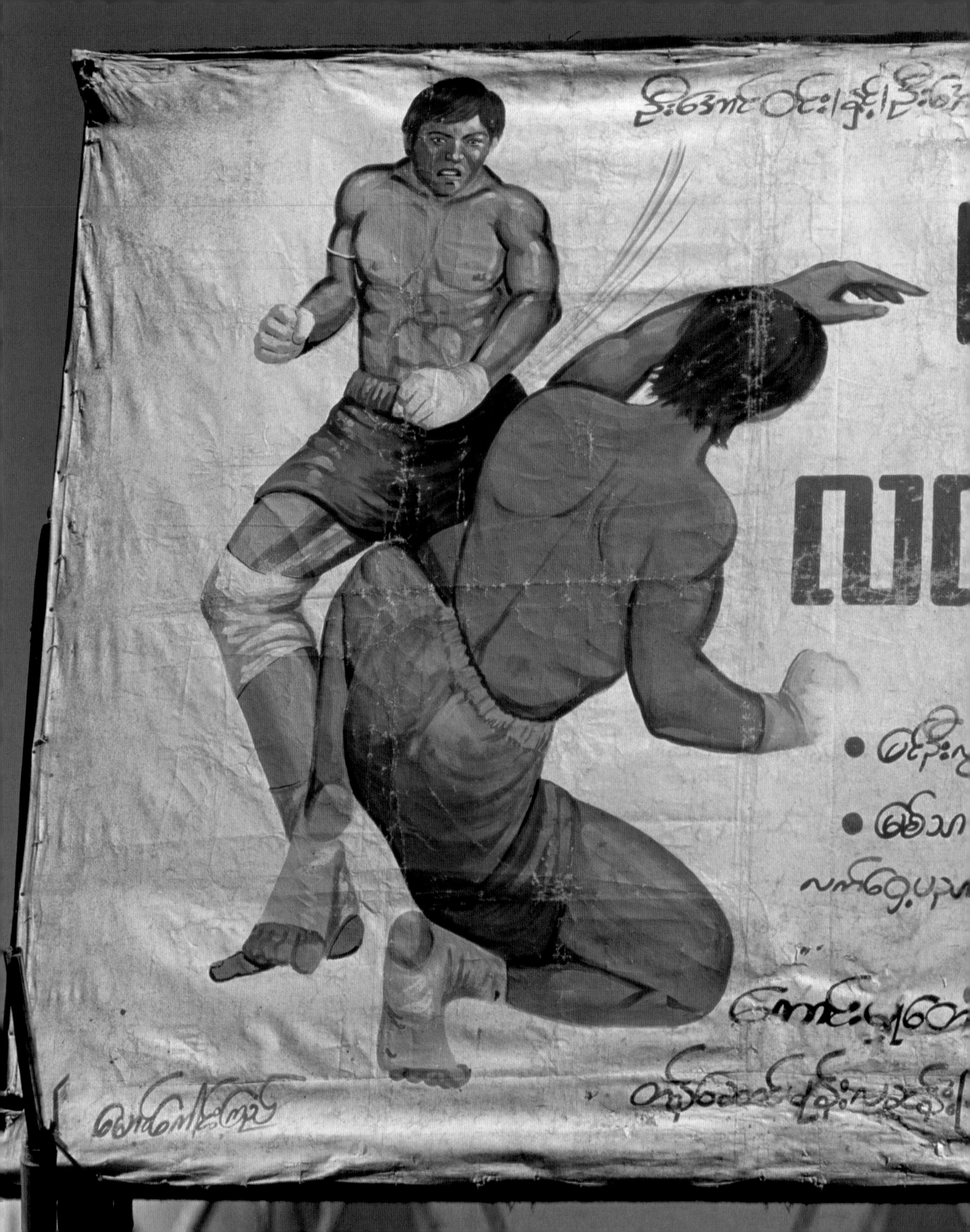

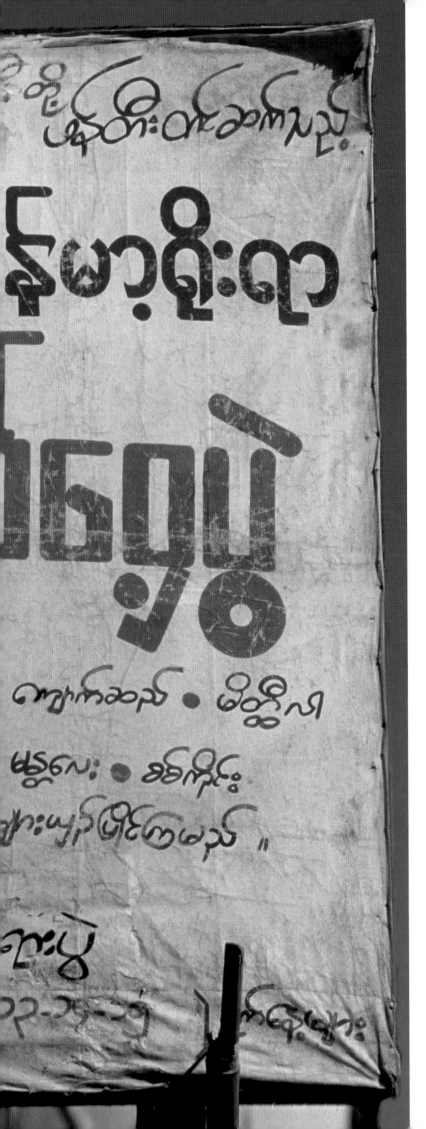

Lethwei

EXPLANATION
BURMESE BOXING
DATE OF ORIGIN
INDIGENOUS ART
FOUNDER
NO KNOWN FOUNDER
PLACE OF ORIGIN
MYANMAR (BURMA)

Lethwei is a traditional kickboxing art similar to its sibling arts of muay Thai, tomoi, and pradal serey (see pp. 158–65, 168–69). While muay Thai is often referred to as the "science of eight limbs," lethwei is sometimes known as the "science of nine limbs" because it incorporates the use of the head-butt, as well as hands, feet, elbows, and knees.

Bare-knuckle tradition
Stylistically, lethwei draws its influences from Indian styles of fighting—and the bare-knuckle origins of Western boxing—rather than from muay Thai or other arts from Southeast Asia. Its moves are typically slow and strong, and lethwei boxers are likely to make heavy strikes aimed at knocking out opponents.

In the past, Burmese boxers wrapped their hands in hemp or cloth. Although the art has recently taken on more sporting and competitive elements, the bare-knuckle or hemp-wrapped fist origins of the style still inform much of the fighting methodology.

Traditionally, lethwei fights were held outdoors in sand pits, where takedowns and sometimes biting or gouging were permitted, and wins were decided by either a clean or a technical knockout (when a fighter could fight no longer). Bloodshed was common and death not uncommon. As a result, boxers concentrated their training on extreme conditioning and absorbing punishing force. They spent a great deal of their training time in preparing to absorb impacts and in conditioning their striking weapons, particularly their fists, knees, and heads.

The modern era
Although the traditional form still flourishes, lethwei was modernized in the 1930s, with the introduction of safety equipment such as head guards and boxing gloves. Fights were held in boxing rings, rounds were timed, and head-butts prohibited. In 1996, a more marketable branch of lethwei was formed, called Myanmar Traditional Boxing. Its goal is to stand alongside muay Thai (see pp. 158–65) in the wider sporting world.

◄ **FIGHT NIGHT ATTRACTION**
Myanmarians are fiercely proud of their nation's kickboxing heritage. Top events are strongly promoted and attract large crowds.

▼ **LEGALIZED VIOLENCE**
A heavily tattooed lethwei boxer aims a left foot to the head of his low-punching opponent during a bout in Rangoon.

Krabi Krabong

EXPLANATION
"SWORD AND STAFF" IN THAI

DATE OF ORIGIN
INDIGENOUS ART

FOUNDER
NO KNOWN FOUNDER

PLACE OF ORIGIN
THAILAND

This weapons-based art is closely related to banshay (see p. 145) and silat (see pp. 172–73). The weapons include "krabi" (a single-edged sword), "krabong" (a staff), "loh" (a buckler), "plong" (a stick), "ngao" (a halberd), "daab song mue" (a pair of swords) held in each hand, and "mai sun fawk" (a pair of clubs) worn on the forearms. The use of a krabi is predominant, although empty-hand forms are included. Krabi krabong was used in the James Bond film *The Man with the Golden Gun* (1974).

History and influences

Weapons training has a long tradition in Thai history, but today's style of krabi krabong is thought to derive from the art of 400 years ago. This was handed down from the "Wat Putthaiswan" (élite bodyguard) of Ayutthaya, a Thai kingdom that thrived from 1350–1767. This lethal and fast-moving art is still taught to the king's bodyguard.

Some experts point to similarities with Chinese and Indian sword-fighting styles, and the bojutsu styles (see p. 219) brought by early Japanese settlers and traders to Indochina and Siam, which have helped to shape stick techniques, in particular, the stances and footwork.

Ritual blessing

An important element of training is the master's ritual blessing, known as the "kru." He uses the sword of Ayutthaya in a blessing to his students who, on reaching a high rank, can carry on the name of the school. Matches are held within a marked circle and are accompanied by music. Weapons are unsheathed but are not used to strike opponents. Judges decide the winner based on technical ability and stamina.

> **DUELING HALBERDS**
Two krabi krabong practitioners train with ngao (halberds), but use dummy blades. As one lunges in a downward chop, the other takes up a defensive position to absorb the oncoming force.

"THE FOUNDATIONAL CONCEPTS [OF KRABI KRABONG] ARE THOSE OF BALANCE AND THE MIDDLE WAY IN THOUGHT, WORD, AND DEED."

MUAY THAI SANGHA

AUTHOR'SNOTE

While in Thailand recently, I had the good fortune to train in krabi krabong using halberd, single, and double sword under Sumi Masamura, who teaches the art to the Thai army. Before training, I observed the ritual dance—accompanied by hypnotic music and performed in unison—which in the past helped warriors prepare their minds for battle. Today, it is performed prior to training to focus the mind. After a grueling half-day introduction, we started outdoor training in the humid midday sun. There was some free sparring with twin swords, but mostly we followed set patterns against single or multiple opponents. Practitioners are expected to quickly memorize movements and sequences of movements, often in excess of 50–60 attack and defending techniques. These are then played out repeatedly at full speed and full contact, which causes a great degree of stress—participants became physically drained and mentally exhausted because of the high degree of focus. It was genuinely good fun, but I stopped after a couple of hours as my accuracy was diminishing—I nearly chopped off one of my opponent's fingers.

BEHIND THE SCENES

KRABI KRABONG

OFTEN REGARDED AS THE "MOTHER" of muay Thai (see pp. 158–65), the origins of krabi krabong can be traced back to the early 1600s. A brutal art featuring lethal force, it thrives in modern Thailand as a ceremonial practice, conducted in homage to past warriors.

Krabi krabong is the art that soldiers would have used to defend themselves on the ancient battlefields of Thailand, and the practice is still taught to the Thai army today. There is a significant spiritual element to the art, which is born of its lethal nature. Before entering battle, former warriors would have spent time in meditation and prayer, knowing there was a strong possibility that they were about to kill or be killed.

This rich history informs many of the practices associated with the art today. Lethal force is no longer used but, before each training session or tournament commences, modern krabi-krabong students pray for the heroes that died for the Thai nation. The training is hard and unrelenting. It focuses on a series of rehearsed moves (the complexity of which are commensurate with the ability of the individual student). Special blunted weapons are used during practice, but sharpened "krabi" (single-edged swords) and "ngao" (halberds) are wielded during tournament play. It is therefore vital that students maintain a calm and focused mind at all times and pay heed to the instructions of their master.

WEAPON SELECTION

Before training commences, krabi-krabong students select from a choice of weapons. All of these are practice weapons—those used by the younger students are made from bamboo, others are covered in rubber. Getting into pairs, the students start the day by using these weapons to rehearse basic manuevers. The sharp blades (below) are used only in competitions and demonstrations.

PRETRAINING RITUAL

Krabi krabong, like other Thai martial arts, is an extension of Buddhism. Before training starts it is traditional for all participants to kneel and pray. During this ritual, the student offers thanks to their master and the disciplines of krabi krabong, and above all praises the bravery of ancient warriors. Following this, the student proceeds with set forms (right).

TRAINING PAIN

Although the competitors use blunt weapons during training, the sessions are full-contact and highly competitive. In this sequence, a female student strikes her opponent with a forceful straight kick to the chest. However, later in the practice bout she sustains an injury to her left leg that requires treatment.

COMPETITION DAY
Tournament bouts are often held outdoors in the afternoon, once gym training is completed. The krabi-krabong students transport all the necessary equipment from the gym to an outside location and then set up. Fortunately, there is then an opportunity for the students to eat and rest before the bouts begin.

SPIRITUAL PRACTICE
With the arena prepared, the competitive action is preceded by a period of group meditation and prayer. All the competitors sit facing a Buddhist shrine; the masters of the school sit in the front row. To musical accompaniment, the masters light incense and bow, and the group dedicates prayers to ancient krabi-krabong masters.

BLESSING FROM MASTER

Before each pair of players takes to the mat, they are greeted by the krabi-krabong master who burns incense and blesses each fighter in turn. Each practitioner wears a special rope around his or her head. This is considered to be a talisman, which both protects the wearer from injury and hexes the opponent.

PREFIGHT RITUAL

Once on the fighting mat, both competitors take part in a prefight dance, accompanied by music, part of which is performed with an ornamental sword, the remainder with empty hands. This ritual is very similar to the "ram muay wai kruh" that is an integral part of muay Thai (see pp. 158–65).

▼ LEAPING KICK
Two krabi krabong fighters rehearse set forms in the glorious surroundings of a Bangkok palace. The player in green first evades a sword strike, before leaping up and delivering a kick to her opponent's upper torso.

▼ NGAO DUEL
A pair of fighters do battle armed with ngao (halberds). The player in red blocks a high attack, then, with a sudden change of direction, he sweeps his ngao at ground level, knocking his adversary to the floor.

WEAPONS AND ARMOR

KRABI KRABONG

KRABI KRABONG TAKES its name from the single-edged sword, known as a "krabi," and the staff, called a "krabong." Other weapons feature also within the art, such as "loh" (shields), "mai sun fawk" (forearm protectors), and "ngao" (halberds—see pp. 148–149, main picture). Generally, the blunter weapons—made from bamboo and rubber—are training weapons used for practice sessions; the sharper swords are reserved for competitions, or for ceremonial use. Although the art is no longer practiced with lethal force, the dangerous nature of the weapons means that it is crucial for practitioners to stay alert and calm at all times in order to avoid injury to themselves or their opponent.

▼ MAI SUN FAWK
Traditionally made from wood, these weapons attach to the forearms and can be used to defend and attack. Worn in pairs—one on each arm—they can be used as clubs or to ward off blows from opponents.

HAND GRIP
The hand grips one bar, and is protected by the other

PROTECTION
Hard wood forms the backbone of the weapon

▲ PRACTICE MAKES PERFECT
A female krabi-krabong student, wearing a traditional green and gold outfit, demonstrates some striking techniques with a blunt practice sword.

> **LOH**
Used as protective devices or to strike, krabi-krabong "loh" or shields are made of various materials, including cane, hide, wood, and metal. They may be circular or rectangular.

PRACTICE SHIELD
These are lightweight and often made from cane

DECORATIVE SHIELD
The shields used in competitions are often painted

LONG SHIELD
Used in battle, these shields are long, thin, and heavy

▼ KRABI AND KRABONG
Ranging from the functional to the ceremonial, a variety of "krabi" (swords) and "krabong" (staves) are available for practice sessions, and for use within tournaments.

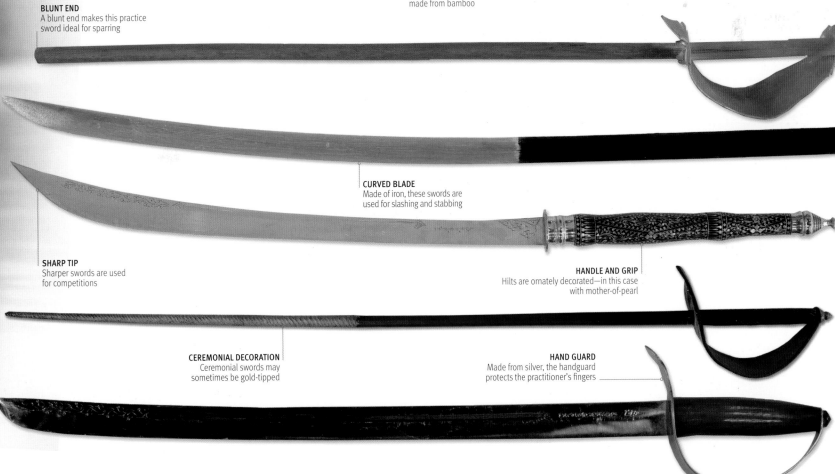

KRABONG
This long fighting staff is made from bamboo

BLUNT END
A blunt end makes this practice sword ideal for sparring

CURVED BLADE
Made of iron, these swords are used for slashing and stabbing

SHARP TIP
Sharper swords are used for competitions

HANDLE AND GRIP
Hilts are ornately decorated—in this case with mother-of-pearl

CEREMONIAL DECORATION
Ceremonial swords may sometimes be gold-tipped

HAND GUARD
Made from silver, the handguard protects the practitioner's fingers

Muay Thai

EXPLANATION
"THAI BOXING" IN THAI

DATE OF ORIGIN
INDIGENOUS ART

FOUNDER
NO KNOWN FOUNDER

PLACE OF ORIGIN
THAILAND

Muay Thai is a hard fighting martial art that resembles pradel serey (see p. 167), tomoi (see p. 169), and muay Lao from Laos. It is probably derived from muay boran (see p. 166) and krabi krabong (see pp. 148–49). Also known as Thai boxing or Thai kickboxing, it is the national sport of Thailand and enjoys worldwide popularity, thanks in part to a daily televised bout in Thailand and the movie *Ong Bak*, starring Tony Jaa in a feature that seamlessly blended acrobatic stunts and Thai boxing.

Muay Thai is often known as the art (or science) of eight limbs, because practitioners use eight points of attack: feet, hands, elbows, and knees. Western boxers by comparison use two points of attack (fists).

The first muay Thai fights
Exact information on muay Thai's origins is sketchy, purportedly because the Burmese destroyed Siamese historical records in 1767. According to popular legend, "Black Prince" Naresuen of Siam defeated the Burmese crown prince in a single bout of muay Thai in 1560, which caused King Bayinnaung of Burma to abandon his attack on Thailand. In 1774, the first recorded muay Thai contest was held in Rangoon at a festival organized by Lord Mangra, king of Burma, to honor the Buddhist faith. A Thai boxer called Nai Khanom Tom defeated nine Burmese boxers in a row, impressing the king with his strength and agility.

Modern fights
Muay Thai fights are generally of five three-minute rounds, with a two-minute rest between each round. Ringcraft (fighting tactics and strategies), conditioning, and fitness are key. As in Western boxing, the referee can end a bout by giving

◀ CAUGHT IN A CLINCH
Thai boxers become entwined on the ropes and clasp one another in a clinch as each struggles to gain the upper hand.

a ten-second count to a knock-down, if he thinks a boxer is in particular danger, or if there have been three knock-downs during a single round.

Traditionally, fighters bound their hands in cloth, dipped them in glue, then sprinkled their fists with broken glass, bringing a frightening and bloody element to matches. This practice was stopped in 1929 and now most fighters wear European standard boxing gloves. Their hands are wrapped in boxing wraps to protect their fists and to harden them by compressing the bones. They also wear groin protection, shorts elasticated at the waist, and optional elasticated ankle supports.

Bouts are accompanied by music "si muay," which is played by a four-piece orchestra consisting of "shing" (cymbals), "klong kaek" and "kon" (drums), and "pi java" (a clarinet).

Ritual dance and fighting stance
In a prefight ritual dance ("ram muay wai kruh," or "kruh," for short). Boxers pay homage to their instructors and hex their opponents with black magic. They often make a loud hissing sound as they exhale air through their teeth, which helps to control breath, oxygenate muscles, and inspire confidence.

Their fighting stance resembles a Western boxer's, except they hold their guard higher and slightly more extended away from their face to protect against elbow and foot strikes. Fighters tend to shuffle forward and back, leading with one foot. They turn their elbows inward to protect the body and to allow for guarding movements that protect the ribs during an onslaught.

Kicking and punching
The signature kick is the low-level roundhouse, or hook, kick at an opponent's thigh. Designed to demoralize an opponent and restrict his mobility, it is often delivered with the shin and the toe hooked inward as opposed to a normal roundhouse in which the toe is pointed back. Boxers precondition the shin over many years by striking it against bamboo trees. Punching resembles the Western boxing techniques of jabs, crosses, hooks, upper cuts, and overhand head punches. Thai boxers use long-range hooks that close the distance after kicking and are often followed by a combination of close-quarter upper cuts, hooks, and jabs.

"THAI BOXING IS ... ALWAYS AT THE READY. IT IS THE ANCESTOR OF ALL OTHER TYPES OF WEAPON AND IS SUPERIOR TO THEM ALL"

THE MOST DISTINGUISHED ART OF FIGHTING BY PANYA & PITISUK KRAITUS

▲ ATTACK AND DEFENSE
As one Thai boxer attacks with a roundhouse kick to the side of the head, his opponent defends with his arm and ducks his head.

AUTHOR'S NOTE

I recently spent a month training in a jungle camp in Phuket in an attempt to understand muay Thai. Not only did I have fun, but I also lost many preconceived ideas about this macho and aggressive art. After intense morning training came shadow boxing, followed by combination work on the pads with an instructor, and ending with an intense sparring match. We were pushed to our physical limits, but always with a calm, purposeful atmosphere. When I injured a shoulder muscle while sparring I expected to continue fighting, but the boxing coach stopped the bout, applied massage and herbal oil, and told me to rest. These tough fighters took injury seriously: small injuries, if untreated or overtrained, can become more serious and prevent a fighter from giving his best in the ring, prematurely ending a successful career that earns a good living.

BEHIND THE SCENES

MUAY-THAI FIGHTERS

IN COMPARISON to the training regime of professional Western boxers—who have periods of inactivity lasting several weeks between bouts—the training schedule of muay-Thai fighters is hard and unremitting. Boxers reside together in the living quarters of the gym, which inevitably means they are completely focused on their art.

Every aspect of a muay-Thai fighter's training is geared toward building speed, accuracy, and power. Fighters must be disciplined, obey the rules of the gym, and pay heed to their master's instruction at all times. Each training day commences at 5 a.m. with a 6–10 mile (10–15 km) run. This is followed by warm-down and stretching exercises, and a nutritious breakfast. Mealtime is an opportunity to chat with fellow boxers and discuss forthcoming bouts.

After a period of rest, the boxers return to the workout area in the early afternoon. There, they engage in prolonged sessions of stretching, weight training, pad and bag work, and sparring—working closely with their trainers throughout. From late afternoon they take a break to eat, and then rest in preparation for the trip to the boxing stadium around 8 p.m. Boxers in peak condition will have scheduled fights on most evenings.

A CHANCE TO RELAX
A muay-Thai fighter's day typically consists of periods of intensive training followed by private rest and recuperation. In fact, one of the few opportunities the boxers have for social interaction is during breakfast, as they relax following their morning run. Living such an insular existence, conversation rarely strays beyond the subject of muay Thai.

STRETCHES AND WEIGHTS
Being a full-contact sport, the muscles and joints of muay Thai fighters are subject to more duress than most athletes. So, at the start of each day, before they commence the rigors of bag work and sparring, the boxers ensure their bodies are fully limbered up. A period of floor work (spent stretching muscles, particularly the legs and arms), is followed by pull-ups and weightlifting to strengthen the upper body, and, finally, some shadow boxing.

PAD AND BAG WORK
The time a muay-Thai practitioner spends working with his trainer (known as a "padman") on the pads and heavy bag is vital to his success in the ring. Pad and bag work enables the fighter to hone his punching and kicking techniques, without the distraction of a sparring partner.

END OF TRAINING

Following an afternoon of intense training, the fighters are permitted a break for food and rest prior to the evening's fight. Boxers are responsible for keeping the gym in good order, so they must first return the gym's equipment before they can enjoy the welcome relief of a cold shower.

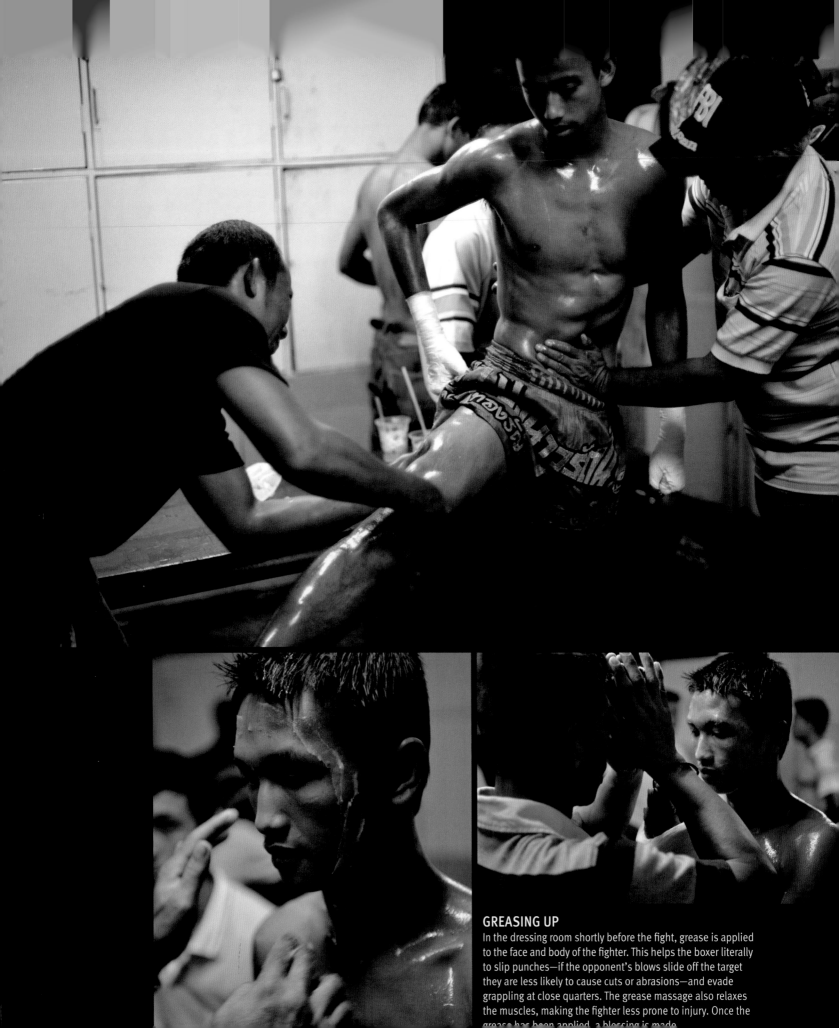

GREASING UP

In the dressing room shortly before the fight, grease is applied
to the face and body of the fighter. This helps the boxer literally
to slip punches—if the opponent's blows slide off the target
they are less likely to cause cuts or abrasions—and evade
grappling at close quarters. The grease massage also relaxes
the muscles, making the fighter less prone to injury. Once the
grease has been applied, a blessing is made.

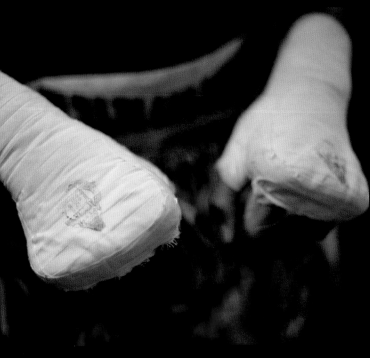

FINAL CHECKS

To guard against foul play—such as illegally weighted gloves—the sport's governing body appoints officials at each contest to oversee preparations backstage. First, hand wraps are inspected and authenticated with a stamp. Then, after boxing gloves are fitted and securing tape applied, the fists are checked again.

LOST IN THOUGHT

After receiving a good luck garland and a blessing, the fighter often spends the final seconds before the ringwalk alone. He uses this time to regulate his breathing, indulge in private prayer, and contemplate the bout ahead.

BEFORE THE BATTLE

The prefight ritual dance known as "ram muay wai kruh"—in which fighters pay tribute to their trainers and invoke a curse on their opponent—is fundamental to the traditions of muay Thai. Once the fight is under way, the contestants usually spend a few seconds sizing each other up, in preparation for delivering the initial blows.

PROBING ATTACK

Contests usually feature intense action and heavy blows from the start. Here, the boxer in red shorts leads the attack. Forcing the pace in a muay-Thai contest is exhausting work so he is thankful for the two-minute break at the end of each round. Cold water is poured over him to cool him down, with the large metal tray keeping the ring dry.

FIGHTING BACK

In the middle rounds, the boxer in the blue shorts goes on the attack. He delivers a clean knee strike (left) to his opponent's midriff. As the contest continues, both fighters become tired and take advantage of opportunities to rest during clinches.

VICTOR AND VANQUISHED

As the fight nears its end, the result becomes increasingly difficult to call—with one fighter, then the other, in the ascendancy. Finally, a thumping overhand right from the boxer in red finds its target and his opponent is floored. When the fallen boxer fails to beat the referee's count his hard-punching adversary is declared the winner. Typically, both fighters will spend the rest of the evening watching their friends' bouts then retire to the gym to sleep. They will need their rest because another day's training begins at 5 a.m.

Muay Boran

EXPLANATION
"ANCIENT BOXING" IN THAI

DATE OF ORIGIN
C. 100 BCE

FOUNDER
NO KNOWN FOUNDER

PLACE OF ORIGIN
THAILAND

A predecessor of muay Thai (see pp. 158–65), muay boran is believed to be more than 2,000 years old. The training regime was probably developed by or borrowed from the ancient military. While different forms have evolved in Thailand, some experts believe the art may have originated in Cambodia.

Originally, fights took place in an improvised space on the ground and lasted until one person gave up. Rules forbade the use of gloves, eye-gouging, hair-pulling, hitting the groin, or hitting a fallen opponent. The style encourages powerful close-quarter knee and elbow techniques aimed at knocking out opponents.

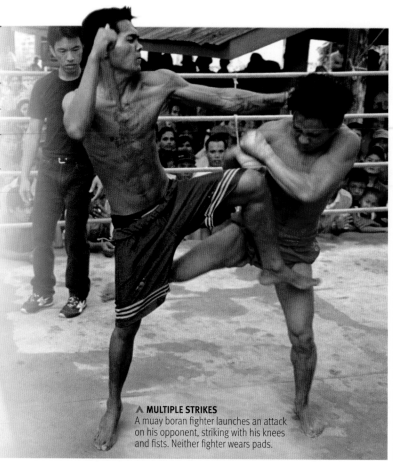

▲ **MULTIPLE STRIKES**
A muay boran fighter launches an attack on his opponent, striking with his knees and fists. Neither fighter wears pads.

Lerdrit

EXPLANATION
"GREAT POWER" IN THAI

DATE OF ORIGIN
1970s

FOUNDER
NO KNOWN FOUNDER

PLACE OF ORIGIN
THAILAND

Lerdrit is a simplified battle version of muay Thai (see pp. 158–65) and is most commonly taught to soldiers in the Royal Thai army. Typically, it includes a range of open-hand techniques, while kicks, knees, locks, grappling methods, and elbows are all essential to the system. Focus tends to be on palm strikes and the use of elbows from the clinch. The Thai police have used lerdrit—including the eight points of attack from muay Thai—since the 1970s. The art's grappling aspect closely resembles muay boran (see left), the parent style of muay Thai.

Tu-Thân

EXPLANATION
"TO IMPROVE ONESELF" IN VIETNAMESE

DATE OF ORIGIN
1970s

FOUNDER
NGUYEN NGOC-THACH

PLACE OF ORIGIN
VIETNAM

Tu-thân is a martial art that aims to increase physical and mental ability and awareness. Practiced regularly with a partner of equal weight, tu-thân's motions of attacking and defending effortlessly let the body develop an instinctive awareness of the flow of power. It also engenders a safe and mostly injury-free way of practicing the interaction of combat without the necessity or intent to hurt one's opponent.

Playful and creative

Movements are conducted in a playful and creative way and classes are held in a focused atmosphere, which can help the student learn how to deal with negative emotions that may arise through the combat process. Practitioners do not gain a ranking in a belt system, nor are there any tu-thân competitions.

Ling Lom

EXPLANATION
MONKEY-STYLE FIGHTING

DATE OF ORIGIN
INDIGENOUS ART

FOUNDER
NO KNOWN FOUNDER

PLACE OF ORIGIN
LAOS

Ling lom is an indigenous martial art that is practiced in Thailand and Laos. It includes traditional muay Thai techniques (see pp. 158–59) and some ground-fighting methods. Many of Tony Jaa's techniques in *Ong Bak*, the Thai movie about a muay Thai warrior, come from ling lom.

Of Hindu origin, the movements of ling lom are believed to be based on Hanuman, the divine monkey in the Indian epic *Ramayana*. The art is also known as "air monkey" or "dancing monkey." Hanuman is considered to be a reincarnation of Shiva, one of the principal Hindu deities. He is also the epitome of wisdom, devotion, faith, valor, strength, and righteousness.

Chinese influence

Early Chinese martial arts may have had an influence on ling lom practitioners, particularly along China's borders with Laos and Myanmar, where systems—particularly hand strikes—resemble early forms of chuan fa, which is a Chinese fist method from the Shaolin tradition.

Though refuted by some practitioners, many believe that muay boran (see above left) and ling lom were originally taught together until around the 1700s, when they started to be taught as separate arts. However, ling lom became more obscure and less practiced than muay boran, which rose to huge popularity after it was transformed into muay Thai boxing.

❯ **DIVINE MONKEY**
The Hindu monkey god Hanuman is known for his ability to lift up the spiritual qualities of humans.

Bokator

EXPLANATION
"FIGHT LIONS" IN CAMBODIAN
DATE OF ORIGIN
INDIGENOUS ART
FOUNDER
NO KNOWN FOUNDER
PLACE OF ORIGIN
CAMBODIA

Bokator is an indigenous martial art that was developed by the Khmer people and used by the ancient armies of Angkor. It is thought to be the predecessor of all Southeast Asian kickboxing styles. Also known as labok katao, it is an extremely complex system that has a total of 341 different styles. It is said to be based on nature and to heavily echo the movements of animals, both real and mythological. These include the dragon, crane, and eagle. Bokator contains a number of locks, strikes, holds, and submissions.

Bokator returns

Jayavarman VII, who ruled the Khmer Empire at the end of the 12th century, was said to be an avid practitioner of bokator. It is widely believed that the art was a key factor in the success of the Angkorian kings who dominated Southeast Asia for six centuries from 800 CE.

ⵥ ELBOW STRIKES
Bokator is renowned for the range of elbow strikes that can be deadly when fighting at close quarters.

Master San Kim Sean is credited with reviving bokator after many practitioners had been killed by the Khmer Rouge in the late 1970s. He returned to Phnom Penh in 2001 and gathered together some very reluctant and very old instructors. In 2006, the first national bokator competition was held in Phnom Penh and featured leading teams from nine different provinces.

Pradel Serey

EXPLANATION
"FIGHT FREELY" IN CAMBODIAN
DATE OF ORIGIN
INDIGENOUS ART
FOUNDER
NO KNOWN FOUNDER
PLACE OF ORIGIN
CAMBODIA

Pradel serey is an Indo-Chinese art based on muay Thai, tomoi, and lethwei (see pp. 158–65, p. 169, and pp. 146–47). Also known as Khmer boxing, pradel serey is a general name for Southeast Asian boxing arts from Thailand, Malaysia, Laos, and Myanmar.

Pradel serey is the national sport of Cambodia. Banned in the 1970s, when many practitioners were executed during the Khmer Rouge regime, it is enjoying a popular resurgence, with televised weekly matches and more than 70 pradel clubs in the country. This is thought to be due, in no small part, to the phenomenal success of muay Thai.

Fists and kicks

A praying ritual, known as the "kun kru," takes place before the bout. The tension-filled atmosphere of the fight is accompanied by traditional Cambodian music played on drums, a stringed instrument, and a flute.

Matches take place in a square boxing ring and last for five three-minute rounds, with either one or two minutes in between. Victory is decided either by points, a ten-second knock-down count, a knockout, or a technical knockout. Modern versions consist of a number of fist-fighting techniques alongside kicks, shin kicks, and strikes with elbows, feet, and knees. Clinches are also widely used, as in other boxing arts, but pradel serey places more emphasis on the use of elbows.

> "EXPONENTS USE MOVES WITH EXOTIC NAMES LIKE 'KLA-KRAB' (TIGER LYING DOWN) AND 'KRAPEU-HA' (CROCODILE OPENING ITS MOUTH)"
>
> MEL KADO, GENERAL SECRETARY, CAMBODIA AMATEUR BOXING ASSOCIATION

Khmer Traditional Wrestling

EXPLANATION
WRESTLING OF KHMER PEOPLE
DATE OF ORIGIN
INDIGENOUS ART
FOUNDER
NO KNOWN FOUNDER
PLACE OF ORIGIN
CAMBODIA

A martial art from Cambodia, Khmer traditional wrestling is believed by experts to have been practiced by both males and females—ancient Angkor temples have murals depicting both sexes fighting in this style.

Dancing, music, and food

Ritual dancing often precedes a bout and dramatic music accompanies the fight, which usually lasts three rounds and is decided when one wrestler holds down his opponent's back on the floor. Traditionally, fights take place during the New Year and other Cambodian national holidays. This competitive sport is also a system of health promotion. During festivals, young wrestlers may invite a competitor to start a match by shouting: "Come and pay for the food, come and pay for the food." When another man replies: "Here is the food payer, here is the food payer," he is taking up the challenge and the match begins. In the past, fights often took place in rice paddies on moonlit nights as a folk sport among villagers. Most participants were farmers, although trained competitors were also free to fight.

ⵥ ACROBATIC SPARRING
Traditional Khmer wrestlers struggle fiercely to become the first to pin their opponent's back to the ground.

Vovinam

EXPLANATION
"MARTIAL ART OF VIETNAM"
IN VIETNAMESE
DATE OF ORIGIN
1938
FOUNDER
NGUYEN LOC
PLACE OF ORIGIN
VIETNAM

Nguyen Loc, the founder of vovinam, grew up in French-occupied Vietnam. His early experiences as a youth, coupled with his patriotic nature, led him to believe that a strong nation could only exist if young people were trained to have a clear mind, pure soul, and strong body.

Loc studied various martial arts, philosophy, theology, and scientific health, before uniting them all into a Vietnamese art designed for the Vietnamese people.

Key techniques
Also known as "vovinam viet vo dao," the art includes training with empty-hand and weapons techniques. Students learn to use unusual weapons, such as the ax and folding fan. Signature moves are diagonal kicks, backfists to the temples, and leg-grappling methods for felling opponents. Elbow and knee strikes, kicks, and wrestling techniques are also included. The art specializes in defensive movements that deal with attacks from behind and weapon-based attacks when the player is empty-handed.

Peace of mind
Vovinam stresses harmony between the Chinese philosophical aspects of yin and yang, which represent the hard and soft elements of physical combat. Students, who often wear a distinctive light-blue training "gi," learn the Buddhist concept of seeing through their ego, freeing themselves from its influence. They become tolerant of—and generous toward – other people, and learn that awareness leads to harmony and peace.

Vovinam's motto and salutation— "iron hand over benevolent heart"— emphasizes the principle that force should only be used as a last resort.

◄ STRENGTH AND FLEXIBILITY
Two experienced vovinam players rehearse set forms with bamboo poles at Quan Thanh temple in Hanoi. With its qualities of flexibility and strength, bamboo is considered by many to be symbolic of vovinam.

Cuong Nhu

EXPLANATION
"HARD AND SOFT"
IN VIETNAMESE
DATE OF ORIGIN
1965
FOUNDER
NGO DONG
PLACE OF ORIGIN
VIETNAM

Cuong nhu is a hybrid Vietnamese martial art developed by Doctor Ngo Dong in 1965, which blends karate techniques with basic grappling methods. It also draws inspiration from taijiquan, wing chun, Shotokan karate, boxing, aikido, and vovinam (see pp. 80–87, 122, 203, 256–63, 238–39, opposite).

The first cuong-nhu dojo in the US opened its doors in 1971 after Ngo Dong escaped from the horrors of the Vietnam War and set up home in the United States.

Basic training takes the hard, external elements of karate—such as kicking and blocking—along with judo takedowns and rolling and throwing techniques. As the student progresses, taijiquan-like elements are included in the curriculum. These stress diversion of thought as opposed to the use of direct blocking moves. Such techniques enable the student to be flexible— he or she responds to the attack appropriately, using either the hard or soft elements of training. Weapons are also taught, usually only to advanced students, and they include the "bo" (staff), the "tonfa" (stick), the "sai" (dagger), and spear.

Ethical art
In keeping with the philosophy of inclusion, alongside martial techniques the art teaches its students public speaking, poetry, philosophy, and painting. A strong element of self-development, through self-control and modesty, informs much of the system. Students are known for developing a positive attitude. A code of ethics governs cuong nhu and the art has a ranking order based on belt colors, similar to Japanese martial arts.

> "TO BUILD A STRONG MORAL AND SPIRITUAL FOUNDATION FOR HIS STYLE, GRAND MASTER DONG INTERJECTED HIS PERSONAL PHILOSOPHY OF SELF-IMPROVEMENT, COMMUNITY SERVICE, AND LOVE AND RESPECT FOR OTHERS."
>
> CUONGNHU.COM

Tomoi

EXPLANATION
"ELBOWS AND KNEES" IN MALAY
DATE OF ORIGIN
C. 1800
FOUNDER
NO KNOWN FOUNDER
PLACE OF ORIGIN
MALAYSIA

Meaning "elbows and knees," tomoi is the Malaysian version of muay Thai (see pp. 158–65). It is also found in Cambodia, where it is called pradel serey (see p. 167), and in Myanmar, where it goes by the name of lethwei (see pp. 146–47). A fighting art and sport based on Indian, Chinese, and Thai martial arts, it is most commonly practiced in northern Malaysia, along the Thai border. It was banned in 1990 along with many other Malay traditions by the government of Kelantan state. As a result, many practitioners began referring to tomoi as muay Thai. However, following the lifting of the ban in 2006, the art has enjoyed greater freedom and most practitioners have reverted back to using the original name for the art.

It is not known exactly how old the art is; experts believe tomoi arrived in Malaysia in approximately 1800, probably as a result of immigration from Thailand, with ethnic Thais introducing their fighting traditions and culture.

FINAL THOUGHTS
Two krabi-krabong (see pp. 148–57) fighters face one another across the competition area. Precombat prayer and contemplation are important in Thai martial arts.

Pencak Silat

EXPLANATION
STYLE OF SELF-DEFENSE FIGHTING

DATE OF ORIGIN
INDIGENOUS ART

FOUNDER
NO KNOWN FOUNDER

PLACE OF ORIGIN
INDONESIA

> "SILAT ENHANCES AND STRENGTHENS SELF-AWARENESS, SELF-DISCIPLINE, INTEGRITY, RESPONSIBILITY, LOYALTY, AND COOPERATION AMONG ITS PRACTITIONERS."
>
> PENCAK SILAT FEDERATION OF THE UK

Pencak silat refers to more than 800 individual schools of martial arts across the 13,000 islands of Indonesia. According to legend, they were used to fight against Dutch invaders. Later outlawed by the Dutch, this hybrid system is known as pencak in Java and Bali, and silat in Sumatra. The single term pencak silat was coined after Indonesia was unified, and then accepted in 1973. Some recent silat systems have adopted the Japanese martial art tradition of denoting rank with different-colored belts. The art has become popular around the world and has also developed a sporting tradition with its own world championships.

Pencak lineage

Knowledge of the art has been passed orally from teacher to student, so written records are few. Soldiers and warriors are known to have trained in silat forms in the Srivijaya kingdom in Sumatra between the 7th and 14th centuries and in the Majapahit kingdom on Java between the 13th and 16th centuries. Yet archeological evidence suggests silat may have been used as early as the 6th century.

Many silat schools trace their lineage to the Buginese warriors, a band of tough mercenaries renowned for their combat skills. When the Dutch occupied the islands between the 17th and 20th centuries, the practice went underground and reemerged only after independence in 1949. Traditional Indonesian dances and rituals are thought to contain aspects of the ancient art.

Styles and weapons

Pencak silat has no standardized techniques, partly due to the fact that differences between schools depend on the environment in which students train. So, for example, the footwork techniques of urban styles differ from those of jungle variants. The Javanese people tend to use the art as a self-defense form. Even so, training regimes all include instruction in empty-hand techniques followed by weapons training.

Weapons include some common Indonesian fighting tools, such as sticks, staves, and rods made of bamboo, steel, or wood. The "cabang" is an unusual, three-pronged knife thought to derive from the trident. The "kerambit" is a small, curved blade that women often conceal in their hair. The "sabit" is a sickle used as a blocking, striking, and slashing weapon. The "keris" is a curving blade that is washed in acid. The "tedang" is a common sword with either a single- or double-sided blade.

Master and student

The large number of distinct pencak silat schools in Indonesia are the result of extremely localized styles that have arisen when a master in a village teaches his own method. This teaching may include aspects of shamanism, animism, healing, and other spiritual practices. Most silat players train in spiritual awareness methods, learning to harness what they believe are supernatural powers.

In general, would-be students offer gifts in order to be accepted by a traditional master. These may include a knife, which symbolizes sharpness of attitude and spirit, and a roll of white cloth, which the master keeps in a sacred place and uses to wrap the corpse of the student should he be killed.

The blood of a ritually slaughtered chicken may be spread on the ground where the student expects to train— this signifies the blood the student would shed in fighting had he decided not to study the art. So, the relationship of master and student becomes akin to a blood relationship, such as that between father and son.

Diverse influences

The hand and foot strikes, locking techniques, and throws suggest the art has had Indian and Chinese influence. The throws—typically launched from a very low stance or a deep crouch—are often thought of as the silat signature move.

Between the 7th and 12th centuries, Indonesia was influenced by Mahayana Buddhism and this, together with the arts, weapons, and philosophies that Indians and Chinese introduced, helped to shape the art. Experts believe that Hindu culture and its grappling techniques influenced silat groundwork and, with the later arrival of Islam, came the distinct "jambia"—the short, curved Arab dagger that probably inspired the pencak silat keris blade.

◀ THE SILAT STANCE
A pencak silat player intercepts a hand strike, then counters with an elbow to his opponent's solar plexus. All techniques are best executed from a solid base, so fighters are taught to maintain a low center of gravity during bouts.

▲ A SIXTH SENSE
A young student practices some prerehearsed techniques in training. From an early age pencak silat fighters are mentored in the art of sensory awareness. During combat they use their hands as eyes, blocking attacks instinctively.

Liu Seong Kuntao

EXPLANATION
HYBRID CLOSE-QUARTERS ART
DATE OF ORIGIN
20TH CENTURY
FOUNDER
WILLEM A. REEDERS
PLACE OF ORIGIN
INDONESIA

A hybrid martial art with Chinese and Indonesian influences, liu seong kuntao is sometimes known as "Chinese hand and Indonesian feet." Its founder, Willem A. Reeders, was of mixed Dutch and Chinese heritage. Raised in Indonesia, he trained in a number of martial disciplines. His great-uncle, Liu Seong, taught him the family's kuntao close-range fighting system, but Reeders drew on many local pencak silat systems (see pp. 172–73) before developing his own version. Later, he took the art to the US, where it has become popular.

Combining principles of anatomy, psychology, and physics, the system's trademark is the rapid

◀ RAPID ATTACK
The closed body movement enables players to strike out, and then arrange their limbs quickly into a protective position.

execution of multiple attacks at close quarters. Postures tend to protect most major vital areas and this protection is maintained at all times. This method is known as "closed body" movement. Weapons training is generally reserved for advanced practitioners, and yet it is an integral aspect of the art and is in keeping with Indonesian traditions, which often focus on being "blade-aware."

Fighting techniques
The open-handed aspects and evasive nature of the strikes have been likened to ba gua zhang (see p. 78), a northern Chinese system that evolved around the "bagua" symbol used in the classic Chinese text *Yi Jing* (*The Book of Changes*). The footwork is Indonesian, favoring mobility and deep, grounded stances.

The training syllabus tends to favor technique application over prearranged fighting sequences ("juru-juru"), which are similar to "kata" in Japanese martial arts. The art promotes self-defense rather than sporting competition. Practitioners do spar, but in a slow and controlled manner to prevent injury. This pace allows students to enhance their ability to move and adapt to the rhythm and flow of combat.

Sindo

EXPLANATION
A STYLE OF SILAT
DATE OF ORIGIN
1972
FOUNDER
KAK JIMMY THAIBSYAH
PLACE OF ORIGIN
INDONESIA

A modern form of pencak silat (see pp. 172–73), Sindo includes a number of self-defense techniques and internal martial-arts' training methods. It was founded by Kak Jimmy Thaibsyah, who trained in the controversial martial art of kateda, which critics have claimed is linked to organized crime and is "cultlike." To date, sindo has been able to avoid similar criticisms and notoriety.

▶ FIST STRIKES
A group of sindo practitioners near Cibogo, Java, take turns executing fist strikes on a solid target. This type of training constitutes excellent but potentially damaging conditioning for the hands.

KAK JIMMY THAIBSYAH

While completing his English degree in Jakarta, in 1972, Kak Jimmy Thaibsyah met Lionel Nasution, the founder of kateda, and began teaching self-defense techniques. He later spent time teaching and studying with Nasution in London, England. In 1987, he opened his first self-defense school in Indonesia, which he called Pencak Silat Tenaga Dasa (PSTD)—others quickly followed. He changed the name of his system to Sindo in 1999.

Bersilat

EXPLANATION
"TO DO FIGHTING" IN MALAYSIAN

DATE OF ORIGIN
15TH CENTURY

FOUNDER
NO KNOWN FOUNDER

PLACE OF ORIGIN
MALAYSIA

An empty-hand martial art derived from pencak silat (see pp. 172–73), bersilat has also drawn influences from a number of Indian arts. It features a dancelike art called "silat pulat." There are several major schools, such as the "lintan," "medan," and "silat buah." The art stresses self-restraint and teaches that it should be used only in self-defense. Teachers are often of high moral standing in their communities.

Before training, students commonly swear an oath that forbids them from divulging the secrets of the art. Training typically includes a number of punches, throws, holds, locks, and chokes. The system features a range of nerve strikes and the curriculum often includes the study of 12 critical nerve centers of the body that are vulnerable to pain when struck by the hand. Such tactics are generally employed when fighting larger opponents who rely on brute strength. It is said that the confidence displayed by a bersilat practitioner is often enough to intimidate a potential attacker into a hasty retreat.

"IN ADDITION TO BEING AN EXCELLENT FORM OF PHYSICAL TRAINING, THE ART OF BERSILAT HAS GREAT SPIRITUAL VALUE, SERVING, ACCORDING TO ITS DEVOTEES, AS AN IMPORTANT AID OF ENHANCING ONE'S SPIRITUAL DEVELOPMENT."

MALAYSIAN MINISTRY OF CULTURE, YOUTH, AND SPORTS

The Ministry of Culture, Youth, and Sports in Malaysia describes bersilat as follows: "As a stance it develops an aesthetic feeling of cultural nature. As a form of physical training it promotes good health, and as a form of spiritual education it develops such qualities as calmness, tolerance, observance, mental efficiency, courage, and self-confidence."

⋀ MUSIC AND DANCE
Silat pulat, the dance element of bersilat, is often performed to musical accompaniment.

⋀ WAITING TO POUNCE
Two bersilat fighters stalk one another warily, prior to engaging in close-quarters combat, during a traditional Malaysian wedding.

Kali Sikaran

EXPLANATION
FILIPINO EMPTY-HAND MARTIAL ART

DATE OF ORIGIN
INDIGENOUS ART

FOUNDER
NO KNOWN FOUNDER

PLACE OF ORIGIN
PHILIPPINES

Kali sikaran is an empty-hand martial art that shares some of the entry techniques (getting past an attacker's blows in order to strike at close range) and footwork and of fencing (see pp. 268–69). It draws on two ancient arts—the weapons art of kali and the kicking art of sikaran—and blends indigenous stick-fighting techniques with fencing techniques introduced by the Spanish during their 400-year occupation of the Philippines. It also uses a number of techniques and training methods from dumog, espada y daga (see pp. 182–83), panantukan, and kadena de mano (see right). Most kali systems can also be used with a machete, as local militia proved when fighting Japanese invaders on the beaches and in the jungles during World War II. Kali's governing body is the International Kali, Arnis, and Eskrima Federation (IKAEF).

Training focuses on developing speed, stamina, strength, and good coordination, and on improving reflexes and the ability to apply the techniques in combat. Practitioners believe that the combination of weapons, empty-hand, and wrestling techniques provide a comprehensive training system for fighters.

Kadena de Mano

EXPLANATION
"CHAIN OF HAND" IN TAGALOG

DATE OF ORIGIN
INDIGENOUS ART

FOUNDER
NO KNOWN FOUNDER

PLACE OF ORIGIN
PHILIPPINES

Kadena de mano is a martial art that combines a number of empty-hand and knife techniques of Filipino origin. A series of short, fast movements delivered with both hands and elbows are designed to serve the purpose of simultaneous strikes and blocks. Combination techniques and reaction flow are the most important aspects of the art—like a musical rhythm, the fighter throws out a strong, interlocking chain of strikes in reaction to an attack or threat. Training focuses on methods to help the fighter shift between a variety of angles in a relaxed state of being, while throwing out powerful bursts of attacks that are effective for close-quarter combat.

The lock flow trap

The system incorporates a number of locking combinations. The most common is the "lock flow trap" practice drill, in which a locking technique is followed by a flowing strike or trapping technique. This helps the students cut down on the reaction time necessary to neutralize an incoming, aggressive threat. These quick-fire combinations of locks, strikes, and traps are extremely difficult to defend against.

▼ TRIBAL ORIGINS
The warriors of the Mangyan tribe from Mindoro Island are the most famous practitioners of buno.

Buno

EXPLANATION
"TO THROW" OR "TO KILL" IN TAGALOG

DATE OF ORIGIN
INDIGENOUS ART

FOUNDER
NO KNOWN FOUNDER

PLACE OF ORIGIN
PHILIPPINES

Buno is a Filipino wrestling art similar to dumog (see p. 183) and is commonly practiced by the Mangyans of Mindoro Island. A common style is "harimaw buno," which combines a number of throwing techniques with controlled locks, joint manipulations, strikes, ground wrestling, and takedowns. Students learn to use a variety of weapons, such as knives, spears, and bows and arrows. Many curriculums include unusual training methods that were once used by indigenous Filipino tribes—for example, mud training, tree climbing, canoe training, and the use of heavy logs to develop strength.

"THERE ARE LITERALLY HUNDREDS OF STYLES OF BUNO PRACTICED THROUGHOUT THE PHILIPPINES. HOWEVER, THE 'HARIMAW BUNO', FORMERLY 'HARIMAW LUMAD' STYLE (KING TIGER WRESTLING), WAS PARTICULAR TO THE MANGYANS OF MINDORO ISLAND."

MARTIAL ARTS DATABASE

▲ LETHAL FORCE
Ground wrestling is a major element in the art of buno. The technique shown here is potentially lethal.

Kuntaw

EXPLANATION
"SACRED STRIKE" IN TAGALOG

DATE OF ORIGIN
INDIGENOUS ART

FOUNDER
NO KNOWN FOUNDER

PLACE OF ORIGIN
PHILIPPINES

Kuntaw is one of the oldest fighting systems in the Philippines (some practitioners claim its origins date back to 1365). The art contains a number of open-hand and foot-striking combinations and includes holds and locks. Experts consider it to be a complete and effective guerrilla fighting system, and it is often used in combination with kali (see p. 175), which is weapons-based. Training syllabuses include a staggering 43 forms. The system was revived during the 1960s and is gaining popularity in the Philippines and in North America. The art may have Chinese origins—its name

LOGO OF THE INTERNATIONAL KUNTAW FEDERATION

could be a different spelling of "kuntao," an ancient Chinese art—and the system has hard and soft elements, and stresses the development of internal and external "qi" or energy. There is a complex system of hitting vital points, similar to those found in acupuncture—these include nerve centers, sensitive bones, easily breakable joints, and vital organs.

Kuntaw Lima-Lima

EXPLANATION
"COMPLETE SACRED STRIKE" IN TAGALOG

DATE OF ORIGIN
1950s

FOUNDER
CARLOS LANADA

PLACE OF ORIGIN
PHILIPPINES

Kuntaw lima-lima is a Filipino martial art also known as "kuntaw arnis." "Kuntaw" is the generic name for hand-and-foot fighting techniques, and "lima" (or "five") refers to the number of weapon forms used by practitioners who have reached brown-belt level or above. "Lima lima" together means "complete." The system is heavily influenced by kuntaw (see left) and uses the hands, feet, and elbows, as well as a dagger or stick. Techniques aim to parry, deflect, and redirect an attack. Students learn 25 basic moves—five strikes, five thrusts, five blocks, five disarms, and five locks—and are encouraged to develop their physical strength through weight training, dynamic tension, and body mechanics. The art has a history of secrecy—being passed on from master to disciple—but is now often taught openly.

> "NO ONE CAN BE SURE EXACTLY HOW KUNTAW … ORIGINATED, BUT IT HAS PROVEN TO BE AN EFFECTIVE FIGHTING ART."
>
> GRAND MASTER LANADA, *KUNTAW—THE ANCIENT FILIPINO MARTIAL ARTS*

Pangamut

EXPLANATION
"UNARMED FIGHTING" IN TAGALOG

DATE OF ORIGIN
UNKNOWN

FOUNDER
NO KNOWN FOUNDER

PLACE OF ORIGIN
PHILIPPINES

Pangamut is an empty-hand fighting art taught by Dan Inosanto. It contains a number of grappling techniques, as well as hand strikes, kicks, leg sweeps, foot traps, biting, and gouging. Students of Filipino martial arts typically learn how to use weapons before learning empty-hand techniques, whereas most other oriental martial arts generally teach empty-hand techniques up to black-belt level and then introduce weapons training. Sticks, knives, and daggers are the most common weapons encountered during confrontations in the Philippines, so these are the ones that are taught. Many martial artists who learn weapon arts in the Philippines have little or no experience of empty-hand training. Pangamut addresses this need by teaching weapon techniques, but with an empty hand. For example, a classic maneuver comes when an opponent thrusts a

knife or stick toward your face—you parry your opponent with your right hand, making contact with their wrist, then your left hand makes contact with their elbow, pushing forward before your right hand goes for a thrusting stab. This stabbing action can be replaced with a punch or a chop, and the move can be performed in exactly the same way unarmed as it can armed. It is this underlying thought and genius that informs many of the empty-hand Filipino fighting arts.

▼ PANGAMUT GURU
Legendary martial-arts instructor Dan Inosanto (right) poses for a photograph at his eponymous academy in Los Angeles, California.

Gokusa

EXPLANATION
A MIX OF KUNTAO AND BALINTAWAK

DATE OF ORIGIN
1960s

FOUNDER
JOSE "JU GO" MILLAN

PLACE OF ORIGIN
PHILIPPINES

Gokusa is a hybrid system formed from kuntao and balintawak (see p. 182). It was founded by Jose Millan, also known as "Ju Go," who was a student of grandmaster Anciong Bacon, a well-known Filipino stick fighter. The system's emphasis is on shifting the body weight and aligning the spine correctly when delivering the force of the system's 12 strikes and defenses.

A change of name

Sometimes referred to as "gokosha," the art was originally known as "tat kon tao" (meaning "the way of the kicking fist" in Mandarin). The name change to gokusa almost certainly reflects the move away from Chinese techniques toward indigenous Filipino techniques, and the increasingly common practice of nationalizing martial arts in the Philippines.

Eskrima

EXPLANATION
FROM "ESGRIMA," MEANING "FENCING" IN SPANISH

DATE OF ORIGIN
INDIGENOUS ART

FOUNDER
NO KNOWN FOUNDER

PLACE OF ORIGIN
PHILIPPINES

A Filipino martial art that focuses on armed combat with a stick, a sword, or a machete, eskrima is characterized by its battle-proven techniques. It is also known as "escrima," "kali"—particularly in the United States and Europe—and "arnis de mano" (meaning "harness of the hand" in Spanish).

Although many eskrima schools can trace their lineage back to different tribes and regions of the Philippines, little is known of the art's origins because it was passed on in an oral tradition. Some people suggest it was influenced by early Indian and Malay martial arts, as well as by silat (see pp. 172–73) from the Malay Archipelago. What is known, however, is that the Spanish conquistadors, after arriving in the Philippines in the 16th century, engaged in skirmishes with tribesmen who used indigenous weapons and techniques.

Order out of chaos
During the country's conflict-wrought history, martial arts developed into highly efficient systems, and recent systemization of the arts has enabled them to be passed on to students in an easily absorbable curriculum. The art is also taught to Filipino military organizations.

Eskrima has many different forms and most emphasize weapons-based training followed by empty-hand movements. The stick is the most common weapon. Students initially train with a padded stick and also a slightly thicker wooden training stick. Then they train with a rattan

cane, which is about 2 ft (0.6 m) in length and which has been fire-hardened and varnished; employed swiftly, it can easily crack a coconut with a flick of the wrist. Students also train with blades—the most common weapon employed in street crime in the Philippines.

Keeping it simple
Eskrima is taught en masse and in a simplified manner. Flashy and spectacular movements are often refined during sparring matches, in which practitioners wear padded body armor, helmets, and hand mitts. However, while simplicity is favored for teaching purposes, the system also has a deeper and more complex methodology that can take decades to master.

Experienced practitioners can fight with either weapons or with empty hands. The system uses any method that might work in a fight, and includes hand and foot strikes, some grappling and throwing moves, biting, and gouging. Practitioners may also include gouging, punching, throwing, or shoving when using weapons.

Common training techniques include the use of the solo stick, double stick, sword and stick, or stick and dagger (known as "espada y daga"). Some systems specialize in other weapons, such as the whip, staff, and a projectile-based weapon that resembles a 9 in (23 cm) nail. It is common to see the latter being thrown into bamboo trees as a way of developing accuracy. When used in combat it is unlikely to kill, but it will distract an opponent long enough to either escape or to draw another weapon.

Diverse beginnings
Eskrima is practiced as a sport in some parts of the Philippines, although there is little standardization of rules. Traditional practitioners claim the set of rules promoted by the World Eskrima Kali Arnis

Federation—in which practitioners fight according to a 10-point system—tends to overemphasize offensive techniques rather than deflective and defensive ones.

Critics also point out the disorganized appearance of the fights, with participants bashing each other as quickly as they can with a stick, as opposed to applying good, solid techniques.

Varying techniques
In combat, a player must study his body alignment in relation to his opponent and ensure that the tip of the weapon strikes vulnerable spots of an opponent's body. In competition, however, points are more likely to be awarded for reasonably effective touches.

Weapons are considered to be an extension of the body, and footwork generally follows a triangular pattern. Thus, when a participant moves in any direction, his two feet always occupy the two corners of an imaginary triangle on the floor. If he steps forward, he steps onto the triangle's imaginary third corner so that no leg ever crosses the other at any time. This ensures a degree of stability and allows the player to use good leverage in his techniques and throw physical force from the ground into his hand or weapon.

AUTHOR'S NOTE

While studying eskrima in Cebu, I trained with an old master who was in his 90s and in perfect physical health, with a sharp eye and a keen sense of humor. When I asked him why he still trained in eskrima every day, he replied with a wry smile: "It is because I cannot play basketball anymore." Clearly uncomfortable talking about his experiences during World War II, I discovered that, as a younger man, he had received training from the American forces based in the Philippines and had later gone on to form a little armed militia group, fighting in guerrilla-type jungle skirmishes against the Japanese armed with little more than a machete—he transferred his eskrima rattan techniques to the machete. As sharp as he was in his early 90s, I can imagine that he would have been a fearsome and highly motivated opponent in his youth.

"A WEAPON HAS NO BONES, NO SKIN, AND FEELS NO PAIN. ESKRIMA TEACHES A PERSON TO USE ANY AVAILABLE OBJECT AS A WEAPON BY EMPHASIZING BASIC AND LOGICAL CONCEPTS."

THE GUIDING PRINCIPLES OF ESKRIMA

Espada Y Daga

EXPLANATION
"SWORD AND DAGGER"
IN SPANISH

DATE OF ORIGIN
16TH CENTURY

FOUNDER
NO KNOWN FOUNDER

PLACE OF ORIGIN
PHILIPPINES

> "IT HAS BEEN SAID BY SOME ARNIS MASTERS THAT ESPADA Y DAGA IS THE ESSENCE OF ARNIS OR FILIPINO MARTIAL ARTS."

ROGER AGBULOS, *CHIEF INSTRUCTOR, ASTIG LAMECO, CALIFORNIA.*

A martial art and discipline of eskrima (see pp. 180–81), Espada y daga is believed to have roots in Spanish swordsmanship. Filipino natives who were sympathetic to the Spanish cause learned the techniques and helped to repel attacks from marauding pirates.

Training is based on the Spanish style of side sword and dagger, and includes three fighting ranges: "corto" (close), "medio" (medium), and "largo" or "larga" (long). Most modern systems include elements of dumog (see opposite). Techniques involve the stronger hand typically holding the longer weapon such as the sword (interchangeable in modern curricula with a rattan stick). The weaker hand fends off and stabs with the shorter weapon, which is most commonly a dagger. Students learn reflex training, speed, and parrying, as well as checking movements, scooping, thrusting, and slashing.

Geometrical footwork patterns and correct angling of the body encourages evasiveness, while at the same time providing a platform for attacks at close quarters without being slashed or cut by an opponent's weapon.

Sagasa

EXPLANATION
"RUNNING OVER"
IN TAGALOG

DATE OF ORIGIN
20TH CENTURY

FOUNDER
GUILLERMO LENGSON

PLACE OF ORIGIN
PHILIPPINES

Sagasa is a Filipino kickboxing art developed by Dr. Guillermo Lengson of the Philippine Karate Federation. Boxing and arnis weapon fighting are complemented by throwing, striking, and grappling techniques. The current system has been evolved over a number of years by senior members of the "bakbakan," a martial-arts group that favors full-contact sparring as a primary training method. Practitioners regularly practice san shou (see p. 120) and enter kickboxing competitions.

Suntukan

EXPLANATION
"BOXING" IN TAGALOG

DATE OF ORIGIN
UNKNOWN

FOUNDER
NO KNOWN FOUNDER

PLACE OF ORIGIN
PHILIPPINES

A Filipino boxing art, suntukan is widely practiced in the north of the country. The system involves a number of empty-hand, flowing, and striking drills, which include chopping maneuvers and close-range "chaining," where punches flow naturally in short bursts. The most notable practitioner is Dan Inosanto, who incorporates much of suntukan into his teaching of Bruce Lee's jeet kune do (see pp. 316–17).

In the few schools that teach suntukan outside the Philippines, the focus tends to be on community-based training, where members of a group get together to explore, trade, and share their knowledge. In some schools, newcomers either have to be sponsored by an existing member or be invited by a member who is considered of good standing.

◄ **MARTIAL-ARTS LEGENDS**
Dan Inosanto (left) was a close friend of the late Bruce Lee, appearing alongside him in the 1973 movie *Game Of Death*.

Dumog

EXPLANATION
"BRAWLING" IN TAGALOG

DATE OF ORIGIN
INDIGENOUS ART

FOUNDER
NO KNOWN FOUNDER

PLACE OF ORIGIN
PHILIPPINES

An indigenous Filipino wrestling art, dumog is often taught alongside eskrima (see pp. 180–81). It is a highly complex form that uses a variety of unbalancing techniques, weight systems, and joint locks in order to effect a victory. Many dumog techniques can be performed from the clinch position, which is a common scenario in many street fights. The art shares a similarity with Western wrestling principles and also with the weight-shifting principles of aikido (see pp. 238–39). The head is often used as a lever and practitioners sometimes use the adage "where the head goes, the body follows."

Suggested origins

Dumog probably developed from the martial arts brought to the country hundreds of years ago by the Indonesians and Malaysians. Some written records suggest that eskrima and dumog close-quarter wrestling techniques were used against Spanish invaders. Legend has it that dumog originated when two natives, who did not have much food on their island, wrestled with each other over a coconut. In memory of this story, some Filipino fiestas feature dumog wrestlers fighting over a coconut. Historians, however, point out that in the Panay region, tribesmen used close-quarter fighting techniques to subdue animal prey when their weapons, such as the "pana" (bow) or "sibat," a spearlike instrument, were broken.

Ernesto Presas is a notable dumog and eskrima practitioner and teacher. He was born in Negros Occidental in 1945, and trained with his father Jose Presas, a well-known stick fighter. In 1970, he popularized the art form at the University of the Philippines, where he has codified many of the systems and techniques into easily learnable formats. Each of the systems is both spectacular to watch and devastatingly effective.

Balintawak

EXPLANATION
NAMED AFTER A STREET IN CEBU

DATE OF ORIGIN
1950s

FOUNDER
VENANCIO BACON

PLACE OF ORIGIN
PHILIPPINES

A Filipino martial art with the motto "economy, elegance, strength, and speed," balintawak draws influence from the Doce Pares systems. It is sometimes referred to as balintawak eskrima and is named after Balintawak Street, in Cebu, where the founder, Venancio Bacon, first set up his school and where many of the system's innovations and developments were created. Bacon studied with a number of well-known practitioners, many of whom had experience of the tradition of fighting death matches with opponents' schools. Standing just 5 ft 2 in (1.57 m) tall and weighing 120 lb (54 kg), Bacon was the veteran of many death matches himself. During the 1950s and 60s, a period known as the golden age of eskrima in Cebu, he was involved in many vicious fights and is said to have killed a number of fighters who challenged for the title of the King of the Eskrimas.

Sikaran

EXPLANATION
"TO KICK" IN TAGALOG

DATE OF ORIGIN
INDIGENOUS ART

FOUNDER
NO KNOWN FOUNDER

PLACE OF ORIGIN
PHILIPPINES

Sikaran is an indigenous Filipino kick-fighting martial art that resembles karate (see pp. 202–03) and predates the arrival of the Spanish. Probably developed by farmers, sikaran was often fought during the good harvest festival and was most commonly practiced by the farmers of Baras Rizal. Immigration of practitioners has spread the art to the US, Canada, UK, Saudi Arabia, and New Zealand.

Entertainment and honor

Sikaran matches, which often took place in circles drawn out on a paddy field, were as much about entertainment and thanksgiving as about tribal ways of settling scores

AGRICULTURAL ART
Wet and uneven conditions like these, often found in the region, typically shaped the fighting style of the peasant farmers.

and restoring honor. Particularly aggrieved participants smeared buffalo feces onto their feet prior to a competition as a way of humiliating and undermining their opponent when they kicked him. A "hari" (victor) was declared when one opponent was either too exhausted, or too hurt, to continue. Participants were not allowed to use their hands to strike an opponent, only to block kicks. Violation of this rule brought instant disqualification.

As practiced today, a signature move is the "biakid"—a spectacular kick, in which the player pivots his entire body in a somersault movement, flailing one leg in a vertical arc over his head and whipping it onto his opponent's face. There are two kinds of attack: the "panghilo" is a paralysing blow usually aimed at the thighs, kidneys, chest, knees, or feet; and the "pamatay" is a lethal blow to the neck, head, groin, heart, or spine.

> **WAITING GAME**
A muay-Thai (see pp. 158–65) fighter at
Lumpini Stadium, Bangkok, waits to enter
the ring. Fighters believe that their special
armbands will protect them from injury.

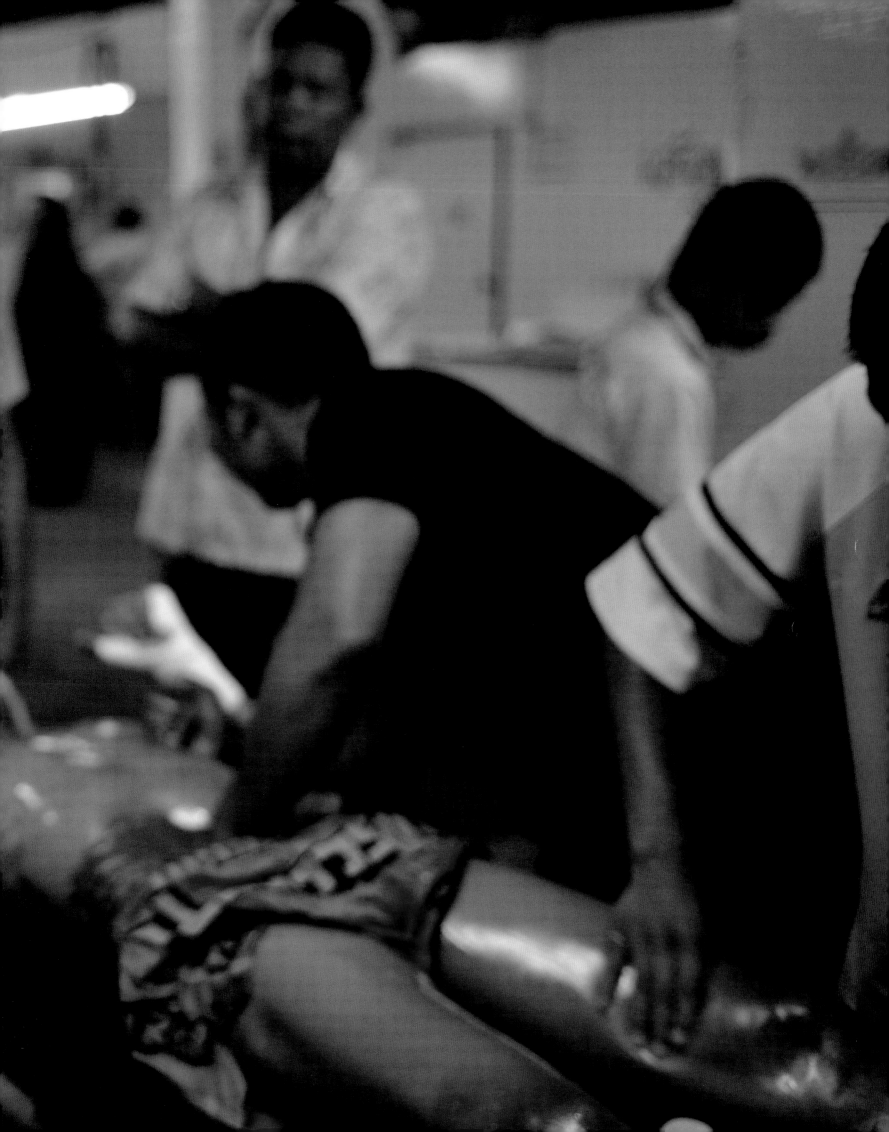

Mau Rakau

EXPLANATION
"TO BEAR A WEAPON"
IN MAORI

DATE OF ORIGIN
INDIGENOUS ART

FOUNDER
NO KNOWN FOUNDER

PLACE OF ORIGIN
NEW ZEALAND

Mau rakau is a traditional Maori martial art that was most popular before the introduction of firearms into New Zealand in the late 18th century. Although difficult to establish its exact origins, legend states that

> FEARSOME ADVERSARY
A Maori warrior wields a taiaha during a tribal ceremony. Mau rakau martial artists pride themselves on their confrontational appearance.

the art was handed down by Tu and Tane, who are the gods of war and forest respectively.

There are a number of groups of mau rakau practitioners in existence, most commonly in and around New Zealand. Although the art is no longer used as a method of tribal warfare training, it is seen as a way of cultivating self-discipline and social responsibility. Many young Maori still tattoo their bodies, often as a sign of defiance to modern society rather than as a spiritual practice.

Weaponry

Tattooed practitioners use various weapons, most commonly clubs made from either wood, whale bone, or green stone, as well as canoe paddles. The weapon of choice is the "tao," a spear 7–8 ft (2–2.5 m) in length that was either thrown or used for blocking, striking, thrusting, and cutting. Other weapons include: the "maripi," a short club with teeth on one edge that is used as a slashing and striking tool; the "taiaha," a staff 5–6 ft (1.5–2 m) long; and the "pou-whenua," a long club fashioned from either the rib or jawbone of a whale.

◀ INDIGENOUS FIGHTING
Before the introduction of firearms to New Zealand, mau rakau fighting was used as a means of settling tribal disputes.

Kombatan

EXPLANATION
FILIPINO MIXED MARTIAL ART

DATE OF ORIGIN
1970s

FOUNDER
ERNESTO PRESAS

PLACE OF ORIGIN
PHILIPPINES

Kombatan is a Filipino martial art founded by Ernesto Presas, and largely based on the teachings of his brother, Remy. It fuses together eskrima (see pp. 180–81) and eclectic elements of judo, karate, jujutsu, (see pp. 234–35, 202–03, 216–17) and Japanese and Filipino weapons systems.

Kombatan also includes a wide-ranging set of Filipino techniques drawn from many indigenous martial arts—the main

influences include espada y daga, dumog (see p. 182, 183), bangkaw, sinawali, and palit palit.

Well-known for its double-stick techniques, kombatan is a highly organized and codified collection of diverse techniques—from stick fighting, knife fighting, and grappling, to throwing, chokes, and holds. The goal of kombatan, like modern arnis (see p. 187), is to modernize the ancient Filipino arts and systemize safe and effective training syllabuses.

Kombatan was first taught in the 1970s at the University of the Philippines. More recently classes have expanded to the University of Santa Tomas, the Central Colleges, and the Philippines' military and police academies. There are also a number of kombatan schools around the world.

Escrido

EXPLANATION
FILIPINO MIXED MARTIAL ART

DATE OF ORIGIN
1980s

FOUNDER
CIRIACO CANETE

PLACE OF ORIGIN
PHILIPPINES

Escrido is a Filipino martial art that largely features eskrima (see pp. 180–81) stick techniques with locks and takedowns commonly found in jujutsu (see pp. 216–17).

Founder Ciriaco "Cacoy" Canete served in the US army during World War II and was a champion of the first modern-arnis (see opposite) tournament in 1979. His stick-work still shows a high degree of influence from sword and knife techniques. Escrido is a combination of the

Canete family system of "doce pares" (12 pairs) as well as aikido and judo, with influences from other Japanese arts. Many Filipino stick masters also fight with the "bolo" (a large machete). The stick and machete are interchangeable during training.

All-around art form

The main goal of the fighting system is to provide an art form that covers all fighting distances from long- and medium-range, to close-quarter and grappling. Training is either one-on-one or with multiple attackers. Although there is a set curriculum, the art encourages each individual to find what works for him or her. Students develop flexibility in their choice of techniques so that, at an advanced level, they can act spontaneously to apply strikes and dancelike throws instinctively.

Lameco Eskrima

EXPLANATION
STICK AND DAGGER
MARTIAL ART

DATE OF ORIGIN
1980s

FOUNDER
EDGAR SULITE

PLACE OF ORIGIN
PHILIPPINES

A hybrid martial art founded by Edgar Sulite, lameco eskrima draws heavily from the eskrima systems (see pp. 180–81) taught by Jose Caballero and Antonio Ilustrisimo. The main weapon is the "baston" (rattan stick) which varies in length, weight, and thickness, according to the preference of the practitioner. Fighters use combinations of the single and double stick, single and double dagger, and the stick and dagger. Other weapons include the sword and staff. Dan Inosanto, who studied directly with Sulite, uses the system in his training (see p. 177).

Like espada y daga (see p. 182), eskrima focuses on the three different ranges of attack and defense—"largo" (long range), "medio" (medium range), and "corto" (close range). Training drills are known as "laban lara," or play fighting, in which students enjoy practicing in a safe, realistic way. This promotes speedy reflexes and a relaxed state of mind—both essential during actual combat.

Yaw-yan

EXPLANATION
"DANCE OF DEATH"
IN TAGALOG

DATE OF ORIGIN
1972

FOUNDER
NAPOLEON "NAP" FERNANDEZ

PLACE OF ORIGIN
PHILIPPINES

Yaw-yan is an external fighting style (driven by speed and muscle power) created by Nap Fernandez, a well-known kickboxing champion from Quezon province, after he studied a number of martial arts, most notably muay Thai (see pp. 158–65). The system follows many of the principles of muay Thai, but differs in its downward cutting kicks and its hip-torquing motions. Yaw-yan has a good reputation on the mixed-martial-arts circuit in the Philippines, although it is relatively unknown outside the country.

Full-contact art
Characteristically, students spend most of their training in full-contact sparring, both inside and outside the ring, where they use elbows, knees, and shins. The system includes a total of 40 basic kicks. Students are expected to develop a high degree of dexterity in their kicking combinations. Advanced kicks are mostly feigning techniques aimed at misleading the opponent before delivering a flow of heavy kicks. An example of this might be a light, low kick to the shin, then a further kick to the face—as the opponent tries to position himself to block the first kick, he leaves an opening in his defense for the second.

Grappling, throwing, and weapons
To cater for the growing interest in mixed martial arts in the Philippines—and the financial rewards on offer—yaw-yan includes a number of grappling and throwing techniques to equip fighters with takedowns, locks, and chokes, as well as "ground and pound," Practitioners are also encouraged to train with traditional Filipino bladed weapons—the bolo knife, machete, and "balisong" (butterfly knife) are favorites. Some schools also incorporate stick fighting, which uses the fire-hardened rattan cane, practiced either in single or double form.

NAP FERNANDEZ

Revered in the Philippines, Napoleon "Nap" Fernandez is a martial arts scholar and innovator. Initially a fine exponent of muay Thai, in later life Master Fernandez was motivated by a desire to create a new martial art—yaw-yan—that was inherently Filipino. In recent years, he has been responsible for introducing "ardigma," a new art that uses the hands and arms (hardened like iron) as a club.

Jendo

EXPLANATION
"THE ECONOMICAL NEW FIST WAY" IN TAGALOG

DATE OF ORIGIN
1973

FOUNDER
JONATHAN MAKILING

PLACE OF ORIGIN
LUZON ISLAND, PHILIPPINES

Created by Jonathan Makiling, jendo utilizes empty hand techniques and traditional Filipino weapons such as the stick and knives. It has been practiced in the central part of Luzon Island since 1973, and was officially recognized in 1996 as a Filipino martial art by the Philippine Sports Commission.

Central to the art's philosophy is the idea of "tres energies," meaning "tri force"—the forces of the normal, the unexpected, and the exceptional. These three interdependent yet complementary forces evolve and shift focus throughout a practitioner's life. Practitioners claim that a deep understanding of them enables individuals to accept all phenomena in nature.

◄ FEEL THE FORCE
A jendo practitioner demonstrates a perfect elbow strike to the back of his opponent's neck, during training.

Modern Arnis

EXPLANATION
STICK-FIGHTING ART

DATE OF ORIGIN
1960s

FOUNDER
REMY PRESAS

PLACE OF ORIGIN
PHILIPPINES

Modern arnis is a Filipino martial art that uses double rattan sticks. Founder Remy Presas turned his back on the death matches and politically fueled in-fighting between various clans of martial-artists, and developed a self-defense system that was holistic, friendly, and injury-free, yet still preserved many traditional Filipino techniques. These included bolo fighting and the stick art of balintawak (see p. 183). In 1969, the Modern Arnis Federation was established in Manila.

The system gained international notoriety when Remy's wife sent a number of modern-arnis instructors to Japan to conduct an exhibition during the 1978 Asaka International Trade Fair.

Key techniques
In modern arnis, emphasis is placed on ensuring correct body alignment before delivering strikes, to allow a maximization of force. Body-shifting in and out of range of the opponent is a key factor in determining success. There are 12 striking techniques in all. The art also includes the stick and knife training of espada y daga (see p. 182).

In 1999, Remy's brother, Ernesto, devised kombatan (see opposite), which retained most of modern arnis' techniques. Since Remy's death in 2001, a number of other splinter groups have emerged.

JAPAN AND OKINAWA

CULTURE AND INFLUENCES

JAPAN AND OKINAWA

MODERN JAPAN BRINGS TO MIND IMAGES of steaming noodle bars, teeming streets, cutting-edge fashion, world-class technology and innovation, and, of course, stunning natural landscapes. Beneath the surface of this diverse culture, however, there beats a very ancient heart. The battlefield arts that have existed in Japan for millennia have greatly influenced Japanese culture, thinking, and history but, in the context of martial-arts history, the permutations that have become incredibly popular around the world—such as karate, aikido, and judo—are relative newcomers.

JAPAN IS ONE OF THE major regions from which most of the martial arts practiced today originate. Only China and Korea can boast a similar heritage. In addition to the influence of its ancient traditions and battlefield arts, Japan has also made many important contributions to modern martial-arts practice. Perhaps the most well-known and widely adopted is the colored belt system—used to grade students according to rank and experience. Belts range in color from white through the spectrum of the rainbow to black, after which different degrees, or "dans," are awarded. Devised in the 19th century by Kano Jigoro, the founder of judo (see p. 234–35), the system is now used in many fields of martial art.

▲ THE FORTY-SEVEN RONIN
This painting shows a group of ronin using grappling hooks and rope ladders to scale the walls of their victim's home. Others stand guard, while the ronin on the left subdues the dogs.

Judo was also one of the first of the martial arts to be thoroughly codified. By combining the throwing and grappling aspects of jujutsu (see pp. 216–17) with elements from other wrestling arts, and standardizing the new art into a coherent system, Jigoro sowed the seeds for the sporting phenomenon that judo has become. Although many of the techniques were already prevalent in wrestling arts around the world, the standardization of the judo training syllabus allowed it to be taught easily, and to a good standard. This undoubtedly led to judo's widespread and rapid popularization.

Voices from the past
The ancient warriors of Japan left behind a fascinating legacy of literature devoted to the martial code and the philosophical thought of the warrior. *Bushido: The Soul of Japan*, written in 1899 by Inazo Nitobe, popularized the term "bushido," meaning "the way of the warrior." As a code, bushido cites seven virtues that are held in the greatest regard within the warrior culture: honor, loyalty, courage, benevolence, justice, veracity, and politeness.

The Forty-Seven Ronin, the true story of an event that came to represent the ideal of how warriors should behave, provides an

SAMURAI HELMET

earlier example of Japan's martial literary legacy and the ethical code of bushido. The story revolves around 47 samurai warriors in the service of Asano Naganori, the Lord of Ako, on the island of Honshu. While on a visit to the court of the Shogun of Tokyo, Naganori was insulted by another Lord, at which point he unsheathed his sword and struck the man who had offended him. It was considered extremely bad manners to draw a sword in the court of the Shogun, and Naganori was ordered to commit "seppuku," a ritualized form of suicide. On his death, the 47 warriors became ronin— samurai without a master—and vowed vengeance on the man who had insulted their master and provoked his suicide. They left their homes and families to enact a plan of revenge. To avoid raising suspicion, they posed as drunkards on the streets of Tokyo for almost two years, until an opportunity arose on December 14, 1702. They crept into the Lord's home and killed him, immediately surrendering themselves to the authorities, even though they knew their actions were punishable by death. They then committed ritual suicide at the tomb of their late master.

Although today we may consider this to be an extreme example of loyalty, it highlights the tradition from which martial artists fashion their attitudes and underlying philosophical principles.

> "THE TEACHING OF ONE VIRTUOUS PERSON CAN INFLUENCE MANY; THAT WHICH HAS BEEN LEARNED WELL BY ONE GENERATION CAN BE PASSED ON TO A HUNDRED."

KANO JIGORO, FOUNDER OF JUDO

6   7   8   9

REGION AT A GLANCE

1 WARRIOR CODE
Bushido, the strict warrior code for living that originated in Japan, has shaped the principles of many martial arts both in Japan and throughout the world.

2 CHINESE HERITAGE
War, trade, and travel between China and Japan has resulted in a cross-fertilization of ideas, with the Chinese influence evident not only in Japan's martial arts, but also in it's culture, religion, architecture, and writing system.

3 THE NATURAL WORLD
An understanding of nature and natural phenomena, living in harmony with the natural world, and observing and learning from it are key elements in many Japanese martial arts.

4 INNOVATION AND PROGRESS
Japan's reputation as an innovator is not new, indeed the colored-belt system—now a universal system of martial-arts grading—was first developed in Japan.

5 LITERARY LEGACY
The ancient warriors of Japan left behind a wealth of literature, from tales of colorful characters and bloody battles to martial ethics and philosophical thought.

6 RELIGION
The idea of personal virtue, and the importance of meditation, loyalty, and sacrifice in the martial code are influenced by the major religions of Japan—Buddhism, Christianity, and Shinto.

7 HONOR AND RESPECT
A cultural emphasis on loyalty, and on the importance of the group over individuals, informs much of Japan's martial-arts philosophy.

8 THE SAMURAI
The emergence, dominance, and eventual decline of the samurai shaped and developed swordsmanship techniques over the years.

9 WEAPONS BAN
One of the key influences on the rise of "empty-hand" martial-arts practices was the ban on carrying bladed weapons, imposed by the government in 1876.

MAP OF JAPAN AND OKINAWA

▼ WIDE-RANGING INFLUENCES
Japan's huge influence on the world of martial arts is well known. However, it was not all one-way traffic. The martial traditions of China and Korea played a part in the evolution of the arts in Japan.

CHINA

RUSSIAN FEDERATION

NORTH KOREA

SOUTH KOREA

Sea of Japan

Korea Strait

East China Sea

Hiroshima

CHUGOKU

Fukuoka

Kochi

KYUSHU

Kyushu

SHIKOKU

HOKURIKU

SHIGA Nagoya

Kobe KINKI

Osaka MIE

TOKAI

SHINETSU

TOHOKU

Sendai

Fukushima

KANTO

TOKYO

Yokohama

CHIBA

La Perouse Strait

Sea of Okhotsk

Hokkaidó

HOKKAIDÓ

Sapporo

PACIFIC OCEAN

JAPAN

Honshū

OKINAWA
Naha

Ryukyu Islands

Philippine Sea

KEY

▷ **Japanese travelers** to China brought karate skills back to Okinawa and the mainland.

▷ **China and Japan** have shared cultural and martial ideas for more than 1,000 years.

▷ **Buddhism arrived** from Korea in 552 CE. Koreans in Japan also brought swordmaking skills and developed one of the fiercest styles of karate known today.

▷ **Japan's occupation** of Korea from 1910–45 had a profound effect on Korea's martial arts.

▷ **European travel** to Japan in the last 100 years has boosted the popularity of Japanese martial arts in the West.

▷ **Since the 1950s**, travel between Japan, Oceania, and Southeast Asia has become commonplace and Japan's influence on the region's martial arts has grown considerably.

▷ **US forces** stationed in Japan and Okinawa during World War II brought martial-arts ideas home with them. Earlier economic migrants from Japan also played an important role.

types of interpersonal relationship: the reciprocal and the asymmetrical. A reciprocal relationship, as the name suggests, is mutually beneficial, with partners aiming to fulfill the reciprocal obligations by agreeing to work together and help each other, for example, in a collaboration between two business partners, or in a marriage between a husband and wife.

An asymmetrical relationship represents an inferior and superior partnership, in which the inferior partner is in debt to the superior partner and neither of them expect that debt to be repaid. Bound to his Master for life, the discipleship that a martial arts' student experiences is a classic example of this. According to the asymmetrical view, the student will never be able to repay the debt he owes for the bestowal of special skills and knowledge upon him by the Master.

The emphasis on both the unity of the group and the asymmetrical relationship is a fundamental element of Japanese martial arts' culture, and understanding its importance goes a long way towards explaining the loyalty that almost all practitioners feel toward their own group, their teacher, and their art.

> ▲ **A LEGEND IN HIS TIME**
Miyamoto Musashi, depicted in this woodblock print wielding two "bokken," is known to the Japanese as "Kinsei," or "Sword Saint," but he was much more than just a swordsman. He was also a master painter, sculptor, and calligrapher.

A unique text

The 17th-century work by Miyamoto Musashi, *Go Rin No Sho*, or *The Book of the Five Rings*, is considered a major classic in martial philosophy and military strategy. Musashi was a samurai warrior, and the book describes his numerous duels and his unique style of twin swordsmanship. It focuses on the spirit of martial arts that can only be attained after rigorous physical and technical training. The text is divided into five scrolls—Earth, Water, Fire, Wind, and Sky— fundamental elements that often feature in Eastern philosophical literature.

Outside influence

Although an island nation, Japan shares much common heritage with China; in fact, its main writing script, Kanji, is derived from Chinese characters. Its major religions include Buddhism, Christianity, and Shinto, which many Buddhists also follow. Buddhism was imported to Japan from Korea in 552 CE. Along with Confucianism (an ancient Chinese philosophical and ethical system that originates from the teachings of the early Chinese philosopher, Confucius) Buddhism has played an important part in the shaping of Japanese thought, culture, and martial arts—in particular the emphasis that many of the arts place on oneness with nature and the universe, and the development of personal virtue.

Enduring loyalty

The Japanese are renowned for placing emphasis on the group as opposed to the individual, and great importance is attached to two very different

> "THE WAY OF THE WARRIOR IS A WAY OF LIFE AND CAN NEVER BE CONSIDERED AS A HOBBY UNLESS YOU ARE SEEKING ONLY TO IMPRESS OTHERS WITH YOUR TECHNIQUES."

MIYAMOTO MUSASHI

> ❯ **SAMURAI HERITAGE**
The era of the samurai—which translates as "one who serves"—spanned almost 1,000 years. Samurai warriors came from the upper class of society, and by the 12th century they had become the ruling elite in Japan. They held this power until the late 1870s.

Evolution of the arts

There are many accounts of how Japanese martial arts evolved into the forms that we recognize today. Japanese interest in Chinese culture began during the Tang dynasty (618–907 CE) and cross-fertilization of ideas between the two countries was widespread during this period, especially concerning architecture and design, religion, and martial arts.

The flowering of Buddhism in Japan had a profound effect on Japanese martial arts, especially during the Nara period (710–784 CE), which represents one of the most active periods of cultural imports into Japan. Many Japanese traveled to China to study Buddhism, some of whom may have brought back kung-fu methods to Japan and Okinawa. Japan also has a long history of Buddhist pilgrims from the Korean peninsula, and they are also likely to have had some influence on Japan's cultural evolution.

Changing times

The Edo period (1603–1867) was another crucial time in the development of Japanese martial arts, particularly the sword arts. Prior to this period, when warriors fought multiple

▲ **CELEBRATING THE PAST**
The Japanese are hugely proud of their rich cultural heritage, as can be winessed at the many festivals held throughout the year to celebrate historical events. Here, some 600 horsemen recreate a samurai battle scene.

opponents on the battlefield, sword techniques naturally favored the use of different angles of attack, various blocking and deflecting techniques, and cuts aimed at the quick kill with the minimum expenditure of energy. However, because the Edo period was largely a peaceful time in Japanese history, dueling between individuals became more common than armed conflict between groups of militia. In swordsmanship, this led to the concept of "one cut, one kill"—whereby two warriors engaged in a duel would intend for the first cut to make the kill. This changed the training focus and techniques used in Japanese martial arts entirely.

Modern developments

The most recent development in Japanese martial history was the ban on the wearing of a sword in public, imposed by the government in 1876, which fueled the growth of unarmed combat. The introduction of this law effectively saw an end to the domination of the samurai, and encouraged an interest among the civilian population in the "empty-hand" methods of Japanese martial arts. It was a very important time in the evolution of many systems.

THE ART OF THE SWORDSMITH

During the era of the samurai, Japanese swordsmiths were responsible for producing what are widely regarded as the finest swords ever made. These highly skilled craftsmen employed a number of complex methods to forge lightweight, exceptionally hard, razor-sharp blades—weapons that helped elevate the samurai to legendary status. Parts of the sword would be embellished with elaborate engraving and inlay work. The scabbard was often made of lacquered wood decorated with designs taken from mythology or nature.

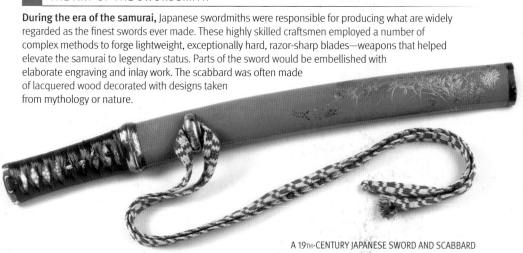

A 19TH-CENTURY JAPANESE SWORD AND SCABBARD

A group of 19th-century samurai warriors pose for the camera. The men at the front and on the right wear ornate helmets, or "kabuto," which were designed to provide visibility and presence on the battlefield. The group carries a variety of weapons, including a yari spear, a wakizashi sword, and a samurai long bow.

WEAPONS AND ARMOR

THE SAMURAI

THE SAMURAI WARRIORS of feudal Japan were trained in the use of numerous fearsome weapons—none more so than the katana. This long, single-edged sword was regarded as an embodiment of the samurai's soul, and the samurai code of honor, known as "bushido," or "the way of the warrior," taught against its misuse. The katana was often worn in conjunction with the shorter wakizashi, and the pair of swords were known as a "daisho," which translates as "big and small." Samurai armor was highly decorative, flexible enough to allow free movement of the sword, and tough enough to easily withstand battlefield conditions.

> **TSUBA**
The tsuba separates the sword's blade from the hilt.

Hole for kogatana (below)
Hole for blade
Hole for kogai

∨ **SEPPA**
A spacer, or "seppa," placed next to the tsuba kept the sword's hilt tight.

∨ **KOGAI**
A tool for arranging a samurai's hair sat next to the wakizashi (see below).

Ear cleaner
Decoration matched the kozuka (below)
Thin end inserted into hair

∨ **KOGATANA**
A small all-purpose knife fitted into a pocket on the scabbard of the wakizashi (see below).

Decorated hilt, or "kozuka"
Small blade

∨ **KATANA AND SCABBARD**
The samurai long sword was worn with the curved, razor-sharp cutting edge uppermost so that the warrior could deliver a devastating cut in one single movement.

MENUKI
Decorative ornaments, or "menuki," on the pommel of the hilt helped to improve grip

SAGEO
A hanging cord, or "sageo," secured the scabbard to the belt

HABAKI
The blade collar, or "habaki," locked the hand guard in position and kept the sword in its scabbard

MUNE
The nonsharp, flat back of the blade, or "mune," was mainly used for deflecting blows. It was made of softer metal than the sharpened edge

> **WAKIZASHI AND SCABBARD**
A shorter sword called the "wakizashi" was usually carried alongside the katana. It was worn indoors when custom dictated that the katana should be left at the entrance.

TSUKA
The wooden hilt, or "tsuka", was covered in rayskin wrapped in braid. The tsuka is always long enough for two hands to grip

SAYA
The wooden scabbard, or "saya," was custom-carved for an individual sword

∨ **YARI**
The spear, or "yari," was the samurai's weapon of choice during the 13th century, before the rise in popularity of the sword and swordmaking during the 17th century.

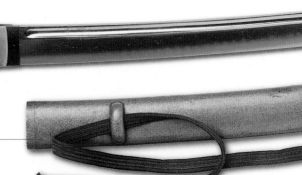

◀ TANTO AND SCABBARD

The tanto was a short knife or dagger used for stabbing, and for ritual suicide, or "seppuku." The strong, lightweight knife was also popular with the ninja.

TANTO
The tanto's stout blade usually had one cutting edge and was 6–12 in (15–30 cm) long

KISSAKI
The curved tip of the blade, or "kissaki," could pierce armor

HI
A groove known as a "hi" was carved into the blade to lighten the sword

STRAIGHT BLADE
The yari's characteristic straight blade was highly durable

▼ SAMURAI BATTLE ARMOR

Consisting of lacquered plates of metal bound together by silk lacing, samurai armor offered excellent protection while being flexible enough for a warrior to wield his sword with ease. This highly decorated tosei armor dates from the 19th century and is a fine example of modern samurai armor. Armor and helmets were intended for display as well as combat, and were especially ornate during the Edo period (1603–1868), after the pacification of Japan.

MEMPO
The fearsome-looking "mempo" protected the lower face and neck

KOTE
The arm defense, or "kote," were made of tiny, interlaced plates

TEKKO
A hand guard, or "tekko," protected the knuckles and fingers

SUNEATE
A samurai would traditionally put on the left shinguard, or "suneate," first

KABUTO
Gilt-wood imitation buffalo horns often adorned the helmet, or "kabuto"

BROWPLATE
Embossed eyebrows on the browplate added to the ferocious look

DO
The main breastplate, or "do," hung from the shoulders

KUSAZURI
A skirt of metal plates, or "kusazuri," protected the samurai's hips and groin

IN ADDITION TO their swords, the samurai also utilized a number of weapons of deception. These disguised or concealed weapons aided surprise attacks and enabled the samurai to arm themselves in places where carrying swords was prohibited.

CONCEALED DAGGER
Instead of a toggle, a dagger was hidden under the samurai's waist sash

▽ SMOKING PIPE
Tobacco was available in Japan in the 16th century, and by the 17th century these "kiserus," or small pipes, were very popular. This one conceals a small dagger inside the shaft.

Dagger concealed

Sheath

Dagger revealed

> TOBACCO POUCHES
These popular articles were worn at the waist and were usually fastened with a "netsuke," or toggle, that slipped under the sash.

LEATHER CASE
This type of tobacco pouch was commonly worn by peasants and travelers

> FAN DISGUISE
This dagger is cleverly designed to look like an ordinary fan. The hilt of the dagger and the sheath are carefully engraved to imitate the closed blades of the fan.

Dagger in the sheath

Dagger unsheathed

Engraved hilt

The empty sheath

Iron bar could be used as a cosh

< TESSEN
This is a solid iron bar shaped like a folding fan. These "tessen," or iron fans, were very popular with the samurai, especially on those occasions when etiquette demanded that they should be unarmed. It allowed them to defend themselves in an emergency, with what appeared to be a common, everyday item.

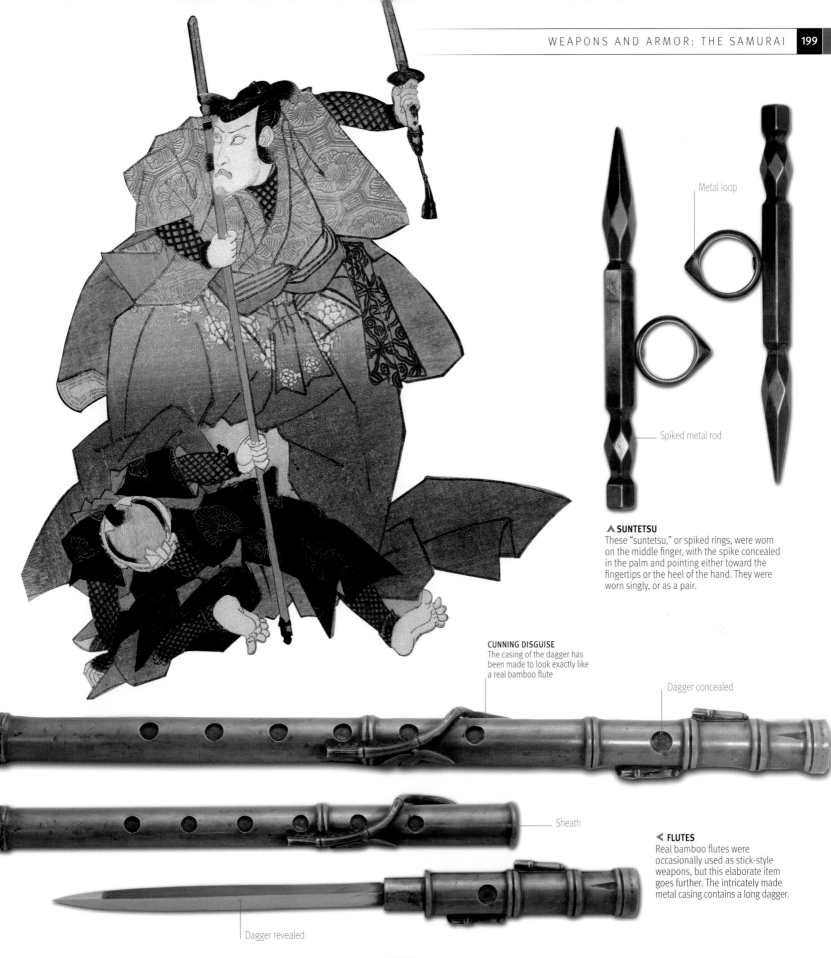

∧ SUNTETSU
These "suntetsu," or spiked rings, were worn on the middle finger, with the spike concealed in the palm and pointing either toward the fingertips or the heel of the hand. They were worn singly, or as a pair.

Metal loop

Spiked metal rod

CUNNING DISGUISE
The casing of the dagger has been made to look exactly like a real bamboo flute

Dagger concealed

Sheath

< FLUTES
Real bamboo flutes were occasionally used as stick-style weapons, but this elaborate item goes further. The intricately made metal casing contains a long dagger.

Dagger revealed

< WALKING CANE
When the Japanese goverment passed an act abolishing the carrying of weapons, the samurai were driven to devise a number of ingenious ways to disguise their blades. For example, this walking cane was made to conceal a sword.

▼ ANCIENT WEAPONS OF WAR

Although the katana is the best-known Japanese battlefield weapon, both samurai and peasants developed a number of other tools for warfare that were as practical as they were deadly. Based upon centuries of experience of hand-to-hand combat, many are still used in martial-arts training today. Some, such as the "kusarigama," a sicklelike tool, derive from farming implements; others utilize hooks and chains and were designed to disarm an enemy from a distance. There are also secret weapons, such as the "suntetsu," a ring that conceals a sharpened metal bar. Some long-handled weapons had blades to stab the enemy, or to cut off his sword hand, while others were spiked so that, if grabbed by the enemy, they could be twisted violently to tear the flesh of his hand, rendering him unable to wield his sword effectively.

Okinawan Karate

EXPLANATION
OKINAWAN "EMPTY HAND" IN JAPANESE

DATE OF ORIGIN
LATE 19TH CENTURY

FOUNDER
THE REVIVERS

PLACE OF ORIGIN
OKINAWA

The development of karate as a form of unarmed combat is, in large part, due to the ban on carrying weapons imposed during the reign of Okinawa's King Shoshin (1477–1526), and following the Satsuma clan's invasion of Okinawa in 1609.

The systemization of modern karate can be credited to a group known as "The Revivers," formed in the late 19th century, which included a panel of experts from various Okinawan martial arts. Originally known as "to-de" or "China hand"

("te" being a word of Chinese origin meaning "hand"), it was not until the early 20th century that the name "karate" was formally adopted.

New heroes

Karate became popular in the West after World War II, when US soldiers who had been stationed in Okinawa brought it back home with them.

Many of the early US practitioners had been raised on stories of macho cowboy culture, and the postwar industrialization of US society had left a vacuum into which tales of amazing characters and astounding feats of strength performed by Oriental karate masters were enthusiastically received. This led to an explosion in popular media of legendary heroes battling against the odds in the name of truth, justice, and honor—characteristics highly valued in the American psyche and in the minds of martial artists.

⋀ EARLY MORNING EXERCISE
Shortly after sunrise, an Okinawan karate master practices a dynamic tension kata, designed to build health and strength.

Ryuei Ryu

EXPLANATION
"RYUEI SCHOOL" IN JAPANESE

DATE OF ORIGIN
1875

FOUNDER
NORISATO NAKAIMA

PLACE OF ORIGIN
OKINAWA

This Okinawan system of karate is believed to have been introduced to Okinawa in 1875 by Norisato Nakaima. The son of wealthy parents, at the age of 19 Nakaima traveled to Fuzhou, in China, to study advanced martial arts. He spent seven years there, during which time he was trained in a number of systems, from physical combat—in particular Chinese boxing—to herbalism. He later journeyed to Fujian, Beijing, and Canton, collecting martial-arts weapons and scrolls.

Shorin Ryu

EXPLANATION
"SHAOLIN SCHOOL" IN JAPANESE

DATE OF ORIGIN
19TH CENTURY

FOUNDER
SOKON MATSUMURA

PLACE OF ORIGIN
OKINAWA

⋁ KARATE CHOP
A shorin ryu master tests his strength in a traditional way, by breaking a stack of tiles with his hand.

Combining elements of shuri-te and tomari-te (see p. 204), this system of karate may have been of Shaolin origin, as the first two characters in Japanese Kanji script are the same as the name of the famed Chinese Shaolin Temple. Its founder, Sokon Matsumura, was a renowned warrior, and bodyguard to three kings of Okinawa.

Natural stances and breathing exercises are characteristic of the training syllabus. Interestingly one of the originator's students, known

as Anko Itosu, developed the "pinan kata," a set of movements that are now popular in a wide range of Japanese-derived systems.

The art form has a self-ranking system, from white to black belt, which was adopted from that set up by the founder of judo, Jigoro Kano (see pp. 234–35). It also includes a number of well-known kata.

Some examples of the more intriguingly named kata are "iron horse" form, "crane on rock" form, and "swallow on the beach" form.

> "A PUNCH SHOULD STAY LIKE A TREASURE IN THE SLEEVE. IT SHOULD NOT BE USED INDISCRIMINATELY."
>
> CHOTOKU KYAN, MASTER IN SHORIN RYU

SOKON MATSUMURA

One of the most renowned martial artists of his time, Sokon Matsumura was chief martial-arts instructor to Okinawa's king, who gave him the title "Bushi," or "Warrior" in recognition of his fighting prowess and samurai qualities of loyalty and honor. The influence of shorin ryu is widespread, with many martial-arts styles tracing their origins back to Matsumura's system.

Shotokan

EXPLANATION
"HOUSE OF SHOTO" IN JAPANESE

DATE OF ORIGIN
20TH CENTURY

FOUNDER
GICHIN FUNAKOSHI

PLACE OF ORIGIN
OKINAWA

The founder of this form of karate is widely considered to be responsible for bringing karate from Okinawa to Japan. The name derives from his pen name, "Shoto," meaning "pine waves," and "kan," meaning "house of."

An external system—driven by speed and muscle power—it emphasizes breathing techniques, long, stable stances, and powerful punches, as well as elements of mind and body control. It is thought that its origins lie in Okinawan te, an ancient fist-fighting technique.

Code and culture

The system is clearly defined in the philosophy's 20 precepts. These are based on bushido, the ancient warrior code and Zen philosophy, and include these instructions:
- Never forget, karate begins and ends with respect.
- There is no first attack in karate.
- The art of developing the mind is more important than the art of applying techniques.
- First understand yourself, then understand others.
- The mind needs to be freed.
- Do not think you have to win, rather think, you do not have to lose.

Wide appeal

In addition to being popular in Japan, shotokan has a large practitioner base in the West and is widely taught in a number of martial-arts schools in both the US and the UK.

> "THE ULTIMATE GOAL OF KARATE LIES NOT IN VICTORY OR DEFEAT BUT IN THE PERFECTION OF THE CHARACTER OF ITS PARTICIPANTS."
>
> GICHIN FUNAKOSHI

GICHIN FUNAKOSHI

Like many of the karate greats, Gichin Funakoshi began life as a weak and sickly child. Born in Okinawa in 1868, he began his karate training with Yasutsune Azato, who taught him shuri te, and Yasutune Itosu, a master of naha te (see p. 205). He traveled to Tokyo in 1922, and became an ambassador for the art of Okinawan karate. Funakoshi was also a poet and philosopher.

▷ **A FLYING LEAP**
The spectacular high leaps seen in many forms of karate were originally employed to kick enemy horsemen from their mounts.

Toyama Ryu

EXPLANATION
"TOYAMA SCHOOL"
IN JAPANESE
DATE OF ORIGIN
1925
FOUNDER
NAKAYAMA HAKUDO

PLACE OF ORIGIN
TOKYO, JAPAN

The principles of this modern battlefield sword art are drawn from the techniques and philosophy of the the samurai era. It is based on the art of drawing a sword from a standing position, but also incorporates some of the mental and spiritual elements that governed the daily lives of swordsmen of ancient Japan.

The art was created by the Japanese Imperial Army. After studying the European close-combat warfare techniques used by troops in the World War I, they adapted these moves for the "katana," the long sword, for use on the battlefield.

The katana, as a national symbol and with its strong association with the samurai tradition of honor and warfare, was particularly important during the World War II.

MILITARY TRAINING

1 An Imperial Army soldier performs toyama-ryu "kata" (set forms), first holding his arms above his head as if about to strike down with his sword.

2 The soldier brings his arms down in a swift diagonal cutting movement, as though he is slicing through his imaginary opponent.

3 Imitating the actions of a soldier beset from all sides, he then turns quickly to his left and thrusts toward another foe.

Uechi Ryu

EXPLANATION
"UECHI SCHOOL" IN JAPANESE
DATE OF ORIGIN
EARLY 20TH CENTURY
FOUNDER
KANBUN UECHI

PLACE OF ORIGIN
OKINAWA

One of the major styles of Okinawan karate, the system was created after its founder, Kanbun Uechi, spent an extended period studying martial arts in Fuzhou, China. He opened his first school in the early 1900s, in Nanjing, but it was closed almost immediately, after one of his students killed a neighbor with an open-hand strike.

System style

Returning to Japan, Uechi eventually started teaching again, and in 1925 he established his institute of martial arts in Wakayama city.

The system is known for its spear hand strikes, toe kicks, and one-knuckle punches. The emphasis is on stability, and on minimizing the size of the striking object to increase the chance of causing serious damage to an opponent.

Tomari Te

EXPLANATION
"TOMARI HAND" IN JAPANESE
DATE OF ORIGIN
UNKNOWN
FOUNDER
NO KNOWN FOUNDER

PLACE OF ORIGIN
TOMARI, OKINAWA

This art form originates from the village of Tomari, in Okinawa, and is part of a collective body of martial arts known as to-de-jutsu, which takes fighting techniques based on Chinese arts and integrates them into Okinawan fighting traditions.

Chinese influence

Surprisingly little is actually known about the art as practiced in its original form. It is known that training involved students walking around the dojo with a companion on their back, and that the use of "kata" (set forms) was important. The style was acrobatic; similar in nature to northern Chinese styles.

Contact was light, quick, and spontaneous, in contrast to modern Japanese karate styles, which favor heavy, focused, and calculated strikes.

Tegumi

EXPLANATION
"GRAPPLING HANDS"
IN JAPANESE
DATE OF ORIGIN
UNKNOWN
FOUNDER
NO KNOWN FOUNDER

PLACE OF ORIGIN
OKINAWA

This traditional form of Okinawan wrestling emphasizes throws, trips, sweeps, joint locks, holds, traps, chokes, and parries. It marries both sporting and self-defense elements, and is believed to be the forerunner of the island's own version of sumo.

Evolved from a very primitive form of grappling, it is arguably one of the earliest forms of unarmed combat in Japan. It is thought that when striking elements were introduced from the Chinese kung fu arts, modern karate was born.

Today, there are many rules that ensure participants' safety. Competitions are refereed and victory is decided by a submission; achieved through either a joint lock, a stranglehold, or a hold-down pinning.

> PREBOUT ADJUSTMENTS
Tegumi contestants take up their starting positions while the referee checks that the waist belts, which are used for leverage, are properly in place.

Okinawan Kobudo

EXPLANATION
"OKINAWAN OLD MARTIAL WAY"
IN JAPANESE

DATE OF ORIGIN
UNKNOWN

FOUNDER
NO KNOWN FOUNDER

PLACE OF ORIGIN
OKINAWA

Sometimes known just as "kobudo," this art is thought to be a forerunner of karate. The techniques of the two arts are closely related in some ways, and kobudo's "kata" (set forms) do include certain empty-hand movements, although they all tend to be based around traditional weapons, such as the bo staff, the tonfa, the sai, the sickle, and the nunchaku, along with improvised farming tools.

Preserving traditions

The kata of kobudo reached their peak between 1600 and 1800, and although the art went into decline, martial-art traditionalists such as Yabiku Moden are credited as being responsible for keeping the art alive through the 20th century to the present day.

Taira Shinken, known as "the father of modern kobudo," is also a well-known practitioner. In a quest to restore and promote traditional Okinawan martial arts, he learned and disseminated the ancient kata after researching and collecting the set movements from the Ryukyu Islands. He selected a total of 42 existing kata, covering eight types of traditional Okinawan weapons. These form the basis of everything known today of the old systems of the Okinawan Islands.

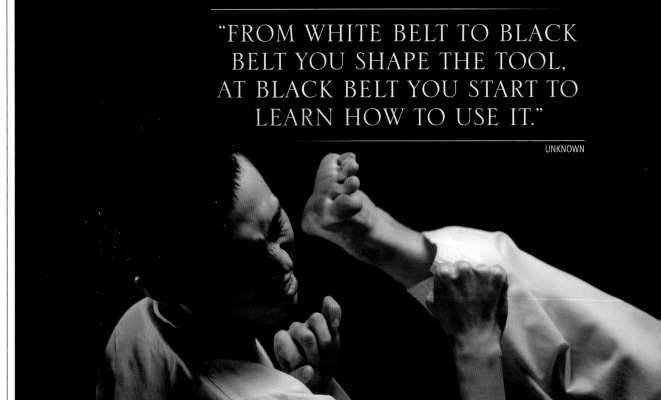

"FROM WHITE BELT TO BLACK BELT YOU SHAPE THE TOOL, AT BLACK BELT YOU START TO LEARN HOW TO USE IT."

UNKNOWN

Wado Ryu

EXPLANATION
"THE WAY OF HARMONY"
IN JAPANESE

DATE OF ORIGIN
1938

FOUNDER
HIRONORI OTSUKA

PLACE OF ORIGIN
JAPAN

This is one of the main systems of karate that is not of Okinawan origin. Although the system bears a resemblance to shotokan (see p. 203), practitioners of wado ryu are more likely to dodge punches rather than block them directly; they believe that correct technique and yielding are sometimes more effective than brute strength alone. The key principle of the system is known as "tai sabaki," meaning "body management," which refers to the technique of moving one's body out of the way of harm and moving along with, rather than against, force.

A belt system, ranging from white to black, and then 10 degrees of black, is standard. The 6th to 10th degree black belts are honorary ranks and are extremely difficult to achieve.

▲ **A GLANCING BLOW**
Despite attempting to dodge, or block the blow with his hands, this practitioner is caught out by an unexpected and well-executed sidekick.

The system draws on a wide range of influences. The "flying swallow" kata is from tomari te (see p. 204), while the "108 hands" is a set of movements that represent the mythological 108 evil spirits of man, said to have been developed by 108 warriors who roamed China in the 1600s robbing from the rich and giving to the poor. There are even stances based on the teachings of a pirate known as "Chinto".

Goju Ryu

EXPLANATION
"THE HARD-SOFT SCHOOL"
IN JAPANESE

DATE OF ORIGIN
20TH CENTURY

FOUNDER
CHOJUN MIYAGI

PLACE OF ORIGIN
OKINAWA

Chojun Miyagi was a disciple of Higaonna, the founder of Naha te (see right), and trained for many years in China before developing this system of karate. Borrowing heavily from Chinese moves and concepts, the style, and indeed the name Miyagi, became synonymous with the *Karate Kid* movies.

The art stresses the importance of blocking softly, yet attacking hard. For example, a soft-palm diverting technique may be countered by a straightforward reverse punch from an opponent, followed by a powerful punch to the opponent's face or head.

Goju is one of the four important systems of karate of Okinawan origin. The system's kata are generally divided into "sanchin" (basic, standard forms), "kaishu-gata" (open-hand forms), and "heishu-gata" (closed-hand forms).

Naha Te

EXPLANATION
"NAHA HAND" IN JAPANESE

DATE OF ORIGIN
19TH CENTURY

FOUNDER
KANYRO HIGAONNA

PLACE OF ORIGIN
OKINAWA

Named after the Okinawan port of Naha, this is an adaptation of a free-flowing style of Chinese boxing.

According to legend, in 1869 Kanyro Higaonna sailed to Fuzhou, in China. An illiterate man, he found employment as a house servant to a wealthy martial arts' master named Lu Lu Ko. He spent years in this lowly position until he saved his master's daughter from drowning during a heavy storm. As a reward his master taught him his system of kung fu.

In the 1880s he returned to Okinawa and started teaching martial arts. His system was heavily influenced by his time spent in China and he became known for the integration of hard and soft techniques. It is said that his kata were so powerful that the wooden floor would become hot to the touch from the gripping action of his feet.

Shukokai

EXPLANATION
"WAYS FOR ALL" IN JAPANESE

DATE OF ORIGIN
1940s

FOUNDER
CHOJIRO TANI

PLACE OF ORIGIN
KOBE, JAPAN

Shukokai is a hard-hitting style of karate in which force is exerted through the correct use of body mechanics. Its double hip twist, which is a way of maximizing punching power, is unique to the system. Mobility and speed are important elements, and a relatively high stance is maintained during fighting. Practitioners typically engage in very long sessions of competitive semicontact sparring, developing power through the use of regular pad work.

Hard hitting

The key to the system's punching power is a combination of the use of the larger muscle groups in the legs, combined with body rotation. The system's chief instructor, Mr. Kimura, spent three years traveling throughout Europe and Africa, studying fighting arts, refining techniques, and incorporating them into the system. Many of these are now included in the syllabus.

⌃ KATORI SHRINE, CHIBA PREFECTURE
The founder of tenshin shoden katori, Lisaza Lenao, was a talented swordsman. It is claimed that he spent 1,000 days and nights practicing martial arts in the Katori shrine.

Tenshin Shoden Katori

EXPLANATION
"THE TRUE AND CORRECT MARTIAL TRADITION OF THE GODS" IN JAPANESE

DATE OF ORIGIN
1480

FOUNDER
IISAZA LENAO

PLACE OF ORIGIN
CHIBA PREFECTURE, JAPAN

This is one of the oldest Japanese martial-arts systems. Although it includes a broad range of skills, the use of the sword is an essential element of the art. Originally, training would have included intelligence-gathering and analysis, warfare strategy, divination, and astronomy, alongside esoteric schools of Buddhism. Although oaths are common in martial-arts circles, the "keppan," the blood oath found in tenshin shoden katori, was extremely stringent.

Modern practice

Today, practitioners use single and double swords of varying lengths at the same time, as well as staves; most schools teach arts that would have been common on the battlefield in the 15th century: sojutsu, jujutsu, shurikenjutsu, and naginatajutsu (see pp. 217–17, 219, 241).

Nippon Kempo

EXPLANATION
"JAPANESE LAW OF THE FIST" IN JAPANESE

DATE OF ORIGIN
1932

FOUNDER
MUNEUMUI SAWAYAMA

PLACE OF ORIGIN
OSAKA, JAPAN

This competitive combat sport utilizes samurai-based armor for full-contact sparring. It employs a wide range of strikes, immobilization techniques, and takedowns. Blocking, diverting, joint locking, and grappling are also used. The main influences on the art are karate, judo, jujutsu, and aikido (see pp. 202, 234–35, 216–17, 238–39), along with a number of wrestling techniques.

Many police forces in Japan use nippon kempo training, both to develop practical martial arts' skills and to build confidence.

Hakko Ryu

EXPLANATION
"STYLE OF THE 8TH LIGHT SCHOOL" IN JAPANESE

DATE OF ORIGIN
1941

FOUNDER
OKUYAMA RYUHO

PLACE OF ORIGIN
JAPAN

A system of jujutsu (see p. 216–17), hakko ryu includes the study of Oriental medicine and philosophy.

The system, founded by a shiatsu master, is related to daito ryu (see p. 203), and is believed to have had a major influence on the founder of shorinji kempo (see p. 240).

Holistic approach

In contrast to most other martial arts, in which students first study how to strike an opponent, the first thing that students of hakko ryu learn is the "hakko dori"—an escape technique. This is a reminder of the art's holistic origins.

Emphasis is placed on the concept of "kan," or feeling and intuition. Interestingly, similar requirements are deemed important in the study of Oriental medicine, in particular massage, in which the practitioner's hands are used almost intuitively to search for physical problems.

Other areas of study that relate to combat include posture and stance work, and engagement strategies.

> "BE MASTER OF MIND RATHER THAN MASTERED BY MIND."
>
> ZEN SAYING

Goshin Jujutsu

EXPLANATION
"PROTECTION OF THE BODY JUJUTSU" IN JAPANESE

DATE OF ORIGIN
UNKNOWN

FOUNDER
NO KNOWN FOUNDER

PLACE OF ORIGIN
JAPAN

Of unknown origin, but similar to other jujutsu systems, goshin jujutsu is most popular outside Japan.

It is a self-defense system with an emphasis on effectiveness over show. The fundamental techniques of the art are strikes, kicks, locks, throws, and ground fighting. Rolling and falling methods, along with stance and footwork, are also key.

The art has a grading system, and the cultivation of the mind—often through meditation or deeper contemplation of the techniques—is an important aspect of training.

Shindo Yoshin Ryu

EXPLANATION
"NEW WAY OF THE WILLOW HEART SCHOOL" IN JAPANESE

DATE OF ORIGIN
1864

FOUNDER
KATSUNOSUKE MATSUOKA

PLACE OF ORIGIN
JAPAN

Consisting mainly of a combination of jujutsu (see p. 216–17) and the type of sword work used in kenjutsu (see p. 219), the school of shindo yoshin was founded by a retainer of the Kuroda samurai clan.

This samurai, Katsunosuke Matsuoka, incorporated facets of many different martial-arts schools into his art, but experts believe he was most heavily influenced by the traditions of the akiyama yoshin and the nakamura yoshin schools.

The art was instrumental in the development of wado ryu karate (see p. 205), one of Japan's most prominent combat systems.

Although it does include the use of classical weapons, the underlying philosophy of shindo yoshin ryu is that gracefulness, and yielding, soft-flowing movements such as those found in nature, are ultimately more powerful and effective than the application of direct brute force.

▼ **HISTORICAL DEPICTION**
In this woodblock print of fighting samurai the defender moves into close range, rendering a sword attack ineffective.

Daito Ryu Aiki Jujutsu

EXPLANATION
"GREAT EASTERN SCHOOL JUJUTSU" IN JAPANESE

DATE OF ORIGIN
11TH CENTURY

FOUNDER
YOSHIMITSU MINAMOTO

PLACE OF ORIGIN
FUKISHIMA PREFECTURE, JAPAN

Until the end of the 19th century, when Sokaku Takeda started to teach the art openly, this substyle of jujutsu (see pp. 216–17), which was founded by Yoshimitsu Minamoto, was practiced only by, and taught only to, the Takeda Samurai family.

It is primarily an unarmed technique utilizing fast, accurate, and relaxed grabs, throws, and holds. Emphasis is placed on using body weight for stability, and to unbalance an opponent before applying a joint lock or throw. In its original form, this would be followed by a strike, aimed at breaking a bone or joint.

Levels of attainment
There are four distinct levels of technique. In "shoden," the basic level, practitioners are taught falling, rolling, and tumbling, technical positions of feet, legs, and hands, defense maneuvers against weapons, and kicks and punches. "Chuden," the advanced level, involves a number of sweeping movements from jujutsu. "Okuden" is the highest level, and is aimed at relaxing the breathing and increasing the ability to act reflexively. Finally, "hiden" are the secret techniques, which are usually only taught to disciples and long-standing practitioners.

SOKAKU TAKEDA

Sokaku Takeda was famed for his astonishing martial-arts skills. While studying for the priesthood he perfected an ability to understand the minds of others, which helped him to develop seemingly supernatural techniques. In his lifetime he taught over 30,000 people.

Ninjutsu

EXPLANATION
"SCHOOL OF ENDURANCE, PERSEVERANCE, AND FORBEARANCE" IN JAPANESE

DATE OF ORIGIN
7TH CENTURY

FOUNDER
EN NO GYOJA

PLACE OF ORIGIN
SHIGA PREFECTURE, JAPAN

The ninja were groups of assassins and spies who fought and hunted in the mountainous regions of Japan. They propagated many myths about themselves, which instilled great fear into their enemies. Those myths still exist today, reinforced by the popular media.

The ninja symbol is the character "nin," which means endurance, tolerance, and strength. The pictograph of a knife above a heart represents self-discipline.

NINJA SYMBOL

Early history
Practitioners credit the origins of the art to En No Gyoja, a warrior monk who set up a training camp in the Togakure mountain range. The sect existed in isolation for 500 years until 1165, when Daisuke Nishina, a clan member, ran away to the Iga province. There he came under the tutorage of Kain Bosm, a mystic warrior and monk, which greatly influenced his training, adding esoteric philosophies to his fighting and tactical guerrilla skills.

Ninjas and samurai
In its original form, the art was geared to the needs of the assassin, with an emphasis on concealment, infiltration, and spying. Opportunities for employment among the ninja peaked during medieval times, when warring factions became better organized and the need for unconventional battle tactics became vital to success.

It is a widely held misconception that the ninja were sworn enemies of the samurai. In fact, many were also samurai who took on assassination jobs or gathered intelligence for opposing samurai clans as a way to raise their status and financial wealth. However, there were many battles between them, largely instigated by warlords who had gathered samurai militia and felt threatened by the ninja's expertise in destabilizing power bases.

Teaching and training
In the past, the art of ninjutsu was practiced and taught in a strict code of secrecy from master to disciple, and teaching as a profession was discouraged by the ninja until quite recently.

Today, there are many different schools of ninjutsu, the majority of which teach skills that originated from samurai fighting arts: spiritual refinement, armed and unarmed combat, explosives training, stealth, water training, military strategy, escape, horsemanship, espionage, geography, and meteorology.

Principles of ninjutsu
Ninjutsu's basic tenets are summed up in a poem, probably composed by a warrior known as Yamabushi.

THE ESSENCE OF NINJUTSU
My parents are the heaven and earth,
My home is my body,
My power is my loyalty,
My magic is my training,
My life and death is breathing,
My body is control,
My eyes are the sun and the moon,
My ears are sensitivity,
My laws are self protection,
My strength is adaptability,
My ambition is taking every
    opportunity with fullness,
My friend is my mind,
My enemy is carelessness,
My protection is right action,
My weapons are everything that exists,
My strategy is one foot in front of
    the other,
My way is ninjutsu.

> "THE ENEMY WHO IS AGAINST THE LAWS OF NATURE WILL LOSE THE BATTLE BEFORE HE BEGINS TO FIGHT."

MASAAKI HATSUMI, NINJUTSU MASTER

AUTHOR'S NOTE

My earliest memories of studying this art still inform much of my own training philosophy today. When I was 12 years old, I had to engage in full-contact fights and wrestling matches with senior students, all of whom were much larger than me. The teachers would encourage us to forget past training with regard to rules, safety, and etiquette, and simply win the fight. So, during one fight with a burly 25-year-old assistant instructor who was pinning me to the ground while delivering painful blows to my ribs and stomach, I rammed my right thumb as hard as I could into his left eye, feeling immediately guilty for my undignified lack of restraint. As he jumped off, screaming, I quickly got to my feet, expecting a severe beating, but to my surprise he gave me a quick slap on the back and a bright smile, declaring, "Well done, that worked!"

> **THE ART OF STEALTH**
Traditional ninja skills included many techniques for surprising the enemy, whether through disguise, unexpected approaches, or unusual methods of attack. Ninjas were trained to be amazingly agile and could make themselves almost invisible in any environment.

BEHIND THE SCENES

NINJA MASTER

IT IS NO SURPRISE that ninja legends abound: the black-clad assassins stalking their prey beneath the moonlight, taking on armies of samurai before disappearing in a puff of smoke. Is it fact or fiction? A behind-the-scenes look at a ninja training camp in Japan provides some answers.

The camp offers a fascinating insight into the life of a modern-day ninja, in which many of the ancient traditions and fighting techniques are still alive and well. Although ninjutsu remains a relatively underground art, it is growing in popularity in both Asia and the West. An important principle in ninjutsu is adaptability. This is the key to survival and, although ninja are rarely found running up and down walls or assassinating Shoguns these days, the codified and clandestine syllabus and training camps are as effective today as they were centuries ago.

"TO DISCOVER THE TRUTH, TO ACHIEVE A HIGHER SPIRITUAL STATE. THAT IS THE TRUE MEANING OF NINJA."

Many schools, such as this one in Chiba prefecture, have a large number of overseas students training alongside local Japanese practitioners. Training may be on an "evening class" basis, or students may opt for more intensive weekend or week-long programs. The ninja master, often assisted by his most experienced students, not only teaches ninjutsu fighting skills, but is also an expert on the philosophies, tactics, and lifestyle of the ancient night warriors. Through him the students explore what it meant to be a true ninja and immerse themselves in all aspects of the ninja culture.

A DEMONSTRATION

The ninja master blocks a straight punch from his student and pushes his arm down. The student's body follows, and finally the master is able to deliver a sharp, decisive kick to the groin, which will incapacitate the student immediately.

THE NINJA ARSENAL

Weapons training is still an important aspect of ninjutsu and, although considered impractical in combat today, nearly all ninja schools keep collections of a wide range of the tools of their former trade; swords, staves, spears, and other long-bladed instruments are staples of the dojo. Ninja also use climbing implements such as ropes, hooks, and hand-and-foot claws in weapons training.

INSTRUCTING THE CLASS

As the students practice their given techniques with their partners, the master paces around the class, spotting any faults with attacks or defensive maneuvers, offering on-the-spot advice for correcting them, and, in some instances, giving an impromptu demonstration of how the technique should be performed.

A NINJA MASTERCLASS

One-on-one training with the master is an important aspect of ninjutsu, as it is with all martial-arts training. Usually performed with a senior student, techniques are polished, and new ideas, principles, or philosophies demonstrated. It is a mini-masterclass in which the student, who may have been practicing alone, can learn directly from the master. A moment of contact with the master can better explain the method of the system than a thousand words.

>>

WEAPONS AND ARMOR

THE NINJA

MANY OF THE WEAPONS used by the ninja were derived from their need for stealth and speed. Although they did use traditional weapons, such as swords and daggers, the ninja also employed an arsenal of other devices designed to stun, delay, distract, and—of course—to kill their enemies. They were masters in the use of gunpowder, which they utilized to create smoke screens, burning projectiles, and even landmines. Many of their weapons had multiple uses and were easily concealed. For example, "shuriken" (small, handheld blades) were usually thrown at the enemy to cause minor injuries and create a distraction, but they could also be used in the hand, to gouge and slash. Ninja clothing was designed for camouflage, with dark colors worn at night, and white worn to blend in with snow. They devised many ingenious ways in which to go about their business undetected. Shaped wooden blocks attached to their shoes imitated the tracks of wild animals, while metal claws strapped to their hands and feet enabled them to climb more easily.

⌃ MANRIKIGUSARI/KUSARIFUNDO
Consisting of a long piece of chain with weights at each end, a "manrikigusari" (sometimes known as a "kasarifundo") was used to disable or to kill outright. The chain was held in the hand and ninja would throw one weighted end into the enemy's face, groin, or solar plexus.

▽ SHINOBI SHOZOKO
When dressed in the "shinobi shozoko"— the uniform that we most commonly associate with the ninja—almost all the ninja's flesh, except for an area around the eyes and the hands, is completely covered. However, it is likely that some ninja would have worn peasant clothing.

OUTER GARMENT
Typically, the ninja shirt or jacket had many pockets, both inside and out, for carrying all their equipment

Weighted ball

⌃ KUSARIGAMA
The chain and blade, or "kusarigama" was used to entangle the enemy or his weapon, making it possible to draw him in and stab him. The weighted end of the chain was swung over the user's head, and then whipped forward. Sometimes the weight itself acted as a lethal weapon.

TABI BOOTS
In common with traditional footwear of the time, the ninja's "tabi" boots had a split toe to improve grip

∨ BO SHURIKEN
Usually sharpened at one end—sometimes both—"bo shuriken" could be thrown in a number of ways: underarm, overarm, sideways, or backward; and with or without spin.

∨ HARIGATA SHURIKEN
The name of this type of shuriken means "needle-shaped." It is thought that they derive from the thick needles that were used to stitch leather armor.

∨ SPIKED SHURIKEN
There are a variety of different small, spiked shuriken, which have sharpened points projecting out on all sides from a central ring.

MIKAZUKI SHURIKEN

HAPPO SHURIKEN

JUJI SHURIKEN

NADEMAJI SHURIKEN

JUJI SHURIKEN

HAPPO SHURIKEN

> KAKUTE
These spiked or bladed rings were favored by female ninja. Sometimes the tips were dipped in poison so the ninja could strangle an enemy while delivering a dose of poison. Alternatively, they could be used to gouge and slash.

Sharpened metal spikes

Curved blade for slashing

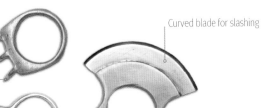

∨ TETSUBISHI
Small, spiked devices, known as "tetsubishi," were used to aid escape. They would be scattered onto the ground to slow down an enemy in pursuit.

METAL SPIKES
The tips were sometimes coated in poison

Forged metal hook

∧∨ KAGINAWA
These hook-ropes, known as "kaginawa," were used primarily as restraining devices. They consist of a hook attached to the end of a long rope with iron rings. Sometimes spiked rings, or "kakute" (see above) were used, to make struggling more painful. Kaginawa could also be used for scaling walls, or swinging from roof to roof, or tree to tree.

Jujutsu

EXPLANATION
"THE ART OF SOFTNESS"
IN JAPANESE

DATE OF ORIGIN
DATE UNKNOWN

FOUNDER
NO KNOWN FOUNDER

PLACE OF ORIGIN
TOKYO, JAPAN

Although the term was not coined until the 17th century, jujutsu is famed for being the unarmed combat method of the samurai. The art forms the basis of judo and Brazilian jujutsu (see pp. 234–35, pp. 342–43) and incorporates pins, joint locks, and throws. It is particularly effective in one-on-one confrontations.

柔術

JAPANESE CHARACTER
FOR JUJUTSU

Techniques

An important aspect of jujutsu training is learning how to break a fall effectively. Practitioners employ a unique method of absorbing force when being thrown; slapping the ground with their free arm so that the shock and disorientation of sudden impact is greatly reduced when the rest of the body makes contact.

> **SELF DEFENSE**
Jujutsu has long been favored by police forces across the world. In this picture from the 1940s, British police officers learn jujutsu techniques as part of a self-defense class.

Although jujutsu means "the art of softness," it is a deadly, combat-orientated art, intended to disable opponents as quickly as possible—often using their own energy, weight, and momentum against them.

The samurai connection

In jujutsu's original form, common samurai battlefield weapons (see pp. 196–97) would have been used. The combat style also comes from its samurai past—the grappling techniques enabled a lightly armed warrior to fight an armor-clad enemy.

Law and order

Modern jujutsu traditions were founded toward the end of the Edo period (1603–1868) when more than 2,000 schools existed in Japan. It was, and remains, an extremely popular art.

Forms of the system are employed by many law-enforcement institutions, the most famous being taiho jutsu (see p. 240), which is used by the Tokyo police. Jujutsu is also used by police forces worldwide.

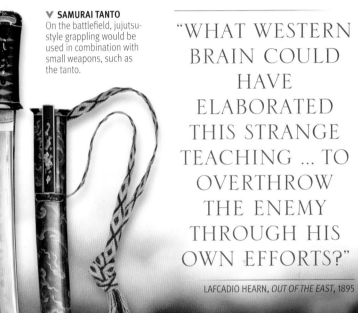

▼ **SAMURAI TANTO**
On the battlefield, jujutsu-style grappling would be used in combination with small weapons, such as the tanto.

"WHAT WESTERN BRAIN COULD HAVE ELABORATED THIS STRANGE TEACHING ... TO OVERTHROW THE ENEMY THROUGH HIS OWN EFFORTS?"

LAFCADIO HEARN, *OUT OF THE EAST*, 1895

◄ **DISABLING TACTIC**
Following an attack, practitioner on the ground has been pinned down in an arm lock, which has incapacitated him. The defender applies pressure to his elbow and shoulder, rendering him unable to move in any direction.

Nakamura Ryu

EXPLANATION
"NAKAMURA SCHOOL" IN JAPANESE

DATE OF ORIGIN
1950s

FOUNDER
NAKAMURA TAIZABURO

PLACE OF ORIGIN
YOKOHAMA, JAPAN

The basis of this modern martial art is best described through the words of its founder, Nakamura Taizaburo: "While teaching kenjutsu in Northern China, I was inspired with the thought that "eiji happo," the eight rules of calligraphy, could also be applied to the rules of swordsmanship. As I practiced the "ei" character [this is to calligraphy what "doh ray me" is to music], I saw in my mind that these eight strokes of the brush traced the trajectories of the sword when cutting. The first brushstroke, "souk," is the thrust of the sword tip; the second, "roku," is the left and right horizontal cuts; the third stroke, "do," is the vertical cut, and so on."

Nakamura was held in high esteem in Japan. In 1992, 11 years before his death, he was given the highest cultural award in Japan—the status of National Living Treasure.

▶ EIGHT STROKES OF CALLIGRAPHY
Nakamura developed his theory while studying calligraphy. Here, each of the major strokes is shown in black, within an actual character.

DOT   HORIZONTAL   VERTICAL   LEFT

RIGHT   RISING   HOOK   TURNING

Iaido

EXPLANATION
"THE WAY OF MENTAL PRESENCE AND IMMEDIATE REACTION" IN JAPANESE

DATE OF ORIGIN
EARLY 16TH CENTURY

FOUNDER
HAYASHIZAKI JINSUKE SHIGENOBU

PLACE OF ORIGIN
TOKYO, JAPAN

More than a century before iaido came into being, a similar art, iaijutsu, had been developed by Iizasa Lenao, the legendary founder of the famed tenshin shoden katori (see p. 206).

Both of these arts involve perfecting control of the sword. In its original form this meant drawing it from its scabbard, then striking, cutting, removing the blood, and replacing the sword—all in one smooth, fluid motion.

Instant reactions

It is likely that the art was developed to save crucial seconds in the event of a surprise attack. A warrior trained in iaido would have lightning-sharp reactions and could respond instantly.

Today, practitioners use either blunt or sharpened metal swords, and are trained to achieve an enhanced state of awareness and sensitivity to the wider environment.

Although modern iaido is a noncompetitive art, competitions do take place, in which set movements are performed in front of a panel of judges.

▼ NO ESCAPE
In this antique painting, a warrior thrusts his enemy to the ground, pushing against his head with one hand to incapacitate him. This will allow the warrior to perform an overhead thrusting maneuver and effect a kill.

Yagyu Shinkage Ryu

EXPLANATION
"YAGYU NEW SHADOW SCHOOL"
IN JAPANESE

DATE OF ORIGIN
16TH CENTURY

FOUNDER
KAMIIZUMI NOBUTSUNA

PLACE OF ORIGIN
JAPAN

The founder of this sword school is credited with bringing radical changes to aspects of swordsmanship, such as posture and grip. He also introduced a type of light armor that gave his men more freedom of movement.

In 1565, Nobutsuna bequeathed his school to his top disciple, Yagyu Muneyoshi, who went on to teach the art to the Shogunate—the military government.

Modern times
The codified forms in the current curriculum, developed by Yagyu Toshikane, the fifth heir to the system, include aspects of bojutsu, kenjutsu, and shurikenjutsu (see below).

> A SIGN OF RESPECT
By offering the sword with the curve of the blade toward his own body, the practitioner shows deference to a higher master.

> "VICTORY GOES TO THE ONE WHO HAS NO THOUGHT OF HIMSELF."
> SAYING FROM THE SHINKAGE SCHOOL OF SWORDSMANSHIP

Kenjutsu

EXPLANATION
"ART OF THE SWORD"
IN JAPANESE

DATE OF ORIGIN
UNKNOWN

FOUNDER
NO KNOWN FOUNDER

PLACE OF ORIGIN
JAPAN

Unlike iaido (see p. 218), kenjutsu utilizes the "katana" (long sword), with a "bokken," a wooden sword of similar size and weight, used in training.

Shurikenjutsu

EXPLANATION
"ART OF THROWING"
IN JAPANESE

DATE OF ORIGIN
UNKNOWN

FOUNDER
NO KNOWN FOUNDER

PLACE OF ORIGIN
JAPAN

A noncompetitive ancient art of knife and spike throwing, shurikenjutsu, although rarely practiced today, is commonly included in a number of other popular arts such as jujutsu,

It is essentially a noncompetitive, demonstrative, performance art, which takes on the form of prearranged set movements between dueling opponents.

The stuff of legend
The most famous practitioner was Miyamoto Musashi, also known as "The God of the Sword," a legendary but real samurai who wrote *The Five Rings*, a tale of his warriorship and his skill in double swordsmanship, to which he attributed his success in over 60 duels to the death.

> SHARP STAR
This type of shuriken is commonly known in the West as the "death star."

kenjutsu, bojutsu (see pp. 216–17, and above) and sojutsu. Practiced by the ninja, it is a secretive art based on stealth and surprise. Weapons are often small and easily concealed. In addition to being thrown, they were also used to stab and slash the enemy.

Bojutsu

EXPLANATION
"ART OF THE STAFF"
IN JAPANESE

DATE OF ORIGIN
UNKNOWN

FOUNDER
NO KNOWN FOUNDER

PLACE OF ORIGIN
JAPAN

Dating back thousands of years, bojutsu was probably a battlefield martial art, used for training troops.

It was adopted by the police in the Edo period (1603–1868) and it is likely that this influenced many of the techniques in existence today, most notably those aimed not at killing, but rather at harming or restraining unruly prisoners. Interestingly, the development of

stick techniques on the battlefield probably came about as a result of warriors having to improvise if the bladed part of a weapon such as the halberd was lost in battle.

Improvised weaponry
Fighting with just the bladeless staff became popular in Okinawa as a stand-alone art form in its own right during the period when the carrying of metal-edged weapons was outlawed.

Many of the grips, thrusts, blocks, parries, sweeps, and deflecting movements were developed among the peasants of Okinawa. It is most likely that the original weapon was the "tenbin," a long wooden pole that was balanced on the shoulders and used to carry buckets containing either grain or water.

> "GO TO THE BATTLEFIELD FIRMLY CONFIDENT OF VICTORY AND YOU WILL COME HOME WITH NO WOUNDS WHATSOEVER."
> SAMURAI GENERAL KENSHIN UESUGI

Kendo

EXPLANATION
"WAY OF THE SWORD"
IN JAPANESE

DATE OF ORIGIN
EARLY 18TH CENTURY

FOUNDER
NAGANUMA SIROZAEMON KUNISATO

PLACE OF ORIGIN
JAPAN

Developed from sword techniques used on the ancient battlefields of Japan, this art of fencing (see p. 268–29) combines philosophical and sporting elements. With the advent of the gun, battlefield training lost much of its practical value and the emphasis changed from warriorship to education and spiritual discipline.

Modern kendo is believed to have been created by Naganuma Sirozaemon Kunisato in the 18th century. It was he who implemented the use of the bamboo sword, known as the "shinai," and the distinctive bogu armor and helmets.

The Zen influence
As a martial art, kendo relies heavily on the Zen philosophy of empty mind, known in Japanese as "mushin." This encourages instinctive actions, bypassing the need for conscious thought, and saving precious moments in conflict situations.

This concept also has practical applications in the day-to-day lives of practitioners, many of whom report an increased ability to deal with unfamiliar or unexpected situations.

剣
道

JAPANESE CHARACTER
FOR KENDO

Technical qualifications
In 1902, the kendo ranking system was created by the Dai Nippon Butoku Kai (an organization set up by the Japanese government in 1895 to solidify, promote, and standardize all martial systems and disciplines) and remains the basis of most curriculums.

There are six ranks, known as "kyu" for beginners and ten "dan," or levels of degree, for advanced players.

The first eight grades are awarded via examination; the latter grades are awarded after nomination and examination. Honorary degrees for instructorship are based on skill, ability to lead and to judge character, and for contributions made toward the advancement of the art of kendo.

⋀ **THE WAY OF THE SWORD**
With Mount Fuji as a backdrop, kendo practitioners in full armor train using "shinai," or bamboo swords.

Practice and competition
The shinai used by junior high school centers in competition training is 44 in (112 cm) long and weighs 13–16 oz (375–450 g). The high school shinai differs slightly, being approximately 45 in (115 cm) long and weighing 16–17½ oz (450–500 g). The adult shinai is slightly larger at 46½ in (118 cm) in length and weighs more than 17½ oz (500 g).

Fights take place in a ring and points are awarded for target strikes to specified parts of the body, and for thrusting movements. The winner is the first competitor to score two points within the maximum five-minute time limit

"IT IS SAID THAT THE IGNORANT ARE OBSTRUCTED BY IGNORANCE, WHILE THE INTELLECTUALS ARE OBSTRUCTED BY INTELLECTUAL KNOWLEDGE. ONE WAY OF GETTING PAST THESE OBSTACLES AND APPROACHING INHERENT KNOWLEDGE IS TO LET GO OF WHATEVER COMES TO MIND."

MUSO KOKUSHI, ADVISER TO EMPERORS AND SHOGUNS

> **PROTECTIVE HEAD GUARD**
Known as a "men," the mask worn by practitioners is made from thick quilted cotton with a steel grille called a "tate-gen."

> **EQUESTRIAN WARRIOR**
A horse-mounted archer in 12th-century battledress
stands against the vivid colors of a Japanese maple
tree. On his back he carries a quiver of arrows, which
would have been used with a longbow more than
7 ft (2 m) in length.

◀ A COLORFUL RITUAL
The costumes worn by the yabusame archers are based on the traditional hunting dress of medieval warriors. As the archer releases the arrow he shouts "Yo-In-Yo," meaning "darkness and light."

▲ YABUSAME ARROWS
Japanese arrow heads are known as "yanone," and this type of forked tip is called a ropecutter. The long pointed shaft, or "tang," slots inside the arrow to provide balance.

Yabusame

EXPLANATION
"RIDER AND HORSE AS ONE" IN JAPANESE
DATE OF ORIGIN
1185–1333
FOUNDER
MINAMOTO NO YORITOMO
PLACE OF ORIGIN
JAPAN

Originally designed to train samurai in bow skills, yabusame is a form of horse-mounted archery. It is still practiced in Japan at ceremonial festivals, where it is believed that, if the archers strike their targets, then the year will be prosperous. Competitions are usually held near Shinto shrines; in the past they were intended as entertainment for the gods as well as local people. Training is intense, and archers—typically from aristocratic families—are treated with great respect. The art is held in high esteem and has been demonstrated during state visits of world leaders and royalty.

Origins of the art
Although there are mentions of the art during the reign of Emperor Shomu in the Nara period (989–1066), yabusame was introduced to the samurai by Minamoto No Yoritomo in the Kamakura period (1185–1333). The style in practice today dates from the 18th century.

Practitioners claim that the art helped the samurai learn focus, while the Zen breathing techniques used in training help stabilize the mind and bring clarity of thought, which is of utmost importance for hitting a target in the heat of battle. It is thought that those who master the art also master their own fear.

AUTHOR'S NOTE

In 2003, I spent some time with the Yabusame. My training included long ritual meditation and holding standing postures, similar to the horse-riding stance in Chinese martial arts. After practicing these postures for hours, I was placed on a wooden horse and rocked and spun while shooting at a target seven yards away. It is vital to go through this type of training before getting on a horse, as falling off at high speed is extremely dangerous and, in feudal days, would have probably meant being killed by an opponent.

Kyudo

EXPLANATION
"WAY OF THE BOW" IN JAPANESE

DATE OF ORIGIN
UNKNOWN

FOUNDER
NO KNOWN FOUNDER

PLACE OF ORIGIN
TOKYO, JAPAN

This archery system is based on the ancient bowmanship techniques of hunters and warriors, but today is practiced primarily for physical and spiritual development.

As traditional battlefield arts declined, military teachers of the arts found themselves unemployed and so began to teach civilians the skills that they had developed. With the advent of this new profession came the birth of artistic, intellectual, and spiritual martial arts.

There are now two important aspects to kyudo, the military branch and the ceremonial branch. Although the study of the art was banned by occupation forces in Japan after World War II, in 1949 the All Nippon Kyudo Federation was formed and a manual was released to codify the practice.

Kyokushin karate

EXPLANATION
"SOCIETY OF THE ULTIMATE TRUTH KARATE" IN JAPANESE

DATE OF ORIGIN
1964

FOUNDER
MASUTATSU OYAMA

PLACE OF ORIGIN
TOKYO, JAPAN

This is a violent, full-contact form of karate that includes kicking to the head, head butts, and punches.

The founder, Masutatsu Oyama, led a colorful life, and believed that self-improvement could be achieved through hard training and discipline. A Korean immigrant to Japan, Oyama suffered a number of humiliating race-related beatings, which led to a mental breakdown. He retreated to the mountains for a number of years, where he put himself through a brutal training regime that included hurling himself against rocks, carrying heavy weights, and fighting with bears and bulls.

Physical punishment

Kyokushin practitioners fight without gloves or protective body armor, believing that protection diminishes the realism. However, in competition, head, elbow, and hand strikes to the head and neck are banned.

Although moderate injuries are common, serious ones are quite rare. The most common injuries sustained by fighters are fractures—particularly to the sternum—broken clavicles, and general bruising.

FIGHTER IN THE WIND

In 2004, a blockbuster movie was made in Korea, based on the life of Masutatsu Oyama. While the movie is not a true biography (the story has all the elements of a Hong Kong action movie, along with a heavy dose of the sentimentality and melodrama often associated with Korean filmmaking), it does capture the spirit of the man and has plenty of awe-inspiring martial-arts sequences. The movie also boasts stunning choreography and cinematography.

Shootfighting

EXPLANATION
MIX OF BOXING AND WRESTLING

DATE OF ORIGIN
1985

FOUNDER
CAESAR TAKESHI

PLACE OF ORIGIN
JAPAN

Created as a response to the wave of popularity of kickboxing in Japan, shoot fighting includes boxing and wrestling techniques.

The governing body, the Shooto Organization, was formed in 1985. International competitions are common and are governed by the International Shoot Fighting Association (ISFA).

Rules of combat

Biting, head butting, and striking in the groin or back of the head are considered fouls, as are attacking an opponent who is falling or recovering from a fall. A victory is decided on points either when a fighter is unfit to continue, a regulation is violated, the referee deems the match too dangerous to continue, or there is a knockout or technical knockout.

Puroresu

EXPLANATION
"PRO WRESTLING" IN JAPANESE

DATE OF ORIGIN
UNKNOWN

FOUNDER
NO KNOWN FOUNDER

PLACE OF ORIGIN
JAPAN

Less gimmicky than its US and UK counterparts, Japan's equivalent of World Wrestling Federation utilizes a number of moves similar to those in shoot fighting.

Japan's first pro wrestler was a former sumo, Sorakichi Matsuda. Although not particularly successful, he is credited with making the sport popular. It was not until the advent of television in 1951 that Japan had its first pro wrestling star, Rikidozan.

Showmanship

Matches take place in a square ring. Like other forms of spectator wrestling, participants often climb onto and jump off the ropes or use the ropes' elasticity as a springboard to launch into their opponent. Matches are won via knockouts, submissions, ring counts, or pinning.

Variations on the standard ring are the six-sided ring, and the ring with barbed wire instead of rope.

This is not considered seriously dangerous to the health of the fighter, but does result in cuts and minor flesh wounds to competitors, adding an element of blood lust.

There is also a female branch of the art that is gaining in popularity, known as joshi puroresu.

▼ SHOOTERS IN ACTION
A masked puroresu fighter launches a devastating dropkick at his opponent's throat as the crowd looks on.

Sumo

EXPLANATION
"WAY OF THE GODS" IN JAPANESE

DATE OF ORIGIN
23 BCE

FOUNDER
NO KNOWN FOUNDER

PLACE OF ORIGIN
JAPAN

The national sport of Japan, sumo has existed since ancient times, when it was performed both as a method of divination and to entertain Shinto gods. It has a huge following and players are treated like living legends.

Messages from the gods

Although its exact origins are unclear, the Japanese record of ancient history, the *Kojiki*, which dates from the 8th century, describes early sumo as a ritualistic practice with the power to halt evil and promote good. Another historical work, the *Nihon Shoki*, describes a battle between two legendary fighters, Taima No Kehaya and

GRAND CHAMPIONS
There are no set criteria for promotion to the rank of Yokozuna, but a wrestler must have power, skill, and dignity to qualify. There are no set quota either—at any time there may be no Yokozuma, or several. Here, a Yokozuma arrives for a dedication ceremony.

SPECTATOR SPORT
Sumo was originally a religious ritual—it was not regarded as a spectator sport until the 17th century. Sumo prints from the 18th and 19th century prove its popularity in the past, and today it still has a huge fan base, with bimonthly tournaments televised from start to finish on Japanese TV .

SUMO IN ART
Sumo was a popular subject in Japanese art. Here, two wrestlers grapple in the ring as referees, one carrying a ceremonial fan, look on.

Nomi No Sukune, that took place in 23 BCE. This fight was to help divine the gods' choice between two warring factions, the Izumo and Yamato. Sukune killed his opponent, and experts believe that sumo gained in popularity as a way of divining the will of the gods, concerning matters as diverse as politics and crop yields.

Women wrestlers

Modern sumo forbids women from entering the ring, but the *Nihon Shoki* records show that ladies-in-waiting to the Emperor Yuryaku held bouts as early as 469 CE, and that a Buddhist nun took on men with some success in Kyoto sometime between 1592 and 1598.

Codes and customs

Since 1960, the system of sumo has been codified as a collection of 70 moves, derived from an original total of 48 moves as practiced in ancient times.

Sumo training stables are notoriously tough and dictated by strict tradition. Training methods are controversial, with wrestlers encouraged to sleep right after huge meals in order to put on weight. Young wrestlers, in keeping with tradition, style their hair into top knots and wear traditional Japanese dress when in public, further signifying their separation from society and their loyalty to the stable.

Reaching the top

The ranking system dating from the Edo period is still in existence. A Yokozuna grand master is the highest sumo position. However, in order to achieve and maintain this status, he must compete regularly and win.

> "SUMO AT ITS FINEST IS A PRIMAL STRUGGLE ... IN A SPLIT SECOND THE STRONGER AND MORE SKILLFUL IS DECIDED. IT IS THE ULTIMATE IN UNARMED COMBAT."

MAKOTO KUBOTA, AUTHOR OF *SUMO*

AUTHOR'S NOTE

Time spent at a Tokyo training stable showed me that there is more to sumo than first meets the eye. The feudal-style ranking system attaches honor to age and experience, and, to me, the experts appeared aloof. I realized that this behavior has developed over millennia as a result of the status given to fighters, and is one of the unique components that makes up the art of sumo. These unlikely athletes do have size on their side, but I was surprised at just how much power they are able to generate through technique too. A common training implement that I used while at the stable was a solid wooden pole, weighing perhaps half a ton, smoothed and varnished and half buried in the ground. Practitioners would slap this solid object repeatedly throughout the day to develop striking strength of titanic proportions.

◁ A WINNING MANEUVER
The sumo ring is called the "dohyo." Wins are decided when a player throws his opponent off balance, forcing him to touch the ground with anything other than the soles of his feet, or pushes him out of the ring.

BEHIND THE SCENES
SUMO WRESTLERS

THE ART OF SUMO and the wrestlers themselves enjoy a high degree of cultural importance in Japan, but their day-to-day lives remain, for the most part, shrouded in mystery. Here we look behind the scenes to shed some light on how these iconic figures live and work.

Sumo wrestlers (or "rikishi") maintain highly disciplined, almost cultlike lifestyles both inside and outside the training stable. Excursions into the outside world are rare, and sumos are expected to adhere to a strict code of behavior when in public. Rules of conduct are laid down by the Sumo Association and any breaches are punished with fines and/or suspension.

Life in the sumo stable is extremely hierarchical, with junior wrestlers—some as young as 13—having to do the "dirty work" of the stable, as well as cater to the needs of more senior wrestlers. To outsiders, the regime seems harsh and outdated, perhaps even brutal, but the rituals and values of sumo have evolved over hundreds of years and those involved take huge pride in their heritage and traditions.

Even the preparations before a bout have a strict routine. The sumo stadium has an east and a west wing and wrestlers do not meet their opponents until the match begins. First, the wrestlers change into their embroidered silk aprons, or "kesho-mawashi," for the ring-entering ceremony. They walk into the ring in procession from east and west and are introduced to the crowd one by one, in order of rank. After the ceremony they return to their dressing-rooms to prepare for their bout.

The famous prebout rituals performed by the wrestlers are derived from Shinto practice and are taken very seriously.

ENTRANCE CEREMONIES
The entrance ceremony is a showcase to introduce the fighters who will be performing in the evening's events. Typically, the wrestlers enter the ring and form a circle around the outside of the ring facing the audience. Then, in a synchronized movement, they turn inward to face each other, clap their hands, raise their kesho-mawashi slightly, and exit the ring.

THE DOHYO

The fighting arena, or "dohyo," is made from rice-straw bales on a large, square platform of clay covered by an even dusting of sand. A new dohyo is built for each tournament and the roof, which is decorated with colored tassels, closely resembles that of a Shinto shrine. The dohyo is considered a sacred place and is blessed by a Shinto priest every morning before a tournament.

THE YOBIDASHI

Regarded as the Sumo Association's "odd job" men, the yobidashi carry out a variety of tasks, including sweeping the ring, providing salt for the purification ceremony, and displaying sponsors' banners. They will often also bang a drum outside a match to attract spectators. One of the yobidashi's most important tasks is the "announcing," or calling the wrestlers to the ring to fight. As he does this, in keeping with tradition, he will hold a fan outstretched in front of him.

PRE-BOUT RITUALS

Before a fight, the wrestlers perform a complex and ancient ritual. First, they raise their legs and stomp down onto the ground to scare away demons. Some then sprinkle salt onto their bodies to ward off injury, but all throw salt into the ring to purify it. Water is sipped from a ladle passed to them by the last winner on their side, to transfer power and luck. On entering the ring the wrestlers crouch opposite each other and stretch out their hands, before bringing them back and placing them on their knees. This signifies that they are ready to fight.

BEFORE A BOUT

The scenes "backstage" on a sumo fight night are much like those of any other performance fighting art—except for the close attention paid to appearance. Since serious injuries are rare, the degree of nervous tension experienced by sumo fighters before a major bout may not be as intense as it is for other fighters, such as boxers. During long waits in the changing room, wrestlers have an opportunity to chat, stretch, check their clothes and hair, and even catch up with the news.

TIME OFF

Although young sumo fighters, for the most part, live a strict, regimented lifestyle, they do enjoy occasional time off from the training stable. They may visit family and friends, go shopping, swim, or play video games—much like any other men of their age. Golf, for example, is an extremely popular pastime in Japan, and is enjoyed by many sumo wrestlers.

"SUMO MAY SEEM ANACHRONISTIC, BUT THE VERY MODERN APPEAL OF THE SPORT INDICATES THAT IT IS NEITHER A RELIC NOR A NOVELTY"

WILL FERGUSON, AUTHOR

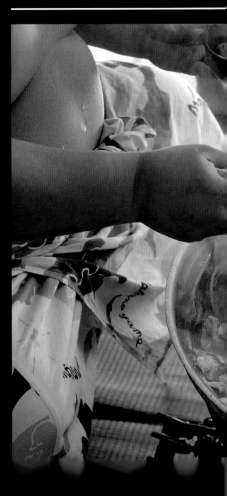

CELEBRITY STATUS

Sumo wrestlers are regarded as major celebrities in Japan. When leaving their camp for excursions to the cities, they wear traditional dress, which further differentiates them from the general public. They will often find themselves mobbed by fans eager for them to sign an autograph or pose for photographs.

IN TRAINING

Building strength and stamina, improving flexibility, and practicing throwing techniques are all part of a sumo's daily training regime. All schools have a sandpit in which to train, where young disciples spend time watching each other wrestling, analyzing moves, and offering advice on strategies.

MEALTIMES

Meals are an important part of the sumo training camp, and are usually prepared by one of the junior wrestlers. Massive, high-calorie, protein-rich stews of meat, tofu, vegetables, and rice—known as "chanko-nabe"—are consumed, along with various side dishes. Eating is a community affair and many sumos, in order to keep the weight on, take a long nap immediately after eating.

Judo

EXPLANATION
"THE GENTLE WAY" IN JAPANESE

DATE OF ORIGIN
LATE 19TH CENTURY

FOUNDER
KANO JIGORO

PLACE OF ORIGIN
JAPAN

Originally named kano jui-do by its founder, judo is based on several schools of jujutsu (see pp. 216–17), including the tenjin shinyo ryu, the kito ryu, and the fusen ryu. Jigoro's system was, in part, born of a strong desire to overcome the disadvantages of his small stature—judo emphasizes the technical study of leverage, which is paramount to the successful felling of opponents of greater stature.

Defensive maneuvers

The different stages of combat in judo include the standing and ground phase, and the guard and body scissors. Techniques include joint locks, chokes, and strangulation. As a form of self defense it is a close-quarter-combat art form, which is both practical and highly effective.

Although players are not allowed to strike or thrust into opponents during competition, these moves are necessary during "kata" (set forms). Due to its excellent grappling techniques, many mixed-martial-arts (see pp. 318–27) fighters use judo as a basis for their groundwork and offensive takedown strategies.

Throwing techniques

Unlike some other wrestling systems, the main principle for throwing an opponent in judo is not to kill, but to shock by smashing the body forcefully to the ground, after which a lock or stranglehold can be more easily applied and victory achieved.

There are four aspects to all throwing techniques. Off-balancing, known in Japanese as "kuzushi," is when a player aims to grab, pull, or

push his opponent, creating a split-second opportunity for forward or backward momentum and unbalancing. Body-positioning is vital during that moment; the player must move into or away from the opponent, preparing to unleash a sudden burst of power and utilize leverage from the ground to unbalance him or her. Next comes the execution, in which the player swiftly executes the chosen technique. The finisher is the application of the final move, whether a smashing into the ground or a follow-up technique, such as a stranglehold, a lock, or a choke.

JAPANESE SYMBOL
FOR JUDO

Evolution of rules

It is interesting to note that over the last century the rules have changed, reflecting the art's growing departure from its original samurai traditions and jujutsu origins. For example, in 1905 the rules stated that in order to effect a victory in a pinning or hold-down technique, it was necessary to hold an opponent down with both shoulder blades touching the ground for only two seconds—the time it would take, in real combat, for a victor to draw a weapon and effect a kill. Now a player must hold down an opponent for the time required to apply an effective barrage of strikes, should this be a real fist fight. The

scoring also differs in that points awarded are determined by how long the opponent is held down.

The points system

Penalties are awarded if a player uses an illegal technique or is inactive for too long, and fighting is stopped if a player falls out of the playing area.

There are four types of point. The "ippon" is a winning point awarded for a perfect throw, a hold of sufficient duration, or a submission. A "waza-ari" is a half-point, awarded for a good throw, or for a 20-second hold (if scored twice this is considered a full point, leading to a win). "Yuko" and "koka" are tiebreakers, awarded for a 15- or 10-second hold.

> "LEARN FROM OTHER PEOPLE'S MISTAKES. YOU MAY NOT LIVE LONG ENOUGH TO LEARN FROM YOUR OWN."
>
> KANO JIGORO

VLADIMIR PUTIN

Vladimir Putin, former President of Russia, is a judo enthusiast. At the age of 14 he began training in the Russian martial art of sambo (see p. 279), a self-defense system similar to aikido (see pp.238–39). He later switched to judo, winning many competitions in his hometown of Leningrad. He is best known for his "harai goshi," a sweeping hip throw. In the picture above he attends a masterclass conducted by his friend, Japanese judo coach Yasuhiro Yamashita.

KANO JIGORO

Born into a well-to-do family in 1860, Kano Jigoro's personal story sheds light on this popular sport. Small in stature, and bullied at school and college, he was unable to defend himself, despite studying jujutsu. At 18 he went to study with Fukuda Hacinosuke, a master of Tenjin shinyo-ryu, who favored technique training over kata. He later studied with a number of reputable masters, many of whom encouraged free practice. This, coupled with Kano's size, sowed the seeds for his system of judo.

◀ **IN COMPETITION**
Participants compete in the Men's 81 kg (178 lb) category during the Good Luck Beijing 2007 Judo Open. The event was held to test the venue for the 2008 Olympic Games.

◀ A MARK OF ACHIEVEMENT
It is a common misconception that the belt system (used to denote rank) is an ancient tradition—it actually dates from the 19th century. The term "black belt" is often used to describe a "master," but there are levels of black belt known as "dan" grades and, in many Japanese arts, very senior grades have belts of a different color.

Aikido

EXPLANATION
"THE WAY OF HARMONY"
IN JAPANESE

DATE OF ORIGIN
1925

FOUNDER
MOREHEI UESHIBA

PLACE OF ORIGIN
HOKKAIDO, JAPAN

The primary goal of aikido is to gain advantage by using an opponent's energy and momentum against him. The art places emphasis on the continuous flow of a combination of movements, and combines physical action with philosophical thought. On the physical side, aikido incorporates a number of locking maneuvers aimed at injuring joints, along with throwing techniques from jujutsu (see pp. 216–17). It draws technical knowledge from kenjutsu (see p. 219) and is influenced in varying degrees by other Japanese weapon-based systems.

Religious influence

The moral element of aikido is equally important. The name, which translates as "the way of harmony," describes the spirit in which training and fighting plays out. Its founder, Morehei Ueshiba, was influenced by the Omoto-kyu religion, which stresses the importance of finding utopia, and extending compassion even to those who do harm.

Early inspiration

Ueshiba's early experiences played a great part in the formation of aikido. As a child he was weak and sickly, so his father, a wealthy landowner,

encouraged him to take up physical sports, such as sumo wrestling and swimming. Ueshiba's grandfather had been a noted samurai, and the young Ueshiba grew up on stories of his great-grandfather's prowess. Tales of his heroism undoubtedly led Ueshiba to the study of Japanese martial arts. His desire to be strong and to protect himself and his family was further galvanized when he witnessed his father suffering a vicious beating at the hands of followers of an opposing politician.

Period of learning

During military service, Ueshiba received sporadic martial training, but in 1912, after moving to Hokkaido with his wife, he began to take his martial arts training to a new level. He traveled widely and studied with a number of renowned teachers, one of whom, Sokaku Takeba Sensei, opened his eyes to the budō. His short study under this master inspired him to look further into Japanese arts.

Throughout the 1920s and 30s Ueshiba taught his system under the name of aiki-jujutsu. This early version included a variety of "atemi," or strikes, aimed at vulnerable points on the body, and its approach to attacking and defending was less circular and flowing than in the later version of the system.

Divine knowledge

As Ueshiba grew in age and experience he became more spiritual. Many experts put the date of the founding of aikido as we know it today to 1925, following an incident in which an unarmed Ueshiba

Born in 1883, in Tanabe Wakayama, Japan, Ueshiba was the only son in a family of five children. Sometimes known by his title, "O'Sensei," or "Great Teacher," Ueshiba became proficient in a number of martial arts during his life, and many myths surround his prowess. Legend has it that he was able to evade a number of students attacking him simultaneously with swords, and that he could knock down opponents with the force of his shout.

defeated, yet did not harm, a naval officer armed with a wooden sword. Later, while walking in the garden, Ueshiba had a spiritual awakening. He said: "I was able to understand the whispering of birds and was clearly aware of the mind of God, the creator of the universe." Another spiritual experience came during World War II, when Ueshiba had a vision of the Great Spirit of Peace. Of this, he said: "The way of the warrior has been misunderstood. It is not a means to kill and destroy others. Those who seek to compete and better one another are making a terrible mistake. To smash, injure, or destroy is the worst thing a human can do. The real way of a warrior is to prevent such slaughter. It is the art of peace, the power of love."

A lasting legacy

Today, aikido is one of the most popular martial arts and is practiced all over the world. Devotees remember its founder as a profound man who transcended the limitations of the technical aspects of martial arts, instead incorporating rigid moral and philosophical elements into his art, which stressed harmony, compassion, and understanding, even in the face of aggression.

Hollywood action man Steven Seagal has built his career around his prowess in aikido. Before he became a movie star Seagal was an aikido instructor and was the first foreigner to own an aikido dojo in Japan. He has starred in numerous martial-arts and action movies, usually as an avenging hero with extraordinary fighting skills.

▼ ON THE FLOOR
A female student throws an instructor to the ground during an exhibition show, held to promote the art of aikido.

"IN TRUE BUDO THERE IS NO ENEMY OR OPPONENT. TRUE BUDO IS TO BECOME ONE WITH THE UNIVERSE, NOT TRAIN TO BECOME POWERFUL OR TO THROW DOWN SOME OPPONENT."

MORIHEI UESHIBA

合氣道

Taiho-jutsu

EXPLANATION
"ARRESTING ART" IN JAPANESE

DATE OF ORIGIN
1947

FOUNDER
NO KNOWN FOUNDER

PLACE OF ORIGIN
JAPAN

Until very recently, taiho-jutsu was practiced exclusively by police officers in Japan, the US, and the UK. It is a form of jujutsu (see p. 216–17) that utilizes a combination of restraining and pain-compliance techniques. Also included in the training are disarming techniques, the use of a baton, handcuffs, and other police weapons, and verbal guidance.

Evolution of style

Alan Cunningham is a key teacher in the US, and is to a great extent responsible for the system's recent growth. Brian Eustace is another key exponent in the West: he teaches the taiho-jutsu system to police forces within the UK.

Taiho-jutsu is now the martial art of choice among many airline security agencies and is also used by a growing number of bodyguards.

The system has undergone numerous changes since its instigation in 1947, the year in which the first official manual of the art was produced. For example, in the early days, officers in Japan were taught to use a five-foot-long staff known as the "jo." However, in 1966, they adopted the extending baton, called the "tokushu keibo." The taiho-jutsu teaching curriculum has been adapted in response to changes such as these.

▼ TOKYO POLICE
Students at Tokyo's Police Academy train in taiho-jutsu mob-control tactics, using old-style fixed batons.

Shorinji Kempo

EXPLANATION
"SHAOLIN LAW OF THE FIST" IN JAPANESE

DATE OF ORIGIN
1947

FOUNDER
DOSHIN SO

PLACE OF ORIGIN
JAPAN

Designed to develop and strengthen mind, body, and spirit, the art of shorinji kempo is based on the belief that everyone has the potential to develop in every direction. Inspired by a variety of martial arts, it includes both hard and soft techniques, offensive and defensive grappling, striking, kicking, and throwing.

Mind control

A pattern of movements known as "hokei" is practiced during free fighting. The goal is to bring order to chaos—chaos being the attacker's inability to control his or her mind, leading to an act of aggression, and order being the defender's ability to bring about a peaceful conclusion through the application of nonlethal self-defense techniques.

Isshin Ryu

EXPLANATION
"ONE HEART METHOD" IN JAPANESE

DATE OF ORIGIN
DATE UNKNOWN

FOUNDER
SHIMABUKU TATSUO

PLACE OF ORIGIN
OKINAWA

This style of Okinawan karate generally includes 14 "kata" or set forms; eight of which are performed empty handed, two with the "sai" (three-pronged weapon), three with the "bo" (staff), and one with the "tonfa" (baton).

Building strength

An unusual aspect of the art is iron-body training, which is aimed at increasing a person's ability to withstand physical punishment. This includes breathing techniques and resistance-based exercises. Many practitioners use the "makiwara," a padded post of solid wood, which is repeatedly struck with the closed fist to develop punching techniques.

Naginatajutsu

EXPLANATION
"ART OF THE NAGINATA"
IN JAPANESE

DATE OF ORIGIN
UNKNOWN

FOUNDER
NO KNOWN FOUNDER

PLACE OF ORIGIN
JAPAN

The naginata, a long pole with a blade at one end, is primarily associated with female samurai. It is often used in combination with the "tanto," a traditional Japanese dagger.

Naginatajutsu competitions take place in Japan regularly. Most are held at high school and college level with students who often have little or no previous martial-arts training, but are interested in the female combat arts.

Weapon development

Although the origins of the weapon are unclear, some experts believe that it may have come about as a result of Japanese warriors altering the design of the Chinese halberd, an infantry weapon that is similar in nature but with a slightly wider blade. Others believe that it developed independently as a modified farming implement. The theory is that samurais returning home from battle found that a longer weapon, fitted with a blade similar to that of a samurai sword, was useful for fighting against cavalrymen, since the length kept the fighter at a reasonable distance from the horse.

▼ SPECTACULAR DISPLAY
Women wearing traditional Japanese dress wield their weapons during an outdoor demonstration of naginatajutsu.

Shintaido

EXPLANATION
"NEW BODY WAY" IN JAPANESE

DATE OF ORIGIN
1965

FOUNDER
HIROYUKI AOKI

PLACE OF ORIGIN
JAPAN

Unlike competitive fighting arts, shintaido is a system of movement based on the principles of martial arts and contemporary performing arts. Its underlying philosophy is peace, harmony, cooperation, and the understanding of the individual and his or her place in nature.

During the 1960s, its founder, Hiroyuki Aoki, formed a group of around 30 people, including some of Japan's top martial-arts instructors, as well as musicians, actors, and artists of all ages, and set about creating his new art.

Pushing the boundaries

Without knowing exactly what they were looking for, the group, known as "ratutenkai" or "meeting of optimists," practiced together, testing the limits of physical and psychological strength. Out of that movement, shintaido was born, incorporating elements of sword work, and martial and performance arts, alongside a number of esoteric practices.

The system is famed for its freezing waterfall training. During the winter participants endure this regime for up to 15 minutes, often experiencing the early stages of hypothermia, which is said to lead to an awakening of spirituality and the development of a sixth sense.

HIROYUKI AOKI

Hiroyuki Aoki was born in Yokahama, Japan, in 1936. He was an actor, painter, and 5th-degree black-belt master (the highest level) of shotokai karate. A devout Christian, in 1965 he set out to create a new martial art designed to encourage peace and communication, and provide a new way to experience nature and the spiritual world.

"THE UNKNOWN WORLD THAT BEGINS AT THE END OF OUR PSYCHOLOGICAL STRENGTH"

HIROYUKI AOKI

Taido

EXPLANATION
"WAY OF THE BODY"
IN JAPANESE
DATE OF ORIGIN
1965
FOUNDER
SEIKEN SHUKUMINE
PLACE OF ORIGIN
JAPAN

Similar to Okinawan karate (see p. 202), this codified fighting art introduced a number of innovative techniques, such as spinning and twisting movements and complex footwork moves.

There are five types of body movement: "ten" involves rolling and tumbling; "nen" is a horizontal spinning movement; "hen" is falling while changing the body's axis; "un" is an ascending or descending movement; and "sen" involves vertical spinning.

Traditional values
Seiken Shukumine believed that his system would benefit both the self and society. There are five principles of the art, which are, in brief: follow the system's precepts and you cannot go wrong; be composed, body and mind as one; with the right spirit you will never fear combat; be adaptable and maintain your physical freedom; having the right state of mind will help you to avoid confusion.

Ready for anything
Students learn to anticipate the flow of multiple opponents' movements and focus on an offensive strategy to neutralize any threats.

▼ **COMPETITIVE BOUT**
A fighter competes in a 30-second bout in front of a judge, who award points based on the range and effectiveness of her techniques.

Kenpo Kai

EXPLANATION
"WAY OF THE GATHERED FIST"
IN JAPANESE
DATE OF ORIGIN
UNKNOWN
FOUNDER
TAWADA ISHIZAKA
PLACE OF ORIGIN
JAPAN

Although considered to be a traditional form of Japanese karate, kenpo kai is actually based closely on Shaolin kung fu, known as "chuan fa" (see p. 57). Its origins are disputed, but legend states that a Chinese family took in a Japanese traveler named Tawada Ishizaka, who ended up staying with them for 20 years, learning the system of Shaolin. On his return to Japan he codified the system and handed its methods down through later generations of his family.

New and old
A number of changes have taken place through the generations, most notably in the late 1960s when two members of Ishizaka's family, Kazuo and Sotoki both traveled back to Shanghai to study with the surviving members of the original Chinese family. On their return to Japan they reintroduced a number of forms and techniques that had been lost as the system had evolved within Japan.

Nanbudo

EXPLANATION
"WAY OF NANBU" IN JAPANESE
DATE OF ORIGIN
1978
FOUNDER
YOSHINAO NANBU
PLACE OF ORIGIN
JAPAN

A relatively new, hybrid martial art, nanbudo uses many techniques that are similar to those found in karate, judo, and aikido (see pp. 202–03, 234–235, 238–239). It was founded by former karate champion, Yoshinao Nanbu, a shito-ryu and shukokai (see p. 206) practitioner. In the early 1970s, Nanbu had developed sankukai,— a similar form of karate—but later withdrew from both his system, and the entire world of martial arts, having become disillusioned with the competition and politics involved.

After moving to France his passion for the arts of his native country was rekindled, and in 1978 he developed the new system of nanbudo. It is considered to be a holistic method of self defense, and, although many of the techniques are based on his early karate career, he also incorporated elements of his own philosophy.

Physical and mental health
The art is divided into four major aspects, "kata," "randori," "ju," and "ki." Basic training in kata—the set forms or patterns—is highly stylized, and bears little resemblance to fighting techniques. There are three levels of kata: basic, advanced, and superior, and, although most techniques are performed unarmed, the system does include training with a six-foot bo staff and a "bokken" (wooden training sword).

In common with the kata of other systems, there are also a number of hidden methods that students are encouraged to discover and develop themselves through the rigorous and repetitive perfection of its moves.

Randori is a formalized set of techniques in which attacker and defender engage in a set of prearranged movements, such as punches and kicks, in order to develop good timing and discipline, and correct distancing.

Ju is a prefix added to other elements of the art, most commonly "jurandori," and indicates a competitive element. Rather than being the practice of movement for movement's sake, in jurandori the set drills between two players are judged on technical criteria.

The last element of the system is ki, which in this system is described as a way of holistically developing the body and physique, allowing ki, or chi—believed by many cultures to be a vital life force—to flow freely through the body. The goal is to enhance physical well-being and prevent disease.

❯ **IN TUNE WITH NATURE**
A group of nanbudo practitioners stand on a beach, facing the sea, to perform kata. The movements and patterns in nature are an important element of the system.

Genbukan

EXPLANATION
"THE PLACE THAT NURTURES THE PROFESSIONAL MARTIAL ARTIST" IN JAPANESE
DATE OF ORIGIN
1984
FOUNDER
SHOTO TANEMURA
PLACE OF ORIGIN
JAPAN

A system of Japanese martial arts divided into 36 categories, genbuken is sometimes called the "ninja sanjurokkei" (sanjurokkei being the Japanese word for "thirty-six").

Shoto Tanemura is credited as being the founder of the system, which he formalized in 1984. A descendant of an old and respected samurai family with roots tracing back to the imperial family of Japan, Tanemura began his training in armed and unarmed techniques at the age of nine. His given name was Tsunehisa, but he later took the name "shoto," meaning "law of the sword."

Armed and unarmed combat

Genbuken focuses on a number of ninjalike skills and includes the study of taijutsu, bojutsu (see p. 219) and the use of traditional weapons.

The unarmed aspects of the art include striking, blocking, kicking, and punching, alongside a number of joint-manipulation and throwing methods. Chokes are a favorite of the system as are nerve and pressure-point attacks and bone breaks.

Weapons grades

There is a ranking system for weapons training that follows a progressive system of colored belts and includes the 10th-dan grading system, which ranks black-belt holders. Those of 4th dan or above are permitted to open schools.

> "IF A HUMAN WHO HAS ACHIEVED GREATNESS DESTROYS HIS LIFE WITH HATE OR ENVY, OR SIMPLY BY FOLLOWING AN EVIL PATH, HE DAMAGES MUCH MORE THAN JUST HIMSELF."
>
> SHOTO TANEMURA

Jinenkan

EXPLANATION
"HALL OF NATURE" IN JAPANESE
DATE OF ORIGIN
1996
FOUNDER
FUMIO MANAKA
PLACE OF ORIGIN
JAPAN

A hybrid system, set up in 1996 by Fumio Manaka, jinenkan is influenced by taijutsu, the unarmed combat of ninjutsu (see pp. 210–211), and the weapons training that Manaka studied under the tutorage of the feted Japanese ninja Masaaki Hatsumi.

Military influence

Manaka spent 39 years in the military, and this training played a part in the formation of jinenkan. Time spent away from his tutor, during which he explored and developed simple techniques, also influenced his system, which stresses the importance of understanding and mastering the basics.

Nature's way

After 37 years studying ninjutsu, he established his own organization, taking on the name "Unsui," meaning "cloud and water." The philosophy of flowing freely informs much of the system, and the symbol of the school has a three-layered cloud, three streams, and the three characters that make up the name "jinenkan," totaling nine objects. The number nine has a mystical meaning in Japanese culture.

∧ **SYMBOLIC LOGO**
"Clouds and water" is a Buddhist term that refers to an itinerant monk who is an independent seeker of enlightenment.

FUMIO MANAKA

Fumio Manaka began training in martial arts at the age of 14 and holds certificates of mastery in a number of the arts, and formal training in many others. He founded jinenkan in 1996 with the goal of allowing students to study the old martial ways (the "Kobudo") of Japan unhindered under his tutelage. He has spent much time in Europe and the United States, in order to raise the level of training in these areas.

EUROPE

EUROPE

THE SECOND-SMALLEST CONTINENT IN THE WORLD, Europe contains a largely wealthy and extremely diverse community of cultures. In most peoples' minds, it is probably not a continent particularly associated with indigenous martial arts. However, Europe has a long and fascinating martial-art history. As power-bases among civilizations came and went—often as a result of violent conflict and large-scale warfare—martial arts developed as a response to the environment in which warriors found themselves.

THE TERM "MARTIAL ART" comes from Latin—it means "the arts of Mars," after the Roman god of war—and was coined to celebrate the martial prowess Roman gladiators displayed during their bloody and brutal battles in the arena. And although most popular Western indigenous martial-art forms have gone on to become sports—such as fencing and many forms of boxing (see pp. 268–69, 256–63)—

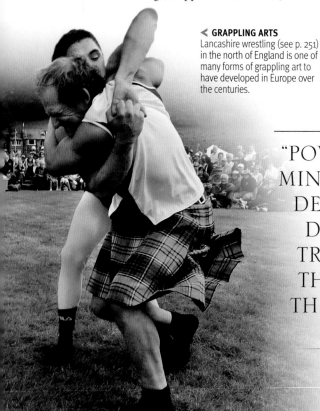

◄ **GRAPPLING ARTS**
Lancashire wrestling (see p. 251) in the north of England is one of many forms of grappling art to have developed in Europe over the centuries.

they really only represent the tip of the iceberg. The European tradition of martial arts is actually as rich and engaging as that found in Asia, and many European art forms offer their practitioners enhanced self-development capabilities.

A founding father

The best-known European martial art is pankration (see p. 276), an unarmed combat technique. A combination of Greek boxing, wrestling, and grappling, it focused on the use of knees, elbows, kicks, punches, and chopping movements, alongside joint-locks and choke-holds. It was a brutal, competitive sport and, although eye-gouging and biting were forbidden,

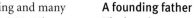

"POWER IS CREATED IN THE MIND, ROOTED IN THE FEET, DEVELOPED IN THE LEGS, DIRECTED BY THE HIPS, TRANSFERRED THROUGH THE TORSO, FOCUSED IN THE FEET OR HANDS, AND FELT IN THE SPIRIT."

UNKNOWN

REGION AT A GLANCE

1 MARTIAL ARTS
The expression "martial arts" has been used since Roman times. It means "the arts of Mars" in Latin and was used to describe the prowess of gladiators in the arena.

2 PANKRATION
The founding father of many forms of wrestling around the world, this martial art from Ancient Greece bears a close resemblance to today's mixed martial arts (see pp. 318–27).

3 ANCIENT SELF-DEFENSE
Archeological evidence suggests that even the Ancient Romans were conscious of the need to defend themselves properly, and they learned various forms of self-defense.

4 INDIGENOUS INFLUENCES
From ancient Celtic and Germanic warrior practices to the traditional fighting arts of wandering shepherds, indigenous arts have done much to shape the European martial-arts scene.

5 MOVING FORWARD
In the 13th century, technological advances and enhanced metal-forging techniques saw an influx of improved weaponry and armor-making techniques.

6 RELIGIOUS CONNECTIONS
As is the case in Asia, many Christian monks were highly proficient in martial arts, both to improve their physical fitness and to defend their churches and their religious beliefs.

7 RICH LITERARY HERITAGE
The existence of centuries-old manuscripts dating back to the 14th century means that many ancient martial arts are still practiced in their original form today.

8 CHANGING TIMES
The introduction of firearms in the 17th century changed the face of the European martial-arts scene forever. As a result, what were once solely battlefield arts evolved into means of self-defense and self-development.

◀ **CLOSE RELATIONS**
The French sport of savate is said to have evolved from a collection of fighting techniques used by sailors, criminals, and soldiers. It bears a close resemblance to the Thai sport of muay Thai (see pp. 158–65).

7

8

MAP OF EUROPE

▼ **NOT SIMPLY ONE-WAY TRAFFIC**
As is the case with many continents, the European martial-art scene has been greatly influenced by the influx of immigrants and philosophies from the East. But the continent has also added to the global martial-arts mix: some of its wrestling styles were exported to other continents and went on to thrive.

KEY

▶ **Immigrants** to the US took elements of catch wrestling with them, which led to the founding of collegiate wrestling.

▶ **Chinese martial arts** became widely practiced in Europe.

▶ **Japanese martial arts** spread widely throughout Europe.

▶ **Roman trading** in Southeast Asia led to a cross-fertilization of ideas.

▶ **Trade with Africa** introduced Europeans to African wrestling arts.

▶ **16th-century** Spanish conquistadors taught sword skills to the Filipinos.

▶ **Early Greek** wrestling styles had an influence throughout Europe.

REYKJAVIK
ICELAND

NORWAY
SWEDEN
FINLAND
OSLO
HELSINKI
St. Petersburg
STOCKHOLM
RUSSIAN FEDERATION
ESTONIA
SCOTLAND
NORTHERN IRELAND
EDINBURGH
LATVIA
MOSCOW
IRELAND
UNITED KINGDOM
North Sea
DENMARK
LITHUANIA
DUBLIN
WALES
ENGLAND
LONDON
NETHERLANDS
BERLIN
BELARUS
BELGIUM
GERMANY
WARSAW
ATLANTIC OCEAN
PARIS
LUXEMBOURG
POLAND
KIEV
Bay of Biscay
FRANCE
CZECH REPUBLIC
UKRAINE
VIENNA
SLOVAKIA
SWITZERLAND
AUSTRIA
BUDAPEST
MOLDOVA
PORTUGAL
SLOVENIA
HUNGARY
MADRID
CROATIA
ROMANIA
LISBON
ITALY
BOSNIA & HERZEGOVINA
Black Sea
SPAIN
Corsica
SERBIA
ROME
MONTENEGRO
Sardinia
KOSOVO
BULGARIA
MACEDONIA
ISTANBUL
ALBANIA
TURKEY
MOROCCO
GREECE
Sicily
ATHENS
anary lands
Mediterranean Sea
TUNISIA
ALGERIA
LIBYA
EGYPT

pretty much anything else was acceptable. The goal of the game was to force an opponent to submit and, in many ways, this 2,000-year-old art bears a striking resemblance to the modern mixed martial arts (see pp. 318–27) and ultimate fighting championship movements prevalent in martial arts today.

Pankration was so effective that the young Alexander the Great, on his conquest to dominate the world, trained his troops rigorously in pankration for close-quarter, hand-to-hand battle with the enemy, along with the use of the spear, the shield, and the sword. His conquest of Asia would certainly have led to a cross-fertilization of fighting techniques between the Greek warriors and the indigenous civilizations with whom they came into contact.

Martial arts were also popular in ancient Rome, not only as a gladiatorial sport but also among civilians of many different social classes, who would engage in knife-fighting for self-defense. Highly codified fighting systems evolved as a result of this fashion and, as the Roman Empire went into decline, other indigenous martial arts started to prosper: records of Germanic and Celtic warrior practices, for example, show detailed training methods and a complex repertoire of movements, in addition to alternative philosophical beliefs.

17TH-CENTURY DAGGER

Moving with the times

The knights of the Middle Ages were the romanticized ideal and embodiment of martial arts and chivalry. They developed a staggering array of weapons for combat, training, and sport, such as those used in jousting (see pp. 266–67). Technological advances and improved metal-forging techniques during this period saw drastic improvements in armor, some of which was so well crafted that the United States' space agency, NASA, still studies medieval plate-armor design when it develops new spacesuits today.

Martial arts and religion

Christian monks have a close connection with European martial-art traditions, much as Buddhist or Daoist monks influenced Asian martial arts. In the 13th century, Germanic monks were well known for practicing martial arts as a sport, a pastime, as a means of improving their fitness, and so that they could defend both their churches and their religious beliefs. Some Western monks were so proficient in unarmed wrestling matches that even knights were often unwilling to challenge them through fear of losing face. If

> ## "WITHOUT KNOWLEDGE, SKILL CANNOT BE FOCUSED. WITHOUT SKILL, STRENGTH CANNOT BE BROUGHT TO BEAR, AND WITHOUT STRENGTH, KNOWLEDGE MAY NOT BE APPLIED."
>
> ALEXANDER THE GREAT'S CHIEF PHYSICIAN

▼ TRADITIONAL ALPINE SPORT
Spectators watch the action in three rinks during the annual Schwing- und Alperfest (the "Swinging and Alps Resident Festival") on the Stoos Mountain in central Switzerland. The Alpine wrestling sport of schwingen (see p. 273) has been practiced since the 13th century.

Eastern European martial arts

Russia has also had a long history of martial-arts practice, both in unarmed wrestling and in weapons-based arts. Some of these arts were so effective that, when Peter the Great assumed power in 1682, one of his first acts of office was to ban stick fighting among the peasants. Banning the practice of martial arts has been a common occurrence throughout the history of many of the world's cultures and was used as a tactic to thwart any possibility of warrior clans challenging the government or power-base in authority at the time.

Change of direction

The biggest change to the face of European martial arts, however, came during the late 1600s with the advent of firearms. This naturally led to a decline in the practice of unarmed martial arts and those employing edged weapons. This technological advancement quickly swept the world and led to an unprecedented transmutation of combat arts. As a result, the emphasis of martial arts shifted more toward self-defense and self-development, as opposed to the previous, more brutal emphasis on battlefield killing.

⋀ THUMBS UP OR THUMBS DOWN?
Jean-Leon Gerome's 1872 painting *Pollice Verso* ("thumbs down") depicts a gladiator standing over his conquered opponent waiting for further orders from the emperor. The painting was the immediate source of the thumbs-down gesture in popular culture.

⋗ MAJOR GLOBAL MARTIAL ART INFLUENCE
Before embarking on his conquest of the ancient world, Alexander the Great trained his troops in pankration (see p. 276). The ancient Greek art has gone on to influence many of the world's grappling martial arts.

⋁ EASTERN TRADITIONS
Russia has a long history of unarmed wrestling arts. Sambo (see p. 279) remains one of the four forms of amateur wrestling practiced internationally today.

challenged by monks, many knights would only engage them in weapons fighting, as traditionally a knight's sword skills were second to none.

Literary resources

Many quality publications, dating back centuries, can be found describing the techniques, philosophy, and tactics of ancient European martial arts. Fabian von Auerswald produced a fascinating illustrated manual in the 1500s, which describes, in good detail, joint-locking techniques, throwing methods, and pin holds, alongside ground grappling and other wrestling tactics.

One of the most famous literary sources, the *Collecteanea*, first published in 1509 by master of arms Pietro Monte, is a body of literature on weapons, mounted fighting, and wrestling. The work outlines the importance of physical fitness in relation to being an effective warrior. The book also describes fighting tactics and the underlying philosophy of exploiting vulnerable areas and openings in the opponent's guard and attack—similar to the philosophies found in Asian martial arts.

An illustrated guide written by Johann Georg Paschen in 1659, *Vollstandiges Ring-Buch*, describes martial-art techniques such as parrying, boxing-like punches, arm locks, and finger jabs, along with submission holds, chokes, and techniques for countering and disarming assailants with edged weapons.

Bataireacht

EXPLANATION
"STICK FIGHTING" IN GAELIC

DATE OF ORIGIN
17TH CENTURY

FOUNDER
NO KNOWN FOUNDER

PLACE OF ORIGIN
IRELAND

Also commonly known as "bata," bataireacht is a traditional stick-fighting martial art originating in Ireland. The term "bata" refers to the primary weapon, the stick—a cudgel-like instrument made from oak, blackthorn, or ash wood. Bata's exact origins are unclear, although many believe it evolved out of the Irish fighters' use of the long and short spear. The three basic sticks used in the art are the long, medium, and short, some of which have a knob of iron at one end, adding weight to the striking area.

Born out of necessity

The art form was commonly practiced during the 18th and 19th centuries to settle scores among Irish men after the 17th-century ban by the British on weapon-carrying saw fighting with a cane or walking stick become a practicality.

Although scant written records of training methodology exist, many of the art's modern practitioners have pieced together what they do know and have created a system that is taught today to great effect.

▷ BADGE OF HONOR
For generations of Irishmen, the bata was a symbol of their courage, martial arts prowess, and willingness to fight for their honor.

Scottish Back Hold

EXPLANATION
SCOTTISH WRESTLING

DATE OF ORIGIN
7TH AND 8TH CENTURIES

FOUNDER
NO KNOWN FOUNDER

PLACE OF ORIGIN
SCOTLAND

Scottish back hold is an ancient wrestling style from Scotland said to have been the fighting style used by the MacGregor clan, who counted Rob Roy among their number. Wrestlers aim to hold their opponent's waist at the back, with the right hand under the opponent's left arm and the chin resting on the opposite shoulder.

Bouts are usually the best of five falls, and wins are awarded when a player throws his opponent so that any part of his body, other than his feet, make contact with the ground.

▽ CONTINUED POPULARITY
Bouts of Scottish back hold are won when a practitioner manages to throw his opponent to the ground.

Lancashire Wrestling

EXPLANATION
N/A

DATE OF ORIGIN
INDIGENOUS ART

FOUNDER
NO KNOWN FOUNDER

PLACE OF ORIGIN
LANCASHIRE, ENGLAND

An extremely violent form of wrestling in which only the deliberate breaking of bones is prohibited, Lancashire wrestling is considered to be the founding art of catch wrestling (see right) and both professional and amateur wrestling.

The style probably evolved out of matches that took place during the 350-year Roman occupation of Britain; the Romans felt the men of Albion (the Roman name for Britain) were rough and did not respect the rules. One of the style's features was that pins (whereby a wrestler holds his opponent to the ground for a prescribed period of time) were not deemed effective finishing techniques—because they relied on the discretion of the referee—so forcing an opponent to submit became the norm.

Only victory matters

Matches were always on a winner-takes-all basis and any money was given to the overall champion. Matches would typically start with players standing about 1½ ft (0.5 m) apart, facing each other, hands straight out and elbows bent in a typical wrestling posture. From here short grips, takedowns, and tussles were employed. Once on the floor, the grapplers constantly moved around trying to apply a hold, a lock, or a choke, with waist holds and throws common.

There were no rounds and no breaks and the fight would typically continue until one of the fighters submitted. Given that matches could last for long periods of time, training for Lancashire wrestling placed an emphasis on physical fitness and conditioning.

◀ **STRICTLY FOR MEN ONLY**
Two wrestlers take part in a Lancashire wrestling bout at the Grasmere Lakeland Sports and Show in the Lake District, England.

Cornish Wrestling

EXPLANATION
N/A

DATE OF ORIGIN
EARLY 15TH CENTURY

FOUNDER
NO KNOWN FOUNDER

PLACE OF ORIGIN
CORNWALL, ENGLAND

Similar to judo (see pp. 234–35), the object of Cornish wrestling is to throw an opponent flat onto his back. The sport achieved its greatest popularity in Cornwall, England, where, in the local dialect, the art is known as "wrasslin."

The Cornish Wrestling Association was formed in 1923 to standardize the sport's rules, which state that the grabbing or breaking of fingers is forbidden and that players are not allowed to grab their opponent's legs, or indeed any part of the body below the waist. A pure, four-pin throw—in which the player throws his opponent so that both shoulder blades and buttocks hit the ground at the same time—is the classic winning technique.

Cornish wrestling bouts can still be seen in the south of England—and in some European countries—demonstrated at local fairs. The most well-known display of the sport takes place every year at the Royal Cornwall Agricultural Show. A feature of the system is that players often swear an oath before the match begins, usually in the Cornish dialect.

◀ **CLASSIC HOLD**
The engraving shows two Cornish wrestlers demonstrating the "inside lock" or "click" hold.

> "ON MY HONOR AND THE HONOR OF MY COUNTRY, I SWEAR TO WRESTLE WITHOUT TREACHERY OR BRUTALITY."
>
> PART OF THE OATH SWORN BY CORNISH WRESTLERS BEFORE A BOUT

Catch Wrestling

EXPLANATION
FROM "CATCH AS CATCH CAN"

DATE OF ORIGIN
19TH CENTURY

FOUNDER
NO KNOWN FOUNDER

PLACE OF ORIGIN
ENGLAND

Catch wrestling is derived from the Lancashire term "catch as catch can," meaning to "hold" an opponent, which was a forbidden rule in the Greco-Roman form of wrestling popular during the Roman occupation of Britain. Catch players typically win a match through submission or a pin down, and matches are usually determined by who wins two out of three bouts.

Notable practitioners

Catch wrestling has enjoyed much popularity in the western world, with Abraham Lincoln, George Washington, and Teddy Roosevelt all notable former catch wrestlers.

Although the original form of the art does not involve any strikes or kicks, it is believed to have been a major influence on today's mixed martial arts movements. The mixed wrestling matches staged during the 20th century (particularly in the 1920s) spurred much legend, with the cross-cultural clashes between Japanese judo players and American wrestlers catching the public's imagination. The art also had a significant influence on the evolution of international mixed martial arts competitions (see pp. 318–27).

▼ **GOING FOR THE KILL**
The wrestler on the right is close to victory after executing a perfect double thigh pick-up on his opponent.

Quarterstaff

EXPLANATION
ENGLISH STICK FIGHTING

DATE OF ORIGIN
16TH CENTURY

FOUNDER
NO KNOWN FOUNDER

PLACE OF ORIGIN
ENGLAND

This traditional English stick-fighting art uses a weapon known as the "quarterstaff"—a hard, wooden staff that sometimes has a reinforced metal tip. It is possible the name evolved because the primary weapon was a staff and, when fighting, was typically held with the right hand in the middle and the left hand a quarter of the way from the end—hence "quarter staff." However, a more probable theory is that the name refers to a fight settled without the use of a lethal sword or knife. In medieval English, "quarter"—

meaning to give mercy—may have referred to the act of pardoning an opponent by not killing him and using the staff as a response to an insult instead of the deadly sword. Typically made from oak, hazel, or ash, they ranged from 6–9 ft (1.8–2.7 m) in length and would have been employed in swinging, arching actions, and poking thrusts.

Easily adaptable

Training was practical and, once mastered, practitioners could utilize a range of improvised weapons in offense and defense, easily adapting the skills they had learned to help effect victory in battle. Most famously used as the favorite weapon and training method of Little John, one of the followers of the legendary Robin Hood, the art was adapted and taught in the late 1800s at Aldershot Military Training School and continued in the early part of the 20th century, when it was simplified and taught as a sport for instilling confidence into young Boy Scouts in England.

▼ **ON THE SMALL SCREEN**
Quarterstaff's most famous practitioner was Little John, one of Robin Hood's men, here portrayed by Clive Mantle (left) during BBC's 1986 television series, *Robin of Sherwood*.

▲ **KEEPING BARTITSU ALIVE**
Thanks to the efforts of numerous teachers, the Victorian martial art of bartitsu is alive and well in the 21st century.

Bartitsu

EXPLANATION
A MIX OF "BARTON-WRIGHT" AND "JUJUTSU"

DATE OF ORIGIN
1898

FOUNDER
E. W. BARTON-WRIGHT

PLACE OF ORIGIN
ENGLAND

Bartitsu is an English martial art founded by E. W. Barton-Wright; the name being a mix of his name and jujutsu (see pp. 216–17). Barton-Wright had studied jujutsu in Japan and, on returning to England in 1898, codified the system and described his new science of self-defense in the following manner: "Bartitsu … comprises not only boxing but also the use of the stick, feet, and a tricky style of Japanese wrestling in which weight and strength play only a very minor part."

Instant attraction

The art quickly caught on for three main reasons: first, there was an increased interest in the Orient; second, at the turn of the century, physical culture had become a popular pastime among many who realized that the Industrial Revolution had led to a decline in the physical health of the sedentary middle and upper classes; and third, there was among the popular media a rising interest in street violence. Newspapers of the time noted that stories about violence, wars, and street crime led to an increase in sales figures. The upshot of the glut of stories, though, was a widespread fear that an epidemic of violence was burgeoning on the streets of England.

E. W. BARTON-WRIGHT

E. W. Barton-Wright led an interesting and colorful life. Born in 1860 in India to a Scottish mother and a northern-English father, he spent the majority of his youth following his father, a railroad engineer, around the world as he moved from job to job. While in Japan, Barton-Wright studied jujutsu and it is likely he also learned judo from Kano Jigoro—the art's founder—during his time there, before returning to England and codifying bartitsu in 1898.

Defendu

EXPLANATION
N/A
DATE OF ORIGIN
1926
FOUNDER
WILLIAM E. FAIRBAIRN

PLACE OF ORIGIN
ENGLAND

Defendu is a close-quarter, hand-to-hand combat system regarded as a systemized method of ending physical confrontation quickly. Englishman William E. Fairbairn borrowed heavily from his training in judo (see p. 234–35) at the famed Kodokan School in Tokyo and added many techniques from jujutsu (see pp. 216–17) and Chinese martial arts. He also incorporated the hand-to-hand fighting techniques he learned while serving with the Shanghai Municipal Police in China.

Evolution of defendu

In 1926 Fairbairn published a book about his methods of defendu, but later modified and refined it into a system known as "Close-Quarter Combat," which he taught to Allied forces in World War II. This second system focused less on restraining techniques and holds, and more on using lethal techniques to end conflict immediately.

Jieishudan

EXPLANATION
"MEASURES TO DEFEND ONESELF" IN JAPANESE
DATE OF ORIGIN
EARLY 1980s
FOUNDER
IAN ZEFF

PLACE OF ORIGIN
ENGLAND

Jieishudan is a UK-based hybrid martial art employing boxing, grappling, and ground-fighting techniques. Developed in the early 1980s, it is an unstructured, nonprofit-making organization that teaches self-defense at youth clubs and is aimed at teenagers who want to learn how to defend themselves and improve their physical health.

In a state of development

It is a constantly evolving system that contains no "katas" (set forms or patterns of movements) or uniform. Sparring is encouraged alongside work on boxing-style bags and physical exercise. Some defenses against knives, sticks, and improvised weapons are taught, and there is a recognized grading system. Practitioners will typically begin with a kick followed by a couple of punches before going to the ground and engaging in a grappling match.

Warrior Wing Chun

EXPLANATION
WARRIOR-STYLE WING CHUN
DATE OF ORIGIN
1990s
FOUNDER
ADRIAN RHODES

PLACE OF ORIGIN
ENGLAND

▼ **DIRECT AND EFFICIENT**
Warrior wing chun practitioners execute a thrusting, darting-finger move known as the "biu jee."

Warrior wing chun is a hybrid martial art that resembles the wing chun system (see pp. 122–23), and also includes a number of locks, holds, and restraining techniques, improvised weapon-disarming, and psychological tactics aimed at providing an enhanced ability to deal with fear during combat.

Adding to the mix

The system's originator, Adrian Rhodes, added boxing techniques and non-lethal compliance methods along with the directness and efficiency-conscious basis of traditional wing chun, and applied the new art while working as a doorman in the north of England.

Sparring between practitioners often takes place in a boxing ring and the system is known for its effective chokeholds that often render opponents unconscious. The "Japanese hold" is a hybrid choke technique, which, once applied, is extremely difficult to escape from and often ends the conflict decisively.

> "KNOW YOURSELF AND YOUR OPPONENT, AND YOU WILL ALWAYS WIN."
>
> CHINESE PROVERB

Jogo Do Pau

EXPLANATION
"GAME OF THE STICK"
IN PORTUGUESE

DATE OF ORIGIN
C. 15TH CENTURY

FOUNDER
NO KNOWN FOUNDER

PLACE OF ORIGIN
PORTUGAL

Jogo do pau is a Portuguese staff-fighting martial art and, although its origins are unclear, it is believed the art was originally used to settle matters of honor between families and village members in the northern states of Portugal. Although there are suggestions jogo do pau's origins may lie in Indian martial arts, it is more likely to have evolved as a form of folk fighting between young men using easily obtainable sticks and canes. There is evidence to suggest

⋀ **NATIVE ART**
Practitioners enjoy a bout of jogo do pau in the northern Portuguese town of Fafe. The art is believed to have originated in the area.

Portuguese guerilla groups used the art form against Napoleon's invading forces during the Napoleonic wars. The advent of firearms, however, saw the art fall into decline. The sport is enjoying a reemergence in some areas of Portugal today.

Zipota

EXPLANATION
"SHOE" IN BASQUE

DATE OF ORIGIN
INDIGENOUS ART

FOUNDER
NO KNOWN FOUNDER

PLACE OF ORIGIN
BASQUE REGION (SPAIN/FRANCE)

Despite zipota's disputed origins, experts believe this little-known Basque fighting style was similar to the French sport of savate (see p. 270) and included stick fighting, mostly with a Basque walking stick. The name probably refers to the Basque word for "shoe," and, although literature on the subject is scarce, it is thought the art probably included a number of leaping and kicking techniques combined with throwing and punching, as seen in savate.

Lutta Corsa

EXPLANATION
"CORSICAN FREE FIGHTING"
IN CORSICAN

DATE OF ORIGIN
INDIGENOUS ART

FOUNDER
NO KNOWN FOUNDER

PLACE OF ORIGIN
CORSICA

Lutta corsa is a free-fighting art believed to have developed from Greek pankration wrestling (see p. 274) and was traditionally practiced by shepherds on the Mediterranean island of Corsica. Although little is known about the art's exact origins, the sport is likely to have evolved among wandering shepherds who used a fighting system that included throws, kicks, chokes, and punches to settle scores, right wrongs, and restore honor.

⋁ **STILL IN THE PUBLIC EYE**
The centuries-old art of juego del palo is still a common sight around the Canary Islands on public holidays and national festivals.

Juego Del Palo

EXPLANATION
"GAME OF THE STICK"
IN SPANISH

DATE OF ORIGIN
INDIGENOUS ART

FOUNDER
NO KNOWN FOUNDER

PLACE OF ORIGIN
CANARY ISLANDS

Juego del palo is a combative stick-fighting art from the Canary Islands that has its roots in the Guanches, the aboriginal inhabitants of the islands prior to the arrival of the Spanish in the early 15th century.

When training for fights, practitioners attack and deflect blows vigorously, while maintaining a loose grip on the stick to reduce the likelihood of injury.

Tools of the trade

Fighting sticks are made from the common woods found on the islands, including bitter almendiero trees, eucalyptus trees, or the wood of the sabina. Two types of stick are used in training: the long and the short. For competition purposes, however, three lengths of stick are used: "chico," short, which is about the length of a walking stick; "medio," medium, which extends from the ground to approximately the level of the player's heart; and the "grande," large, which can reach up to 13 ft (4 m) in length.

La Scuola della Spada Italiana

EXPLANATION
"THE ITALIAN SCHOOL OF SWORDSMANSHIP" IN ITALIAN

DATE OF ORIGIN
EARLY 15TH CENTURY

FOUNDER
NO KNOWN FOUNDER

PLACE OF ORIGIN
ITALY

An Italian style of fencing popular from 1400 to 1900, the Italian School of Swordsmanship has undergone several changes throughout its colorful history.

The school laid the foundations for many other European fencing arts and, although the earliest record of it was written by Fiore Dei Liberi in 1409, it seems the history of the art is much older. The original system included the use of the dagger, spear, long sword, short sword, and ax, along with a number of unarmed and wrestling techniques.

∧ FROM ANCIENT TO MODERN
The weapons, and reasons for their use, may have changed over the centuries, but many of the La Scuola della Spada Italiana's ancient fundamentals remain to this day.

The first English translations of Italian swordsmanship training manuals appeared in the 1590s, and the four distinctive guarding positions of that time remain today: the "prima," the "seconda," the "terza," and the "quarta." The governing body, the Accademia Nazionale (National Academy), certifies masters in systems that follow the original principles of the art.

> "NONE BEARS A MORE ARDENT HEART THAN ME, A LION, AND I CHALLENGE ANYONE TO BATTLE."
>
> FIORE DEI LIBERI FROM HIS BOOK *FLOS DUELLATORUM*

Lucha Canaria

EXPLANATION
"CANARIAN WRESTLING" IN SPANISH

DATE OF ORIGIN
INDIGENOUS ART

FOUNDER
NO KNOWN FOUNDER

PLACE OF ORIGIN
CANARY ISLANDS

A form of wrestling native to the Guanches, the inhabitants of the Canary Islands prior to the arrival of the Spanish, the first recorded mention of lucha canaria came in an essay written by Alvar Garcia De Santa Maria in 1420. Official rules for the sport were created in 1872, and some of the art's original techniques still survive today.

Contests are fought in sandy circles and the goal is to throw an opponent to the ground: if any part of his body, other than his feet, touches the sand, a point is awarded,

∧ NO WAY BACK
The wrestler on the left has his opponent in enormous trouble during this bout of lucha canaria on the island of Gran Canaria.

with two points required to win the overall bout. The various throwing techniques are known as "manas."

Playing in the right spirit

A good sporting attitude, good health, and respect for others are fundamental to the sport and, consequently, punches, strikes, and strangleholds are considered illegal. Players wear a uniform made of a strong fabric commonly consisting of two parts, a short-sleeved shirt and rolled-up trousers, known as "calzon." There are no weight categories and fights generally last between one-and-a-half and two minutes. Team bouts usually consist of 12 members. The sport is still a common sight on the islands on public holidays and national festivals.

Liu-Bo

EXPLANATION
FROM "LIU," TO HONOR SICILY'S SICULAN ROOTS, AND "BO," "STAFF" IN JAPANESE

DATE OF ORIGIN
INDIGENOUS ART

FOUNDER
NOT KNOWN

PLACE OF ORIGIN
SICILY, ITALY

Liu-bo is an Italian staff-fighting martial art that has its roots in Sicily. Originally a shepherd art handed down from father to son through the generations, it has now become an official sport in Italy and is codified by the Centro Sportivo Educativo Nazionale (CSEN). Although there were originally no restrictions on which parts of the body could be struck, in competitions today practitioners are only allowed to hit an opponent's chest in thrustinglike moves. A point is awarded following

∧ TAKING LIU-BO TO THE PEOPLE
Practitioners demonstrate the techniques of liu-bo at a summer camp in Lignano Sabbia d'Oro in northeastern Italy.

a clean strike to an opponent's legs, arms, chest, or shoulders, and a point is taken away from a player who behaves in an unsporting manner, such as shouting at, or insulting, his opponent. Strikes to the groin area lead to instant disqualification. Fights take place in an 26 ft x 26 ft (8 m x 8 m) square surrounded by a 6 ft (2 m) safety space.

Boxing

EXPLANATION	N/A
DATE OF ORIGIN	UNKNOWN
FOUNDER	NO KNOWN FOUNDER

PLACE OF ORIGIN
NO KNOWN ORIGIN

Boxing, or pugilism, is a common combat sport in the West, possibly born from the Greek pankration arts (see p. 276), and was first accepted as an Olympic sport in 688 BCE. Opponents punch each other using a variety of combinations and victory is decided if a player knocks down his opponent for a set period of time (usually ten seconds). Other ways of achieving victory come with a clean knockout (KO), or with a technical knockout (TKO), in which the fight is stopped either by a referee or by a member of the player's team.

Ancient roots

The ancient Greeks and Romans, the Minoans (1500 BCE), and the early Egyptians and Berbers (3000 BCE) all practiced forms of pugilism. It is thought that original matches had no weight categories or rounds, and fighters would typically wrap

▲ **BORN IN ANTIQUITY**
A fresco depicting two boys fighting, discovered on the Greek island of Santorini and dating back to the 16th century BCE.

their hands in hardened leather to protect them from fractures, broken bones, and dislocated fingers.

Two distinct forms of boxing emerged during the days of the Roman Empire. The first, influenced by the Greeks, stressed boxing as a leisure activity; the latter, from the Roman gladiatorial matches, saw

fighters fight viciously—sometimes to the death—in order to gain freedom, respect, and money.

Codifying the sport

Boxing has taken various forms in different countries through the years, but modern Western boxing grew out of London prize-ring fighting, a bare-knuckle form of the sport. The first record of these matches appeared in 1681 in the *London Protestant Mercury* and later, in 1719, the term "boxing" was used for the first time.

In 1743, a later champion, Jack Broughton, introduced a number of rules, and mufflers—the first form of boxing gloves—were also introduced around this time.

By 1838 the rules had tightened further and biting, head-butting, and hitting below the belt were deemed illegal. Later, in 1867, with the formation of the Marquess of Queensberry Rules, modern boxing, as we know it today, was born. Fights, it was stated, should take place in a 24 ft by 24 ft (7.3 m by 7.3 m) square

ring, and rounds should last three minutes with a one-minute interval in between. If a fighter was knocked down, he would be allowed 10 seconds to get himself together, stand back up, and reengage in the fight.

A shift in emphasis

The introduction of what would now be seen as modern boxing gloves saw the sport undertake another dramatic change: because the gloves could be used as a defensive weapon, a more complex set of strategies was required to knock out an opponent.

Boxers employ a range of tactics, such as feigning, and gambits like the "rope-a-dope," in which they allow themselves to be hit in order to wear down their opponent and open up holes in their opponent's defense.

When fighting, the boxer shuffles forward, backward, and sideways in small steps, pushing off his back

▼ **THE GREATEST**
Muhammad Ali stands over Sonny Liston after knocking him down in the first round of their 1965 world heavyweight fight in Maine, USA.

> "FLOAT LIKE A BUTTERFLY,
> STING LIKE A BEE
> YOUR HANDS CAN'T HIT
> WHAT YOUR EYES
> CAN'T SEE."

MUHAMMAD ALI

THE ONE-TWO PUNCH

1 From the classic guard position, the boxer aims a left jab at his opponent's face.

2 Then, for a split second, he retreats back into the guard position for protection.

3 He shifts his body weight low, constantly maintaining a good defensive guard to protect himself from any of his opponent's blows.

4 As he leans forward, he fires a strong straight punch to the midsection, causing his opponent instinctively to drop his guard.

5 Springing back into the upright position, he delivers what he hopes will be a decisive left hook to his opponent's now-unguarded jaw.

6 Then it's back to the guard position, as he considers what action is required next.

BOXING IN THE MOVIES

Boxing's dynamic nature has made it an ideal vehicle for several blockbuster Hollywood films. Marlon Brando (*On the Waterfront*), Robert de Niro (*Raging Bull*), Sylvester Stallone (*Rocky I–VI*), Will Smith (*Ali*), and Russell Crowe (*Cinderella Man*) have all appeared as boxers, and, in 2004, *Million Dollar Baby* won Oscars for the Best Motion Picture, Best Director (Clint Eastwood), and Best Actress (Hilary Swank).

leg, punching forward from a crouched position, hands held up high to protect the face, elbows close in to protect the ribs, while at the same time protecting himself from blows to the jaw. The boxer must learn to use leverage, gravity, and momentum to his advantage.

The boxer's weapons

The jab is the most well-known boxing technique and is used to probe weaknesses in the opponent's defense and to feel for range before delivering a heavy knockout blow, often a hook—a swinging punch thrown by either the lead or rear hand. The most basic boxing combination is the one-two punch—a left jab followed by a straight right fist (see below left). Targets for boxers include vulnerable parts of the body, such as the solar plexus, the ribs, kidney, liver, jaw, and nose. Although officially discouraged, it is not unusual to find a boxer using a hip throw, an arm lock, or a wrestling maneuver to try to throw his opponent to the floor. Eye-gouging and punches to the back of the neck are illegal and deemed unsportsmanlike, as are head-butting maneuvers.

Preparing for a fight

Road work is a basic prerequisite of the boxer's training routine and it is common to see professionals completing 100–150 miles (160–240 km) of road running per week in addition to their normal gym work and fight training. Full-contact, heavy sparring is a must, and additional padding, including head padding, is often worn for protection. Other training methods include jumping rope—to keep the boxer light on his feet—and punching on what is known as the "heavy bag."

Shadow boxing is another basic training method and, in some ways, is similar to the "katas" found in oriental martial arts, because both see the practitioner perform set moves while visualizing an opponent and refining the techniques. Push-ups, sit-ups, weight training, and general physical fitness are the foundations upon which a successful boxer learns and carries out his craft.

◄ **FINDING THE TARGET**
Lennox Lewis lands a right hook during his 1999 world heavyweight fight against Evander Holyfield.

PROFESSIONAL BOXER

TWENTY-FIVE-YEAR-OLD DARREN BARKER is one of the UK's most exciting boxing prospects. After taking up the sport at the age of 13, he reached the pinnacle of his amateur career when he beat Uganda's Mohammed Kayongo to win light-welterweight gold at the 2002 Commonwealth Games in Manchester.

Darren turned professional immediately after his gold medal-winning performance and made an impressive unbeaten start to his career (notching up 15 straight wins—ten of them by knockout), including a solid points victory over veteran Hussain Osman for the vacant British Boxing Board of Control Southern Area middleweight title. His star was on the rise. But then Darren's life was thrown into turmoil when his younger brother Gary, a promising boxer who had

> "MY BROTHER'S DEATH LAST YEAR GAVE ME A DIFFERENT MENTAL OUTLOOK ... BEING IN TOUCH WITH THE MOMENT. I WILL HOME IN ON THAT ASPECT FROM NOW UNTIL THE FIGHT."

been tipped for medal glory at the 2012 Olympic Games, was tragically killed in a car accident. Darren spent nine months out of the ring, but in just his second fight back, he defeated unbeaten Australian fighter Ben Crompton by a unanimous points decision to claim the vacant Commonwealth middleweight title belt. Darren is seen here three days before the first defense of his Commonwealth crown, against experienced 34-year-old Steven Bendall.

THE GYM

Darren's gym is located at the back of a North London rugby club. It is equipped with only a ring, a couple of heavy bags, speed balls, and floor-to-ceiling balls, but it is a place Darren loves: "Training five days a week at the same gym with the same people really builds an atmosphere. I look forward to every day."

SHADOW BOXING

Darren finishes his warm-up routine with three three-minute bursts of shadow boxing. Similar to "katas" found in Oriental martial arts, shadow boxing allows Darren to run through some of the moves he will use during the fight, visualizing his opponent in the ring. He then does another three three-minute set, this time holding light weights.

THE RUN

Darren would normally go for a 40-minute run at 6 a.m. every day, but fight night is fast approaching, so running is kept at a minimum as Darren winds down the intensity of his training. In the run-up to a fight, he concentrates on increasing his intake of carbohydrate-rich foods, so that his body will be able to produce the steady stream of fuel required during the fight. Today's pregym workout starts with 10 chin-ups, 10 minutes' light stretching, and a gentle 15-minute run.

WRAPPING HANDS

Back in the gym, Tony Sims, Darren's trainer, winds two layers of strapping around his protégé's hands and wrists for protection. He then tapes the wraps together and ensures that Darren's fingers are separated. Darren's hands are the tools of his trade, and every effort is made to protect them.

STRETCHING

Darren undergoes a series of stretching routines before the training session gets under way. Stretching improves muscle balance, aids flexibility, increases the supply of blood to the muscles, and reduces the chance of injury.

>>>

TRAINING WITH PUNCH BAGS

The warm-up now complete, Darren puts on his sparring gloves and starts the intensive part of the session. He starts with 10 three-minute rounds on the heavy bag, with each round broken up by a 60-second burst on the focus mitts to sharpen his reflexes and condition his fast-twitch muscle fibers. He then completes three three-minute rounds on the floor-to-ceiling ball, a piece of apparatus that hones a boxer's speed, accuracy, and precision.

CONDITIONING WORK

Jumping rope gives Darren's shoulders, calves, and quads a serious workout. He jumps rope on a rubber mat to minimize the impact on his feet and ankles. Then it's on to the medicine ball, one of the oldest forms of strength and conditioning training. Darren performs 100 sit-ups while his trainer Tony pounds his stomach with the heavy ball: the intention is to condition Darren's body to the punishment it will take during the rigors of the fight.

COOLING OFF

Darren winds down with a series of sit-ups and stretches. His training session is over, there is nothing left for him to do before the fight, and now he has time for a non-boxing-related chat with trainer, friend, and mentor Tony. After rehydrating and having a shower, Darren will now rest before the biggest fight of his career.

THE WEIGH-IN

The day before the fight, Darren arrives for the official weigh-in. He steps on the scales: 158½ lb (71.9 kg). He may be slightly lighter than his opponent, but he is well inside the 160 lb (72.6 kg) weight limit. Darren and Steven Bendall pose for the cameras. The next time they meet will be in the ring.

PRE-FIGHT BUILD-UP

Darren's bout with Steve Bendall is the main attraction on the fight card, and is scheduled for 12 three-minute rounds. The commentators and cameramen gather around the ring; there is a buzz in the crowd. This is a much-anticipated fight and will be screened live on television. The fight is being staged at York Hall in Bethnal Green, London, one of the UK's best-known boxing venues, with a capacity of 1,200—and tonight it is full to the brim.

THE FIGHT: PART TWO

With the words of encouragement from his corner ringing in his ears, Darren starts to dominate the fight and his 34-year-old opponent seems to have no answer to his speed and precision. Darren works well behind his jab and lands meaningful punches at will. It seems as though the prefight predictions of a win for Darren in eight rounds might not be wide of the mark.

THE FIGHT: PART ONE

Darren makes an impressive start to the fight. A left, followed by a right, followed by a left hook leaves Steven Bendall on the canvas after just 20 seconds of the opening round, but he recovers after an eight-second count from the referee. By the end of the third round, Darren seems to be gaining the upper hand in the fight, but his corner reminds him of the importance of remaining focused and getting the job done.

THE VICTOR

Midway through the seventh round the referee calls time to inspect a cut that has developed over Bendall's right eye following a clash of heads between the two fighters. The bout resumes—but only for 30 seconds before the referee calls a halt to the fight. It's official: Darren has retained his Commonwealth title with a technical knockout.

"I NEVER OVERLOOKED STEVE BENDALL. HE IS A QUALITY OPPONENT. IT WAS A MATTER OF BOXING SMARTLY, SO THIS WAS A GOOD PERFORMANCE AT THIS STAGE OF MY CAREER."

DARREN BARKER SPEAKING AFTER THE FIGHT

Jousting

EXPLANATION
FROM "JUSTER" IN ANCIENT FRENCH

DATE OF ORIGIN
10TH CENTURY

FOUNDER
GODFREY DE PREUILLY

PLACE OF ORIGIN
FRANCE

Jousting was a medieval equestrian sport designed to demonstrate a warrior's suitability for battle. It was originally conducted with three different weapons: the lance, the battleaxe, and the knife or sword. Although the earliest record of jousting as a sport came in 1066, it did not gain widespread popularity until the 13th century, before its decline during the 17th and 18th centuries.

Competitive jousting

In its prime, regular jousting competitions were held across Europe and often involved large prizes, as well as frequent injuries. In order to win, a jouster would aim to "til" (unseat) his opponent. Common types of horse used were either agile, medium-sized horses, or heavier steeds bred for war. They would typically wear long-necked furs, a saddle with a high back so that the jouster would not easily be thrown, and armor that would often feature ornamental signs.

The armor worn by knights was interchangeable so that it could be replaced quickly and easily if damaged. Breastplates were attached to the general armor and, as they took the brunt of the blow, were heavier and stronger; the helmet was known as "The Great Helm"—a solid-metal coverall helmet with a thin strip at the front to allow vision. The lances were often painted with stripes and symbols of a knight's coat of armor and were fashioned from solid oak.

Modern jousting

Jousting is still popular around the world today and the sport's governing body, the International Jousting Association, regulates rules and is responsible for safety in modern competition.

> "IS THERE AMONG YOU ANY GENTLEMEN WHO, FOR THE LOVE OF HIS LADY, IS WILLING TO TRY WITH ME SOME FEAT OF ARMS?"
>
> GAUVAIN MICAILLE'S CHALLENGE TO ENGLISH SOLDIERS DURING THE 100 YEARS' WAR

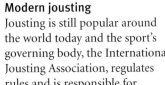

▼ **BULL'S EYE**
The lance shatters as a jouster scores a direct hit on his opponent's shield during a modern jousting match.

MEDIEVAL TOURNAMENTS

There were three types of tournament prior to the 17th century. The first was the "mêlée," popular in the 12th and 13th centuries, in which participants gathered and fought until just one knight remained astride his horse. The second type of tournament was the "individual joust": a face-off between two knights on horseback with each trying to unseat the other by a judicious strike of the lance to an opponent's shield. The third was the "practice tournament," in which participants aimed the lance at practice targets such as wooden dummies or rings.

Kinomichi

EXPLANATION
"THE WAY OF BREATH"
IN JAPANESE

DATE OF ORIGIN
1979

FOUNDER
MASAMICHI NORO

PLACE OF ORIGIN
FRANCE

Kinomichi is a grappling system from France believed to have originated from aikido (see pp. 238–39), and was created by Masamichi Noro, a disciple of aikido's founder Morihei Ueshiba, in Paris in 1979. The art emphasizes the natural order and flow of "qi" and key elements are the link between man, heaven, and earth. The ultimate aim is to realize and achieve a sense of harmonious peace through the codified practice of fighting.

Baton Français

EXPLANATION
FRENCH STICK FIGHTING

DATE OF ORIGIN
EARLY 19TH CENTURY

FOUNDER
NO KNOWN FOUNDER

PLACE OF ORIGIN
FRANCE

Baton français, also known as French stick fighting, is a historical fencing discipline that utilizes a 4 ft (1.2 m) long pole. Although the origins of the art form are unclear, the system's techniques resemble those found in other European stick-fighting systems, such as jogo do pau and juego del palo (see p. 254), quarterstaff (see p. 252), and long-sword fighting arts. Codified in the early 1800s, many French savate boxers (see p. 270) still train with the baton today.

Gouren

EXPLANATION
"WRESTLING" IN BRETON

DATE OF ORIGIN
4TH CENTURY

FOUNDER
NO KNOWN FOUNDER

PLACE OF ORIGIN
BRITTANY, FRANCE

Gouren is a barefoot wrestling form from Brittany that dates back to the 4th century. It is thought to have been practiced as a way of enhancing chivalry between people of noble descent and, in particular, the Bretons, a distinct ethnic group located in Brittany, France, who originally came from Britain. The sport remained popular until the early 20th century, but declined with the growth of interest in new sports, such as soccer and cycling.

Back in the public eye

The re-emergence of interest in European martial arts, however, has seen gouren federations spring up

▲ ON THE POINT OF VICTORY
The wrestler on the left gains the upper hand in this gouren bout in Brittany, France. The aim is to throw an opponent onto his back.

across Europe, and championships are now held every two years. Matches often take place alongside music and dance, and players typically wear white shirts with short, black pants tied around the waist with a belt. Bouts start with the fighters swearing an oath, and victory is achieved by throwing an opponent cleanly to the ground so that they land on their back.

"AS A WITNESS TO MY SINCERITY, AND TO FOLLOW THE CUSTOMS OF MY ANCESTORS, I HOLD OUT MY HAND TO MY ADVERSARY."

PART OF THE OATH SWORN BY GOUREN WRESTLERS BEFORE A BOUT

WEAPONS AND ARMOR

THE MEDIEVAL JOUSTER

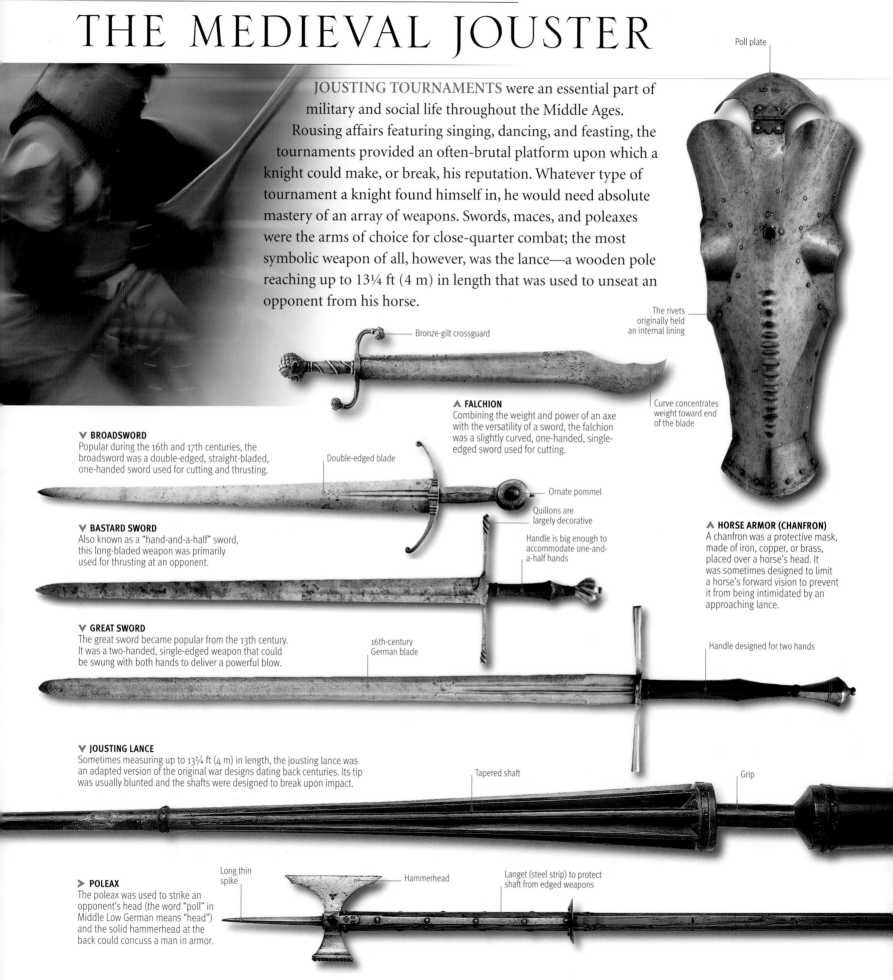

JOUSTING TOURNAMENTS were an essential part of military and social life throughout the Middle Ages. Rousing affairs featuring singing, dancing, and feasting, the tournaments provided an often-brutal platform upon which a knight could make, or break, his reputation. Whatever type of tournament a knight found himself in, he would need absolute mastery of an array of weapons. Swords, maces, and poleaxes were the arms of choice for close-quarter combat; the most symbolic weapon of all, however, was the lance—a wooden pole reaching up to 13¼ ft (4 m) in length that was used to unseat an opponent from his horse.

Poll plate

The rivets originally held an internal lining

Bronze-gilt crossguard

△ FALCHION
Combining the weight and power of an axe with the versatility of a sword, the falchion was a slightly curved, one-handed, single-edged sword used for cutting.

Curve concentrates weight toward end of the blade

▽ BROADSWORD
Popular during the 16th and 17th centuries, the broadsword was a double-edged, straight-bladed, one-handed sword used for cutting and thrusting.

Double-edged blade

Ornate pommel

Quillons are largely decorative

Handle is big enough to accommodate one-and-a-half hands

△ HORSE ARMOR (CHANFRON)
A chanfron was a protective mask, made of iron, copper, or brass, placed over a horse's head. It was sometimes designed to limit a horse's forward vision to prevent it from being intimidated by an approaching lance.

▽ BASTARD SWORD
Also known as a "hand-and-a-half" sword, this long-bladed weapon was primarily used for thrusting at an opponent.

▽ GREAT SWORD
The great sword became popular from the 13th century. It was a two-handed, single-edged weapon that could be swung with both hands to deliver a powerful blow.

16th-century German blade

Handle designed for two hands

▽ JOUSTING LANCE
Sometimes measuring up to 13¼ ft (4 m) in length, the jousting lance was an adapted version of the original war designs dating back centuries. Its tip was usually blunted and the shafts were designed to break upon impact.

Tapered shaft

Grip

▷ POLEAX
The poleax was used to strike an opponent's head (the word "poll" in Middle Low German means "head") and the solid hammerhead at the back could concuss a man in armor.

Long thin spike

Hammerhead

Langet (steel strip) to protect shaft from edged weapons

"Roped" comb

Holes for ventilation

Eagle's beak

16TH-CENTURY HELMET
The fashion in the early 16th century was to wear helmets with strange, masklike visors in the parades during tournaments. This one resembles an eagle's head.

Eye slit

Rounded skull

FROG-MOUTHED HELM
The wearer of this 15th-century helmet could see his opponent by leaning forward during the charge. At the moment of impact he straightened up, so that the "frog-mouthed" lower lip protected his eyes from splinters of the breaking lance.

Armor-piercing spikes

MEDIEVAL MACE
One of the oldest battlefield weapons, the mace became popular in Europe by the 12th century and was extremely effective in close-quarter combat.

ARMOR
By the 15th century, knights were protected by full suits of plate armor designed to make the edges and points of weapons glance from their smooth surface. A full suit of armor could weigh up to 44–55 lb (20–25 kg).

Visor

Bevor

Vambrace

Chain mail

Gauntlet

Cuisse

Poleyn

Greave

Spur

Sabaton

Etched and gilt decoration

Hole to take lance

HAND GUARD
The vamplate was fixed over the lance to guard the knight's hand and prevent it from sliding up the lance's shaft.

LOCKING GAUNTLET
Once the knight had gripped his sword, the locking gauntlet was locked shut so that the sword was not lost in combat.

Pauldron

Besagew

Breastplate

Hole for staples

Protruding arm to support lance

LANCE REST
This was fixed to the breastplate by staples. It helped to take the weight of the lance and stopped it from sliding back through the armpit on impact.

SHIELD
This 15th-century wooden shield is covered in leather. The lance could be placed in the recess in the side. The shield was attached to the breastplate by means of a staple nailed to the rear.

Curved edge to support lance

ROWEL SPUR
Spurs with a rotating spiked rowel on the end of the arm had replaced prick spurs by the end of the early 14th century.

Rotating rowel

Western Archery

EXPLANATION
N/A

DATE OF ORIGIN
FROM 9000 BCE

FOUNDER
NO KNOWN FOUNDER

PLACE OF ORIGIN
WESTERN EUROPE

Western archery involves using a bow to shoot arrows and is popular in the West, particularly in Europe and the United States, and first appeared as an Olympic sport at the 1900 Games in Paris. Participants shoot arrows at targets from various distances and it is as much a mental activity as a physical one. Although many regulatory bodies exist, the Federation Internationale de Tir a L'Arc (FITA) is the most common. Born from the ancient battlefield skills required before the invention of the gun, archery is often taught as a prerequisite in many martial arts around the world.

Although not a practical weapon for use in modern warfare, the benefits of practicing archery

▼ **ALL IN THE MIND**
Before releasing the arrow, the archer will already have its flight path to the target pictured in her mind.

include a stilling of the mind similar to meditation and an enhanced ability to focus. Many skilled practitioners also claim to experience a spiritual state of mind and body in which they direct their attention toward a target, release the arrow, and find that the arrow follows the mind toward the target. This is known as a "state of void" in Buddhist thought and is referred to as "duende" in Spanish dance, a term describing the state of fusion between mind, body, and spirit.

AUTHOR'S NOTE

Intrigued to find out more about this ancient battlefield art, I took myself to a small club in north London expecting to be trained in only the physical movements and technical aspects of the art form. I was delighted to find Western archery had more in common with the esoteric forms of philosophy and Zen Buddhism I had encountered in Asia. We were encouraged not to focus on hitting the target with the arrow, but instead to acquire the target in our mind's eye and allow the arrow to find its own way there, free of judgment, hope, and desire. On adopting these principles when firing or releasing the arrow, I noted a marked improvement almost instantly in my scores. It was almost as if someone had turned on the light and we were shooting arrows instinctively.

Fencing

EXPLANATION
FROM "DEFENS" IN MEDIEVAL ENGLISH

DATE OF ORIGIN
UNKNOWN

FOUNDER
NO KNOWN FOUNDER

PLACE OF ORIGIN
WESTERN EUROPE

Fencing is the ancient art of combat using weapons such as daggers, swords, knives, and bayonets. However, the term "fencing" generally refers to the European school of swordsmanship and the Olympic sport, where the three main weapons used are the épée, the foil, and the saber.

Olympic fencing is governed by the Federation Internationale d'Escrime (FIE) and the rules

evolved from guidelines laid down in the 17th century. Bouts in Olympic competition are judged by an electronic scoring system; when competitors touch their opponent with the sword in a specific area, they register a score. The total number of points is added up electronically through a sensory device, and the fencer with the most points at the end of the bout is deemed the winner.

Common origins

Often thought of as a Western martial art, there are a number of different branches of fencing practiced today. They all share the common value born from the original fighting and dueling art in which efficiency and speed are the keys to effective combat and survival. The classical fencing

> "FENCING IS A GAME OF SUBTLETY, AND BLUFF CAN BE MET WITH COUNTERBLUFF."

CHARLES L. DE BEAUMONT

movement places emphasis on original techniques found in European fencing training of the 19th and 20th centuries. Some schools also teach the saber, a heavier battlefield sword. However, because of its unwieldy nature, teaching methods for the saber concentrate less on sporting strikes, focusing instead on the killing cuts—techniques that include stabbing, slashing, cutting, and feigning.

Weapon types

The foil, a flexible and light weapon thought to have originated during the 17th century, is the most common weapon and is used for thrusting, the main way to score points in modern fencing. The épée, which, according to legend, was developed during the 19th century by a French student who felt the foil was too light and unrealistic, is another common weapon. Similar in nature to the small sword, players generally thrust it at any part of their opponent's body. The saber is a cutting and slashing weapon, although competition blades are lighter and more flexible than real blades.

Scene of battle

Bouts are contested on a piste or strip 5–6½ ft (1.5–2 m) wide by 46 ft (14 m) long and, although the advent of electronic scoring devices has diminished the need for referees, players can still ask for them to be present to help assess any technical infringements. Matches

MAKING A POINT
Fencers score points by making contact with predetermined areas of their opponent's body. The fighter with the most points wins.

start when the referee calls "play" and end when they call "halt." Rounds are generally three minutes in length and, in multiround matches, one-minute breaks occur between every three-minute round. French is the international language of the sport and in official matches refereeing is conducted in French.

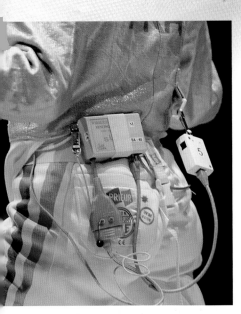

AUTOMATIC TOUCH
Electronic scoring was first introduced into fencing at the 1936 Olympic Games and has remained in the sport ever since.

SAFETY FIRST
FIE regulations state that masks worn during training and competition must be able to withstand a force of at least 60 lb (27 kg).

Greco-Roman Wrestling

EXPLANATION
N/A

DATE OF ORIGIN
1848

FOUNDER
EXBROYAT

PLACE OF ORIGIN
FRANCE

Greco-Roman wrestling is based on an ancient form of wrestling, a version of which is practiced as an Olympic sport today. Headlocks and bear hugs are common, and throws are the favored techniques, although players are not allowed to attack below the waist. The system evolved from a wrestling system developed by a Napoleonic soldier called Exbroyat, who established the rules in 1848.

Continental appeal

Although popular in mainland Europe, the art did not enjoy the same level of success in the United Kingdom or the United States. As a result, freestyle wrestling became the more popular form in both countries, and that led to the development of collegiate wrestling (see p. 328).

Although early Greco-Roman wrestling matches lasted for an unusually long time—sometimes up to two or three hours—modern bouts are far shorter. With competitors separated by weight categories, most victories are earned by a fall or throw, with technical superiority being more important than brute strength.

Rules of engagement

Fights take place on a thick, rubber mat to ensure the participants' physical safety and are played out in a 29½ ft (9 m) square surrounded by a 5 ft (1.5m) border, known as the "protection area." Practitioners wear a special type of shoe, which is light and flexible, along with a singlet. Head gear is also sometimes worn to protect the wrestlers' heads and ears.

Victories are decided by a fall; by a pin, whereby one player holds down his opponent's two shoulders on the mat simultaneously; by decision, whereby the wrestler with the most points at the end of a set period is declared the winner; by default, whereby the wrestler is unable to continue; by technical superiority, sometimes known as a "technical fall," where a wrestler gains a six-point lead over his opponent; by disqualification; or by injury, where a medical practitioner deems the injuries sustained by a player serious enough to halt the bout.

▼ FIGHTING TO GAIN THE UPPER HAND
The United States' Cael Sanderson and Belarus' Siarhei Borchanka fight for supremacy in the men's 185 lb (84 kg) elimination round at the 2004 Olympic Games in Athens.

▲ FRENCH BOXING
Savate, also known as "boxe française," combines elements of Western boxing with numerous graceful kicking techniques.

Savate

EXPLANATION
"OLD BOOT" IN FRENCH

DATE OF ORIGIN
AROUND 16TH CENTURY

FOUNDER
NO KNOWN FOUNDER

PLACE OF ORIGIN
FRANCE

Savate is a full-contact boxing and kicking art, indigenous to France and some other parts of southwest Europe. It is believed to have evolved from a collection of fighting techniques used by sailors, criminals, and soldiers. The art form also includes a number of grappling maneuvers and involves weapons training, most notably with staffs such as the "baton" and "la canne de combat."

Rise in popularity

The earliest recorded information on savate dates from the 18th century, although it is probable that the system was in existence two or three centuries earlier.

Savate's popularity in France rose again during the 1800s and, by the 1870s, Joseph Charlemont systemized the teaching of the art, developed the use of gloves in training, and introduced a ranking system whereby students could wear either a colored sash denoting their grade or a colored band around the cuff of their boxing gloves. Charlemont's son was arguably the best savate player of all time and due to his successes the system went on to be taught to the military in both the United Kingdom and the United States under the name of "Automatic Defense."

Savate today

The system as codified today usually contains 14 different hand strikes. Head, shoulders, elbows, hip strikes, and knees are also used alongside weapons, including firearms, whips, a staff, and razors. A number of kicks are employed and one particular kick, "savate," is well known as the "hand-on-the-floor kick," whereby practitioners use the hand as leverage while spinning or jumping and kicking to great effect. In keeping with oriental tradition, those who learn the art are classified in three sections. There are three levels of practitioner: "élèves" (students) "disciples," and "donneurs" (teachers). Students may practice two, three, or four times a week, but disciples usually train full-time and enjoy a close relationship with their teacher, who will often introduce them to teachings of life and philosophy.

◄ MASS APPEAL
A publicity drawing, created by the French artist Guillaume in the early 20th century, depicts a woman practicing savate.

Parkour

EXPLANATION
"OBSTACLE COURSE" IN FRENCH
DATE OF ORIGIN
MID-1990s
FOUNDER
DAVID BELLE
PLACE OF ORIGIN
FRANCE

DAVID BELLE

Parkour was founded by David Belle in the mid-1990s and focuses on the most efficient movement of the body and mind. The originator noted that in a hostile confrontation one might be able to do three things in order to survive: speak, fight, or flee. Most martial arts do not have any set curriculum or training methodology to enhance a participant's ability to escape, thus parkour was an answer to this need.

Military origins

The name "parcours" refers to the obstacle courses used by French soldiers and was a natural choice of name for the later art, parkour. Known popularly as a jumping art form practiced by young people in Europe, the most important training techniques are jumping, landing, and learning to roll and absorb force

▼ THE SKY'S THE LIMIT
No limits and no fear. A traceur performs a spectacular back flip on the roof of the London School of Economics in England.

Born in 1973 and raised in Seine Maritime, Normandy, France, David Belle showed an amazing gymnastic ability during his childhood and went on to make close friends with a group of teenagers (among them Sébastien Foucan, who would go on to found free running). Belle joined the fire brigade, then the French marines, but found his taste for adventure did not sit well with the austere discipline of the military. In 1997 he made a documentary about parkour and from that moment on the sport's popularity took off.

while, at the same time, taking advantage of momentum to create spectacular moves; players often engage in 180- or 360-degree rotation turns, known as "turn vaults," while leaping from or toward objects such as walls or buildings. Vaulting techniques, whereby practitioners dive forward over an obstacle, body horizontal, pushing from the hands and then tucking the legs in and landing safely in a vertical position again, are a staple of the art.

▲ CLEARING HURDLES
A parkour practitioner, known as a "traceur," shows his natural athleticism in the streets of Helsinki, Finland.

"WE AIM TO TAKE OUR ART TO THE WORLD AND MAKE PEOPLE UNDERSTAND WHAT IT IS TO MOVE."

DAVID BELLE

Deutscher Jujutsu

EXPLANATION
GERMAN JUJUTSU
DATE OF ORIGIN
1967
FOUNDER
GERMAN DAN COUNCIL
PLACE OF ORIGIN
GERMANY

Based on aikido, judo, and karate (see pp. 238–39, 234–35, 202–03), Deutscher jujutsu is the main form of jujutsu practiced in Germany. The system emphasizes a number of techniques created for real-life situations, including various kicks, knee strikes, and throws, as well as pressure-point techniques, armed techniques, unarmed techniques, and restraining techniques covering

> ▲ **LEARNING THE ROPES**
> Two students get to grips with German jujutsu throwing techniques at a German Dan Council-promoted summer school.

both one-on-one situations and those with multiple opponents. The Jujutsu International Federation (JJIF) is the art form's international governing body and now has a recognized presence in over 70 countries worldwide.

Kampfringen

EXPLANATION
"COMBAT GRAPPLING" IN GERMAN
DATE OF ORIGIN
EARLY 15TH CENTURY
FOUNDER
OTT JUD
PLACE OF ORIGIN
SOUTHERN GERMANY

Kampfringen is a mostly unarmed combat system that employs joint throws, leverage throws, and pain-compliance grips, alongside striking techniques. Although the term is also a generic one for the unarmed combat systems that originated from the Roman Empire and remained popular throughout the Middle Ages, it is also a stand-alone system

in its own right. It is thought the Austrian Ott Jud, a master of the fighting arts during the 15th century, was the forefather of modern kampfringen. While Ott is not credited with documenting his own system, numerous accounts exist that suggest he taught the system to many Austrian lords.

Varied paths of development
Kampfringen has evolved over the centuries, with later masters all placing emphasis on different aspects of the art. Sword and weapon seizures, and weapon-aided joint locks, along with specific stabbing actions aimed at particularly vulnerable areas of an opponent's armor, were popular during the 15th and 16th centuries.

Deutsche Fechtschule

EXPLANATION
"GERMAN SCHOOL OF FENCING" IN GERMAN
DATE OF ORIGIN
14TH CENTURY
FOUNDER
NO KNOWN FOUNDER
PLACE OF ORIGIN
GERMANY

The Deutsche Fechtschule was a sword-fighting movement popular from the 14th to 17th centuries. Its principles are still practiced today.

Between 1487 and 1570 the Brotherhood of St. Mark—the most important organization of German fencers—was responsible for teaching sword arts in the country, and it is due to their efforts that a canon of literature detailing ancient techniques, methodology, and weaponry still survives to this day.

Multifaceted art
An interesting aspect of the art is that, although fighting is primarily conducted with the long sword, principles of wrestling are also employed. Practitioners will use their body weight to gain leverage against their opponent and, once contact has been made with the opponent's sword, will then employ a clever set of moves, similar to some Japanese systems, to manipulate the sword quickly into another position to achieve advantage and, ultimately, a cut to the opponent. Part of the training involves practicing with the

sword alongside the dagger. Stafflike weapons are also used, as is the large shield. Today most of the art's practitioners train in a semicontact fashion with blunted swords. Armor, including headgear, is common.

Using the force
The idea of using weakness to overcome strength and strength to overcome weakness underpins much of the art. The experienced practitioner, once he has made contact with his opponent's sword, will sense immediately whether he has to make a strong move or a weak one in order to execute a winning strike or cut.

The still-prevalent drive to achieve a winning cut suggests that duels in the past were not uncommon and, although the art has evolved into a sport over the centuries, the central theme has always been to end a life-threatening, armed encounter quickly.

> ➤ **ANCIENT TECHNIQUES**
> The swordsman on the right uses a "zwerch hau" move to defend himself from a downward blow.

> "PRACTICE KNIGHTHOOD
> AND LEARN THE ART THAT
> DIGNIFIES YOU AND BRINGS
> YOU HONOR IN BATTLE."
>
> MASTER JOHANNES LIECHTENAUER, A 14TH CENTURY GERMAN FENCING MASTER

Schwingen

EXPLANATION
"SWINGING" IN GERMAN

DATE OF ORIGIN
13TH CENTURY

FOUNDER
NO KNOWN FOUNDER

PLACE OF ORIGIN
SWITZERLAND

Schwingen, a sport practiced by herders of the Swiss Alps since at least the 13th century, is a type of Swiss folk wrestling. It is considered to be the country's national sport and is still a common sight at public festivals to this day.

Into the arena

Fights take place in circular areas that measure 39 ft 5 in (12 m) in diameter and that are usually covered with sawdust to protect participants from hard falls. The goal is to throw an opponent onto his back, and some of the techniques resemble those found in judo (see pp. 234–35) and shuai jiao (see p. 103). Schwingen is known as a gentlemanly sport and, in keeping with tradition, the winner should brush the dust from the loser's back at the end of a match.

Steeped in tradition

There are no weight classes or categories and it is often the stronger men who win in competition. Although the awarding of prize money is discouraged, traditional gifts—such as furniture, livestock, or cowbells—may be presented to successful wrestlers. It is likely that the art became popular not just as a means of self-defense, but as a way for young men to show off their strength to prospective partners.

> **THE NAME OF THE GAME**
Sometimes referred to as "trouser lifting," the object of schwingen is to throw an opponent onto his back.

⌃ CAPTURING THE PUBLIC'S IMAGINATION
Up to 8,000 spectators flock to the mountains to watch the annual schwingen festival in Muotathal, Switzerland.

▼ CHASING THE OLYMPIC DREAM
Japan's Makoto Sasamoto (red) and
Kazakhstan's Nurlan Koizhaiganov (blue)
battle it out in the men's Greco-Roman
132 lb (60 kg) final elimination round at
the 2004 Olympic Games in Athens.

Pankration

EXPLANATION
"ALL POWER" OR "ALL STRENGTH" IN ANCIENT GREEK
DATE OF ORIGIN
INDIGENOUS ART
FOUNDER
NO KNOWN FOUNDER
PLACE OF ORIGIN
GREECE

Pankration, the ancient full-contact fighting art, which became an Olympic sport in 648 BCE, is one of the world's oldest martial arts. Mythology maintains that it was invented by Hercules and Theseus, although it is more likely to have developed as a training method for Greek soldiers, who noted that, by combining boxing techniques and groundwork as both sport and exercise, they could keep themselves battle-ready and still fight effectively should they lose their weapon during the heat of battle.

Brutal beginnings

In the early days of the sport, contests would run uninterrupted, deaths were not uncommon, and a bout was ended either by surrender, by

> **ANCIENT ART FORM**
This 3rd century BCE Greek sculpture shows a pankrationist performing an arm lock on his opponent during a wrestling bout.

knocking an opponent unconscious, or by killing him. The most common cause of death during matches was strangulation with a violent chokehold across the windpipe or carotid artery.

Renewed interest

Modern pankration is enjoying increased popularity in the West, with schools emerging in both the United States and Europe. However, the modern systems differ from ancient ones and are hybrid inventions influenced by both freestyle and catch wrestling, karate, jujutsu, boxing (see pp. 251, 202–03, 216–17, 256–63), and other ancient techniques taken from various sculptures and paintings.

Although the biting of fingers and joints, as well as eye-gouging, were common occurrences in the art's original form, they are generally prohibited from modern-day competition.

PANKRATION IN ANCIENT GREECE

By the time pankration became an Olympic sport in 648 BCE, there is evidence to suggest it was already an ancient sport. Pankrationists would display one of a variety of styles, many of which had been passed down through the generations. Master teachers were called "Thaskalos," while students were referred to as "Pankriatists." To help hone breathing techniques and power-striking, exercises known as "pyrrics" were used: these were similar to the "katas" (set forms) of Oriental martial arts.

> ## "THAT NEW AND TERRIBLE CONTEST OF ALL HOLDS."
>
> GREEK PHILOSOPHER AND POET XENOPHANES, ON PANKRATION

Svebor

EXPLANATION
"ALL TYPES OF FIGHTING" IN SERBIAN

DATE OF ORIGIN
INDIGENOUS ART

FOUNDER
NO KNOWN FOUNDER

PLACE OF ORIGIN
SERBIA

Svebor is an ancient Serbian combat art that places strong emphasis on efficiency and practicality, with techniques including head butts and stone throwing. The origins of the sport are believed to lie in the Balkan martial arts—said to be the chosen warrior arts of the Serbian knights of medieval times—and the art has strong links with the Serbian Orthodox Christian religion. Little value is placed on aesthetics, and the art contains a number of leaps, jumps, falls, rolls, arm strikes, and other techniques all aimed at knocking men from their horses.

> **UPHOLDING TRADITION**
Members of a Serbian svebor club clash with broad axes in the shadow of the medieval fortress in Belgrade.

Realnog Aikidoa

EXPLANATION
"REAL AIKIDO" IN SERBIAN

DATE OF ORIGIN
1990s

FOUNDER
LJUBOMIR VRACEREVIC

PLACE OF ORIGIN
SERBIA

Realnog aikidoa (known as Real aikido) is a Serbian martial art and, although some modifications have been made, it is based largely on

▲ SHOWING THE WAY
Ljubomir Vracerevic, the founder of real aikido, leads a training session at the World Center of Real Aikido in Belgrade, Serbia.

aikido (see pp. 238–39). For the most part, the curriculum follows that of aikido, with a dan system of grading (ranging from 1st through to 10th dan), but the similarity of the organization's name to aikido has led to much discord among both the martial art and aikido communities, with numerous accusations being leveled at the art form.

Combat 56

EXPLANATION
NAMED AFTER ELITE POLISH ARMY UNIT, 56TH COMPANY

DATE OF ORIGIN
1990s

FOUNDER
MAJOR ARKADIUSZ KUPS

PLACE OF ORIGIN
POLAND

Founded by Major Arkadiusz Kups, Combat 56 is a Polish close-quarter combat, self-defense art similar to judo (see pp. 234–35). It is named after an elite troop known as the 56th Company, a secretive unit thought to have operated behind enemy lines during a number of recent conflicts. Kups quickly recognized the need to equip his troops with a quick-to-learn, lethal range of close-quarter combat techniques that could be employed effectively on operations, and, although little is officially known about the system, it is reasonable to conclude that it contains knife-fighting elements, breaks, chokes, throws, and striking movements to vulnerable points of the body.

Khridoli

EXPLANATION
GEORGIAN MARTIAL ARTS

DATE OF ORIGIN
INDIGENOUS ART

FOUNDER
NO KNOWN FOUNDER

PLACE OF ORIGIN
GEORGIA

Khridoli is an ancient Georgian martial art that includes weapons training. Its central tenets are wisdom, truth, and strength. Georgian warriors have a long tradition of fighting—stretching back some 3,500 years—and experts believe that over 30 forms of wrestling and boxing were practiced in ancient Georgia. As the country found itself on near-constant military alert throughout the centuries, the highly respected art of the warriors was considered central to the civilization's survival. The Russian occupation of Georgia in 1921 saw a decline in native martial arts, and sambo (see p. 279) became the art of choice for many interested in learning the fighting arts.

Systema

EXPLANATION
"THE SYSTEM" IN RUSSIAN

DATE OF ORIGIN
INDIGENOUS ART

FOUNDER
NO KNOWN FOUNDER

PLACE OF ORIGIN
RUSSIA

Systema is a Russian martial art taught to military Special Forces that aims to give practitioners a framework of self-defense techniques that are easy to apply and remember. It has its roots in the numerous wars to have taken place in Russia and in the ancient fighting traditions of many Russian tribes. No uniforms are required for training and, although the art has close associations with the orthodox Russian Christian Church, being religious is not a prerequisite of training.

▼ PERSONAL SAFETY IN MIND
Although its aims are non-sporting in nature, systema provides practitioners with an ability to defend themselves in many types of situation.

◀ R.O.S.S. TRAINING
Members of the pro-Kremlin Nashi youth movement practice R.O.S.S. at Lake Seliger, north of Moscow.

R.O.S.S.

EXPLANATION
ACRONYM OF "RUSSIAN OWN SYSTEM OF SELF-DEFENSE"

DATE OF ORIGIN
INDIGENOUS ART

FOUNDER
NO KNOWN FOUNDER

PLACE OF ORIGIN
RUSSIA

R.O.S.S. combines elements of Russian close-quarter combat and survival techniques, including sambo, bayonet fencing, acrobatics, dance, stunt-style combat, holistic health, and street-fighting techniques known as "Russian fisticuffs."

Although it is extremely difficult to verify its origins, some practitioners assert that the art is an

> "THE LIFE THAT BELONGS TO EACH OF US IS OUR OWN, AND EACH OF US DEFENDS IT IN OUR OWN WAY."
>
> ALEXANDER RETUINSKIH

evolution of traditions dating back to the nomadic Steppe warriors. It is thought the system was passed on through families to the modern day and, in keeping with Cossack esoteric and philosophical traditions, a strong emphasis is placed on introspection and the exploration of human potential, the laws of nature, and ancient Slavic folklore and traditions.

The modern version of R.O.S.S. was developed by Commander Alexander Retuinskih and it is claimed that the system is taught to Spetsnaz Russian Special Forces instructors—the Alpha unit of Byelorussia frontier troops in Lithuania—as part of their training regime, as well as to units of the ministries of internal affairs, defense, and protection services.

Buza

EXPLANATION
N/A

DATE OF ORIGIN
INDIGENOUS ART

FOUNDER
NO KNOWN FOUNDER

PLACE OF ORIGIN
NOVGOROD, NORTHWEST RUSSIA

Buza, also known as "Tverian buza," is an ancient, native, unarmed, all-around fighting system thought to have evolved among the villages of the Novgorod area in northwest Russia. Training for the system includes empty-hand fighting techniques, moves for disarming an opponent brandishing a weapon, war dances, and training in ancient Russian edged weapons. The system achieved its greatest widespread popularity in the latter half of the 20th century.

Sambo

EXPLANATION
"SELF-DEFENSE WITHOUT A WEAPON" IN RUSSIAN

DATE OF ORIGIN
1930

FOUNDER
ANATOLY KHARLAMPIEV

PLACE OF ORIGIN
RUSSIA

An acronym of two Russian words meaning "self-defense without a weapon," sambo was created in 1930. It is heavily influenced by Japanese, Chinese, Mongol, Armenian, Georgian, and Russian martial arts, in addition to French wrestling and a hand-to-hand combat system known as "tested," as used by the Soviet army during World War II.

Made up of three different aspects—self-defense, special combat, and the sporting variation—sambo is similar to the Japanese martial art of daito ryu aiki jujutsu (see p. 207). The self-defense elements include methods for escaping from chokeholds, and locks, punches, kicks, and empty-hand weapon-disarming techniques.

Abiding by the law

The self-defense methods are informed by strict Russian laws, which hand down a five-year prison sentence to anybody found to have used excessive violence during a self-defense situation. As a result, sambo aims only to defend the life of a practitioner with the minimum force required.

The training elements used by the Russian army and police, however, come from a different viewpoint. Their philosophy is that a practitioner must not allow an attacker to cause them injury.

A number of eye gouges, hair-pulling, dislocating maneuvers, and throws are used, but as well as throwing an opponent, military practitioners have the specific intention of simultaneously dislocating or breaking a joint.

In competition, practitioners wear either a red or blue jacket, shorts, and a grappling belt. The uniform does not denote rank; the colors, as in

> ## "IT INVOLVES … PUTTING HIM UNDER PRESSURE TO MAKE A MISTAKE."
>
> P. SEISENBUCHER AND G. KERR IN *MODERN JUDO, TECHNIQUES OF EAST AND WEST*

boxing, are used to differentiate the fighters. Sambo remains one of the four main forms of amateur wrestling practiced internationally and is governed by the International Amateur Sambo Federation (FIAS), which sanctions official competitions.

Sambo practitioners enjoy success in a number of wrestling and mixed martial art championships (see pp. 318–27), and the sport's popularity has also been recognized in the computer-gaming world, with some characters adopting sambo styles.

▼ **GETTING A FIRM GRIP**
Russia's Alsim Chernoskulov (red) and Georgia's Mindia Bodaveli (blue) battle it out at the Presidential International Sambo Tournament.

Russian All-Round Fighting

EXPLANATION
N/A

DATE OF ORIGIN
1998

FOUNDER
MAXIM SHATUNOV

PLACE OF ORIGIN
RUSSIA

Russian All-Round Fighting is a hybrid martial art that has been heavily influenced by Russian traditions of hand-to-hand fighting, swordsmanship, and wrestling. Regular sporting competitions are encouraged, and the system also includes hand-to-hand combat techniques aimed at bringing street-based violence to a decisive end. The art claims not to have taken any principles from Oriental or other non-European martial arts and is said to be specifically designed to meet the temperament and cultural traditions of men of Indo-European descent.

> FROM RUSSIA WITH INTENT
Hand-to-hand fighting in Russian All-Round Fighting is typified by lashing swings followed by an instant change of the angle of attack.

Stav

EXPLANATION
"STAFF" IN NORWEGIAN

DATE OF ORIGIN
C. 6TH CENTURY

FOUNDER
THE HAFSKJOLD FAMILY

PLACE OF ORIGIN
NORWAY

A Nordic martial art that resembles taijiquan (see pp. 80–87), stav uses weapons, rune stones, Norse mythology, mystic teachings, and traditions dating back to the 6th century. Although impossible to pinpoint its exact origin, the art

> KEEPING TRADITIONS ALIVE
Practitioners from the Oxford Stav Club in England demonstrate stav's ancient staff-fighting techniques.

is mentioned in the practical book *The Nordic Culture Historical Lexicon*, an ancient work chronicling writings, life, and behavior in the region.

Learning Viking arts
Students are taught how to handle staffs and cudgels, as well as battle axes, swords, and wands—weapons that would have been common among fighting Viking warriors through the centuries. The

art also includes several esoteric elements, with the particular goal of getting practitioners to achieve an integration with the "Web of Orlog," a traditional concept that explains the primal law of the universe and how all actions—described as "threads of life"—are connected. It is hoped that, through achieving a basic understanding of this concept, practitioners can be more responsible with their choices about how they interact in the world, and recognize that each action has an equal and opposite reaction.

> "THE WHOLE SYSTEM CAN BE TAUGHT IN AN AFTERNOON, THOUGH IT MIGHT TAKE A LIFETIME TO UNDERSTAND WHAT HAS BEEN TAUGHT."

STAV PRACTITIONER IVAR HAFSKJOLD

Han Moo Do

EXPLANATION
"THE WAY OF KOREAN MARTIAL ART" IN KOREAN

DATE OF ORIGIN
1989

FOUNDER
YOUNG SUK

PLACE OF ORIGIN
FINLAND

Han moo do is a Korean-based martial art founded in Finland that now enjoys growing popularity among the Nordic countries. Not to be confused with the similar-sounding han mu do (see p. 136), the system incorporates a number of full-contact, competition-based fighting techniques and was developed by Young Suk in 1989. Thought to be based on hoi jeon moo sool (see p. 137) and tae kwon do (see pp. 134–35), the system also bears a resemblance to aikido (see pp. 238–39) and, in addition to competition techniques, joint locks, kicks, punches, throws, and grapples are also commonplace.

Glima

EXPLANATION
"TO STRUGGLE WITH SOMETHING" IN ICELANDIC
DATE OF ORIGIN
12TH CENTURY
FOUNDER
NO KNOWN FOUNDER
PLACE OF ORIGIN
ICELAND

Glima is an Icelandic folk wrestling art known as a friendly form of recreation and a sport of gentlemen. Unusually for a martial art, there is little pushing or eye contact and no groundwork. Fighters waltz around each other in a clockwise direction, always standing erect, which, it is believed, creates opportunities for both offense and defense. In that respect, it is a part-physical, part-mental game and one not known for causing physical injuries to practitioners. However, its ancient heritage was probably quite different. It is believed to have originated in the 12th century and writings describing the art can be found in the ancient Icelandic sagas. In Icelandic the word "glima" means "to struggle with something," and has connotations with the struggles presented by life.

Fairness and respect are central to the system's values. Wrestlers wear a belt around the waist and thighs, which is used as a leverage point to hold and throw opponents. Inside their shoes, some practitioners wear runes that are believed to invoke magical powers and, although many modern practitioners do not believe in the runes' symbolism, some still continue the tradition of wearing them while wrestling.

◀ AN UPLIFTING TRADITION
A glima wrestler gains the upper hand by hoisting his opponent high into the air; his next move will be to slam him into the ground.

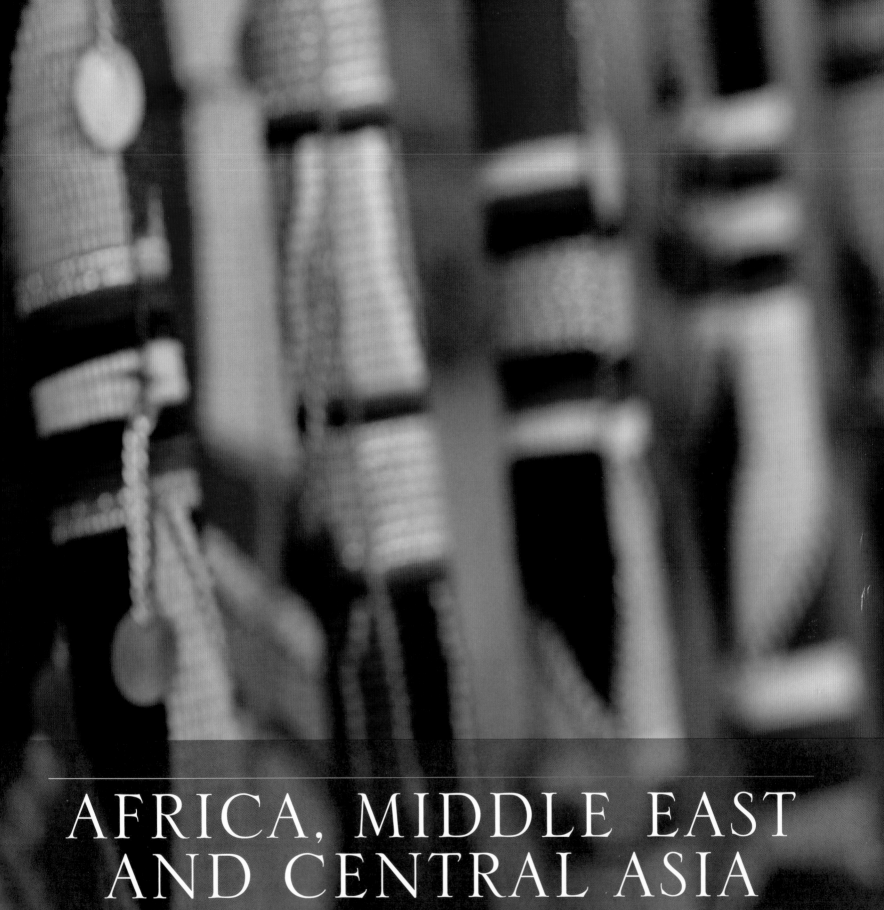

AFRICA, MIDDLE EAST AND CENTRAL ASIA

CULTURE AND INFLUENCES

AFRICA, MIDDLE EAST AND CENTRAL ASIA

THE AFRICAN CONTINENT is rich in history and it is perhaps not surprising that it boasts one of the oldest martial arts in existence. Its varied landscape—the massive expanses of deserts, the lush green jungles, and the amazing vistas and fauna—is reflected in the diversity of its martial arts, which, along with those of the Middle East and central Asia, are arguably among the most captivating in the world.

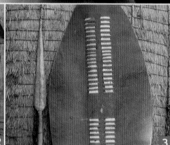

THE EARLIEST EVIDENCE of martial arts in Africa was discovered in the Beni Hasan tombs in Egypt, which date back to between 2040 and 1785BCE, during the Middle Kingdom. In the tombs, archaeologists found paintings of wrestlers displaying techniques such as punching, kicking, throwing, and locking of their opponents' joints. There is also evidence to suggest that ancient Egyptians performed stick fencing as a tribute to the Pharoah. Modern Egyptian stick fencing (see p. 289)—the highly codified system of combat with its own methodology, weaponry, and training syllabus—was developed to keep the Egyptian armed forces trained and ready for battle.

Wrestling and grappling arts are popular throughout Africa and have been likened to European catch wrestling and pankration (see pp. 251, 276). These were traditionally associated with agricultural ceremonies and courtship rituals, most commonly in Nigeria, Sudan, Senegal, Cameroon, and the Gambia.

Tribal arts

Tribal fighting arts were originally practiced as a method of survival because, prior to colonization, the greatest danger to sub-Saharan Africans was

> "DO NOT TRY TO FIGHT A LION IF YOU ARE NOT ONE YOURSELF."
>
> AFRICAN PROVERB

< ZULU WARRIOR
A Zulu warrior from South Africa holding aloft a shield, club and spear. Native costume and traditional weapons form a key part of African tribal martial arts.

REGION AT A GLANCE

1 BIRTHPLACE OF THE WORLD
Thought by many to be the oldest inhabited territory on Earth, Africa is a continent of tradition, where ancient martial arts survive and flourish alongside modern styles.

2 BENI HASAN TOMBS
Some of the earliest historical evidence of martial arts anywhere in the world was discovered in the form of paintings on the walls of these ancient Egyptian tombs.

3 INDIGENOUS TRIBES
The division of precolonial Africa into separate clans and tribes allowed many different martial arts to develop. Conflict between tribes also helped to shape these fighting styles.

4 FIGHTING METHODS
Originally practiced as a means of survival, the use of weapons and shields in early African martial arts reflects the need for both attack and protection.

5 RELIGION AND SPIRITUALISM
Ritual plays a key role in many tribal fighting arts, and many African martial arts include rite-of-passage, prayer, or shamanic elements.

6 MUSIC AND DANCE
The reliance on memorizing attacking and defensive movements using performing art forms is a captivating and common aspect of African martial arts.

7 THE SLAVE TRADE
The influence of African martial arts has spread to other areas of the world. African slaves first practiced Capoeira, the music and dance-based martial art, now popular in Brazil.

8 COLONIALISM
The introduction of firearms and new religious beliefs had a profound effect on African martial arts. It became more common for tribal disputes to be settled with guns, rather than with the more traditional methods such as stick fighting.

▲ WEAPONS OF WARFARE
The weapons used in traditional African martial arts are primitive yet effective. Often used by warriors to ensure their own survival, they are designed to seriously injure opponents in warfare.

MAP OF AFRICA & THE MIDDLE EAST

▼ MARTIAL ARTS AND MUSIC
The enforced movement of Africans into the Americas through the slave trade saw the music and dance elements of African arts assimilated into a number of hybrid American arts. As well as its indigenous arts, Africa has been influenced by the martial arts of China and Japan.

KEY

▶ **In the 16th century,** the slave trade brought African martial arts to the Americas. These helped to shape music- and dance-based arts, such as capoeira in Brazil.

▶ **European traders** traveling to North Africa saw and were influenced by wrestling and stick-fighting styles.

▶ **Elements of** Japanese martial arts have been assimilated into Africa's hybrid arts.

▶ **South African** hybrid arts, such as RAT, draw on martial arts from China.

"TO SUBDUE
ANOTHER TRIBE
YOU MUST STRIKE
IT ONCE AND FOR
ALL ... THERE'S NO
OTHER WAY."

SHAKA ZULU

▲ MARTIAL ARTS AND RESPECT
Martial arts also provide Africans with a means of earning respect within their tribes. The Zulus sparred with sticks to develop their battle skills and enhance their reputations.

the threat from other tribes. Tribal rivals would have been equally matched as hunters, gatherers, and fighters. The most renowned of the African warrior tribes was the Zulu of South Africa, who still represent South Africa's largest ethnic group. Historically, their primary arts included the spear, shield, and club, and they made clever use of all three during strategic advancement.

▼ EARLY EVIDENCE OF MARTIAL ARTS
These ancient Egyptian paintings, discovered in the Beni Hasan tombs on the east bank of the Nile, clearly depict wrestling moves. Their discovery revealed the rich and long history within which African martial arts are rooted.

African Weapons

African tribal weapons were designed for warfare and survival and, as such, were brutal. Historically, the Zulus initiated combat by first throwing their spears from a distance or charging at opponents with them, using their shield as a blocking device. When the use of a spear became impractical at close quarters, they would switch to a club. However, Shaka Zulu, the revolutionary leader of the Zulus during the early 19th century, changed indigenous warfare when he introduced the "iklwa," a stabbing spear that proved highly effective in combat when combined with a tall shield.

Many other clever instruments of war were developed in Africa. The throwing iron, for example, known as the "mongwanga," was a spiked throwing implement that could be employed

effectively from distances of 82 yd (75 m). When thrown with force at a closer range of 27 yd (25 m), this multi-bladed instrument could easily impale a victim, sometimes with lethal consequences. It also had a handle so that it could be used to stab and thrash at close quarters. Another interesting weapon used by certain tribes was the bladed bracelet (see below)—a wrist bracelet with a sharpened outer edge.

➤ BLADED BRACELET
If sharpened, this could be used for slicing an opponent at close quarters, blocking a bladed instrument, or for heavily striking a vulnerable target on the opponent's body.

∧ ZULU DANCERS
Music and dance play crucial roles in the lives of indigenous tribespeople, especially when preparing for battle. Some African martial arts also use music and dance as a means of memorizing attacking or defensive maneuvers.

Dance and music

Perhaps the most interesting aspect of early African martial arts was the reliance on memorizing attacking and defensive maneuvers by setting them to patterns of dance, accompanied by music. These artistic elements of African martial arts have also influenced other arts, such as Capoeira, the Brazilian dance- and music-based martial art (see pp. 340–41), which was originally practiced by African slaves.

Colonization and change

Throughout Africa's long history, martial arts have largely remained unchanged until relatively recently. From the mid-18th century, the European introduction of firearms in exchange for West African slaves threatened the continuation of traditional martial arts in Africa. The introduction of the gun changed the face of warfare entirely, leading to an emphasis on different battlefield skills. Furthermore, in the late 19th century, the Islamic revitalization of many African countries led to the reduction of a lot of martial arts that contained pagan or shamanic elements.

Although the term "witch doctor" is often used negatively in the developed world to imply a lack of expertise, the belief in traditional, ritualistic healing over science is prevalent in many African shamanic societies. Many tribal communities believe that illness, disease, and even death are caused by evil sorcery or offended spirits, and will therefore consult a traditional healer before attending a western-style physician. They will also often visit a "medicine man" before a stick fight, wrestling bout, or battle, in order to obtain strength and protection from the spirits. These "shamans" communicate with the spirit world on behalf of the community, using highly ritualistic divination processes. In South Africa, they are known as "sangomas," and form a crucial part of tribal life.

▼ NATIONAL SPORT
In many areas of Senegal, Laamb wrestling is considered a people's sport and is more popular than soccer or baseball.

Laamb Wrestling

EXPLANATION
"TO FIGHT" IN WOLOF

DATE OF ORIGIN
INDIGENOUS ART

FOUNDER
NO KNOWN FOUNDER

PLACE OF ORIGIN
SENEGAL

Incorporating both striking and grappling techniques, Laamb wrestling is a highly ritualized art form. Practitioners wear loincloth wrappers provided by their fiancés or female relatives, and perform a stylized dance around the ring before combat commences. The drum beat and accompanying music creates an almost hypnotic atmosphere for spectators who gather around the sand-filled pits.

In order to win a Laamb match, a practitioner must force his opponent's knee or back to the ground. Successful fighters are notorious in their region and young men often engage in these types of fights to prove themselves as men and to bring honor to their families, themselves, and their village.

A fighter never enters the ring without the presence of his spiritual leader, known as a "marabout" or "juju man." It is believed they have the power to exorcise evil demons and break spells that may have been cast on the fighter by his opponent. The art is now also starting to gain interest from business promoters, who offer financial rewards to the winners.

Evala Wrestling

EXPLANATION
WRESTLING STYLE OF THE
KABYÉ PEOPLE

DATE OF ORIGIN
INDIGENOUS ART

FOUNDER
NO KNOWN FOUNDER

PLACE OF ORIGIN
TOGO

▲ **TALCUM POWDER**
Evala wrestlers cover themselves with talcum
powder to make it harder for their opponents
to get a firm grasp.

Most commonly practiced by the
Kabyé people in Togo, Evala is a
traditional wrestling art from west
Africa. For young men in the area,
it is considered the penultimate
element in a rite of passage into
adulthood, which includes climbing
three mountains, intensive mental
and physical training, and
circumcision. Those who fail the
training are not initiated into
adulthood. Fights take place on a
yearly basis at the Evala festival.

Although wrestlers are initiated
regardless of whether they win or
not, winning the fight is of primary
importance—a loss is considered to
bring shame on the participant and
his family. This encourages the fighter
to train hard and focus on his
master's teachings.

◄ **GRASS HUTS**
Separated from their
families approximately
a week before the fight,
young warriors reside
in grass huts, where
they are subjected to
intensive mental and
physical training.

Dambe

EXPLANATION
"TO HAVE INTEGRITY IN THE LIGHT
OF THE CREATOR" IN HAUSA

DATE OF ORIGIN
INDIGENOUS ART

FOUNDER
NO KNOWN FOUNDER

PLACE OF ORIGIN
NIGERIA

Also known as "Hausa boxing,"
Dambe is practiced by the Hausa
people, who reside mainly in
Nigeria, but are also prevalent in
large groups across Chad, Ghana,
Sudan, and Cameroon.

Predominantly a brutal fist-
fighting art, in the past it included a
wrestling component—known as
"Kokawa"—but many of the original
wrestling moves have now been lost.
Accompanied by percussive music,
contests consist of three rounds and
take place on a flat, mud-baked
surface; the fighters create plumes of
dust as they brawl.

Traditionally, participants wrap
their dominant leg in a metal chain
and bind their fighting fist, called
the "spear," in rough twine. Fighters
are taught to adopt a wide stance,
with their guard raised high above
their heads. They aim to use a single
strike with the spear to knock down
their opponent, known as "killing."
Usually the left hand, referred to as
the "shield," is used to parry or
block. Roundhouse-style kicks are
also sometimes employed. A match
is won when a fighter forces his
opponent to touch the ground.

Fights usually occur during
harvest time, when competitors—
often farmers or butchers—come
together and fight, wearing traditional
loincloths. There is a spiritual
element to the art and practitioners
wear amulets, which they believe
give them supernatural protection.

Dambe is starting to gain
commercial interest and is often used
to advertise products. With money
now on offer for some bouts, fighters
travel from far and wide to compete.

> ## "LET THOSE WHO DARE, COME BATTLE WITH ME."
>
> EXCERPT FROM A KIRARI PRAISE CHANT, SUNG TO HONOR THE GREAT DAMBE FIGHTER, SHAGO

Egyptian Stick Fencing

EXPLANATION
STICK-FIGHTING STYLE OF THE
EGYPTIANS

DATE OF ORIGIN
C. 2000 BCE

FOUNDER
NO KNOWN FOUNDER

PLACE OF ORIGIN
EGYPT

Egyptian stick fencing dates back to
the time of the Pharaohs and is one of
the oldest recorded arts. The stick,
known as the "asa" or "nabboot," is 4 ft
(1.22 m) long, and fighting moves are
based on sword and shield strikes and
blocks, as used in actual combat.

In common with many stick-
fighting arts around the world, it is
likely that the sporting element
developed as a practical training
method for warriors who, before
gaining mastery of the sword, could
practice techniques using sticks
without causing too much physical
harm to their training partners.

Training safely was particularly
important prior to the advent of
modern medicine and antibiotics, as
a minor cut with a sword could easily
become infected and cause a fatality.

The art is most commonly
witnessed during festivals and the
month of Ramadan, and
demonstrations still take place at
marriage ceremonies around the
country. Modern stick fencing is
also taught to the Egyptian army.

A popular variant is "Tahtib," a
stick-fighting dance performed by
martial artists, usually accompanied
by musicians.

▼ **NOBLE ART**
Wielding rough wooden staves, two participants
wearing traditional robes and turbans compete
in the ancient sport of Egyptian stick fencing.

Nuba Fighting

EXPLANATION
FIGHTING STYLE OF THE
NUBA PEOPLE

DATE OF ORIGIN
INDIGENOUS ART

FOUNDER
NO KNOWN FOUNDER

PLACE OF ORIGIN
SUDAN

Nuba fighting includes both wrestling and stick-fighting elements, and is practiced by the Nuba people, who live in the Kurdufan hill country of central Sudan. Contests are regularly

▲ **TRIBAL CONFLICT**
A crowd of spectators form a human circle around the fighters, while girls from the village sing to praise one fighter and deride the other.

organized between male members of neighboring communities, who aim to bring honor to their village, rather than to achieve personal success. When wrestling, a fighter wins the match by throwing his opponent to the ground; pinning is not allowed and there are no submissions.

Tournaments are usually held after the harvest to offer thanks to the spirit world for a plentiful crop, and are accompanied by feasting.

Testa

EXPLANATION
HAND-TO-HAND FIGHTING
STYLE

DATE OF ORIGIN
INDIGENOUS ART

FOUNDER
NO KNOWN FOUNDER

PLACE OF ORIGIN
ETHIOPIA

Testa is a hand-to-hand combat art popular in Ethiopia and Eritrea. It places an emphasis on dirty fighting techniques, such as gouging, biting, and head-butting. Unusual techniques include biting an opponent's windpipe or groin. The main goal, however, is to knock out an opponent with the head, which is known as the "big knuckle."

Rough and Tumble

EXPLANATION
HYBRID FIGHTING
STYLE

DATE OF ORIGIN
1990s

FOUNDER
NO KNOWN FOUNDER

PLACE OF ORIGIN
SOUTH AFRICA

Also known by the acronym RAT, Rough and Tumble was formulated to teach armed and unarmed combat skills to the South African Special Forces, although it is now widely practiced by civilians. A hybrid system that has drawn influence from many other martial arts, it has no official technical structure and may be difficult to distinguish from other hybrid styles.

Common striking techniques used include punches, kicks, knee strikes, elbow strikes, head-butts, and finger gouges, but fighters are also able to utilize grappling methods, such as tripping, throwing, locking, choking, and trapping. Along with the physical basics, practitioners study ethics, law, strategy, and psychology, in the hope that they will become open-minded and humble fighters. Fitness is a key element of the art, which has a rank and belt system similar to the Japanese grading systems.

Suri Stick Fighting

EXPLANATION
STICK-FIGHTING STYLE OF
THE SURI PEOPLE

DATE OF ORIGIN
INDIGENOUS ART

FOUNDER
NO KNOWN FOUNDER

PLACE OF ORIGIN
SOUTHWEST ETHIOPIA

▼ **GAINING RESPECT**
Suri stick fighters—protected only by a thick cloth, wrapped around their head and arms—strive to win the fight and improve their social standing.

The Suri are a seminomadic people whose livelihood revolves around herding cattle. Each Suri male carries a long stick—known as a "donga"—as he walks through the bush and tends to his cows.

The Suri people view themselves as warriors, and stick fighting plays a crucial part in their culture. It is also a major spectator sport. Huge crowds gather to watch the contests, which generally occur after the rainy season when food is plentiful and energy levels among the tribe are high. It is common for around 20 to 30 fighters from each side to participate, taking it in turns to fight one-on-one.

Bloodshed is common—the only rule of combat is not to kill your opponent—and the atmosphere is highly volatile. The violence often erupts beyond the arena and, with firearms readily available in the region, shootings among spectators are becoming an increasingly common problem at these events.

▼ **PAINTED FACES**
A Suri stick fighter displays the intricate, fingerpainted designs that have been applied to his face using white clay.

▼ TRADITIONAL WEAPONS
A Nguni stick fighter levels an "induku"—a heavy, carved stick used for attack—at his opponent's head. The shield and slender stick for blocking are carried in the left hand.

Nguni Stick Fighting

EXPLANATION
STICK-FIGHTING STYLE OF NGUNI TRIBES

DATE OF ORIGIN
INDIGENOUS ART

FOUNDER
THE ZULU KING SHAKA

PLACE OF ORIGIN
SOUTH AFRICA

Developed to teach self-defense and tribal warfare techniques to teenage herdboys, Nguni stick fighting is an often brutal sport. The original Zulu fighting system, it is said to have been practiced by Nelson Mandela as a child. Stick fighting also plays a vital role in tribal ceremonies, including the initiation ritual that marks a boy's transition from childhood and adolescence to manhood.

Fighters use two sticks—one for attack and one for defense—and a small cowhide shield to parry and block attacks. The objective is for each combatant to strike his opponent until he falls to the ground, or surrenders, or until first blood is drawn. Strength, agility, and the ability to take pain are the ultimate defining characteristics that allow fighters to win stick battles, and training for the art, though varied, always aims to engender these qualities. Over the years fighters develop rhythm, timing, speed, and an enhanced spacial awareness that helps them to block incoming attacks.

In recent years, the sport has become more codified, with regular competitions, rules, and safety procedures in place. As such, it has enjoyed a resurgence in popularity.

> ❯ COWHIDE SHIELD
> A small shield protects a fighter's hand and wrist from incoming strikes without hindering his movements.

"A MAN CHOSEN TO WIELD LIFE AND DEATH ON THE BATTLEFIELD MUST BE AN ARTIST. IF HE ISN'T, HE IS SIMPLY A MURDERER."

SHAKA ZULU

BEHIND THE SCENES

NGUNI STICK FIGHTERS

THROUGHOUT HISTORY, STICK FIGHTING has played a central role in the lives of the Nguni people, providing the opportunity for men to develop their battle skills and earn respect within the community. Living mainly within the KwaZulu-Natal province in South Africa, the Zulus represent the largest Nguni tribe.

Stick fighting is ingrained within Zulu culture and traditions. Although it plays an important part in certain tribal rituals—such as initiation ceremonies—its main objective is to teach self-defense and battle techniques to male members of the tribe so they are prepared and able to fight in battle situations. As such, training forms a crucial part of their lives, yet must fit around other tasks within the homestead, such as cattle herding and hut maintenance. Training begins when teenage herdboys reach puberty: at this point they are divided into groups and taken under the care of an older boy leader. It is

> "IT IS VITAL THAT ZULUS LEARN AND MAINTAIN FIGHTING SKILLS TO A HIGH STANDARD. AS THEY MAY SOON BE RISKING THEIR LIVES IN REAL WARFARE SITUATIONS."

vital that Zulus learn and maintain skills to a high standard, as they may soon be risking their lives in real warfare situations. Although there is no specific time set aside for training or battle, it is common for boys and men to spar on a daily basis, in order to keep their skills as sharp as possible. Sparring also helps them to establish and enhance their stick-fighting reputations, thereby proving their manliness and earning them respect. Traditional outfits and weapons are utilized for both stick fighting and battle. Furthermore, as with many African tribal arts, dancing and rituals are key elements of fight preparations.

GRASS HUTS

Zulu warriors and their families live in "beehive" grass huts, constructed from poles and thatch. The hut floors are reinforced using a densely compacted combination of cow dung and sand, polished to resemble dark, green marble. Food is stored in pots and baskets outside the huts, and the homesteads are entirely self-sufficient.

NGUNI VILLAGE

Commonly arranged around a central, circular cattle fold, Nguni huts are typically arranged in a crescent shape, at the higher end of a sloping area of land. Fields for growing crops and grazing cattle are located nearby.

DAILY LIFE

A tribe's strength is measured by the amount of cattle it herds, and, accordingly, cattle form a crucial aspect of the Zulu way of life. Herding cattle to and from pasture takes up the majority of most typical mornings, and beef is only eaten on special occasions. Other daily tasks include building and repairing huts, making weapons, digging storage pits, and producing handicrafts. When circumstances demand, Zulu men practice their stick-fighting techniques and, as warriors, take part in battles against other tribes.

SPIRITUAL BELIEFS

Zulus worship one creationist god known as "Nkulunkulu." They appeal to Nkulunkulu and converse with the spirit world through a member of the tribe called the "sangoma"—and through the sacrifice of cattle. The sangoma uses divination processes to invoke ancestral spirits, believing that all misfortunes—including death—are the work of evil sorcery or offended spirits.

MAKING WEAPONS

Using locally sourced materials and skills passed down from generation to generation, the manufacture of weapons is an important feature of Zulu life. Weapons are generally made from animal skin, wood, iron, wire, and rope. Fighting sticks are cut from local trees.

> "A WARRIOR IS NOT A WRESTLER; HE'S KILLED THE MOMENT HIS SPEAR AND SHIELD ARE OVERPOWERED."
>
> AFRICAN PROVERB

TRAINING SESSIONS

Stick fighting, though also a sport in its own right, is practiced primarily by male members of the tribe as a means of obtaining and improving warrior skills for battle. Boys start their training during puberty, when they are also taught how to hunt and throw a spear.

PREPARING FOR BATTLE

Traditionally, it is important for Zulu warriors to undergo certain cleansing rituals when preparing to fight. The night before a battle, a herbalist, known as the "inyanga," sprinkles medicine called "intelezi" over the fighters and their weapons that fortifies the warriors for the day ahead. A sangoma may also be consulted.

"A MAN WHO IS PUTTING ON HIS ARMOR FOR WAR SHOULD NOT BOAST LIKE A MAN WHO'S TAKING IT OFF."

AFRICAN PROVERB

BATTLE

Preparing to charge into battle, Zulu warriors let out a battle cry and perform a ritualistic dance, with the goal of raising morale and intimidating their opponents. Under King Shaka's reign in the early 19th century—and with the introduction of new weapons and tactics—warfare was brutal. Battles are primarily fought to settle disputes, perhaps over land, with neighboring tribes.

WEAPONS AND ARMOR

ZULU WEAPONS

DECORATION
The tips of shields and sticks are often decorated with animal tails and hides

SIMPLE YET EXTREMELY EFFECTIVE, the weapons utilized by Zulu warriors helped them to become a fearsome and brutal fighting force. The Zulu King Shaka revolutionized the face of warfare when he popularized the use of the "iklwa," or stabbing spear, which warriors used in addition to their traditional "assegais," or throwing spears. In battle situations, warriors would first use their throwing spears to weaken enemy lines from a distance, after which they would advance as soon as possible in formation. Stabbing spears and clubs were then used to deliver further injuries to their opponents at close quarters.

∨ CEREMONIAL DRESS
Warriors wear full ceremonial dress for stick-fighting ceremonies and tribal events; a scaled down version of this would be worn for actual battle.

SHIELD
It was considered to be a disgrace for a Zulu to lose his shield to an enemy

∨ ASSEGAI
These throwing spears—designed to be thrown from a distance—have slim handles that allow warriors to hold multiple spears in their shield hands, ready for casting. They are usually the first weapons used in battle.

IRON TIP
Iron blades are sharpened to inflict the greatest possible injury

FUR
The type of animal hide worn reveals the warrior's status in the tribe—the royal family and chiefs wear leopard skins

BRACELET
Jewelry is used to identify different regiments of warriors, as well as a warrior's status

INDUKO
An offensive fighting stick is used in stick-fighting practice and ceremonial demonstrations

LOINCLOTH
These knee-length skirts are made from animal hides and fur

LONG SHAFT
A long shaft makes the weapon aerodynamic, enabling it to travel farther when thrown

UBHOKO
A long blocking stick is used to ward off or parry opposition blows

GRIP
Wrapping the shaft in woven wire ensures that it is easy to grip and throw

◄ IKLWA
So called because of the sound they make when withdrawn from an opponent's body, these short stabbing spears are the Zulu's weapon of choice in close-combat situations.

IRON TIP
Iklwa blades are slightly shorter than assegai blades, but just as sharp

COW HIDE
A small, oval-shaped piece of skin stretched over the frame forms the front of the shield

WRAPPING
Animal skin is used to reinforce and decorate the joint

SHAFT
Local wood is shaped so as to ensure a good grip

UMSILA
A short stick forms the backbone of the shield and is often decorated with strings of animal skin

▼ IHAWU
Warriors used shields for protection during battle and stick fighting. During Shaka's reign, the color of the shield denoted the rank of the warrior.

NOOSE
The umsila (see below left) is attached to the back of the cow hide using four triangular nooses

ROUNDED KNOB
Heavily weighted and designed for maximum impact, rounded ends are carved from local hard wood

▼ SHORT CLUB
Used for very close combat, short clubs are held in one hand and deliver a heavy blow, making them simple yet powerful weapons.

▼ ISIWA
Also known as "knobkerries" these longer clubs—usually wielded in the right hand—are used by warriors as missiles or when fighting one-on-one against an opponent.

DECORATIONS
Although primarily used for aesthetic purposes, in some cases markings help to distinguish between different tribes

LENGTH
The length of the wooden staff is determined by the stature of the warrior

CARVINGS
Zulus often use longer clubs as staves during peacetime, hence the ornate nature of this weapon

◄ **BRUTAL ART**
Waiting for their turn to join the fray, Suri stick fighters form a ring around the fighting arena and offer support to fellow villagers. Fights are extremely fierce and often little protection is worn against injury.

Krav Maga

EXPLANATION
"CONTACT COMBAT" IN HEBREW

DATE OF ORIGIN
1930s

FOUNDER
IMI LICHTENFELD

PLACE OF ORIGIN
ISRAEL

The official hand-to-hand combat art of the Israeli Defense Force, krav maga is exploding in popularity throughout Europe, Australia, and the US—especially in California, where it is fast becoming a fitness and self-defense craze among the Hollywood elite. Developed by Imi Lichtenfeld in the 1930s, it was originally taught to soldiers in the newly formed state of Israel as a method of defense against inevitable attacks. Now adapted for use in civilian situations, krav maga teaches practitioners how to manage stress effectively so they can function normally in threatening situations. It is often thought of as a natural system that is easy to learn and simple to retain. Performed intuitively, these qualities should help its growth. The art is not practiced as a sport and there are no specific uniforms or officially recognized competitions.

Guiding principles

Krav maga is based on simple principles and instinctive rules, such as "there are no rules in a real fight" and "do not injure your partner when training." The guiding principles are sixfold: to neutralize any threat; to go from defending to attacking quickly; to avoid injury; to use improvised weapons; to strike vulnerable parts of the opponent's body; and to use the body's natural reflexes. There are no set movements and practitioners are urged to use whatever works. "Retzef"—the concept of continuous combat motion—is also crucial in krav maga, teaching practitioners to incorporate effective movements in a rapid and continuous fashion until the opponent has been neutralized.

Training techniques

The main areas of study are prevention, escape, evasion, and avoidance. Training involves practical self-defense techniques that allow followers to defend themselves against choke-holds and grabs, as well as against weapons, such as pistols, machine guns, and knives. Because of its origins and use in the

IMI LICHTENFELD

Raised in Slovakia, Hungarian-born Imi Lichtenfeld formulated krav maga in the 1930s to protect his Jewish neighbors from fascist thugs. Under Nazi persecution, he fled to Palestine, joined Haganah (see opposite), and fought for the creation of Israel. He taught krav maga to soldiers until his retirement, and then adapted it for everyday life.

> **NEGOTIATING A THREAT**
A krav-maga instructor demonstrates one of the techniques for disarming an assailant. Weapon maneuvers are crucial elements of krav maga, because of its origins and use in the military.

GUN-DISARMING TECHNIQUE

1
Standing in their starting positions, the defender (left) faces the attacker and prepares to redirect the line of fire by grabbing the muzzle of the gun.

2
He takes control of the weapon and pushes it downward, while simultaneously launching a powerful counterattack by punching the attacker in the face.

3
By disarming the attacker quickly with strong snapping movements, he gains control of the weapon and keeps his body out of the line of fire.

4
Only when he is sure that the gun is completely in his possession does he retreat to a safe distance. Stepping back too soon could jeopardize his safety.

5
With the weapon and the defender now safe, the balance of power has shifted, and the threat from the attacker is successfully overcome.

military, the system has also evolved a number of more specific techniques, for example, extracting a hand grenade from the hand of a terrorist when the pin has already been removed. This is a particularly risky maneuver, for which good technical knowledge and a high degree of skill must be employed.

A crucial difference between krav-maga training and training for other martial arts is that all attacks and defenses are applied as if under life-threatening circumstances. Techniques are regularly performed under worst-case-scenario conditions, such as fighting in confined spaces (alleyways, staircases, and vehicles), in the dark, against multiple attackers, or against an attacker approaching from behind. In all of these situations, physical and mental control is key.

"MOVE QUICKLY FROM DEFENSE TO ATTACK BY BECOMING THE AGGRESSOR AS FAST AS POSSIBLE."

IMI LICHTENFELD

Haganah System

EXPLANATION
"DEFENSE" IN HEBREW
DATE OF ORIGIN
1920s
FOUNDER
NO KNOWN FOUNDER
PLACE OF ORIGIN
ISRAEL

"Haganah" was a paramilitary Jewish organization—formed during the British mandate of Palestine (1920–1948)—that later became the Israeli Defense Force (IDF). It defeated better-equipped opponents to establish the state of Israel. The Haganah system evolved from these military beginnings, adapting armed and unarmed tactics for civilian needs. It is based around two major components: Fierce Israeli Guerrilla Hand-to-hand Tactics (FIGHT) and Israeli Tactical Knife and Combat Shooting—and is constantly updated to keep up with the ever-changing face of warfare. The basic principles are to "avoid," "escape," and "demolish." If a situation can be avoided then it should be; the next recourse is to escape. If neither option is viable, practitioners are urged to incapacitate their opponent. If forced to fight, there are no rules and no limits. Controversially, some practitioners claim not to need a teacher, believing that DVDs and books will suffice.

▼ IN TRAINING
A row of female Haganah fighters during a training exercise. Both men and women fought in the underground army.

Kapap

EXPLANATION
"FACE-TO-FACE" COMBAT IN HEBREW
DATE OF ORIGIN
1930s
FOUNDER
NO KNOWN FOUNDER
PLACE OF ORIGIN
ISRAEL

Developed in the 1930s and based on concepts rather than techniques, the term "kapap" is an acronym of "krav panim el panim," which translates as "face-to-face combat." It was adopted by the Pal'mach—a separate, elite fighting branch of Haganah (see above), established in 1941 by the British military and Haganah to protect Palestine from the Nazis—and formed a crucial part of their training. The fighting spirit is central to the art, and training is not geared toward sport but is solely used as a form of self-defense. Key elements include proper body posture, correct movement on striking, appropriate striking method, positioning, and stick and baton defense and attack. Experience is deemed more valuable than title, and it is vital for kapap instructors to have had practical experience of warfare.

Although kapap methods were still considered relevant, the term itself went into decline after the 1940s. However, a group headed by Lieutenant Colonel Chaim Peer and Major Avi Nardia reintroduced it in 2000 by establishing an international kapap federation. Aiming to popularize the military techniques they had learned and taught while serving in Israel among civilians, it is largely due to their efforts that the system has become popular in Europe and America.

"ALWAYS A STUDENT, SOMETIMES A TEACHER."

Sayokan

EXPLANATION
"THE WAY OF THE WARRIOR" IN TURKISH

DATE OF ORIGIN
1999

FOUNDER
NIHAT YIGIT

PLACE OF ORIGIN
TURKEY

Founded by Nihat Yigit, sayokan is a hybrid martial art of Turkish origin that combines various elements of Shaolin kung fu, tae kwon do, and kyokushin karate (see p. 57, 134–35, 225).

The system describes itself as a reformist art and, alongside technical, physical movements, incorporates two separate training programs, known as "bravery program A" and "bravery program B." This interesting addition to the art helps participants to develop physical and mental confidence, along with resilience and determination.

The first training program ("A") places emphasis on the participants' ability to respond to attacks, and is performed without the protection of pads or body armor, usually in five-minute fighting bouts. The second program ("B") is a 108-hour course, including one-on-one and multiple-opponent sparring. Weapons are usually introduced at this level, and successful candidates achieve a black belt (1st Dan).

> "DON'T CARRY YOUR ART ON YOUR BACK, LET SAYOKAN CARRY YOU ON ITS BACK."
>
> SAYOKAN MOTTO

Kurash

EXPLANATION
"REACHING THE GOAL WITH THE JUST OR FAIR WAY" IN UZBEK

DATE OF ORIGIN
INDIGENOUS ART

FOUNDER
NO KNOWN FOUNDER

PLACE OF ORIGIN
UZBEKISTAN

Kurash is a Turkic wrestling art, most commonly practiced in Uzbekistan. Although the art has developed over millennia, many of its original tactics and philosophies remain in place. Kurash is not an Olympic sport, but it is included in the Asian Games. A victory is achieved by throwing an

Yagh Gures

EXPLANATION
"OIL WRESTLING" IN TURKISH

DATE OF ORIGIN
14TH CENTURY

FOUNDER
NO KNOWN FOUNDER

PLACE OF ORIGIN
TURKEY

> **TRADITIONAL OUTFITS**
> Slathered in oil, bare-chested competitors wear only hand-stitched garments called "kisbet." Traditionally made using water-buffalo hide, modern outfits are commonly made of calf leather.

Also known as "Turkish oil wrestling," yagh gures is a wrestling art in which wrestlers, known as "pehlivan" (which means "hero"), cover their bodies with olive oil, thus making it more difficult for their opponents to apply holds and locks.

Before entering the ring, the wrestlers oil each other as a mark of respect and to demonstrate friendship and harmony. If a younger man competes and is victorious over an older man, he kisses the older man's hand, a common sign of respect in Turkish communities.

A victory is achieved when a wrestler manages to hold down his opponent in a position from which it is reasonable to expect him not to be able to extricate himself.

Traditionally, this ancient wrestling art had no time limits, and it was not uncommon for matches to last up to two days in length. Today, wrestling bouts are stopped at between 30–40 minutes, depending on region or category.

A popular place to witness the art is at the Kirkpinar tournament, which has been held annually since 1362 and is the oldest continual sporting competition in existence.

opponent onto his back, and points are awarded if he is thrown onto his belly, buttocks, or side.

This upright style of wrestling discourages ground fighting; it was traditionally a battlefield art, and once a fighter was on the ground he was more vulnerable to attack and weapon thrusts from opponents. Balance and quick footwork—enabling practitioners to stay on their feet while wrestling, and undermining the balance of their opponent—is central to the martial application of throws and trips.

> **BALANCE AND FOOTWORK**
A kurash practitioner demonstrates the importance of balance and footwork when tackling his opponent.

"KURASH INCORPORATES FEATURES CLOSE TO THE SPIRIT AND CHARACTER OF THE UZBEK PEOPLE, NAMELY COURAGE, BRAVERY, SPIRITUAL GENEROSITY, FAIRNESS AND HUMANISM."

ISLAM KARIMOV, PRESIDENT OF UZBEKISTAN, HONORARY PRESIDENT OF THE INTERNATIONAL KURASH ASSOCIATION

THE AMERICAS

THE AMERICAS

TO MOST PEOPLE, the continents of North and South America are not immediately associated with the martial arts. On closer inspection, however, the region reveals itself as a cultural melting pot in which vibrant, indigenous, tribal fighting methods stand side-by-side with martial-arts traditions from Europe and Asia. Central and North America's most popular martial arts are hybrid systems that have emerged through the continual evolution and amalgamation of indigenous and imported systems.

MARTIAL ARTS have become an increasingly essential part of the fabric of modern, urban society in many corners of North, Central, and South America. This has been encouraged by the demands of live TV broadcasts that have turned some arts into sports watched by millions—for example, the spectacular mixed-martial-arts competitions of the Ultimate Fighting Championships (see pp. 318–27). Movies, too, have popularized other arts among younger generations eager to learn self-defense techniques or to imitate their screen heroes.

> "WHEN PURE KNUCKLES MEET PURE FLESH, THAT'S PURE KARATE, NO MATTER WHO EXECUTES IT OR WHATEVER STYLE IS INVOLVED."
>
> ED PARKER, AMERICAN MARTIAL ARTIST, PROMOTER, TEACHER, AND AUTHOR

▼ CAPOEIRA AT SUNDOWN
Practitioners on a beach in Brazil take it in turns to play a variety of musical instruments, dance, perform acrobatics, and spar.

The African connection

The early martial arts of the Americas emerged among the communities of African slaves who brought their fighting and dancing skills to Brazil and the Caribbean. They created martial arts such as capoeira (see pp. 340–43), which involves a multitude of powerful punches, kicks, and head butts. Capoeira was outlawed, but the slaves continued to practice their art under the guise of music and dance performances—the blows were disguised among hypnotic dance movements. Slave communities also created mani stick fighting in Cuba and calinda in the Caribbean and New Orleans (see p. 338), and these were also fought with a musical accompaniment, often at festivals and carnivals. The no-holds-barred wrestling matches of Brazilian vale tudo and Brazilian jujutsu (see pp. 339, 344–49) are forerunners of mixed martial arts (see pp. 318–27), which saw a huge surge in popularity in the early 1990s. All these systems have left an indelible imprint on the martial-arts landscape in the Americas.

A fusion of styles

Perhaps the best example of the hybrid influences that distinguish a truly American martial art is jeet kune do (see pp. 316–17). The legendary martial-arts movie star Bruce Lee (see p. 313), who was born in San Francisco and raised in

1 OPPRESSION OF SLAVERY
Africans brought their fighting techniques with them when they were sold into slavery in the Americas. The techniques evolved under conditions of oppression in Brazil and the Caribbean.

2 RETURNING MARINES
US marines serving in Korea and Japan learned martial arts from local people. On their return to the US, some set up schools to promote their own version of the arts.

3 ASIAN IMMIGRATION
Immigrants from China, Japan, and Korea introduced their particular martial arts to urban communities in Brazil and the US.

4 THE POWER OF TELEVISION
The development and popularity of sports such as mixed martial arts owe much to the power and reach of television and the money it provides.

5 THE INFLUENCE OF THE MOVIES
The US movie industry, and especially the movies featuring martial-arts legends such as Bruce Lee, has had a profound effect on the spread of martial arts.

6 THE MELTING POT OF HAWAII
Several important martial-arts systems evolved in Hawaii, where the culture of the Pacific Islanders met the urban culture of the US.

7 URBAN VIOLENCE
The widespread increase in urban violence has encouraged more and more people to learn self-defense techniques in order to protect themselves.

8 MUSICAL RHYTHM
The accompaniment of rythmical music, especially drum beats, and dance is integral to the movements and techniques of several martial arts.

> **A CULTURAL MELTING POT**
There is no doubt that the greatest influence on the development of martial arts in the Americas is the diverse mix of people from all over the world who have settled there.

MAP OF THE AMERICAS

KEY

The Americas were heavily influenced by the music- and dance-based arts brought to their shores by African slaves.

At the turn of the 20th century, economic migrants arrived in the Americas from Japan. This led to the development of various hybrid systems, including Brazilian jujutsu.

Chinese migration, especially during the 19th-century gold rush, saw the growth of Chinese-based martial arts in America.

Elements of Brazilian jujutsu have found their way into mixed martial arts in the US.

Collegiate wrestling is based on elements of catch wrestling, brought to the US by UK immigrants.

Hong Kong, developed this system from techniques of Chinese wing chun, Japanese judo, Western boxing, European fencing (see pp. 122, 234–35, 256–65, 268–69), and Filipino arts. Lee drew on philosophies from around the world to express his thinking. His innovative martial-arts training program was modern and scientific and emphasized the practical value of nonclassical and traditional routines. The US culture of freedom, creativity, and a can-do attitude no doubt played a large part in shaping his thinking. Lee's legacy also includes a number of hugely successful movies, almost all of which highlight his exceptional physical conditioning and martial-arts prowess.

Burgeoning success

The proud martial tradition in America extends from collegiate wrestling (see p. 328), which is largely based on catch wrestling from Europe (see p. 251), to the kickboxing phenomena of the 1970s and 80s that transformed the public perception of martial arts. Other examples include lua (see p.334), a unique and exotic combat art from Hawaii, and American kempo (see p. 315), which is based on Chinese fighting methods but has a purely English-language syllabus, is taught in an American cultural context, and was popular with celebrities such as Elvis Presley.

The success of martial arts in the Americas has extended to the military, security services, and police, all of whom have recognized the benefits of martial techniques in their field of work. The US armed forces have extensively researched and developed a number of noteworthy combat systems. For example, two highly codified, close-quarter combat systems—the Marine Corps Martial Arts Program and the LINE system—are specifically designed for teaching recruits in a limited time-frame and to maximum effect.

⌃ THE CALM BEFORE THE BRAWL
A group of men gather in the streets for the annual tinku festival in Mancha, in the Bolivian Andes. During the festival men will square up to each other in the streets and engage in bloody, often bare-knuckle, fighting.

"IF YOU ALWAYS PUT A LIMIT ON EVERYTHING YOU DO ... IT WILL SPREAD INTO YOUR WORK AND INTO YOUR LIFE. THERE ARE NO LIMITS. THERE ARE ONLY PLATEAUS, AND YOU MUST NOT STAY THERE, YOU MUST GO BEYOND THEM."

BRUCE LEE

⟨ COLLEGIATE WRESTLING
With great effort, a practitioner pins his opponent to the mat—the ultimate aim in collegiate wrestling, and a maneuver that guarantees a win. The wrestling style has evolved from a wide variety of styles brought into America from all over the world.

> **ANYTHING GOES**
The name of the Brazillian martial art of vale tudo translates from Portuguese as "everything allowed." This reflects the fact that the sport has fewer rules regarding safety than many other martial arts in America.

HAWAIIAN WEAPON USED IN LIMALAMA

A MARTIAL-ARTS ICON

Bruce Lee (far right, with his mother and siblings) was born Lee Juan Fan, in 1940, in San Francisco. He took up martial arts after being set upon by a gang when he was 12 years old. Lee began his Hollywood career teaching martial arts to other actors, but was destined to become a star in his own right. He is widely regarded as being the catalyst for the success of martial-arts movies in the West.

Wen-Do

EXPLANATION
WOMEN'S SELF-DEFENSE

DATE OF ORIGIN
1972

FOUNDER
NED AND ANNE PAIGE

PLACE OF ORIGIN
TORONTO, CANADA

▼ **DEALING WITH AN ATTACKER**
In wen-do, women learn to deal with an attacker by escaping from body and arm holds, wrist grabs, and front and back chokeholds.

Wen-do is not considered by practitioners to be a martial art form, but rather an organization dedicated to practicing self-defense techniques for women. Wen-do was founded by Ned and Anne Paige, who are skilled practitioners in judo, karate, and jujutsu (see pp. 234–35, 202–03, 216–17). It draws from all martial arts and provides women with knowledge, skills, self-defense ability, and personal power. This feminist organization celebrates survival and a resistance to injustice. Its core philosophy of hybrid self-defense techniques, underpinned by a belief in personal self-development, makes wen-do an important addition to the growing body of hybrid martial arts.

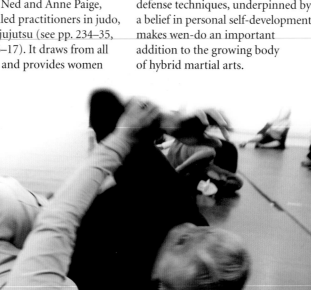

Defendo

EXPLANATION
THE WAY OF SELF-DEFENSE

DATE OF ORIGIN
1945

FOUNDER
BILL UNDERWOOD

PLACE OF ORIGIN
TORONTO, CANADA

Englishman Bill Underwood developed an unarmed combat system called combato (later renamed defendo) after learning basic jujutsu (see pp. 216–17) and other grappling skills. He became a Canadian citizen and taught his system of close-quarter striking and jujutsu-style grappling to North American Allied soldiers during World War II.

Restraint and self-defense

In 1945, he changed the name of his system, removed the more lethal techniques, and focused instead on restraint and self-defense. The changes made the system more acceptable to the general public and among police forces.

At its heart, the system features the defendo "triad," which essentially combines four leverages, twelve pressure points, and five grips. The systematic nature of training and teaching mean that defendo can be categorized as a martial art.

Hurricane Combat Art

EXPLANATION
FIGHTING LIKE A HURRICANE

DATE OF ORIGIN
1993

FOUNDER
FRANK MONSALVE

PLACE OF ORIGIN
LAS VEGAS, USA

This hybrid martial art was founded by Frank Monsalve in Las Vegas for military, security protection, and self-defense purposes. Monsalve trained in various martial arts, such as American taiho-jitsu and hung gar (see p. 111).

Hurricane combat art also draws on various theories from Russian systema (see p. 278) and incorporates jeet kune do (see pp. 316–17) and muay Thai (see pp. 158–65) as well as hand-to-hand combat methods used by the American military.

The origins of the system, it is claimed, lie in pencak silat (see pp. 172–73). Like a hurricane, this system incorporates fast and violent flurries of attacks that are aimed at maiming or neutralizing opponents in the shortest time possible.

Practitioners are taught to "read" weaknesses or openings and apply attacks in a fluid and consistent manner. "Kata"—set patterns and forms—are not encouraged.

> "EYES NEVER BEHELD THE SEAS SO HIGH, ANGRY, AND COVERED BY FOAM ... WE WERE FORCED TO KEEP OUT IN THIS BLOODY OCEAN, SEETHING LIKE A POT ON A HOT FIRE."

CHRISTOPHER COLUMBUS WITNESSING A HURRICANE IN THE CARIBBEAN, 1503

GUN-DISARMING TECHNIQUE

1 The attacker raises and aims a pistol at the defender's head. The latter exaggerates his own sense of fear and shock as a way of distracting his assailant's mindset.

2 The defender quickly raises his hands directly up the center line of his body and lowers his head at the same time. He traps the gun with both hands, and points its muzzle upward.

3 Next, the defender forces the gun straight downward and rolls it backward, twisting the assailant's wrist and hand, and making sure the gun points away from him.

4 The defender torques violently to the left, wrenching the gun hand. At the same time he smashes a right elbow to the attacker's head and sets him up for a knee strike.

Shaolin Kempo Karate

EXPLANATION
SHAOLIN-STYLE FIGHTING

DATE OF ORIGIN
1970s

FOUNDER
FREDERICK VILLARI

PLACE OF ORIGIN
CALIFORNIA, USA

Despite the unusual name, which combines both Chinese and Japanese transliterations, the training syllabus of this system has a distinctly Chinese flavor, with technique names that include "the eleven hands of Buddha," "the blood palm," and the "poison-finger techniques."

Founded by Frederick Villari, who trained under Shaolin instructor

William K. S. Chow, the school's main body of teaching draws on techniques from Shaolin kung fu, kempo, and karate (see p. 57–67, 206, 202–03).

Shaolin kempo karate revolves around a principle called "the four ways of fighting." The four ways of achieving success in combat are by using the hands (including any part of the arms) or the feet (and legs), by knocking an opponent over, or by grappling.

◀ **FRED VILLARI**
Villari's integrated Shaolin style of fighting promotes good health, long life, and wisdom.

Shingitai Jujutsu

EXPLANATION
SELF-DEFENSE SKILLS

DATE OF ORIGIN
1984

FOUNDER
JOHN SAYLOR

PLACE OF ORIGIN
COLORADO SPRINGS, COLORADO, USA

Shingitai jujutsu is a form of jujutsu grappling (see pp. 216–17) that blends various strikes and submissions. The founder, John Saylor, was influenced by his experiences in the early 1980s when he ran the judo (see pp. 234–235) coaching at the US Olympics training center in Colorado Springs.

A former US heavyweight judo champion, he had officially retired in 1982 because of a shoulder injury. While competing at the Olympic training center he was able to train with some of the best judo fighters of the time. He witnessed the effects

of physical fitness and strength on the success of martial artists. He also recognized that an unhealthy lifestyle weakened the body and was detrimental to the martial artist's skills. Saylor compares shingitai jujutsu to the decathlon event—a successful decathlete must train in a wide variety of skills, never neglecting one aspect of training for another.

Three key aspects

The name "shingitai" encapsulates the three key aspects to training: "shin," or the mental approach and character of a fighting spirit; "gi," or the functional use of techniques applied through competition; and "tai," which refers to the physical body fitness and strength that are key elements to this system's fighting methods. Overall balance in striking, throwing, grappling, and groundwork are fundamental to achieving technical success.

American Kempo

EXPLANATION
AMERICAN-STYLE KARATE

DATE OF ORIGIN
1956

FOUNDER
ED PARKER

PLACE OF ORIGIN
PASADENA, CALIFORNIA, USA

American kempo, or kempo karate, is characterized by successions of quick-fire movements designed to disable and overwhelm opponents. Although essentially a nonviolent system of self-defense, its ethos is highlighted by a quote from founder Ed Parker: "Whatever the attitude, so is the response."

Parker, who was born and raised in Hawaii, learnt judo and boxing (see pp. 234–35, 256–63) at an early age. One of his lasting contributions was his striving to translate concepts and technical information from martial arts into a Western cultural context. Two of his well-known students were Elvis Presley and Robert Wagner.

Chinese and Japanese influences

The training syllabus of American kempo is similar to that of other southern Chinese kung-fu systems, such as choy li fut (see p. 114) and hung gar (see p. 111). The Chinese influences came from Parker's tutorage under William K. S. Chow,

who was an instructor in Shaolin kung fu (see p. 57–67). In 1954, Parker opened a commercial karate school in Provo, Utah. He went on to modify his early training in these Chinese systems by adding techniques from boxing and judo.

American kempo was influenced by James Masayoshi Mitose, who taught kosho ryu kempo. Parker's famous quote (see right) underlines the influence of circular-type Chinese moves and the linear nature of the hard Japanese moves.

The creed

In 1957, Ed Parker wrote the American kempo creed: "I come to you with only karate [meaning empty hands]. I have no weapons but, should I be forced to defend myself, my principles, or my honor, should it be a matter of life or death, of right or wrong, then here are my weapons—karate, my empty hands."

▶ **PARKER AND PRESLEY**
Ed Parker was Elvis Presley's lifelong trainer—he taught the singer American kempo, awarding him a black belt, and became his bodyguard.

"WHEN CIRCULAR MOVES END, LINEAR MOVES BEGIN. WHEN LINEAR MOVES END, CIRCULAR MOVES REOCCUR."

ED PARKER, 1930

Jeet Kune Do

EXPLANATION
"THE WAY OF THE INTERCEPTING FIST" IN CANTONESE

DATE OF ORIGIN
1967

FOUNDER
BRUCE LEE

PLACE OF ORIGIN
CALIFORNIA, USA

Jeet kune do (JKD), also commonly known as "jun fan jeet kune do," is a hybrid martial art with direct, nonclassical, and straightforward movements influenced by boxing, fencing, judo, and wing chun (see pp. 256–63, 268–69, 234–35, 122).

Due to its central philosophy of using what is useful and disregarding what is superfluous, jeet kune do is considered by many to be one of the fathers, philosophically, of the mixed-martial-arts movement (see pp. 318–27). However, Bruce Lee went to great lengths to promote the fact that he was neither an inventor nor a modifier. He stressed that his goal was not to create a fixed or

THE NUNCHAKU
This lethal weapon probably originated in Okinawa in Japan. It usually consists of two sticks joined by a rope or chain. Ideally, the length of each stick is about the same as the length of a man's forearm.

ENTER THE DRAGON

The first kung-fu movie to be made by Hollywood, *Enter the Dragon* tells the story of a Shaolin martial artist who, in search of honor and vengeance, infiltrates the island fortress of a criminal warlord and defeats him. Bruce Lee died six days before the movie was released in 1973, but it went on to establish him as an icon of popular culture and to trigger a worldwide interest in kung fu and other martial arts.

hybrid system, but to free martial artists from the bondage placed upon them by the rigors of following and practicing a systemized doctrine.

JKD's innovations
Lee's early training in wing chun, with its fixed and rigid stances, formed the basis of JKD. He added the mobility afforded by Western boxing's footwork and the "quick-entrance" technique based on the lunge from fencing. He turned to Zen Buddhism and Daoism for philosophical inspiration, and encouraged practitioners to adapt and interpret techniques for themselves. Lee taught that no art is superior to any other, and that the only limitation is self-limitation.

Rather than training by practicing "kata" (forms or set patterns of moves), Lee promoted the reliance on applied technique so that sparring dominates JKD training. He compared traditional martial arts, many of which do not encourage sparring as a training method, to dry-land swimming. Full-contact fighting or sparring is now considered the best way for a student

to gain close-to-reality combat experience. Although many of Lee's principles have become commonplace among a large number of hybrid and mixed-martial-arts styles, at the time his methods were seen as radically controversial and many traditionalists criticized his efforts to move away from the traditional and into the modern.

Two JKD branches
Currently, there are two main branches of JKD. The "concept" branch, whose main teachers are Dan Inosanto and Larry Hartsell, believes in the constant evolution of the system and has added further grappling as well as kali, eskrima, and arnis techniques (see p. 175, 180–81, 187) from Filipino traditions.

The "original" branch, which is sometimes known as jun fan jeet kune do, teaches that students should learn the basic founding principles of the art and then expand their own individual knowledge by studying other martial arts with other teachers. Its main teachers include James Lee, Andy Kimura, Ted Wong, and Jerry Poteet, who were also students of Bruce Lee.

AUTHOR'S NOTE

I am a huge fan of Bruce Lee's martial arts and film work, and while in Hong Kong I had the pleasure of learning from Yip Chun, who is the head of the wing chun style. His father, Grandmaster Yip Man, taught wing chun to Bruce Lee. Although Yip Chun is slight, in his 80s, and perhaps no taller than 5 ft 2 in (1.57 m), he demonstrated to me painfully a number of awe-inspiring movements and techniques that his father would have taught to Bruce Lee. These techniques included strikes, pushes, and unbalancing maneuvers that required a deep knowledge of human biomechanics and physics. Lee used this understanding—combined with a study of philosophy, anatomy, nutrition, weight training, and boxing—to form a unique expression of fighting he called JKD.

> **BRUCE LEE WITH NUNCHAKU**
Through his movies, Bruce Lee made the nunchaku famous. Once mastered, it can be useful for disarming an opponent who attacks with a weapon such as a sword.

Three aspects
JKD has three central aspects: efficiency, directness, and simplicity. Efficiency stresses that an attack must do the job it is intended to do. Directness means that the techniques must be as direct as possible. Simplicity requires that the art must not be overcomplicated, and it must be easy to learn and apply.

Studying movements
Lee's intuition and highly developed sense of body language—particularly his inherent understanding of nonverbal and telegraphed movements prior to an opponent launching an attack—enabled him to move quickly and effectively.

His training manuals and notes show that, during an important phase of jeet kune do's development, he became obsessed with studying the movements of other people. For hours on end he would wander the city streets and follow complete strangers, mimicking their exact

movements—the way they walked, where they placed their weight, as well as their bearing and mannerisms.

While studying European fencing techniques Lee noted that, prior to making an effective attack, a fencer must move forward into range. The initial movement in fact provides an opportunity to intercept that attack, to change its direction, and to reply with force. This is one reason why Lee called his system jeet kune do— "the way of the intercepting fist."

JKD's five ways of offensive attack borrow movements from fencing. One way is "attack by drawing": by leaving an opening a fighter draws his opponent into attack, then counters and gains the upper hand. Another way is "progressive indirect attack": as an opponent's attention is diverted when an area of his body is attacked, a fighter follows by attacking another area that has become exposed.

"PATTERNS, TECHNIQUES, OR FORMS TOUCH ONLY THE FRINGE OF GENUINE UNDERSTANDING … TRUTH CANNOT BE PERCEIVED UNTIL WE COME TO FULLY UNDERSTAND OURSELVES AND OUR POTENTIALS. AFTER ALL, KNOWLEDGE IN THE MARTIAL ARTS ULTIMATELY MEANS SELF-KNOWLEDGE."

BRUCE LEE, *BLACK BELT* MAGAZINE, 1971

Mixed Martial Arts (MMA)

EXPLANATION
A MIXTURE OF VARIOUS
MARTIAL-ART STYLES

DATE OF ORIGIN
1993

FOUNDER
NO SINGLE FOUNDER

PLACE OF ORIGIN
LAS VEGAS, USA

Mixed martial arts is a combat sport in which fighters compete in a ring using full-contact techniques, such as grappling and striking, that are derived from a variety of martial arts. While the concept of combining techniques from different art forms has existed for millennia, the terms "mixed martial arts" and "MMA" only became popular in 1993 with the emergence of the Ultimate Fighting Championship (UFC). As MMA's popularity—and levels of sponsorship—have escalated, so the

> **INSIDE THE OCTAGON**
Bouts between mixed martial artists take place inside an octagon-shaped ring, while the crowd and television cameras remain glued to the action.

movement has disassociated itself from the "free-for-all" tradition of Brazilian vale tudo (see p. 339) fights, and has spawned a mini-revolution among martial-arts communities across the world. Ground fighting, a key element of MMA, has received renewed attention, and many martial arts' syllabuses now include grappling and groundwork to give students a well-rounded education in combat. Although MMA is a brutal sport, there has only been one recorded death during an official competition.

While it is hard to establish the exact evolution of the

> **ANCIENT FIGHTERS**
A Greek vase shows two pankration wrestlers fighting in one of the earliest forms of mixed martial arts.

modern MMA movement, many trace its origins to the Gracie family and their work since 1920 in Brazil. In Japan, where players are referred to as "shoot fighters," the art has also become a popular form of entertainment and sport.

Bruce Lee's philosophy

With his philosophy of "absorbing what is useful and disregarding what is not," Bruce Lee's influence can also be seen in the development of MMA. Lee moved away from traditional forms of combat in favor of efficiency gained through full-contact sparring.

Ancient history

MMA has its roots in ancient Greece and the pankration championships (see p. 276), which were no-

holds-barred, full-contact fights, often conducted without padding. Grappling was heavily utilized and deaths were not uncommon. Successful fighters were legends in their lifetimes, much like the MMA champions of today.

Over the last 20 years, MMA has evolved rapidly from its groundwork jujutsu base (see pp. 216–17) to incorporate a range of powerful strikes, such as the classic technique "ground and pound" (see opposite). When performed successfully, this brutal technique often leads to either a knockout or a technical knockout.

Three areas of training

MMA fighters focus their training on three main areas: groundwork, clinch work, and stand-up work.

Groundwork may involve elements and techniques from other styles, such as judo, catch wrestling, sambo, Brazilian jujutsu, and Greco-Roman wrestling (see pp. 234–35, 251, 279, 344–45, 270). MMA

fighters also use submission holds and mounting techniques.

Clinch work focuses on throws and takedowns, and also the muay Thai (see pp. 158–65) specialty of striking while holding the clinch. Knees and elbows are also employed.

Stand-up work focuses on boxing (see pp. 256–63), kickboxing (see p. 331), muay Thai, and any other striking martial art that utilizes quick, powerful entry techniques in order to disable or disorientate opponents. Grappling techniques from jujutsu and judo are adapted for use in the ring because players do not wear a "gi" (traditional uniform) and so cannot grab the lapels of a jacket.

Victory in competitions

Competition rules vary according to which body is hosting the event. An MMA fighter achieves victory by either a submission, a technical knockout, or a knockout. Some fights are decided by three judges

using a ten-point system. However, there can also be a no-contest (when both fighters violate the rules) or a disqualification, whereby fighters have received three warnings. A warning is given for disobeying the referee or for committing an illegal movement, such as a head-butt or an eye gouge, or attacks to the groin, throat, or back of the neck.

⋏ EYEBALL TO EYEBALL
Aggressive face-to-face confrontations are common in the highly charged atmosphere of many no-holds-barred MMA fights.

⋗ GROUND AND POUND
MMA fighters aim to get the upper hand by grounding their opponent and then pounding the head with a shower of punches.

BEHIND THE SCENES

MMA FIGHTERS

AT THE TOP OF EVERY MMA FIGHTER'S AGENDA is the need to be in peak physical and mental condition on the night of a crucial bout. The best-prepared competitor is the one most likely to win—he comes equipped with grappling, punching, and kicking skills, as well as all-around strength and fitness.

MMA fighters ideally follow a daily regime of training that enables them to concentrate on developing their fitness and to learn and fine-tune their technical skills. Even the fittest fighters need to stay in great shape because they know that there comes a point—usually late on in a match—when energy levels can start to fade and technical ability begins to take second place.

> "MIXED MARTIAL ARTISTS FOCUS THEIR TRAINING ON GROUNDWORK, SUCH AS SUBMISSION HOLDS, CLINCH WORK, SUCH AS THROWS, AND STAND-UP WORK, SUCH AS BOXING."

Training often means a grueling program of early morning runs, intense workouts in the gym, sparring in the practice ring, and strictly following a nutritious diet that will not only help with body conditioning but will also enable a specific weight to be reached. In order to be the best at a certain weight—and MMA is organized according to weight classes—fighters need endurance, stamina, power, and speed. They must also be mentally alert so that they can adapt their skills to gain the upper hand—from stand-up contests, in which boxing and muay Thai skills are key, to takedowns and groundwork, where judo, Brazilian jujutsu, and Greco-Roman wrestling come into their own. It is in the heat of the moment that MMA fights are won or lost, where accomplished holds or chokes lead to submissions and ultimate victory.

BIG FIGHT NIGHT
The climax of a fighter's training comes with an MMA match inside the caged ring. The thrilling occasion is watched by a large TV audience and witnessed by an excited crowd that increasingly is joined by celebrities from other sports.

TECHNICAL TRAINING
MMA fights may sometimes look like no-holds-barred contests, but in reality they are skillful combats between two technically trained competitors. Often, an MMA fighter starts his career from a platform in which he has experience of one or two specialties, such as muay Thai, kickboxing, or Brazilian jujutsu. He builds on his technical skills base and focuses on developing three main areas of expertise— stand-up work, groundwork, and clinch work—that will pay dividends during his fights as they move through their many different phases.

GETTING INTO SHAPE

Every MMA fighter works on their conditioning, pushing themselves harder and harder until they are in great shape for fight night. Often, this is a solitary business that means missing social occasions and starting training at daybreak. Intense workouts involve running, jumping rope, cycling, push-ups, weight-lifting, and ringwork. Fighters build up their aerobic and anaerobic capacity, and work on extending their power, endurance, and stamina.

WEIGHING-IN

Within 24 hours of a bout, the two contestants meet at an authorized weigh-in, where officials check that their weight is appropriate for the scheduled class of fight. There are six classes—from featherweight, lightweight, and welterweight to middleweight, light heavyweight, and heavyweight. These occasions are usually accompanied by a faceoff between the protagonists, which adds to the tension and expectation of the fight.

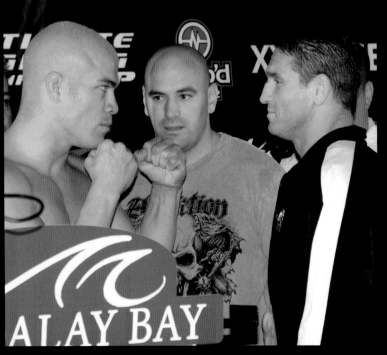

GETTING READY FOR THE RING

Fighters put a great deal of hard work and dedicated training into preparing for a big fight. With the bout fast approaching, it's important that the pressure of the occasion doesn't affect a fighter's mental outlook. They learn to relax in their dressing room, aided and abetted by their training assistants, who spend time massaging muscles and joints as well as helping to motivate them with commonsense advice aimed at focusing their minds on the fight ahead.

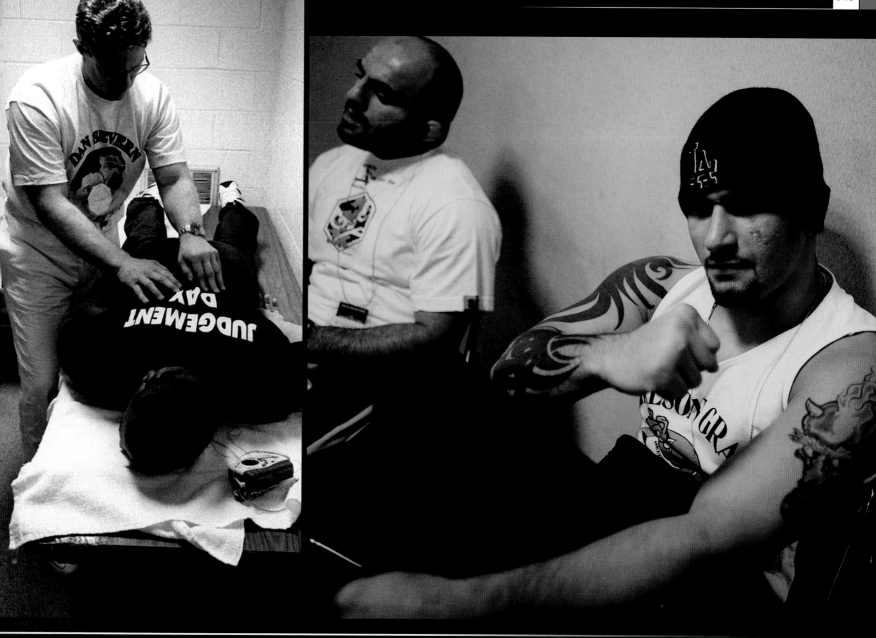

GLOVES AND HAND WRAPS

In a rare moment of calm before entering the packed arena, an MMA fighter adjusts his gloves—which are closely regulated. They have to be clean and in good condition, with a smooth surface and without any compacting of the stuffing inside. The wrist straps must be fixed with adhesive tape. Underneath the gloves the fighters can wrap their hands in medical gauze or tape so long as it does not cover their knuckles.

NO HIDING PLACE

During a fight, the entrance to the fenced octagonal ring is bolted and the competitors come face to face in full, close-quarter combat. The floor is covered with a shock-absorbing mat beneath the canvas, and the uprights and cross-beams of the fence are padded. Grappling, clinching, striking, kicking—the fight goes on until one or other fighter submits, is knocked out, or is considered by the judges to have suffered a technical knockout.

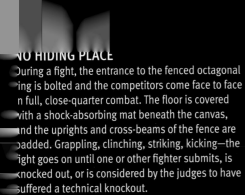

ROUNDS AND BREAKS

Usually, for nontitle fights there are three rounds that last five minutes, with a one-minute break between each round in which fighters return to their corner. Here, they can drink water and receive basic treatment for wounds until a crowd-pleasing octagon hostess parades around the ring with the number of the next round above her head. For title fights, there may be a maximum of two extra rounds—in the event of a draw—after the first three rounds. Alternatively, a title bout might start out having five rounds of five minutes

"MMA IS AN ADRENALIN-
FUELED EXPERIENCE—
EXCITING,
UNPREDICTABLE,
AND FRESH."

HYWEL TEAGUE, *PROFESSIONAL FIGHT PHOTOGRAPHER*

WINNERS AND LOSERS

Victory can be sweet for a winner, a reason to celebrate with a roar to
raise the roof while his dazed and defeated opponent can barely lift
himself from the canvas. The octagon doctor is always on hand to
check the health of a fighter and to assess the seriousness of an injury.
For all-or-nothing title fights, the victor's ultimate prize can be the
much-heralded UFC Champions Belt.

> **AGGRESSION IN THE CAGE**
Croatian Mirko Cro Cop withstands the attack of
American Eddie Sanchez before cruising to victory
with a technical knockout in the first round during
this UFC mixed-martial-arts bout at the Mandalay
Hotel in Las Vegas in 2007.

Collegiate Wrestling

EXPLANATION
AMERICAN COLLEGE WRESTLING
DATE OF ORIGIN
1905
FOUNDER
EDWARD GALLAGHER
PLACE OF ORIGIN
OKLAHOMA, USA

Sometimes known as "scholastic wrestling," collegiate wrestling is a grappling art practiced in US universities, colleges, high schools, and middle schools. Its origins are in catch wrestling (see p. 251), although, for safety, emphasis is placed on learning how to control an opponent rather than developing explosive offensive techniques.

▼ **ACHIEVING A BREAKDOWN**
A collegiate wrestler struggles to achieve a breakdown as he forces his opponent either onto his side or his stomach.

Events are governed by the National Collegiate Wrestling Association (NCWA) and the National Collegiate Athletic Association (NCAA).

Bouts are usually of three rounds, during which a wrestler tries to pin down his opponent. A pin, or a "fall," occurs when one wrestler manages to hold both his opponent's shoulders—or a part of them—on the mat for a full second. If he stays in a mounted or riding position on top of his opponent for more than a minute he earns a point. Points can be accumulated until a technical fall is achieved.

An official varsity sport

In 1900, the first collegiate match took place between Yale University and the University of Pennsylvania. Then, in 1905, the Eastern inter-Collegiate Wrestling Association held its first tournament. Shortly before World War I, Edward Gallagher, a track, field, and football coach from Oklahoma State University, launched wrestling as an official varsity sport.

The rules in use today evolved gradually over the first half of the 20th century. In 1911, a rule was introduced that allowed a referee to determine the winner if there was no fall within 15 minutes. By 1941, a point system had gained wider acceptance and, in 1942, bouts were held on open mats laid onto a gym floor. In the 1960s, 70s, and 80s, collegiate wrestlers had successes in international bouts. Notably, Dan Gable won Olympic gold for freestyle wrestling (collegiate wrestling's international counterpart) in 1972.

> "WRESTLING IS THE ONLY SPORT I'VE EVER COMPETED IN THAT PUTS YOU TOTALLY IN A SITUATION OF CONSTANT MOTION WITHOUT BREAKS."
>
> DAN GABLE, FREESTYLE (LIGHTWEIGHT) OLYMPIC CHAMPION, 1972

Hoshin Roshi Ryu

EXPLANATION
"THE SCHOOL OF THE MASTER GUIDE" IN JAPANESE

DATE OF ORIGIN
1980

FOUNDER
GLENN MORRIS

PLACE OF ORIGIN
MICHIGAN, USA

Hoshin roshi ryu combines mental and physical self-protection and uses techniques drawn from ninjutsu and jujutsu (see pp. 208–9, 216–17).

Founder Glenn Morris was an organizational psychologist interested in Daoist philosophy and esoteric writings. Courses on reiki, shamanism, massage, and meditation, are taught alongside simple yet effective self-defense techniques. Physical combat is only used as a last resort and showing kindness and consideration to others is key. Student training focuses on practicing techniques and learning how to apply them in real-life situations, rather than memorizing individual "kata" (set forms).

▼ KNIFE EXERCISES
Two hoshin roshi ryu practitioners demonstrate knife-on-knife exercises that enable them to develop confidence in self-protection.

Shen Lung Kung Fu

EXPLANATION
INVISIBLE-DRAGON STYLE KUNG FU

DATE OF ORIGIN
1960s

FOUNDER
FU XI WEN

PLACE OF ORIGIN
USA

This style of kung fu was developed by Grand Master Fu Xi Wen, who based it on five animals—the snake, mantis, tiger, crane, and monkey. It places equal emphasis on martial technique and character building.

Philosophical aspects

A unique aspect of this art is that philosophical and intellectual teachings are encouraged. After a year, students are expected to study the *Tao Te Ching*, *The Art of War*, and *The Analects* of Confucius. These classics were once essential in the training of Daoist-based martial arts. The ultimate goal of shen lung kung fu is to encapsulate the spirit of a priest and the mind of a scholar in the body of a warrior.

To Shin Do

EXPLANATION
"THE WAY OF MENTAL SHARPNESS" IN JAPANESE

DATE OF ORIGIN
1996

FOUNDER
STEPHEN K. HAYES

PLACE OF ORIGIN
USA

To shin do was founded by the legendary US ninja Stephen K. Hayes. The system is a departure from ninjutsu (see pp. 208–9) as taught by the Bujinkan organization in Japan, differentiating itself by focusing on threats more likely to be encountered in modern-day life in the US. Students learn to handle surprise attacks from multiple assailants through the use of strikes, punches, kicks, grappling techniques, chokes, and joint locks. They also learn how to overcome fear and develop a psychological advantage in combat. Advanced students are

◄ THE SWORD
Stephen K. Hayes demonstrates his swordsmanship with a traditional Japanese sword.

offered optional courses on the use of classical Japanese weapons, meditation and yoga, classes on how to instruct effectively, as well as courses aimed at the security and protection industries.

Hatsumi tradition

Founder Stephen K. Hayes helped to introduce ninjutsu to the US and Western Europe. In fact, he and his close friend Bud Malmstrom are credited with initiating the ninja boom of the 1980s. A former student of Masaaki Hatsumi, Hayes says that breaking away from ninjutsu and developing to shin do is the greatest tribute he can pay to Hatsumi. Central to the ethos of ninjutsu is the need to constantly strive to update its techniques, making to shin do the latest adapted version in the evolution of the assassin's art.

Choi Kwang Do

EXPLANATION
"THE WAY OF KWANG CHOI" IN KOREAN

DATE OF ORIGIN
1988

FOUNDER
KWANG JO CHOI

PLACE OF ORIGIN
USA

Choi kwang do shares similarities with tae kwon do (see pp. 134–35). It was invented in the US by Grand Master Kwang Jo Choi after he developed problems with his joints. He removed what is known as the "locking out" action in tae kwon do techniques, whereby joints are fully extended and susceptible to damage. The philosophy of choi kwang do emphasizes the development of character and mental strength rather than focusing on competition, self-defense, and fighting. Family-orientated classes offer a less intensive training program than other martial arts, and students are encouraged to train over a long period of time.

American Karate System

EXPLANATION
N/A

DATE OF ORIGIN
1973

FOUNDER
ERNEST LIEB

PLACE OF ORIGIN
MICHIGAN, USA

The American karate system (AKS) is essentially a blend of Japanese and Korean martial arts adapted for the American physiology and psyche by Ernest Lieb. On returning from Korea, where he was stationed as a US marine in 1964, his goal was to form an organization that promoted brotherhood as opposed to rivalry. Lieb's slight stature made it hard for him to succeed against bigger

opponents in his early training in judo (see pp. 234–35). However, karate (see p. 202) taught him that he could overcome this through hard work and dedication, combined with timing, speed, and accuracy.

Seeking perfection

AKS practitioners employ a range of blocks, punches, kicks, throws, joint locks, and breaking techniques. They strive at all times to seek perfection and self-enlightenment through physical and mental techniques.

Students wear traditional white suits, whether training or taking part in tournaments, gradings, or official functions. They are graded using four different colored belts prior to gaining a black belt (for which they must be 18 or over to be eligible). The highest rank is the black belt (10th Dan), which was held by Lieb.

ERNEST LIEB

Born in Germany, Ernest Lieb immigrated to the US in 1952. He studied chi do quan under Mr Kim in Korea, and competed very successfully in many tournaments. He was tragically killed in a train accident while traveling in Germany in 2006.

Progressive Fighting System

EXPLANATION
FIGHTING FOR SELF-DEFENSE
DATE OF ORIGIN
1983
FOUNDER
PAUL VUNAK

PLACE OF ORIGIN
CALIFORNIA, USA

Progressive fighting system (PFS) helps people to learn self-defense so they can deal with armed and unarmed assailants. Developed by Paul Vunak, PFS is a version of jeet kune do (see pp. 316–17) that uses head-butts, knees, and elbows delivered at very close quarters.

Street-based reality

PFS techniques distilled into another system called RAT, or Rapid Assault Tactics, have been taught to US law-enforcement agencies. Training involves baton and handcuffing techniques, restraint, and locks and throws drawn from dumog (see p. 183). Filipino stick and knife techniques also feature strongly.

PFS stresses street-based reality. Students turn everyday objects, such as pool cues, keys, and coins, into weapons. Sparring teaches students how to react under real circumstances—they learn to be aware of other potential threats while engaging an opponent. To motivate students PFS uses the 80–20 rule— a student is given 80 percent encouragement while 20 percent of their mistakes are pointed out.

LINE System

EXPLANATION
ACRONYM OF "LINEAR INFIGHTING NEURAL-OVERRIDE ENGAGEMENT"
DATE OF ORIGIN
1978
FOUNDER
RON DONVITO

PLACE OF ORIGIN
VIRGINIA, USA

The LINE system is a collection of close-combat skills and techniques developed by Ron Donvito before he joined the US Marine Corps in 1978. The standardized system contains grappling and striking techniques that resemble many other martial arts and are nearly all designed to kill an enemy. Donvito has summed up its ethos as: "Get them on the ground, stamp on their head."

Confidence and aggressiveness

Between 1989 and 1998 the US Marine Corps used LINE system to train 750,000 military personnel. It instilled both confidence and aggression, and taught hand-to-

⋀ ATTACKING THE ELBOW
A LINE system instructor demonstrates the technique of damaging the elbow joint by striking it on the outside with sufficient force.

hand, close-quarter skills. Soldiers are tested on the techniques when they are very tired. After 4–6 hours of taxing aerobic and anaerobic work in full battle dress, the soldiers must prove they can demonstrate the techniques quickly, powerfully, and effectively. All LINE system techniques are tested in poor visibility, too—such as at night or in smoke-filled environments.

Kokondo

EXPLANATION
"THE WAY OF THE PAST AND THE PRESENT" IN JAPANESE
DATE OF ORIGIN
1970
FOUNDER
PAUL AREL

PLACE OF ORIGIN
CONNECTICUT, USA

Kokondo is a self-defense system that emphasizes body dynamics and fast, powerful techniques. The term kokondo describes the martial arts of kondo karate and its sister style, jukido jujutsu, developed earlier in 1959. Founder Paul Arel studied sanzyu ryu jujutsu and, while in Japan with the US Marines, jujutsu and karate (see pp. 216–17, 202).

"THE SEVEN IDEALS OF PRACTICE
ARE BENEVOLENCE,
JUSTICE, HONOR, COURAGE,
LOYALTY, POLITENESS,
AND VERACITY."

THE BUDO CODE OF THE WARRIOR

Kokondo's main philosophy comes from the "budo" code of the warrior, and ideals such as honor, justice, and loyalty are encouraged. Its practice derives from three key principles: focus on an opponent's center line (an imaginary vertical line that divides the body in two) while throwing or striking; emphasize the circular-style movements commonly found in many Chinese systems when striking; and, most importantly, try to create an imbalance in an opponent before attempting a strike or a throw.

⋗ THROWING AN OPPONENT
The kokondo way of throwing an opponent involves creating an imbalance and focusing power on their center line.

Jailhouse Rock

EXPLANATION
PRISONER FIGHTING STYLE

DATE OF ORIGIN
UNKNOWN

FOUNDER
NO KNOWN FOUNDER

PLACE OF ORIGIN
USA

According to both practitioners and popular legend, jailhouse rock (JHR) is a hybrid African-American style developed among prisoners and urban gang members. Others dispute that it is a real martial-art form. There are different regional styles, such as "52 hand blocks," "gorilla," "baryard," and "strato;" these vary greatly in content and methodology. JHR's overriding principle seems to be the promotion of constant improvization, deflection, and effectiveness in nonsporting confrontations. Originally a fighting system typically used by criminals, it has become more mainstream and accessible due to its codification.

Media attention
The popularity of JHR has gathered pace, largely due to media attention. References can be found in the world of boxing, popular rap songs, and in crime books, graphic novels, and various essays on African-American culture. Although its history is unclear, JHR probably has historical links with indigenous African fighting arts, slave arts, and European bare-knuckled boxing.

◀ **SAN QUENTIN**
Inmates at prisons, such as San Quentin in California, have developed a fighting style that has become renowned in urban culture.

CUS D'AMATO

According to legend, US heavyweight boxing champion Floyd Patterson learned a style of jailhouse rock when he was in Coxsacki Penal Institution, New York. His distinctive "peek-a-boo" style of fighting, in which he held his gloves in front of his face, may have been influenced by JHR, although his trainer Cus D'Amato (above left) is usually credited with inventing it and passing it on to other American boxers, such as Mike Tyson.

Kickboxing

EXPLANATION
N/A

DATE OF ORIGIN
1970s

FOUNDER
NO KNOWN FOUNDER

PLACE OF ORIGIN
USA

Kickboxing is a contact martial art that combines Western-style boxing with kicks. During the 1970s, kickboxing as we know it today became popular in the US, due largely to the success of Bill "Superfoot" Wallace, who won many professional fights between 1974 and 1980. An injury to his right knee meant he relied heavily on his left leg. His specialities were roundhouse kicks, hook kicks, and precise kicks in quick succession.

American and Japanese styles
The sport is renowned for its American and Japanese styles. The term "kickboxing" was probably coined when kyokushin karate fighters (see p. 224) invited muay Thai experts (see pp. 158–59) to Japan in the late 1950s and early 60s. Other forms of kickboxing include shoot fighting, yaw yan, muay Thai, pradal serey, and lethwei (see p. 225, p. 187, pp. 158–59, p. 167, pp. 146–47).

Techniques and competitions
The most common techniques range from the "cross hook jab," "under cut," and "upper cut" of classical boxing to the "roundhouse kick," "front kick," and "side kick" of muay Thai. A unique technique is the "spinning back fist," whereby a boxer violently rotates his body in a 180-degree turn, allowing the fist of his right or left arm to flail out and strike his opponent's jaw or body. This spectacular skill can be devastatingly effective, often resulting in a decisive victory.

Competitions usually consist of between three and 12 three-minute rounds. Fights are won by a straight knockout (KO) or a technical knockout (TKO), if one of the fighters quits or if a fighter's corner throws in the towel, or by a points decision from a team of three judges. Punches and kicks are awarded points equally, unlike muay Thai, in which kicks to the body and head are highly scored, regardless of whether or not they are clean strikes. Typically, the competitive sport of kickboxing does not allow elbow or knee strikes, head-butting, locking, or throwing.

▼ **KICK AND THRUST**
A kickboxer attempts a roundhouse kick but his opponent thrusts his body forward in defense. Kickboxers wear gloves and pads that protect their shins and feet.

Chu Fen Do

EXPLANATION
HYBRID SELF-DEFENCE SYSTEM
DATE OF ORIGIN
1979
FOUNDER
TONY BLAUER
PLACE OF ORIGIN
USA

Sometimes known as the "panic attack system," chu fen do was founded by self-defense psychologist Tony Blauer. The art classifies itself as a combination of inter-dependent techniques that form a unified whole. The techniques employed are influenced by moves from Western boxing, muay Thai, jujutsu, and wrestling (see pp. 256–63, 158–65, 216–17, 270). Training equips students with a psychological understanding of fear and how it affects performance.

American Combat Judo

EXPLANATION
JUDO FOR COMBAT
DATE OF ORIGIN
1944
FOUNDER
BERNARD COSNECK
PLACE OF ORIGIN
USA

This art form combines self-defense and offense. Sometimes known as "judo with an attitude," it was developed by combat instructor Bernard Cosneck to quickly train American Coast Guards during World War II. He removed the complicated blocks and chokes from judo (see pp. 234–35) and included certain strikes.

> **DEVASTATING TECHNIQUES**
Combat judo moves can be devastating—rule number two says, "Always finish a technique by kicking your opponent in the head."

Model Mugging

EXPLANATION
SELF-DEFENCE FOR WOMEN
DATE OF ORIGIN
1971
FOUNDER
MATT THOMAS
PLACE OF ORIGIN
USA

Sometimes known as "impact," this hybrid system of self-defense is designed primarily for women. It was developed after a high-profile rape and beating of a female, black-belt martial artist in 1971 in Palo Alto, California. Popular in the US and Europe, it is taught by different organizations, but its underlying philosophy is to emancipate women from the myth of fragility.

The switch mechanism
A constantly developing system that absorbs techniques from a range of martial arts, it focuses on "the switch"—a mental mechanism of turning from one state of mind to another. It allows people to switch from "everyday life mode" to "facing an aggressive attacker mode." Role play helps to emotionally charge the students, creating an adrenalized state of mind and body that prepares students for real combat.

Students learn the "Mind, Body, and Voice" method of self-defense. This teaches them to defend themselves verbally against an assault, and provides an emboldening psychological advantage.

> **STRIKE TO THE THROAT**
The techniques of model mugging are simple to learn and effective, often focusing on highly aggressive strikes to the throat or groin.

Neko Ryu Goshinjitsu

EXPLANATION
"CAT-STYLE SELF-DEFENCE" IN JAPANESE
DATE OF ORIGIN
1970s
FOUNDER
ERNIE CATES
PLACE OF ORIGIN
USA

Neko ryu goshinjitsu is a self-defense system based on the relaxed power, natural movement, and cunning of the cat. It includes adversarial psychology techniques, grappling techniques, elements of judo (see pp. 234–35), and the development of "qi."

Japanese businessmen
Little is known about Nakabiyashi Sensei, the legendary founder of the original concept on which this art was based. He developed the cat-style, self-defense movement for Japanese businessmen, who it is said could learn the system reasonably effectively within four hours.

The teachings eventually made their way into the US Marine Corps training program. One marine in particular, Ernie Cates, also known as Professor Cates and holder of a number of rankings in different arts, studied under Nakabiyashi Sensei and created the current form.

SCARS

EXPLANATION
ACRONYM FOR "SPECIAL
COMBAT AGGRESSION
REACTIONARY SYSTEM"

DATE OF ORIGIN
1970s

FOUNDER
JERRY PETERSON

PLACE OF ORIGIN
USA

Sometimes known as "Special Combat Agression Reactionary System," the SCARS combat system was created by Jerry Peterson, using his training in san soo kung fu and his combat experiences in the late 1960s during the Vietnam War. The main aspect of the system, which differentiates it from other similar systems, is that it claims to have no blocking moves—although it does include attacking maneuvers that resemble blocks. The underlying principle behind every contact is that the practitioner should attempt to cause injury to his opponent.

Expensive training
Although a highly streamlined course, the expensive nature of SCARS training has led to criticism from the martial-arts community.

It is arguably the most expensive self-defense training program available. Due to an excellent marketing campaign, it is estimated that, in 1993 when training tapes were promoted in national magazines in the US, the system grossed one million dollars in the first nine months of trading. Taught on 40-hour retreat programs, it is clearly a successful enterprise.

Marine Corps Martial Arts Programme

EXPLANATION
N/A

DATE OF ORIGIN
2001

FOUNDER
US MARINE CORPS

PLACE OF ORIGIN
USA

The Marine Corps Martial Arts Program (MCMAP) was created to instill into troops the warrior ethos, and to teach them close-quarter combat techniques. It also serves as a way of building team cohesion and morale. MCMAP replaced former programs such as the LINE system (see p. 330) and may be referred to as a synergy of mental character and physical disciplines, with applications across the full spectrum of violence.

Peace-keeping techniques
As well as being employed in combat situations, MCMAP techniques can also be used during peacekeeping operations. In these situations, wrestling moves and locking and restraining techniques are intended solely to restrain an opponent, rather than to kill.

The martial program includes full-contact wrestling and sparring training, and makes good use of safety equipment such as padding, helmets, and mouth guards. Weapons training is also incorporated into the regime, with emphasis placed on bayonet, handgun, and rifle techniques.

The structure of the course is rigid and MCMAP is graded by the use of five different colored belts: tan, gray, green, brown, and black. The black belt is further graded into six degrees or levels or attainment.

> "I WANT THE MARINES WHO TAKE THIS COURSE AND THEN RETURN TO DUTY FEELING 'NOW PEOPLE ARE SAFER BECAUSE I'M HERE."
>
> LT. COL. JOSEPH C. SHUSKO, 2005

The first and lowest rank (tan belt) is awarded after 27.5 hours of training, whereas troops must complete 71.5 hours of training to achieve the first-degree black belt.

▼ MARINE TRAINING
A marine demonstrates an MCMAP ground-fighting technique for subduing an opponent.

Grappling Inoue Wrestling

EXPLANATION
INOUE-STYLE WRESTLING
DATE OF ORIGIN
1990s
FOUNDER
EGAN INOUE

PLACE OF ORIGIN
HAWAII

Grappling Inoue wrestling is a hybrid martial art based on Brazilian jujutsu and incorporating techniques from boxing (see pp. 344–49, 256–63) and from other wrestling styles. It was developed by Egan Inoue, a Japanese-American who has become an accomplished mixed martial artist (see pp. 318–27) and a former world racketball champion. His brother Enson is also a successful mixed martial artist and a former world champion of shooto (see p. 225).

After studying with the Gracies—the founding family of Brazillian jujutsu—and following a succession of decisive wins at the open-weight category in that sport, Egan Inoue set up his own school, Grappling Unlimited, in Hawaii.

Although his style of grappling does not receive as much publicity as other mixed martial arts, Egan is well known in martial-arts circles for his perfectly executed arm bar methods. International fame came when he won a mixed martial arts match against the champion's champion, Randy Couture.

> "YOU THINK OF MIXED MARTIAL ARTS IN HAWAII, YOU THINK OF EGAN INOUE. HE BUILT THE SPORT IN HAWAII."
>
> ENSON INOUE, *THE HONOLULU ADVERTISER*, 2004

◀ **EGAN INOUE**
With a black belt in Brazilian jujutsu and a grappling style all of his own, Egan Inoue is a formidable opponent in any competition that features mixed martial arts.

Limalama

EXPLANATION
"THE HAND OF WISDOM"
IN HAWAIIAN AND SAMOAN
DATE OF ORIGIN
1950s
FOUNDER
TU'UMAMAO TUIOLOSEGA

PLACE OF ORIGIN
HAWAII

A hybrid martial art, limalama was developed from the traditions of the Polynesian islands of American Samoa by Tu'umamao Tuiolosega. It is a self-defense system that is sometimes considered to be a branch of American kempo (see p. 315).

An all-inclusive system
The life experiences and personal battles of the founder are distilled into limalama's 13 principles. For example, a principle called "amofoe," states that a fighter must understand how to manipulate his bodyweight and use swaying tactics in order to improve balance. Limalama also makes use of street-fighting techniques and can be described as an all-inclusive system that addresses every kind of attack. These include grabs, tackles, pushes, punches, kicks, and hugs, as well as a range of holds, locks, chokes, and the use of assorted weapons—and various combinations of all of the above.

TU'UMAMAO TUIOLOSEGA

Tu'umamao "Tino" Tuiolosega, who founded limalama, was born of royal lineage in 1931 in American Samoa and later moved to Hawaii. He took with him his Polynesian martial-arts experience as well as influences from boxing, judo, and the five-animal systems of Shaolin kung fu (see pp. 256–63, 234–35, 57–67). During the 1950s, he served with the US Marine Corps and fought at the bloody but decisive battle of Inchon in Korea. He became a chief instructor in hand-to-hand combat training to the US Marines.

Lua

EXPLANATION
"FORBIDDEN WAY TO FIGHT"
IN HAWAIIAN

DATE OF ORIGIN
INDIGENOUS ART

FOUNDER
NO KNOWN FOUNDER

PLACE OF ORIGIN
HAWAII

Also known as "kapu kuialua", lua is a fighting style that features joint locks, breaks, and strikes delivered with lethal force. According to legend, it is the ancient Hawaiian art of kings, taught only to the royal family. Before entering battle, ancient warriors shaved their hair and oiled their bodies so that their opponents could not grab any part of them. They performed dances of death to embolden themselves and to intimidate opponents, and they worshipped Ku, the Hawaiian god of war (see box right).

> "THE BODY IS LIKE A TREE TRUNK WITH BRANCHES, STEMS, AND LEAVES REPRESENTING HOW WE WALK, JUMP, RUN, AND KICK: THEY MUST BE NURTURED."
>
> FROM *THE MANA OF THE KAIHEWALU 'OHANA LUA*

The modern form of lua has been influenced by karate (see p. 202) and jujutsu (see pp. 216–17). As a result it is as much a martial art as a cultural legacy. In addition to fighting techniques, students are encouraged to learn massage, holistic traditional practices, and ritual forms of dance, to instill into them the psychological components of battle. Practitioners are taught to be positive in all things.

A range of weapons

Common lua weapons include the "palua puili" (a double club), the "pahoa" (a single-edged dagger), and the double-edged dagger. Other weapons are the "ma'a" (a sling), the "polo-u" (a long spear), and the "pohaku" (a stone). Training emphasizes the use of various body parts—elbow, palm, fingers, knees, hand, feet, forehead, shoulder, forearm, and chest—as offensive weapons. In one early training method, devotees walked along

narrow branches in order to develop balance and coordination. Certainly stalking and pouncing were vitally important in early Hawaiian culture. Although modern lua does not use such training, it still incorporates a number of brutal and dirty fighting techniques ("mokomoko"), such as biting, poking, pushing, and pulling.

A BLOODTHIRSTY GOD

Lua practitioners follow a philosophy of dualism that is similar to Daoism. The goal of this philosophy is to balance the powers of good and evil, light and dark, male and female, destruction and healing. The top half of the body (soft, feminine) has to be unified with the bottom half (hard, masculine). The lua fighting sytem sought to combine the ethereal characteristics of Ku, the god of war (right), and his wife Hina, the goddess of the moon. In Hawaiian mythology, Ku was one of the four great gods, and the only one who demanded human sacrifice.

▼ **ARMED COMBAT**
Two practitioners dressed as warriors attack each other with distinctive weapons on the side of a mountain.

> **FIGHT TO THE FINISH**
A violent bare-knuckle fight between two men at the
Tinku festival in Macha, Bolivia, is watched over by
the police. The sport is banned by the government
and the Catholic Church, but only rarely do the police
intervene to stop the bloodshed.

Calinda

EXPLANATION
STICK-FIGHTING DANCE
DATE OF ORIGIN
18TH CENTURY
FOUNDER
NO KNOWN FOUNDER

PLACE OF ORIGIN
CARIBBEAN

Also known as "kalenda," calinda is a form of stick fighting that is practiced on islands such as Haiti, Martinique, and Trinidad and Tobago in the Caribbean. Calinda probably evolved among African slaves and can be seen in various dance forms at festivals and carnivals, particularly at the annual carnival in Trinidad and Tobago. Calinda is also the name of a popular dance performed by former Afro-Caribbean slaves throughout New Orleans during the early part of the 20th century.

> **CARNIVAL TIME**
To the accompaniment of drums and chants, agile dancers take part in mock-combat displays using sticks over 3½ ft (1 m) long.

Mani Stick Fighting

EXPLANATION
CUBAN STICK FIGHTING
DATE OF ORIGIN
19TH CENTURY
FOUNDER
NO KNOWN FOUNDER

PLACE OF ORIGIN
CUBA

This little-known stick-fighting martial art evolved during the 19th century among the sugar plantations of Cuba and it is still practiced on the island. It is said that the Spanish slave owners encouraged their male slaves to fight to the death as a form of entertainment. A pair of men follow choreographed patterns as they dance and fight in a circle. The stick they use is about as thick as a sugar cane and about 16 in (40 cm) long. There are also techniques for knife fighting as well as head-butting, punching, foot-sweeping, and elbow strikes.

Tinku

EXPLANATION
"ENCOUNTER" IN QUECHUA
DATE OF ORIGIN
INDIGENOUS ART
FOUNDER
NO KNOWN FOUNDER

PLACE OF ORIGIN
BOLIVIA

Tinku is both a ritualized form of combat and a festival celebrated in Bolivia. Tinku battles take place at holiday times when different tribes wearing brightly colored cloaks and woven hats get together to eat, drink, play music, and fight.

Raw and primal

Tinku is one of the world's most bizarre and violent forms of ritual combat, and it is very raw and very primal. Groups of men may engage in bloody close-quarter fighting in the streets. Single combatants chosen from different tribes fight until one or the other is either knocked down, knocked out, or killed. Even women battle with each other. Combatants do not wear mouth shields, body pads, or head guards.

> **A RITUAL FREE-FOR-ALL**
Fists fly in the narrow streets during the Tinku festival as random running battles erupt and bystanders are drawn into the fray.

Often, they fight simply with their fists, elbows, and feet, but it is not unusual for them to use whips, clubs, slingshots, and rocks as weapons. Death, serious maiming, and injury are common.

Tinku probably predates the arrival of Europeans in South America. For centuries neighboring tribes have fought to right old wrongs or gain prestige. They believe the winners will have a bumper harvest and a

prosperous year. Anthropologists have pointed out that such fights may prevent all-out war between tribes and establish a pattern of tribal dominance that ensures the successful survival of every tribe.

Vale Tudo

EXPLANATION
"ANYTHING GOES"
IN PORTUGUESE

DATE OF ORIGIN
1960s

FOUNDER
NO KNOWN FOUNDER

PLACE OF ORIGIN
BRAZIL

Vale tudo is a grappling art that was born from the "all comers welcome" fighting that was common in Brazilian circuses in the 1920s. It was later popularized in a 1960s Brazilian television show, *Heróis do Ringue (Ring Heroes)*—but it was taken off air after one competitor suffered an exposed arm fracture. Although vale tudo means "anything goes," modern competitions have rules, such as no eye gouges or groin strikes.

Many different styles

Vale tudo uses techniques from many styles including jujutsu, muay Thai, wrestling, Western boxing, and sambo (see pp. 216–17, 158–65, 256–63, 279). Training is heavily physical and geared toward fighting in the ring. The overall ethos of vale tudo, like many Brazilian wrestling forms, is that techniques must be tested in full-contact fighting conditions in

> **CLOSE TO THE ACTION**
An eager audience watches with rapt attention as two vale tudo fighters engage in close-quarter combat inside a cage.

order to be considered useful and legitimate. Individual techniques are practiced repeatedly until they become instinctive.

An example of the "all comers welcome" style of the 1920s was printed in the Japanese-American *Courier* newspaper on 4 October,

1928. It reads: "One report from San Paulo declares that Jiu-Jitsu is truly an art and that in an interesting exhibition in the side tents to the big circus a Bahian Negro of multiplous dimensions met his Waterloo at the hand of the diminutive Japanese wrestler. The Negro was an expert at

Capoeira, an old South American style of fighting, but after putting the Japanese on his back and trying to kick his head, the little Oriental by the use of a Jiu-Jitsu hold threw the Bahian and after a short struggle he was found sitting on the silent frame of the massive opponent."

Kombato

EXPLANATION
SELF-DEFENSE COMBAT

DATE OF ORIGIN
1980s

FOUNDER
PAULO ALBUQUERQUE

PLACE OF ORIGIN
BRAZIL

A hybrid martial art, kombato is geared toward defending against armed and unarmed attackers. It is used by bodyguards, law enforcers, and military personnel, and is gaining popularity as a self-defense system. It uses grappling, joint locks, punches, and kicks. Emphasis is placed upon intuitive understanding of the triggers that spark aggression and violence—a key principle is to avoid those situations in the first instance and to resort to a physical response only as a secondary tactic.

Luta Livre

EXPLANATION
"FREE WRESTLING"
IN PORTUGUESE

DATE OF ORIGIN
1927

FOUNDER
NO KNOWN FOUNDER

PLACE OF ORIGIN
BRAZIL

Luta livre is an energetic and highly effective form of grappling and sport wrestling that has been practiced in Brazil since 1927. Fighters do not wear any protection, and rely on correct and superior technique to defeat a foe. They use throws, locks, and holds to devastating effect, but never punch or kick. Strength and conditioning are vital. Luta livre is constantly evolving, absorbing techniques from other wrestling and grappling arts.

Luta livre has ten key principles. The most fundamental is, "If I don't know, I won't allow." This means that, no matter what an opponent tries to do, he must always be opposed and never allowed to gain the upper hand.

Keep moving and changing

There are many ways of making this principle work. For example, fighters should use the element of surprise and vary their techniques constantly. Fighters are encouraged to keep moving, changing their position and their angles of attack and defense.

If a fighter controls the space, he can control his opponent's actions—for example, using his body to block their movement and intentions can undermine their ability to execute techniques effectively. A fighter should always be doing something in a match—constantly strategizing, fighting, pushing, and moving.

El Juego Del Garrote

EXPLANATION
"GAME OF THE STAFF"
IN SPANISH

DATE OF ORIGIN
UNKNOWN

FOUNDER
NO KNOWN FOUNDER

PLACE OF ORIGIN
VENEZUELA

This martial art is practiced, albeit rarely, in Venezuela and the island of Gran Canaria. The garrote is a staff or stick that is heavier at the striking end. This slows down the combatant's ability to strike a target quickly, but does maximize the impact. Masters of the art secretly teach students the skills to fight with the staff, machete, and knife, and to unbalance and throw their opponents by locking their limbs in order to gain a victory.

Capoeira

EXPLANATION
"COCKEREL'S CAGE" IN
PORTUGUESE

DATE OF ORIGIN
16TH CENTURY

FOUNDER
NO KNOWN FOUNDER

PLACE OF ORIGIN
BRAZIL

Capoeira is a blend of combat, dance, music, and singing that originated among African slaves who were brought to Brazil by the Portuguese during the 16th century. The earliest form of capoeira became known as "capoeira angola." Its traditions were passed orally from one generation to the next and it was associated with the fight against slavery.

By the early 20th century, capoeira had developed a bad reputation because it was often used by petty criminals on the streets. Eventually, however, it grew into an acceptable

▼ IN THE RODA
In an urban street in Brazil two capoeiristas show off their skills in front of a circle of onlookers and enthusiasts known as a "roda."

and systematic art form known as "capoeira regional," which is now practiced around the world.

One theory states that the name capoeira is derived from the culture of cockfighting. "Capoeira" translates as "rooster's cage" in Portuguese and "capao" means "rooster." Indeed, capoeira matches are held in a circle of people, called a "roda," resembling the crowds that would surround a pair of fighting roosters.

Positive sense of energy

Music and singing are an integral part of the practice of capoeira. Typically, when players enter the roda to fight—or "play" as it is called—the music takes on a tempo that dictates their speed, actions, and even proximity. The music can be fast and aggressive, while at other times it is slow and melancholy. The ultimate goal of the music, chorus, singing, and movement is to generate a positive sense of energy.

When the musicians play slower rhythms known as "angola," the players' actions may be slower, less aggressive, softer, and more dancelike.

▲ CAPOEIRA'S ROOTS
A painting by English artist Augustus Earle depicts two slaves engaged in an illegal demonstration of capoeira in 1824.

"Jogo de dentro" is a faster-paced rhythm that makes the fighters adopt a more exciting, aggressive style. The lyrics of capoeira songs are blueslike and tell stories to highlight or illustrate the feelings of either the singers or the practitioners.

Capoeira angola

Ritualized games that mix elements of dancing and combat performed to a musical accompaniment are the main feature of capoeira angola. It stresses the interaction between combatant, musician, and observer.

Combatants, known as "capoeiristas," often fight at close quarters as they try to bring their opponent to the ground, using acrobatic kicks, trips, sweeps, and head-butts. Capoeira angola contains many sneaky and aggressive tactics that hark back to its violent origins. Many movements, such as some kicks and head-butts, may have evolved from the slaves trying to escape from their chains.

Two masters

The man most associated with capoeira angola was Mestre Pastinha, who lived in Salvador in the Brazilian state of Bahia. He opened an academy in 1942 to preserve the tradition of capoeira from more modern forms. He popularized the art overseas and many practitioners in the US and the UK can trace their lineage back to his system.

Mestre Bimba (see right) created capoeira regional to systematize the art and disassociate it from criminal elements. In 1932 he opened an academy called "The Regional Physical and Cultural Center"— hence the name capoeira regional.

Capoeira contemporanea

A blend of angola and regional forms, capoeira contemporanea is not technically a style in its own right. Its practitioners combine regional's focus on speed, power, and reflex, with angola's focus on strategies and tactics. They can employ both forms at will, thus making them more rounded players and martial artists.

Mestre Bimba was born in the state of Bahia in 1900 and learned capoeira at the age of 12. He became a feared fighter who promoted the philosophy of brain over brawn. He introduced techniques such as the martelo (the roundhouse kick) and the galopante (a slapping strike with a cupped hand). In 1937, his art and academy received national recognition and, in 1953, the then president, Gertulio Vargas, declared capoeira as the national sport.

Maculelê

EXPLANATION
AFRO-BRAZILIAN DANCE
DATE OF ORIGIN
INDIGENOUS ART
FOUNDER
NO KNOWN FOUNDER

PLACE OF ORIGIN
BRAZIL

Maculelê is an Afro-Brazilian dance and martial art that almost died out after the abolition of slavery in 1888. No one knows when or how it began, nor what the word maculelê means. It may have featured in a harvest festival celebrated by sugar workers, who fought and danced with cane sticks as well as the machetes and straight-bladed razors they used in the fields. Revived in the mid-1900s by Mestre Popo of Santa Amaro in Bahia, maculelê is practiced by capoeira groups and, occasionally, as an art form in its own right.

Pair of sticks or machetes

Maculelê is accompanied by singing and "atabaques" (drums). Players traditionally wear dried grass skirts, similar to those their forefathers would have worn before they were enslaved. They dance and fight with a pair of sticks called "grimas" that are about 1 in (2.5 cm) thick and 24 in (60 cm) long. Some capoeira schools switch the sticks and use machete-type knives about 16 in (40 cm) long.

Players train with sticks made of biriba wood, machetes, and knives, giving them experience of the weapons wielded by urban gangs. A maculelê training session may start with a group of players standing in a

circle, or roda— the leader sings a song while the rest join in with choruses and a rhythm. On an agreed signal two players enter the ring and dance.

> MACHETES
A pair of machetes or long knives that resemble machetes may be used instead of the more traditional sticks.

Rhythm and harmony

As they dance, they strike their sticks to the prevailing rhythm. During a four-beat sequence players hit their own sticks together on the first three beats and, on the fourth beat, strike each other's sticks. Their movements are athletic, strong, and expressive. They dance in harmony rather than attacking decisively with the intent of doing harm. Maculelê improves the participants' rhythm, timing, speed, technique, and ability to perform set movements, such as attacks and blocks under pressure. As a result they learn to relax and overcome their natural fear of encountering live weapons, so improving their ability to defend themselves against armed assailants.

▼ ACROBATIC DISPLAY
Two maculelê players dance together in harmony as they wield their knives and perform acrobatic techniques.

> "YOU ENTER HEAVEN ON YOUR MERITS;
> HERE ON EARTH WHAT YOU OWN IS ALL THAT COUNTS.
> FARE YOU WELL OR FARE YOU POORLY,
> ALL ON THIS EARTH IS BUT FAREWELL, COMRADE."
>
> TRADITIONAL CAPOEIRA SONG

Capoeira instruments are played in a line called a "bateria." The chief instrument is the "berimbau" (pictured below), which is made of a Brazilian wood called biriba and a calabash gourd. There are usually several berimbau players in a roda, and each one holds a wooden stick and a small shaker, or "caxixi," containing beans or pebbles in his right hand. He hits a steel string (often simply a wire taken from a vehicle tire) with the stick and the sound resonates inside the gourd. The instrument creates different pitches to which the players respond instinctively. Other instruments include tambourines, a rasp, a cowbell, and the "atabaque," which is a kind of conga drum (left).

◀ CAPOEIRA ON THE BEACH
Two capoeiristas practice their defensive and offensive moves on an Atlantic beach in the state of Bahia, Brazil. As one swings his outstretched leg in an arc, the other takes evasive action.

Brazilian Jujutsu

EXPLANATION
JUJUTSU DEVELOPED IN BRAZIL
DATE OF ORIGIN
1925
FOUNDER
CARLOS AND HELIO GRACIE
PLACE OF ORIGIN
BRAZIL

This grappling art evolved from Kodokan judo, thanks largely to the efforts of Mitsuo Maeda, a Japanese immigrant to Brazil (see opposite). The art has become synonymous with the Gracie family, who developed the art and gained success in the early days of mixed martial arts (MMA) and the Ultimate Fighting Championships (UFC) in the US (see pp. 318–27).

A more practical edge

Gracie jujutsu is the most well-known form of Brazilian jujutsu. The latter is more of a sport, so training is geared toward point-scoring and competition. By contrast, the Gracie style focuses on self defense, giving it a more practical edge in both street combat and MMA competitions.

Classic techniques

To some extent, Brazilian jujutsu reflects the philosophies of the founder of judo, Kano Jigoro (see pp. 234–35), who believed that his art should be character building and promote physical fitness. One way in which the combat element of Brazilian jujutsu differs from judo is in its emphasis on ground fighting. The rules of judo state that a player must recommence in a standing position, but in Brazilian jujutsu there are no such rules. Competitors are permitted to drag opponents to the ground, and points are awarded according to the ease at which he could further strike the opponent from that position—in other words, for the dominance of his position.

The guard and the mount are two classic techniques. The guard is a defensive posture—when one player is on top of another, the player underneath clamps his legs around the waist and arms, the head, or the head and body of his opponent. The mount is a method of straddling an opponent quickly in order to set up a joint lock, such as an arm bar, or a head lock or choke out, or to further deliver punishing strikes. In common with many Japanese arts, Brazilian jujutsu employs the belt system as a way of grading players. However, the art is unusual in that the criteria for grading is based on

---

> "KNOWING HOW TO PUNCH AND KICK IS VERY IMPORTANT ... BUT YOU MUST BACK YOURSELF UP WITH KNOWLEDGE OF GROUND FIGHTING."

RORION GRACIE, 2003

▲ HELIO GRACIE
The man many consider to be the founder of Brazilian jujutsu, Helio Gracie fathered four sons—Rickson, Royler, Royce, and Rorion—who went on to become fighters.

a practitioner's expertise in free sparring and on championship results, and belts are awarded at the discretion of the instructor.

Maeda travels the world
In 1904, Mitsuo Maeda went to the US, to demonstrate judo to President Teddy Roosevelt.

His traveling companion, Tsunejiro Tomita, was an original student of judo's founder. When Tsunejiro was defeated in a wrestling match with an American football player, Maeda was deeply embarassed and vowed to become a professional wrestler. He later joined a circus and competed in wrestling matches in Europe and the US. During this tour he adopted the name Conde Koma, meaning "Count of Combat."

Between 1909 and 1913 he wrestled in Mexico, Costa Rica, Cuba, and Brazil, where he eventually settled. He was undefeated in approximately 1,000 matches fighting under judolike rules, and is said to have been defeated only twice in

MITSUO MAEDA

Mitsuo Maeda was born in Hirosaki City in Japan in 1878 and learned sumo wrestling (see pp. 226–33), but did not have the right physique. His parents sent him to school in Tokyo when he was 17. He joined the famous Kodokan school of judo under the direction of Sakujiro Yokoyama, who was famous for challenging other martial artists and had a relatively good record of success. Maeda achieved a 4th Dan, which, for the time, suggests an extremely high level of skill. He began his travels in 1904 (see left), went to Brazil in 1914, and died in Belém in 1941.

other forms of wrestling. Maeda delighted in issuing challenges—including one to Jack Johnson, who was at that time the heavyweight boxing champion of the world.

The dawn of Gracie jujutsu
The exact date of Maeda's first meeting with the Gracie family is not known for sure. It is thought that Gastão Gracie was managing an Italian boxer who was associated with the circus with whom Maeda had traveled. Some time after their

initial meeting, Gastão's son Carlos became a disciple of Maeda and learned the basics of his Kodokan judo wrestling style.

By 1925, Carlos Gracie had opened his first wrestling gym in Rio de Janeiro. Helio Gracie, who was the youngest and weakest of his five brothers, probably influenced the art's emphasis on groundwork. He relied more on technique than strength, and quickly found that fighting from the ground helped to balance out the weight and size problems associated with bigger, stronger opponents.

The California school
During the 1980s, Helio Gracie's sons took Brazilian jujutsu to California and opened a school. During the 1990s, Rorion and Royce Gracie had great successes in the UFC championships. In 1994, the US Army training facility at Fort Benning introduced Gracie jujutsu as a training method for building self-confidence into recruits.

Later in the 1990s, as a result of the Gracie brothers' experience in the UFC, punches and kicks were added to the Gracie jujutsu system.

Issuing challenges
It is interesting to note that the Gracies took on Maeda's tradition of issuing challenges. Helio Gracie once challenged the heavyweight boxer Joe Louis. His son Royce challenged Mike Tyson. While the challenges generated publicity for the art, they didn't take place because too little money was on offer to the boxers.

◀ **HEAD-TO-HEAD**
Experienced fighter Renzo Gracie (top) employs Brazilian jujutsu ground-fighting techniques in a recent mixed-martial-arts championship.

▼ KICKING AND CHOKING
In front of a crowd of 54,000 at the Los Angeles Coliseum, Royce Gracie kicks out at his Japanese opponent Kazushi Sakuraba, but is then caught in a Brazilian jujutsu choke hold. He frees himself to go on and win the mixed-martial-arts bout with a unanimous decision.

◄ GUARD POSITION

GUARD POSITION
As two fighters struggle for supremacy in a mixed-martial-arts contest, the fighter underneath uses a common Brazilian jujutsu technique—the guard. By wrapping his legs around his opponent to constrict his movements, he can gain the advantage.

GLOSSARY

Aikidoka A practitioner of aikido.

Angle of attack The angle and trajectory of an opponent's attacking move, made with the fist, foot, or a weapon.

Ashiwaza A Japanese word used in judo for all foot throwing techniques where the foot is used to sweep or hook the leg or foot of an opponent. It is also used in karate to mean any leg or foot technique.

Ax kick A martial-arts kick in which the straightened leg is brought down on an opponent as though it were the blade of an ax. It is common in tae kwon do.

Ayurvedic techniques The traditional Hindu methods of medicine and healing that are incorporated into many Indian martial arts.

Backfist A martial-arts technique in which the back of the fist is used to either block the blows of an opponent or to strike an opponent.

Balisong A butterfly knife that originated in the Philippines. The blade can be extended with just a flick of the holder's wrist.

Belt Worn by a martial artist around his or her waist. In some systems of martial arts the colour of the belt refers to a practitioner's rank.

Bo A long wooden staff used in the Japanese martial art of bojutsu.

Bodhidharma An Indian monk—also known as Da Mo—who is credited as the originator of Zen Buddhism. He traveled to China in the 6th century CE and settled in the Shaolin temple, where he taught martial exercises to the monks. Some experts believe that these exercises evolved into Shaolin kung fu.

Bokken A Japanese word for a type of wooden sword used for training.

Bolo A heavy machete used in the Philippines for fighting and for practical purposes.

Boxer Rebellion A rebellion that took place in China in 1899–1901 by members of the Righteous Harmony Society against foreign influence in China. The society, a peasant organization that originated in northern China, would attack foreigners involved in trade, politics, and building projects such as the railroads. In 1900, the so-called "Boxers" killed 230 diplomats. Their name (given to them by foreigners in the region) derives from the martial-arts techniques they used.

Broadsword A type of sword with a broad blade that is commonly used in a slashing manner.

Buddhism A philosophy—often regarded as a religion—that stresses that individuals have a "seed" of goodness within themselves, and that the practice of Buddhism aims to allow this goodness to "flower." It is a philosophy that actively advocates peace and harmony over judgement. It is central to the ethos of many martial arts, and many Buddhist monks created their own styles of martial arts.

Budo Meaning "the way of war" in Japanese, budo is a description of the martial arts as a way of life.

Bushido An ethical code followed by the samurai warriors of ancient Japan. It is often translated as "the way of the warrior."

Center line A notion, which is key to most martial arts, that describes an imaginary line running between, and relating to, the position of the practitioner's body and that of an opponent.

Chi See *qi*.

Circular motion Any strike or block that is performed using a circular movement of the limbs, as opposed to a linear movement.

Codified system An art form or style of art form in which fighting techniques, traditions, and philosophies have been organized into a recognizable code or system.

Cultural Revolution A period of internal struggle inside the Chinese Communist Party that took place between 1966 and 1976. Chairman Mao, fearing that he was losing his grip on the party, encouraged the party's youth militia to take control of party committees and replace them with revolutionary ones. Across China, the party purged many of the "bourgeoisie"—artists, writers and party officials were killed, and many millions of people persecuted.

Daga A bladed weapon, daga is the Philippine spelling of the word "dagger."

Da Mo See *Bodhidharma*.

Dan A black-belt ranking—commonly used in Japanese martial arts—that often starts at "1st Dan" and rises to "10th Dan."

Danjon The Korean term for the location of *qi* energy in the abdomen.

Dan tien The Chinese term for the location of *qi* energy in the abdomen.

Degree A black-belt ranking that is commonly used in non-Japanese martial arts.

Dit-dar medicine Traditional Chinese methods of healing and bonesetting.

Do The Korean and Japanese word that translates as "path" or "way." It is often a suffix to art forms such as tae kwon do or aikido.

Dobok The traditional Korean uniform.

Dojang A Korean martial-arts training hall.

Dojo A Japanese martial-arts training hall. Also commonly used as a generic term for any martial-arts training hall.

Dropkick A technique that involves the attacker jumping in the air and using both feet to kick an opponent. It is commonly used in forms of wrestling.

Dynamic tension A self-resistance exercise that involves tensing a group of muscles and then moving against those muscles as if a weight was being lifted.

Edged weapon Any weapon that has a blade, such as a knife or sword.

Eighteen weapons The "18" traditional Chinese martial-arts weapons. Common since the early 13th century, they include the spear, staff, hook, sword, and a number of other bladed weapons.

Elbow strike A strike to an opponent using the elbow. The technique is not allowed in many martial arts, though it is permitted in muay Thai.

Empty hand A term that refers to techniques performed without a weapon or systems that are predominantly not weapons based.

Escrimador A term from the Tagalog language in the Philippines that describes an escrima practitioner.

Escrima stick A short stick made of hardened bamboo or rattan cane. It is the primary weapon of choice in the Philippine art of escrima.

Etiquette In martial-arts terms, etiquette describes the courtesy, respect, and appropriate behavior expected in the *dojo*.

External system A term used to describe martial arts that use a system of hard, vigorous linear strikes, for example, karate or tae kwon do (see also *internal system*).

Footwork A general term to describe the position and movement of the feet and legs in martial arts and combat sports.

Form A set pattern of movements performed to help martial artists memorize abstract combat techniques (see also *kata*).

Free sparring A method of teaching used in karate, which allows students to learn particular techniques by using them in informal fight training (see also *kumite*).

Front kick A basic martial-arts kick that involves raising the knee in front of the body and then straightening the leg to strike an opponent with the foot.

Fudoshin A Japanese word to describe the ability of a practitioner to remain detached from a situation, regardless of the nature of the situation.

Gi A Japanese word to describe the traditional martial-arts uniform.

Grappling Techniques that focus on holding, throwing, and locking the joints of an opponent, as commonly found in wrestling-based arts.

Groundwork The hand-to-hand combat techniques employed by practitioners on the ground, as opposed to those used while standing up.

Guan-do The Chinese word for *halberd*.

Guan jang A Chinese term to describe the head of a martial-arts school, or the instructor of a school.

Gup A Korean word to describe a student of any ranking below the level of black belt.

Guru An Indian word to describe a master or teacher. It is sometimes also used in Filipino martial arts.

Halberd An ax blade topped with a spike mounted on a long shaft.

Hanshi A Japanese word to describe high-ranking, black-belt masters.

Hara A Japanese word to describe the location of *qi* energy in the abdomen.

Haragei A Japanese word to describe the ability of a martial-arts master who can locate and direct his own *qi* energy force.

Hard style A term usually applied to striking arts that focus on power and conditioning as opposed to arts that use an opponent's own force against them (see also *soft style*).

Harmony A principle of balance commonly described as the ultimate goal of martial arts.

Hidden techniques or teachings Techniques that are reserved for advanced students.

Hogu A Korean word to describe safety equipment used in martial arts.

Hook A term used to describe a punch involving a short lateral movement of arm and fist, with a bent elbow and with a wrist that twists inward at the moment of impact. It can be delivered with either the left or right hand.

Internal system A term used to describe martial arts that use a system of soft, circular movements (see also *external system*).

In-yo A Japanese term that means "light and dark." It was used as a traditional cry from the samurai, and is now used by yabusame practitioners before they shoot an arrow.

Iron body A system of martial-arts training that increases bone density, allowing practitioners to strike and be struck with increased force and not be injured.

Iron palm A system of martial-arts training that strengthens the limbs used for striking an opponent so that more powerful strikes can be employed.

Isometric stretching A system of developing muscle tissue by stretching or flexing one set of muscles to counter the force of another set of muscles.

Jab A term used to describe a straight punch delivered with the lead hand, which moves directly out from the shoulder.

Jian A straight sword of Chinese origin that is often used by the military elite.

Jo A short staff used in some Japanese martial arts.

Joint lock A technique, used in many types of martial arts, that involves manipulating an opponent's limbs to a point where they cannot move anymore. Joint locks are generally used to restrain opponents but can cause damage such as tears to muscles or broken bones.

Judoka A Japanese word for a practitioner of judo.

Jutsu A Japanese word meaning "style," "system" or "art."

Ka The suffix used to indicate that a person is a practitioner of a specific art. A karate practitioner, for example, is known as a "karateka."

Kaiken A small traditional Japanese dagger that was often carried by Japanese women for self-defence or ritual suicide. It was easily hidden in clothing.

Kanji The Japanese term for the set of Chinese letters used in the modern Japanese writing system.

Kata A Japanese word to describe a choreographed sequence of movements that help the martial artist remember abstract techniques (see also *form*).

Katana A long, single-edged traditional Japanese sword that was commonly used by the samurai.

Kensei A silent shout or *kiai* used to focus the mind of a practitioner when a loud, vocal shout cannot be executed.

Ki The Japanese word for *qi*.

Kiai A Japanese word used to describe the shout common among martial artists that aims to release *qi* on the execution of a technique.

Kihop A Korean word to describe the shout common among martial artists that aims to release *qi* on the execution of a technique.

Kime A Japanese word to describe the martial artist's ability to focus the mind.

Knockout Also known as a "KO," a knockout is a winning criteria in several full-contact sports, such as boxing, kickboxing, muay Thai, and mixed martial arts. It is awarded when one of the players fails to rise from the canvas after being knocked down.

Kris A bladed weapon common in Indonesia and Malaysia, and which is sometimes used in the Philippines. It has a wavy, snakelike blade and is often thought to be imbued with voodoolike qualities.

Kumite A Japanese word to describe *free sparring*.

Kup so A Korean term to describe vital points on the body that are targets for striking.

Kusarigama A Japanese word to describe a bladed weapon that resembles a sickle, to which a weighted chain is often attached.

Kwoon A Chinese word to describe a martial-arts school.

Kyu A student who ranks below the grade of black belt, usually used in reference to Japanese martial arts.

Lance A spearlike weapon that is often employed from horseback. It is common in many of the world's fighting traditions.

Lathi An Indian staff made from bamboo or cane.

Lei-tei A Chinese word to describe a raised platform used for fighting.

Linear motion A term used to describe moves and techniques that are performed, and directed toward their given target, in a straight line.

Makiwara A conditioning instrument, constructed from a block of wood tied around with rope, that is used to train the knuckles of the fists. A practitioner repeatedly punches the block to harden the hands.

Martial arts A term derived from Mars, the Roman god of war, that describes arts of a martial or warlike nature.

Mushin A Japanese word to describe a state of "no mind." It is taken from the Buddhist concept of "void," and it means to possess an open-minded, nonjudgmental attitude that is responsive to any given situation.

Naginata A bladed, Japanese *halberd*, which was often used by the wives of samurai warriors to protect their homes.

Nerve-point technique See *pressure-point technique*.

Ninja-to The sword used by the ninja of Japan. It is multi-functional and could also be used as a climbing tool. The scabbard has a snorkel or blowpipe and, for ease of use indoors, it is typically shorter in length than the *katana*.

Northern style A term used to describe Chinese martial arts originating north of the Yangtze River. Northern styles tend to emphasize fast and powerful kicks, high jumps, and fluid, rapid movement.

Nunchaku A weapon, developed from a type of flail used to beat the husks from rice, that consists of two short, thick sticks attached by a chain.

Overhand punch A martial-arts punch that involves a circular upward motion of the arm from the shoulder and finishes with a blow to the top of an opponent's head.

Pain-compliance technique A type of martial-arts technique used specifically to control a person and force them into submission. A selection of these techniques has been universally adapted for use by law-enforcement agencies around the world.

Parang A heavy bladed instrument used in the Philippines and Indonesia for practical and combat purposes.

Pin A generic term used to describe the action of pinning an opponent to the ground. In judo, for example, it is the desired outcome for many holds used in *groundwork*.

Poomse A Korean term used to describe a *kata* or set *form* of movements.

Pressure-point technique A martial-arts technique that focuses on striking specific points on an opponent's body known to produce the highest levels of pain.

Qi Also commonly spelt *chi*, qi is an ethereal force that permeates both animate and inanimate objects. The ultimate purpose of many martial arts is to accumulate and learn to direct qi energy through the power of thought. Many martial artists believe that it is stored in the abdomen. Traditional Chinese medicine and acupuncture work on the belief that when the meridians of qi, which act as highways in the body, become blocked or the qi becomes stagnant in a given area, illness will manifest itself. Only the clearing of the meridians will lead to the restoration of health and vitality. Many martial artists believe that by using qi to focus on objects they will have an enhanced reservoir of strength and will be able to perform a given technique to maximum efficiency.

Qi gong A Chinese collective term for a variety of therapeutic practices involving movement and regulated breathing. Its purpose is to aid both physical and spiritual well-being.

Rank A term that describes the level of mastery of an art or style that a martial artist has achieved.

Reflex training A term that describes the training used to learn martial arts, such as wing chun, that rely primarily on reflex actions.

Ringcraft A term, typically used in boxing, that describes the techniques and tactics employed by a practitioner.

Roundhouse kick A martial-arts kick that involves swinging the leg in a semicircular movement and striking an opponent with the front of the leg or foot.

Safety equipment This usually refers to the protective gear used by students when sparring, often consisting of a head guard, mouth shield, gloves, and foot pads.

Samurai Ancient Japanese warriors who belonged to the military aristocracy.

Sensei A Japanese word that means "teacher" or "master."

Seven Stars A term used in Chinese martial arts to describe the seven common weapons of the human body: the hands, feet, head, knees, elbows, shoulders, and thighs.

Shaolin temple A Zen Buddhist monastery regarded by many experts as the birthplace of Buddhist martial arts.

Shinai A bamboo training sword used for martial arts training, most commonly seen in kendo.

Shuriken A spiked, metal throwing implement, commonly seen in the form of a disk with spikes, that was used by the ninja.

Side kick A basic martial-arts kick that involves drawing up the leg, pivoting on the other leg, and then thrusting out with the raised leg to strike an opponent.

Sifu A Chinese word that means "teacher" or "master."

Soft style A term used to describe techniques that divert incoming force as opposed to countering it with powerful, linear striking actions (see also *hard style*).

Sojo The originator of a martial system or school.

Southern style A term used to describe Chinese martial arts originating south of the Yangtze River. Southern styles emphasize strong arm and hand techniques, stable stances, and fast footwork.

Spear A weapon, common throughout the world's fighting traditions, that is thrown, or used for thrusting and slashing. There are more than 700 different types of spears in Asia alone.

System A term used to describe differing martial-arts styles that may have evolved within a specific discipline or art form. For example, a family system describes styles that have been developed within one family or clan.

Steel whip A weapon that often consists of nine separate, linked sections, with a bladed dart instrument at one end. It can be thrown over an opponent's weapon to disarm him and can also be used for slashing, blocking or throwing from a distance.

Stranglehold A martial-arts grappling hold that is used to strangle an opponent.

Style A generic term used to describe variations within a specific martial-arts discipline.

Sutemi A Japanese word to describe a warrior's enhanced awareness of self-sacrifice in order to achieve an objective. It is mainly associated with aikido.

Tanto A short, Japanese dagger that was often worn on the belt of a *samurai*.

Tao Also spelt "Dao," this is a Daoist word that translates as "way" or "path" and is often used as a suffix in Chinese martial-arts systems.

Te The Japanese word for "hand" that often indicates, when used as a suffix in the name of a system, that the art form was of Okinawan origin.

Technical knockout Also known as a "TKO," a technical knockout is a term used in several full-contact sports. It is declared when a referee, or another fight official, declares that one of the fighters is in no fit state to continue a fight.

Telegraphing A generic sporting term to describe unintentionally alerting an opponent to a practitioner's next move. In the sphere of martial arts, this commonly occurs when a practitioner looks first at the target he intends to strike on an opponent's body.

Tenbin An ancient farming implement from which the *bo* was developed.

Tengu Mythical Japanese creatures who are said to have taught martial arts to humans.

Tonfa A weapon that evolved from an Okinawan farming tool, which is thought to have been the handle of a rice mill. It is approximately 2 ft (60 cm) in length and has a handle set at 90 degrees to the main striking arm. The tonfa is commonly employed by American police forces as a blocking and striking implement.

Under cut A punch that involves a semicircular vertical motion of the arm from the shoulder and finishes with a rear-hand blow to an opponent's head.

Upper cut A punch that involves an upward motion of the arm from the shoulder and finishes with the fist striking an opponent's chin.

Vital points Specific points on the human body that, when struck, yield damage in excess of that which would be expected for the force of the strike.

Yin and yang A Chinese philosophy central to Daoist thinking. It was originally used to describe the Sun and the Moon but has evolved into a term that describes the dualistic nature of the universe, such as male and female, light and dark, hard and soft, and up and down.

Zazen A type of meditation in which students are encouraged to empty their mind and so be free of any thoughts.

Zen Buddhism A school of Mahayana Buddhism that came into existence in the 6th century CE. It emphasizes a system of assessing individual experience as opposed to studying religious theory.

INDEX

Page numbers in **bold** indicate main entries. Refer to main entries for the history, training, and practice of an art.

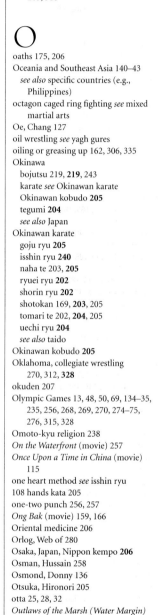
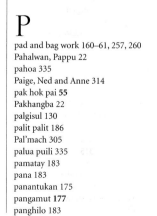